The Restoration

To Ken Wolf

Good luck & good reading

Dave Bean

Sept. 06

DAVID J. BEAN

The Restoration

The story of a special-mission, World War II airplane and its crew and how the plane's restoration also restored the team spirit that had produced the plane and won the war, to enable new cycles of restoration.

Published by

Ho Logos Press, a Division of

∝ *Ho Logos Group*

Cypress, California

MMII

E-mail hlpress@aol.com
Website www.hlpress.com

Grateful acknowledgement is made to the celebrities and personages quoted from
various media sources and for the short excerpts of text quoted from duly cited
sources.

Library of Congress Card No. 2002107923
ISBN 0970209819

The Restoration
Author: Bean, David J., 1923-
1st ed. October 2002
Includes bibliographical references.

For Librarian cataloging:
Dewey Decimal 629.1309, Aviators in History

Book design by Ho Logos Press
Cover design by Ho Logos Press
Edited by Bob Hougland

Cover note: The winged figure is Icarus, the 6th Century BC legend who crashed into
the Icarian Sea after flying too near the sun with waxen wings. Artwork based on a
painting by Charles-Paul Landon, 1760-1826.

First Edition. Manufactured in the United States of America, October 2002, by KNI,
Inc. Printed on acid-free paper.

DEDICATION

This book is dedicated to the memory of John K. Northrop, a man I worked for, admired, and tried to emulate.

David J. Bean
September 2, 2002

FOREWORD
By John H. Northrop

Even as a child I realized that my father designed beautiful and advanced aircraft that were quite different from others I saw. Photos taken of his aircraft sitting next to other contemporary aircraft made the difference evident. As I grew I learned that his design talents extended to many other fields as well, including marine hull and equipment design, artificial limbs, hydraulic brakes, and modular, thermally efficient, concrete panels for building construction. Thus although noted historically for total design of high-performance aircraft, his design innovativeness spread from this common root to find application wherever functional complexity had to be met with reliable, lightweight, low-cost design.

It was much later, after I had my own family and had worked at other companies that I realized his executive management talents in leading people rivaled those he demonstrated so well in the aircraft systems field; for example, I remember well the many times my father returned to the plant on the graveyard shift, after sleeping a few hours, to speak to employees on the third shift just as he had spoken to the preceding shifts, when he felt it was important to keep all the employees informed of the company's growth and how their team effort was contributing to that growth and their own. Even those who swept up rivets learned directly from him that they too were an important part of the overall team contributing to company and individual success.

The author has done exceptionally well in chronicling these talents, which were so well known and appreciated by Northrop employees and the industry in general.

I can add from my own experience a particular incident to further illustrate the author's story. When I was 16 years old, Northrop Aircraft, Inc., the parent company of the present Northrop Grumman Corporation, was just in the early planning stage of becoming operational. LaMotte Cohu, who was to become the company's first General Manager, had come to our home to have an informal talk with my father. I was in a nearby room and heard them conversing. The one thing I remember my father saying was, "I want Northrop to be a GOOD place to work." The words and the emphasis are exactly as I heard them. He always seemed to have kept this goal foremost in his management approach; it was more than policy: it was procedure, too. It was an approach that was both derived from the spirit of the generous talent bestowed upon him by God and that established a team spirit for which the company became noted among employees, suppliers, and customers.

The words, "I want Northrop to be a GOOD place to work," and the spirit they engendered were at the root of the design and manufacture of the N-3PB airplane that is the subject of this book. The same words became the basis of the motto of Northrop Corporation over the years: *Northrop is a good place to work*. That this motto was more than a slogan is evident in the unselfish time and effort expended by all those who became caught up in the restoration of the N-3PB almost 40 years after it was built, whether they were volunteers, paid employees, or vendors; whether they punched the clock or were executives.

My father became aware of the magnitude of the restoration work required on this particular N-3PB when Leo Gay brought over snapshots of the plane as it looked just pulled from the Thjorsa River in Iceland. As the photos in this book show, it looked like part plane and part spaghetti. Dad was never informed of the special deadline that had been set so that the restoration would be completed in synch with his 85th birthday.

Although my father had a much-appreciated tour of the restoration facility at the Northrop plant when the work had progressed beyond the cleanup stage and the plane began to take on the configuration and aerodynamic beauty of the original, by the time of the rollout of the restored airplane he was hospitalized. A tracheotomy prevented him from speaking, but it was evident to us that he was delighted and grateful to be honored in this particularly special way. Later that same day, Dad was taken from his bed and, in a wheel chair, rolled up to a reception room in the hospital. There he met some of those personnel involved in the restoration and the foreign dignitaries who were attending the rollout ceremony. He was very pleased but of course frustrated and distressed that he could not vocalize his thoughts and feelings at this meeting. Even so, this meeting and the video later shown to him of the rollout were certainly the highpoints of his final months in the hospital.

Immediately following the meeting in the hospital, my wife Mary and I entertained the same group of visitors at a quickly devised reception at our home just blocks away. It was a memorable opportunity and occasion to get to know all these fine people directly and to hear from them how much they admired and respected my father. The beverage of choice was referred to euphemistically as Scandinavian aqua vitae ('Akvavit,' similar to vodka).

While this is the story ostensibly of the restoration of an airplane, it is obviously, in the author's telling of it, a story of the restoration of people and, more importantly and subtlety, of the spirit, which finds tangible expression, as the author notes, in teaming and the team efforts of people. As the author concludes, such expression requires freedom. In trying to capture the essence of my father, as foreword to the author's detailed explication, I'll relate a couple of anecdotes that have not as yet been documented. In these stories, I hope the reader will see that his essence was to ensure the freedom for people to express their team spirit as the way to individual and group excellence.

A Northrop security guard told the first to me many years after it happened. My father had arrived at the plant before finding that he had left his required identification badge at home. Even though the guard recognized him and had spoken to him on many occasions – and was ready to admit him on his personal recognizance – he insisted on driving back home to get the badge. For one thing, he did not put himself above the rules that all the other employees had to comply with; but, in addition, as the premier role model for the company, he did not want to spend the day wearing a "Temporary" badge. As leader, he had to meet company standards as impeccably as he designed and built aircraft that met the standards people wanted to know were being met. This was not perfectionism driven by want but by substance.

The next anecdote certainly must have been widely known early on in his career, but may have gotten left behind as he moved the aircraft industry ahead so quickly with one innovation after the other during the decade prior to World War II; and it shows the kind of resilience and restorative grace he had under even personally awkward circumstances. The incident goes back to the early days at one of the Douglas plants in El Segundo, California. I believe it was on the "swing shift." My Dad, going down to the assembly line, had climbed to the top of a short ladder to check something about the rudder of an airplane model then being produced. Out of sight to each other, an assembler was at that very moment in the cockpit completing the installation of the rudder pedals. Just as Dad began inspecting the rudder, the assembler tromped on the pedals to check out his own handy work. The assembler felt the rudder impact something and standing up in the cockpit saw that he had knocked the famous designer off the ladder and onto the floor. Suddenly filled with trepidation at what he had done to the "boss," the assembler apologized profusely. The "boss" picked himself up, dusted himself off, and said, "You're lucky it was me. Don't ever do that to your foreman."

A final story is about a still earlier, perhaps more historical, event. Claude Ryan (shown later in this book), who was founder and president of the aircraft company in San Diego that bore his name (now an important part of Northrop Grumman), had a serious weight problem with the wings of a nice looking monoplane his company was building. Ryan contacted my father, who was working for Douglas Aircraft at that time in the mid-1920s, and wanted him to do some "moonlighting" to redesign the wings to remove weight and make the plane more efficient. Dad agreed to do the work if Douglas would give his approval, for he had a third child on the way and could use the money. Douglas agreed to the arrangement; so for several weekends Dad made the 120-mile trip to San Diego – an excursion which would take four to five hours in those days, motoring along the Pacific-ocean-hugging highway today known as the PCH.

The redesigned wings saved about 200 pounds that would be converted into the plane's useful load-carrying ability for equipment, fuel, and people. These same wings, lengthened slightly, became those of "The Spirit of St. Louis" – that not-so-good-looking, but mission-perfect Ryan monoplane in which Charles Lindbergh launched modern aviation.

FOREWORD
By Roy P. Jackson

Restoration of the Norwegian N-3PB airplane was performed at a time when I was vice president and general manager of the Northrop Corporation's Aircraft Division. The restoration occurred 40 years after Northrop's production of the plane – an event preceding by many years my association with the company. Yet during my assignment as general manager of the Aircraft Division, from 1979 to 1982, I became quite familiar with the plane and came to see it as one of the premier examples of Jack Northrop's prodigious output of increasingly higher performance aircraft.

It has a unique role in the evolution of Jack Northrop's career and is an especially unique airplane, in that it was designed for peacetime patrol of Norway's thousand mile coastline so as to maintain the country's neutrality during WWII, yet even before the production contract had been signed, Norway had been occupied and the airplane was relegated to its unintended use as air cover for Allied convoys crossing the open sea between Iceland and its distant neighbors, Greenland and the Shetland Islands. Its improvised mission occurred at a great moment in history and elevated it to a place in that history that it would not otherwise have. It is this uniqueness, I think, that sets the airplane apart from more widely used and known Northrop aircraft, because it reflects the basic philosophy of Jack Northrop and the people who joined him in his commitment to not only advance man's ability to fly, but to design and produce the best aircraft for that advancement. In this sense, as David J. Bean so well conveys, Jack Northrop's philosophy was that of the team.

It is interesting that while Northrop as a company played a significant role in the recovery and restoration of the particular N-3PB that was restored, the restoration itself was undertaken as an all-volunteer effort, partly as a matter of company policy regarding legal risk, but also because the company at that time was in a major transition to higher and more sustained growth. In business parlance, the restoration was simply not a budgetary line item in the company's strategic business plan. It is notable that so many people, both inside and outside the company, signed up to volunteer their leisure time to undertake what from the beginning, in Iceland, had been referred to as a "mission impossible." The author captures this mounting sense of the impossible as the project proceeds from the recovery phase in Iceland to the restoration at the Northrop Aircraft Division. There's one comment the author records that especially captures this theme of the impossible, when an Icelandic farmer, who lived along the river where the plane was discovered, tells the recovery team they don't stand a chance, because, "What the Thjorsa takes, it never gives back." But the team won over the forces of nature; as the author says, "Over time and the river."

I'm impressed with this book for a number of reasons, two of which I will share with the readers, one of which may even seem somewhat vain; but, after all I was there, cheering on this overcoming of the impossible and actively supporting its fulfillment in everyway possible. Surprisingly, and to his credit, the author has taken what most would consider a rather specialized, aficionado type subject and discovered and expressed through it a theme that is essentially philosophic. The restoration in this context takes the airplane beyond the level of mere artifact for museum display to one in which past meaning is restored for future contemplation and action. By the time Jack Northrop is restored by virtue of the flying wing having been restored to its ordained place in the annals of aviation advancements, Icarus, whose wings failed, is restored.

This book offers great hope for a better future. Nothing really fails, for if only one thing is restored it means that everything is restorable. What seems to be a "mission impossible" is quite doable, if one perseveres as the people in this book did.

The second reason this book impresses me is personal. The author invited me to write this foreword, because I did actively participate in the restoration by going to Iceland to represent Northrop Corporation in the opening of the exhibit of the airplane there; in fact, this exhibit was in the capitol, Reykjavik, where the plane's historic mission in WWII began. Two things I remember most about this trip were that the weather was beautifully clear but cold and the people were beautifully warm and gracious hosts. The trip exhilarated, enthused, and refreshed me at a time when my responsibilities at Northrop were quite challenging and possessive of my time and thoughts. Normally, an aerospace executive today seldom receives much acclaim or claim to fame, since the historic days of aviation's pioneers are past. I am once again exhilarated, enthused, and refreshed to know that this Jack Northrop airplane, which marked the beginning of the modern Northrop Grumman Corporation, should also mark a high point in my aerospace career. Now I see that through this book I too have been restored.

Personal thoughts aside, if one person were to be singled out, on the Northrop side at least, as key to making possible this "mission impossible," it would be Darrell G. McNeal, who was the manager responsible for aircraft prototyping at Northrop throughout my tenure at the division and corporate levels. McNeal had that essential management quality of being imperturbable in the midst of critical situations – which prototyping of aircraft does not lack and which the restoration of the N-3PB certainly did not lack. It was his way, I think, of coming up with the right questions to ask at just the right time and knowing whether the answers were right. As one learns in life, the right questions always precede the right answers.

The author is to be congratulated on proceeding in the same mode in his thematic development of a most interesting, exciting, and meaningful story. The story unfolds in many levels, proceeding from the need for the airplane, its production, its unusual mission during WWII, its crash landing, its recovery, its restoration, and finally its takeoff again in a new dimension of meaning that, while mythical on the surface, climbs yet higher, transcending the purely physical. It is a pleasant, enlightening flight – even a modern odyssey. Most positively, it shows that if Icarus crashed, he too is restorable. Since such myths apply to all mankind, it portends well for all of us.

PREFACE
By David J. Bean

Though World War II leaped onto the world stage with a sudden blitzkrieg of Poland, for most of the eventual major Allied participants it was slow in gathering true "world war" scope and magnitude. For England, the period from September 1939 to early 1940 is often referred to as the "Phony War." For Norway, this period of relative rest ended shortly after the blitzkrieg of Poland when, in early 1940, the country was overrun. The slow start for the Allies in no way diminished the ferocity and suffering that was to follow and the heartbreak, agony, and heroism demanded of all participants.

Though in the early stage of the war the United States remained neutral, President Franklin Roosevelt transformed the country into an arsenal of democracy as the defense business geared up to supply the weapons that the future Allies would require. One of those companies was a little-known startup called Northrop Aircraft, Inc., formed by a well-known aircraft designer, John Knudsen Northrop, who since his earliest days in the industry had become popularly known as "Jack Northrop."

Concurrent with the invasion of Norway, as its first business activity, Northrop won a contract to supply that country with a coastal patrol aircraft capable of operating from the smooth-water fjords that dominate Norway's coasts. For the most part the people who would build that airplane were new to the aircraft industry and were essentially learning on the job. In fact, Jack Northrop established a school for the training of aircraft mechanics in order to assure a constant supply for his plant.

The working atmosphere around Northrop was one of camaraderie and cooperation even though the United States was not yet in the war. With war seemingly imminent, business growth was so fast that the company awarded subcontracts to other manufacturers as a way of increasing its manufacturing area virtually overnight from 216,000 to approximately 500,000 square feet. The company had been formed with the idea that if the U.S. joined the war there would be a surge in business growth and that if it didn't join, the presence of Jack Northrop as chief engineer would attract business anyway. World conditions had greatly accelerated the need for expansion, and having control of the company was the best way to respond to the business opportunities. Even though the number of employees increased dramatically during this period everyone sensed that, because of Jack Northrop, they were "present at the creation" and this feeling permeated the entire company. Efforts to unionize the employees were never successful; the workers just didn't see the need for a union to get them benefits the company already provided.

Norway's N-3PB seaplane patrol bomber was created in this environment of patriotic, close company team identification. As news reached the Northrop team about Norway's occupation and the courageous escape of large numbers of its armed forces determined to continue fighting from friendly bases, the team immediately identified with the cause and needs of the refugees. The employees working on the airplane, knowing it was going to join the Norwegian cause, followed the news of the Norwegian's exploits closely as they were transmitted back to the factory.

That the airplane could and would be used to fulfill a mission it was not designed for is itself a minor miracle for this airplane or any small seaplane, for it was never intended or thought able to operate off the open sea. High waves and small floats are simply not compatible. Yet these courageous, determined men and the rugged little airplane did exactly that to the ever-lasting astonishment of people who followed the outcome.

This book tells the story of that airplane and of the people who built it, flew it, crashed it, found it, and restored it. There is a time gap in the story because after it crashed in 1943, the airplane lay buried in the bed of the Thjorsa River in Iceland for almost 37 years. There are only a few references regarding the aircraft during this period when the local farmers made abortive attempts to remove it from the river's icy burial. It would have stayed in the riverbed had not the war also opened up Iceland's highly conservative culture for opportunities of growth internationally. The war and the growth in aviation worldwide gave Iceland an opportunity to turn a new page in its history. Dedicated Icelandic aviation historians became aware of the plane and, using their newly acquired international awareness, initiated formation of a multi-nation task force to recover and restore the airplane. It was not an overnight victory. There were major unknowns concerning the location, situation, and condition of the buried airplane. After multiple surveys over a three-year period, a detailed approach was determined for the recovery. The pieces were restored to pristine though non-flyable condition by an all-volunteer team at Northrop, inspired once more by the memory of the importance of the plane to Norway and its historical importance as the first one designed and produced under Jack Northrop at his new company – a memory especially shared by those who had worked on the airplane during its production.

From the standpoint of aircraft design history, the airplane itself is not especially noteworthy since its design by then was standard technology and its operational life was relatively short (though exceptionally demanding) and included no historically significant accomplishments. Yet the airplane signified a synthesis of meaning to those participating on the international team. To each team member, Iceland, Norway, Britain, and Northrop, the airplane had a meaning that went beyond the object itself. It was this immanent sense of transcendence the plane signified that compelled the formation of a team of dedicated people from nations thousands of miles apart to work together and overcome the physical, legal, financial, and bureaucratic obstacles to locating, recovering, and restoring the airplane.

ACKNOWLEDGEMENTS

This book is the product of a number of years of reflection on my career in the aerospace industry – a career that included the project described in *The Restoration* and that became both my vocation and avocation. I have to thank John K. "Jack" Northrop, first of all for creating a company like Northrop Corporation as a base from which a project like this could proceed. Without Ragnar J. Ragnarsson and his associates at the Icelandic Aviation Historical Society, the basis of the book (the recovered airplane) would not have come into being and without the hundreds of people at Northrop who volunteered time and material the restoration of the plane would not have been possible. Among these people, the one I worked most closely with during the restoration and continue to work with in various similar projects is Oliver H. "Bub" Larsen. Bub reviewed the entire book and made key changes and suggestions to keep the book historically correct.

I was fortunate also to locate some of the key people who worked on the restoration or who were even associated with the production and flight test of the airplane in 1940, just before the U.S. entered WWII. Dale T. Brownlow, John Hardman, Harris Stone, Murray LaHue, and Gene Smith provided historical inputs that were not in the record and that added human dimension unobtainable in any other way than by personal reminiscence. Roy Wolford knew Jack Northrop personally even before 1940, worked for him at Douglas Aircraft in the 1930s, and completed his aerospace career at Northrop Corporation. Roy is one of those rare treasures for the historian, in that he flew as aerial photographer in the flight tests of the N-3PB airplane in 1941. Roy also reviewed the book and provided valuable original photographs of the airplane and key personnel from his historical file.

These Northrop personnel who had helped restore the airplane volunteered once again to provide information and documentation from their personnel historical files and memory of the great team effort put forth. Eugene Smith and his wife Naomi provided noteworthy support in this regard. The fact that they had saved copies of documentation no longer extant anywhere else shows how important their participation was to them. John Williams, a longtime Northrop friend and restoration volunteer, also provided photos via e-mail.

As Roy P. Jackson notes in his foreword, Darryl McNeal was the key person in managing the restoration and restoring as an integrated airplane what arrived at the Northrop plant in 1979 in sundered pieces. I am pleased to acknowledge my very good fortune in having Darryl's wife, Elizabeth, as a source of information about Darryl's early life and his beginning years at Northrop, plus her vivid memory of his unflagging personal commitment to the restoration. Their son, Gary, who still works for Northrop Grumman Corporation, also shared his recollections of having worked as a volunteer on the restoration.

Throughout the writing of the book, Ragnar J. Ragnarsson provided invaluable historical details, not in the record, that would not otherwise have been available. As could be expected, writing a book based on historical fact depends a lot on what you know, but if it's contemporary history the 'what' becomes inextricably linked with 'who' you know. The author was fortunate in having met Ragnar during the formal rollout of the restored N-3PB; and subsequently, during the final writing of this book, in coordinating regularly with him, via e-mail, on questions concerning the key phase of the story, the recovery. His personal review and commentary on those historical events, activities, and people pertinent to the recovery phase are duly acknowledged and appreciated.

That Ragnar was pivotal in the entire story is shown by the fact that he was awarded, by the King of Norway, the Order of St. Olav, Knight 1st Class, for his work in enabling the N-3PB to be restored as emblematic of Norway's own great saga of restoration during WWII. Also, Ragnar directed the author to Jan Bulukin in Norway who, as the surviving son of the Norwegian air force pilot whose destiny was to include the crash-landing that originated the subject for this book, not only participated in the recovery, but provided first-hand information about his father's military career and the recovery itself. Jan Bulukin also obtained photographs of the N-3PB airplane as it looks today, on exhibit in Oslo at the Air Museum.

Also in Iceland, Fridthor Eydal, of the Icelandic Defense Force, provided previously unpublished photographs of the early attempts to recover the plane and a rare photograph of the historic Balbo Hangar, plus maps of the Reykjavik peninsula and that bend in the Thjorsa River where the pivotal event on which this book is based occurred. In addition, Hakon Adalsteinsson, of the Icelandic Hydropower & Environmental Resources Agency, provided hydrodynamics data on the Thorjsa River for the period of concern.

In Norway, Cato Guhnfeldt, author and journalist, was a most valuable contributor of information on the Free Norwegian Air Force, its aircraft fleet during WWII and afterwards, photographs of the operations and maintenance phase of the N-3PB in Iceland, and the history of Squadron 330(N) from its formation to the present. Cato had represented the Norwegian Aviation Historical Society at the recovery in Iceland and was to do so again at the rollout of the restored airplane. Following the restoration, he authored a history of Norwegian Squadron 330(N) and its wartime operations with the N-3PB.

Also in Norway, the author extends a very special acknowledgement to Oluf Reed-Olsen, a highly talented and heroic aviator, seaman, and artist, who was a pilot in N-3PB Squadron 330(N) during its operations out of Iceland during WWII and also a member of the Norwegian secret service. He wrote two best-selling books about his wartime experiences, one of which was made into a popular movie. Many of the photographs shown herein were shot by him during Squadron 330(N) operations in Iceland. Well known by both Cato Guhnfeldt and Jan Bulukin, Oluf Reed-Olsen is now 96 years old. In the early 1960s, he managed a summer camp for boys on an island off the southern coast of Norway and Jan Bulukin says he got his "life long passion" for scuba diving under Reed-Olsen's tutelage. The author salutes him for his rare combination of viking energy and rennaissance spirit.

Even before we were finished with the restoration of the N-3PB in 1980, I had started collecting and storing data pertaining to its history. Shortly after the restoration, I began writing about the whole experience and after a few months I had completed a preliminary draft of the main elements of the story that my then-secretary typed into initial manuscript form. But about this time an article by Ragnar J. Ragnarsson appeared in *Wings* magazine, telling about the N-3PB's WWII origin and service in Iceland with RAF Squadron 330(N), so I set my project aside. About a year ago I met my former secretary at a luncheon meeting and she asked about the manuscript. When I told her it was filed away she was very disappointed and urged me to dig it out and finish it. Thanks to her recall and suggestion, I proceeded accordingly.

Thanks also to my editor, Bob Hougland, at Ho Logos Press, whose own unflagging professional work and attitude not only restored my confidence in the value of the story told by this book, but helped bring my manuscript to final form for publication. He researched much of the bibiliographic data for detailed attribution, and assisted in researching information on the Northrop F-20 aircraft through James O. Young, PhD, Chief Historian, Department of the Air Force, Headquarters Air Force Flight Test Center (AFMC), Edwards Air Force Base, California. Dr. Young provided valuable background information on the F-20 program.

One caveat is essential in any book that has a historical basis. The validity of such works depends on the extent to which the facts presented have a valid source. Historians rank such sources in the order that they proceed from first-hand accounts by witnesses or participants in the events recorded, to secondary sources, and finally to opinions. The reader will find that all facts that are not generally known have been documented as to their authoritative sources. In wanting to write this book over a number of years, the author himself obtained many documents of a first-hand witness nature as a result of his participation in the N-3PB restoration and also as a result of having worked at Northrop since the days of its founder Jack Northrop. These are vital first-hand records that would have gone unnoticed without this book. The author's final acknowledgement, therefore, is owed to those writers and eyewitnesses whose accounts became the primary sources for this history called *The Restoration*. Whenever and wherever there was a difference of opinion as to the factuality of this history, as author I assume final responsibility for the choice made.

The fact that I am most certain of is that my wife Bettie, in seeing me work over this subject for a number of years and in particular the past year and continuing to encourage the effort, was the catalyst that made the book possible. If an author is married and writes a great book, it is axiomatic that a great woman was behind him.

EDITORIAL NOTE

Glossaries are appended to aid the reader who may want more specific definition of certain terms used in the text. Appendix L provides a glossary of U.S. aerospace industry acronyms and standard units of measure for terms used in the book. To simplify the presentation of quantitative measurements, all such information is presented in English units or in both English and metric units where the original was metric. Appendix M provides a glossary showing the standard conversion factors for changing from one measurement system to the other.

All other appendices are referred to in the text as applicable.

CONTENTS

APPENDICES

Part I - Background

CHAPTER 1 - A CLASSIC RESTORATION

This is the story of an unusual military airplane, the N-3PB seaplane that, almost accidentally, performed a very important mission during the Second World War. Forty years later, after its important mission was long over and largely forgotten, the plane arose again to become the subject of a concentrated, coordinated effort of the same group of nations and people who had designed, built, operated, and given it a home base. It is a story, above all, of how this airplane – though only a machine – brought humans together as a team, one version of which is shown by the N-3PB crew in Figure 1 on the airplane's first flight in California.

The "restoration" therefore is an encompassing, even mythic one, in that it signifies more than just putting the pieces back together. The point of the story is perhaps not so much to restore or preserve but to create, to grow something so greatly experienced during the war, but since then found missing in everyday life. This "restoration" was a form of odyssey – a search, discovery, and re-creation of a time past when the team effort surpassed any individual goal, because there was a commonly shared threat to freedom. It was so different and significant that it makes a story worth retelling.

Roy L. Wolford

Figure 1. Operated by a team of three, the N-3PB, intended for coastal reconnaissance in a neutral Norway, became an Antisubmarine/Antiship Weapon System during the 1941-43 Battle of the Atlantic, flying out of Iceland to protect Allied shipping in the northern sealanes to Russia and Britain.

For one thing, this restoration required finding the aircraft, which was not even visible to the outside world. In fact, if one had walked by the site where it had crashed not looking for it – or even intentionally looked for surface signs of it, nothing would have been seen or espied. It was difficult even systematically to prove its existence. For this airplane was not only submerged in frigid waters but buried in the lava silt and clay of a glacial riverbed just below the Arctic Circle. In effect, the airplane no longer existed.

So given such difficult circumstances and uncertainty, why would anyone want to find and restore this airplane? There would have to be compelling reason well beyond mere curiosity or an opportunity for adventure. First the airplane would have to be found; and after 40 years that would not be easy. Given the wintry intemperance of the general location of the crash and the uncertainty of even the existence of the airplane, why bother? The war was over long ago, and the airplane had performed a relatively remote mission that went unnoted in the day-to-day news coverage of the war. The effort required could be likened to that of an archeological dig – or would it be more likely, anthropological? It certainly went beyond the material form of the aircraft. Once again, as in the war, it was a time when men and women had a sense of mission in which every person was an important member of the team and every task a team objective toward success.

Through this restoration, perhaps unconsciously, the same men and women wanted to recapture that team feeling, to win again, this time against the forces of nature and not against a human threat: it was this reunified force of mankind that made it both necessary and sufficient.

But was this the only goal that inspired the search, detection, survey, recovery, transport, and restoration of an airplane of which there was no visible evidence of existence and that, in the worldwide scope and magnitude of the war, had low visibility of operational presence? It was only in the retelling of the story that the author found an answer to this more fundamental question. For one thing, this airplane and the people who operated it had been thrown into an unbelievably hostile environment; the airplane was not even designed for the mission it was given – to patrol the North Atlantic and protect troop ships and war material convoys against submarine attack. In succeeding, however, the airplane and the people established a reputation that became legend among the Icelanders and the Norwegians and contributed to Allied victory in "The Battle of the Atlantic."

But having a unique mission that was successfully accomplished still does not justify all the effort put forth to find and restore the airplane. So, why was this relatively obscure airplane worth all the effort put forth to restore it? Obviously, there is something grander but just as obscure behind the airplane and the effort. It has all the overtones and proportions of a myth. Like light shimmering on a pool of water, there is a glimmer of something both deeper and scintillating – and yet very alive and significantly more revealing. Like a myth that is durably meaningful from generation to generation, the N-3PB was a focal point of a past of quiet greatness and meaning. It was a classic.

St. Exupery's *Night Flight*, a classic novel about the beginnings of commercial aviation in South America in the 1920's, touches thematically on this meaning. The story is about the air service operator and his crew of aviators who are initiating air mail delivery at night, flying long hours under adverse weather conditions, in darkness, to prove that mail delivery by air could be much faster and more efficient than by land or sea. It is the beginning of airmail, delivered in rickety, open cockpit airplanes by men who love their airborne freedom amidst the wind and stars and at the same time are being driven to perform rigidly on schedule every day. The chief operator of the service believes that the only way mail delivery by ground can be beat is to fly at night so the mail arrives the very next day. In the preface by Andre Gide the essence of this historical effort and its telling by St. Exupery is captured as only one captivated by his subject can do:

> Aviation, like the exploration of uncharted lands, has its early heroic age and *Night Flight*, which describes the tragic adventure of one of these pioneers of the air, sounds, naturally enough, the authentic epic note. The hero of *Night Flight*, though human through and through, rises to superhuman heights of valor. The quality which I think delights one most of all in this stirring narrative is its nobility. Too well we know man's failings, his cowardice and lapses, and our writers of today are only too proficient in exposing these; but stood in need of one to tell us how a man may be lifted far above himself, by his sheer force of will.

> More striking than the aviator himself is, in my opinion, Riviere, his chief. The latter does not act, himself; he impels to action, breathes into his pilots his own virtue and exacts the utmost from them, constraining them to dare greatly . . . . At first sight his severity may seem inhuman and excessive. But its target is not the man himself, whom Riviere aspires to mold, but the man's blemishes. In his portrayal of this character we feel the author's profound admiration. I am especially grateful to him for bringing out a paradoxical truth which seems to me of great psychological import: that man's happiness lies not in freedom but in his acceptance of a duty. Each of the characters in this book is wholeheartedly, passionately devoted to that which duty bids him to do, and it is in fulfilling this perilous task, and only thus, that he attains contentedness and peace . . . .

> A sense of duty commands Riviere in all things, (as St. Exupery says) "the dark sense of duty, greater than that of love." Man is not to seek an end within himself but to submit and sacrifice his all to some strange thing that commands him and lives through him . . . . This is the mainspring of every act of heroism. 'We behave,' thought Riviere, 'as if there were something of higher value than human life . . . . But what thing?' And again (St. Exupery): "There is perhaps something else, something more lasting to be saved; and perhaps it was to save this part of man that Riviere was working."[1]

---

[1] Antoine De Saint Exupery, *Night Flight*, a Harvest/HJB Book (New York: Harcourt Brace Jovanovich Publishers, 1973), "Preface" by Andre Gide: pp. 3-5.

Riviere was obviously fighting a war. The applicability of this story to the N-3PB history and its restoration is evident if "War" is substituted as the main character. For it was the war that brought the airplane into being and that instilled the men who flew and supported it with that sense of duty that went beyond love or life itself. This airplane, therefore, signifies the highest form of duty – that "something else, something more lasting, to be saved."

Gide goes on in his preface to note that the idea of heroism may play little or no part in future wars, because warfare was becoming virtually a computer game in which, with automatic target location, identification, and weapon delivery, man would no longer be at the same risk as before. Yet aviation, he believed, would continue to provide "the most admirable and worthy field for the display of prowess." So the N-3PB – assigned a very high risk mission in the war, though being a relatively obscure airplane – signifies not only the high sense of duty of its flight and ground crews, but the lineage of manned aircraft designed to enter extremely risky war zones – zones , as the Germans found, defended by increasingly sophisticated air defenses. The restoration of this airplane therefore can be likened to an archeological dig in which the remains of some remote yet historically significant artifact are the objective. Once the artifact is restored for viewing, everyone who knows or is aware of its history can look at it in picture or actual form and reminisce or imagine what life had been like then; and that, what once was, had been restored anew. The battle fought and the victory won is memorialized in honor of the duty past and in anticipation of the duty ahead.

That the N-3PB restoration was made possible by the initiative of an emerging nation of historically noted people adds further significance to its meaning. For just one of many notable things, Iceland has the oldest parliament system of government in the world – originating in 930 AD. On September 1, 1939, when Germany started World War II by invading Poland (in, as few people now remember or know, an alliance with Russia), Iceland was a sovereign, independent state under the King of Denmark. The country had been first settled in 874 AD by a Norwegian looking for freedom from monarchial despotism in his homeland. Others followed and by 1262 the population was sufficient that one of the more enterprising settlers, who was of a group of feudal lords reigning on the island, entered into a pact of allegiance with the Norwegian king in exchange for support in taking over Iceland. Thus, Iceland lost its independence and the freedom of its individuals in one step. In 1381, control was relinquished by Norway to Denmark as part of a larger alliance to ward off aggressor nations on the continent of Europe, particularly in Scandinavia. Iceland became free of this bipartite alliance in 1918, when the Treaty of Versailles reduced the tie with Denmark to that of monarchial representative solely for Icelandic foreign affairs and defense.

As shown in Figure 2, Iceland, from a spacecraft, appears as a large snowflake lying in the North Atlantic just below the Arctic Circle and approximately midway between Greenland, 300 miles to the west, and the Faeroe Islands and Scotland, 500 miles to the east. At 39,709 square miles (102,845 square kilometers) in area, it is about the size of the State of Virginia. But size alone does not set value. As Winston Churchill noted in his history of "The Battle of the Atlantic, 1941,"

Whoever possesses Iceland, holds a pistol firmly pointed at England, America, and Canada.[2]

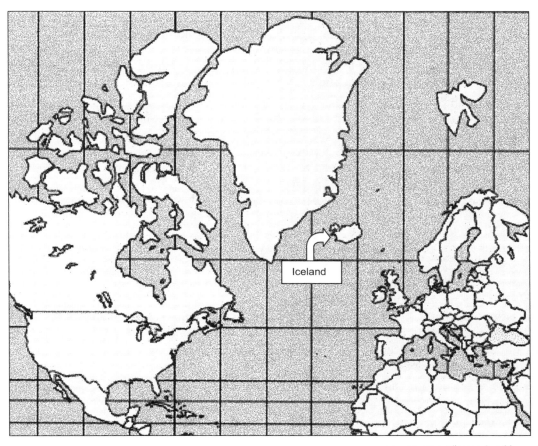

www.comm.org/images/world

Figure 2. Iceland, strategically situated midway between Britain and the U.S., was figuratively a refuge, a shield, and a gun in the hand of whoever occupied her, while watching sentiently over the North Atlantic and the Greenland and Norwegian Seas.

Germany felt the same way, for following Hitler's unilateral termination on April 28, 1939 of the Anglo-German Naval Agreement (entered into with Britain on June 21, 1935) within a month the Third Reich pressed the Icelandic government for aircraft landing rights on the island. The purported reason was to enable Lufthansa's commercial aircraft

---

[2] Winston S. Churchill, The Grand Alliance, Vol. III of The Second World War, (Boston: Houghton Mifflin Company, 1950) p. 138. Note: Churchill was quoting one of Hitler's master strategists, as shown in Chapter 4, though without attribution.

to make transatlantic flights. Because Hitler already had taken over Austria the previous year and invaded Czechoslovakia just two months before, the Icelandic government turned down the request, so as to stick to the policy of neutrality that it had announced and followed since becoming an independent state in 1918. In fact, Iceland has no military forces to this day. Even the British were denied bases by Iceland in April 1940, though the bases were requested for use to protect North Atlantic sea-lanes as lines of maritime supply after German forces occupied Denmark and Norway. Again, the request was turned down, so as to stay neutral.

But Iceland's strategic importance has remained evident to all nations. In 1949, it became one of the founding members of NATO. Because it has no military forces of its own, Iceland entered into a defense agreement with the U.S. in 1951, at which time the Iceland Defense Force (IDF) was formed. The IDF mission is to keep the sea and air transport routes and communications open between North America and Europe. There are 25 different NATO military commands linked with the IDF base and international airport at Keflavik, a fishing town 22 miles west-southwest of Reykjavik, the capitol. Military personnel from the U.S. forces and from The Netherlands, Norway, and Denmark are located at the base, along with Icelandic civilians who work there. Norway and Denmark, of course, are associates of many centuries.

The strategic importance of Iceland, due to its location, was never so pronounced as during World War II. In fact, it can be said that, while Churchill's observation quoted above is certainly a truism, it turned out that the Icelandic pistol was actually pointed directly at the Third Reich in every part of its military force, in particular directly at the German navy and air force and indirectly at the army. How this reversal came about involves the N-3PB, because for a critical time during the first two years of the war, this airplane became the pistol.

The next question, however, is how did a Norwegian military seaplane get based in Iceland, which is neutral?

From a technical standpoint, the potential for the N-3PB mission capability began 10 years before World War II. John Knudsen Northrop, part Norwegian by maternal ancestry but also paternally English and an American aircraft design genius by birth, had been a leading aircraft company chief engineering executive since 1930. Before Northrop, aircraft airframes had been built using the same beefy truss design typically found in bridges. It was his breakthrough technology in designing all-metal, multicellular, stressed-aluminum-skin structure and construction techniques to achieve unusually high strength, low-weight airframes that made the high-performance seaplane patrol bomber feasible. By 1939, when traditionally neutral Norway saw that it needed to prepare against a possible German invasion, John ("Jack") Northrop was ready with just the right mission design solution. He proposed a float-equipped airplane capable of carrying a crew of three (pilot, bombardier-radioman, and gunner) with a full bomb, torpedo, or depth-charge load, plus wing-mounted and cockpit flexible-mounted machine guns, and fuel for a 750-mile flight range.

The plane's mission need had developed in parallel with the rapid political changes in the national structure of Teutonic Europe following Hitler's appointment as Chancellor of

Germany by President Hindenberg on January 30, 1933. Hindenberg, who had initially rejected Hitler as suited only to be a postmaster, soon realized that Hitler and his Nazi troopers, fomenting daily in the streets for national socialism, were the only means for keeping the Communists from taking over Germany. If the Communists won, Russia would not be far behind.

Hitler initiated his political control and expansionist strategy from the first day in office. Within two days he issued an order that all meetings or demonstrations of the Communist Party were forbidden. Within the next three weeks, 4,000 party members, including the entire Central Committee of the Communist Party, were arrested. By July, he was pressuring the Allied Disarmament Conference at Geneva for equality in weapons and in the organization of armies and fleets. Not surprisingly, the French and the British tended toward an accommodation of Hitler's demands, because they too were intimidated by the appeal that emerging Communism had for the common man. Both Britain and France were still relatively encumbered with the monarchial, aristocratic traditions that had dominated Europe since feudal times. In Russia, in 1917, the serfs, seizing on Marx's concept of Communism as the way to utopia – and seizing also on the vulnerability of the Czarist army as it fought the German invader, had violently taken over the government by killing the entire royal family. This cataclysmic emergence of Communism occurred at a time when the Western Allies were still trying to win the First World War, which, once won, effectively ended monarchial government in Germany and the other Teutonic nations. Thus the Teutonic monarchy, in starting the war, ended itself. Henceforth, the lure of Communism was perceived by the West to be a real threat to their emerging democracies and their pragmatic compromise between aristocratic elites and the plurality of the common man. At the other extreme of course was Fascism which, perversely like Communism, was simply another guise for control by an aristocratic elite. So it wasn't monarchy per se that was being contested; rather, it was who was going to be "king. "

Still not officially permitted to re-arm and re-militarize Germany, Hitler ironically began using Russia as a surrogate base for training ground and air forces, getting Russia to favor and encourage such an arrangement by supplying it military equipment; and this surreptitious teaming led finally, on August 23, 1939, to a formal Non-Aggression Pact under which the two nations attacked Poland and Finland nine days later, beginning World War II. So two opposing political ideologies found a basis for cooperation of the most extreme sort in finding a common, though supplementary, interest.

It was the combination of this sudden surprise attack on Poland and Finland at the easternmost end of the Baltic Sea (along with the pattern of Hitler's preceding strategy of scooping up the Teutonic nations one by one) that alerted the King of Norway and his government as to what was coming to the North Atlantic end of the Baltic. Norway was the westernmost of the three major Scandinavian countries (Norway, Sweden, and Finland) and alone faced the North Atlantic and Hitler's fleet of battleships, cruisers, destroyers, and U-boats on their emergence from the Baltic. Hence Norway's growing concern about having an airborne capability, such as represented by the N-3PB seaplane, to maintain surveillance over its thousand-mile Atlantic coastline to deter and, if necessary, prevent covert intrusion by German ships.

Hitler, by the time of the attack on Poland, had violated every provision of the Treaty of Locarno, signed by Britain, France, Germany, Belgium, and Italy on December 25, 1925 to formalize the national boundaries set by the Treaty of Versailles in 1919 to end World War I and stabilize Western Europe. (And it was the Treaty of Locarno, in excluding Russia, that ironically initiated its preference for an alliance with Germany.) Hitler's plan of progressive territorial expansion, counterclockwise around Europe, was clearly revealed in that on March 7, 1936, he had reoccupied the Rhineland; on February 12, 1938, Austria; and on March 14, 1939, Czechoslovakia. In five years, Hitler had doubled the size and population of Germany.

Beyond a certain size of territorial expansion, Hitler no longer needed manpower, but natural resources in the form of iron ore and oil to build military equipment, operate it, and conduct a world war. It was the need for ore that necessitated control of Norway and compelled him to invade it. The ore originated in north central Sweden in the great iron region of Gellivare, but in winter the port of entry at Lulea was inaccessible due to ice in the Bay of Bothnia, which separates Sweden and Finland from the Baltic. Ore shipments then had to be re-routed by railroad to the port at Narvik on the North Atlantic coast of Norway and thence to Germany through Skagerrak passage to the Baltic and the Kiel Canal, which Churchill called "that side-door from the Baltic"[3] that had to be closed.

Thus Norway was indispensable for transshipment of ore needed to supply the German war industry. Since Britain was also vitally interested in Norway as a base for maritime operations against German ships (a base that would prevent Germany's access to Narvik – which connected with the railroad from the Gellivare iron ore fields in Sweden), Hitler actually had to invade Norway, despite its policy of neutrality, to keep the super-aggressive Britain out. The Norwegian government meanwhile knew that if Britain set up bases there, Hitler would be sure to invade.

So to secure its traditional neutrality, Norway needed military equipment, especially aircraft; hence in early 1939, Norway began specifying the military seaplane it required to establish a military presence along its thousand-mile North Atlantic coastline, which was serrated by thousands of fjords, bays, and offshore islands and islets. In February 1940, Commander Kristian Ostby of the Royal Norwegian Naval Air Force found the precise aircraft required at Northrop Aircraft Company in Hawthorne, Los Angeles County, California, when he met Jack Northrop.

While the design of any airplane is not a trivial problem, a military seaplane multiplies the design complexity. It must carry a crew, fuel for extended patrol at sea and return to base, plus munitions for strafing and bombing engagement of the enemy. The landing gear in the form of pontoons generate unwanted aerodynamic drag drawing down on fuel, speed, and flight time and transmit extremely high landing loads to the primary structure of the airframe. The N-3PB was a design challenge of the highest order, further complicated by the urgency of its need: Norway required the airplane *now*, if not yesterday. When Commander Ostby walked in the door at Northrop Aircraft, Inc., on February 14, 1940, his homeland was less than two months from invasion by Germany.

---

[3] Loc. Cit., Vol. I, *The Gathering Storm*, page 414.

He had already been to United Aircraft and Douglas Aircraft companies, but neither could meet the performance Norway specified for its pontoon-seaplane patrol bomber – performance capped by a minimum speed of 200 miles per hour and operating range of 750 miles carrying a torpedo or bomb load of 2,000 pounds. But the way to proceed was indicated by the fact that everywhere he went Jack Northrop-designed airplanes were all he saw and that everyone he talked to, in private at least, said Jack Northrop was the only one who might be able to meet both the design requirements and delivery schedule. It all came down to a high-performance military airplane that didn't yet exist (in even design form) that was needed immediately. Such a design entailed a performance that could only be met by a high-performance person – one whose visionary concepts for aircraft were matched by his demonstrated capabilities. Commander Ostby was in luck, because Jack Northrop had resigned from Douglas Aircraft a year earlier to form Northrop Aircraft, Inc., and was ready to meet all the requirements.

That John K. Northrop was a genius at aircraft design everyone agreed. Like Einstein, formally he had only a high school education, but what he lacked in scholastic credentials was amply provided in natural talent and his use of it in a concentrated pursuit of success. Aviation historian Thurman Jacobs noted that "Northrop's lack of formal education far from being a handicap may actually have been an asset. After all, what school could have taught him to be an aircraft engineer?" Donald Douglas, Sr., expressed the same thought, saying, "Any formal education he lacked he didn't need." He began his aircraft industry career in 1916 at age 21 as a draftsman. By 1923, he was a project engineer at Douglas, a job he left in 1926 to co-found Lockheed Aircraft Company and serve as chief engineer.

He demonstrated the feasibility of his lightweight stressed-skin approach to airframe design and manufacture in the all-wood Lockheed Vega, which set both speed and endurance records for the time. Amelia Earhart demonstrated the aircraft's superiority in her record flight across the Atlantic in 1932. Eager to operate more freely, Northrop left Lockheed in 1928 to form Avion Corporation and apply these advanced airframe and performance concepts in metal in his first flying wing design and in the first modern low wing monoplane, the Alpha. After Avion merged with United Aircraft in 1930, he formed his first Northrop Corporation, in 1931 and under his engineering direction the Northrop Gamma and Delta commercial planes were built, followed by the Army's A-17 and A-17A attack planes, the Navy's BT-1 dive bomber, and export models for other countries, such as China, Sweden, Argentina, Iraq, The Netherlands, and, as reported by Robert McLarren in 1941, even Norway.[4]

---

[4] *Model Airplane News*, April 1941, "Norwegian Nemesis," by Robert McLarren. McLarren's article was written during the crisis of Norway's invasion by Germany and suffers from some confusion as to exactly what aircraft Norway had purchased from Northrop or Douglas prior to the invasion and where they were delivered afterwards. The author has clarified this matter through Cato Guhnfeldt, Norwegian aviation historian, journalist for Norway's *Aftenposten*, and president of the Norwegian Aviation Historical Society, as documented in Chapter 3. (See Footnote 28, p. 42.)

These aircraft constituted a progressive evolution of a baseline high-strength, lightweight airframe technology that, in the A-17A U.S. Army attack bomber, became the first all-metal military aircraft with retractable landing gear. This same design was upgraded further in strength for the U.S. Navy to use in aircraft carrier operations, which impose higher loadings during landing due to the short landing distance and use of an arresting cable to stop the airplane's rollout immediately after touchdown. This impact shock capability is similar to what a military float-type seaplane required.

It was this breakthrough in high-strength, lightweight design – particularly applicable in the wing – that made the N-3PB readily designable by Jack Northrop. His engineering and technological approach enabled the seaplane, equipped with floats, to achieve a top speed of over 250 miles per hour fully loaded for its 750-mile- range mission.

In January 1938, after Northrop Corporation had been bought and integrated by Douglas Aircraft Company as its El Segundo Division, he had resigned and joined with a small group of leading avaation investors to start his second Northrop company, incorporated as Northrop Aircraft, Inc. The N-3PB seaplane was the first airplane designed by him at the new company, which during 1939 had operated its engineering department out of the Hawthorne Hotel while its first production plant was being built on vacant land adjacent to Hawthorne Airport. A contract for 24 of the N-3PB airplanes was signed between Norway and the new company on 12 March 1940, one month after Commander Ostby's arrival and 27 days before Germany invaded Norway and Denmark.

Then, without warning, just one month after the invasion of the Baltic countries by Germany, Britain "invaded" Iceland. As noted above, Britain's request to establish bases in Iceland had been turned down due to the island's neutrality policy and so Churchill abandoned diplomacy and arbitrarily took over that portion of the Island needed to support British operations for control of the North Atlantic. The British objective was to pre-empt a takeover of the island by Germany, because it was now clear that Britain, though it had tried to counter the German invasion, would not be able to stop it from occupying Norway. On the morning of May 10, 1940 the people of Reykjavik were rudely awakened by the sound and sight of a British invasion force landing at the docks and taking over operational control of the entire island.

Icelanders were doubly consternated at being invaded, because, without any military force, they were now also without a defender, because Denmark, Iceland's historical protector, had been occupied by Germany concurrently with its invasion of Norway. In reaction, the British, having failed to deter Germany in Norway, despite an attempt to land at Narvik (on the North Atlantic coast) at the same time Germany was landing at Oslo (on the Baltic coast), had immediately invaded Iceland so as to ensure its use as a mid-Atlantic seabase by the Allies.

Both Britain's try at stopping the Germans in Norway and its heading them off in Iceland were previews and rehearsals of what was to come on D-Day when the allies invaded the European mainland. When it became clear that the Germans had an overwhelming advantage throughout Norway, the British, instead of trying to land an army and fight head-on, improvised the first "commando" type tactics of the war by using

Roy L. Wolford

Figure 3. John K. Northrop, pioneering U.S. aeronautical engineering design genius and innovator whose lightweight, high-strength, durable airframe technology – demonstrated in six similar commercial and military models over the previous 10 years – made the first Norwegian N-3PB deliverable nine months after contract signing. (Northrop shown here at his drafting board in 1941, studying map of Iceland – also note first N-3PB in photo on wall.)

a small, covert force that quickly infiltrated and temporarily took over the port to destroy its docks and the railroad terminal before letting Norway slip into German hands. The objective was to deter shipments of iron ore to Germany out of Narvik.

The British "invasion" of Iceland ensured that the Icelandic pistol alluded to by Churchill would henceforth be pointed in the direction of the Third Reich, away from England, Canada, and the U.S. The loading and firing of the pistol was still to come. In looking about for aircraft and manpower to utilize this base properly, they were helped when the Norwegian government (now removed by the British to London) asked permission of the British to locate the freed Norwegians and their soon-to-be-available N-3PB squadron in Iceland, where the Royal Norwegian Air Force could then train for an eventual return to Norway and, in the interim, be operationally available for missions at sea.[5]

The British urgently needed air coverage of its convoys in the North Atlantic to protect its logistics lifeline, and this need became doubly manifest when Russia severed its tie with Germany and joined the U.S. and Britain in the Western Alliance. Now, besides sailing to England, U.S. convoys loaded with tanks, trucks, artillery, rifles, ordnance, troops, and aircraft would be sailing to, from, and past Iceland on their way to Murmansk in northwest Russia, north around Norway, Sweden, and Finland and through the Barents Sea. The N-3PB seaplane, loaded with bombs, depth charges, or torpedoes, could patrol almost halfway to Norway or 300 miles in any direction from its Icelandic bases to strike enemy surface ships or U-boats trying to intercept and sink those convoys. Iceland now would be a loaded pistol pointing directly and firmly at the Third Reich – all because of the availability of the N-3PB military seaplane, its Norwegian operators, and Iceland's ideal North Atlantic location for its operational deployment by the Norwegian Royal Air Force under control of the British Royal Air Force.

The day of May 10, 1940 was historical, for as the British "invaded" Iceland, Germany invaded France, Holland, and Belgium. On the same day Neville Chamberlain ("Peace in our time") resigned as Prime Minister and Churchill was asked by the King to form a new Government. In the context of these events, the strategic importance of the N-3PB and Iceland became immediately clear and gained in criticality as the war progressed toward its ultimate scope and magnitude as a World War. With Germany occupying Norway, German warships, formerly restrained to the Baltic Sea, could now directly access the North Atlantic and threaten supply convoys coming from Canada or the U.S. Over a year before the U.S. officially entered the war when Pearl Harbor was struck, the U.S. and Britain were in direct consultation and coordination for their joint defense of the Atlantic Ocean. As Churchill noted, Iceland, properly equipped, could be turned to "good account":

> It was upon this thought that, . . . we had occupied Iceland . . . . Now we could use it against the U-boats, and in April 1941, we established bases there for the use of our escort ships and aircraft.[6]

On December 13, 1940, nine months after the N-3PB contract was signed between Norway and Northrop, the first of the 24 aircraft was ready for flight test. In March 1941, the British gave Norway go-ahead to establish an N-3PB squadron in Iceland for convoy escort and antisubmarine patrol. The first flight mission was conducted on June 23, 1941. As the Royal Air Force's confidence in the Norwegian squadron grew, the airplane became fully accepted and integrated in anti-sub/-ship patrol and attack. During August 26-29, 1941, the Norwegian squadron flew 10 sorties in which 4 U-boats were

---

[5] This proposal by Norway was welcomed by the British because at that point there were no other aircraft, ready and available in any quantity, remotely capable of performing that mission.
[6] Ibid.

attacked. As Ragnar Ragnarsson, Vice President of the Iceland Aviation Historical Society (IAHS) and Project Manager of the recovery effort on the restored N-3PB, has written about the life of this airplane:

> During the month of August a large concentration of German U-boats was detected in the waters south and southeast of Iceland . . . . The Norwegian's, eager to see some action, persuaded the British to employ them in the hunt, ... From then on the squadron's capability was firmly acknowledged and during the next eighteen months its "Northrop's" were to play an active role in World War II's most crucial battle of all: "The Battle of the Atlantic."[7]

The Battle of the Atlantic refers to that intense period of U-boat activity and sinking of Allied shipping during WWII from June 22, 1941, when Germany launched its surprise attack on Russia – its former ally – to July 9, 1943, when the Allies invaded Italy at Sicily. Although the U-boat attacks and sinkings went on for the duration of the war, Churchill refers to the Atlantic at that particular time as "U-Boat Paradise."[8] He further states:

> The Battle of the Atlantic was the dominating factor all through the war. Never for one moment could we forget that everything happening elsewhere, on land, at sea, or in the air, depended ultimately on its outcome, and amid all other cares we viewed its changing fortunes day by day with hope or apprehension.[9]

Admiral Karl Doenitz, head of the Third Reich naval forces from January 1943 through April 1945, noted the effectiveness of the German U-boats during the war, in tabulating the number of merchant ships confirmed by Allied forces as sunk by his U-boats at 2,759 ships representing 14,119,413 tons of cargo,[10] valued today at about a trillion dollars. In addition, there were thousands of lives lost on both sides. There were so many U-boats deployed in the Atlantic and so much shipping that the Germans devised "Wolf Pack" strategies and tactics to maximize sinkings through coordinated attacks of convoys by multiple U-boat squadrons.

Churchill calls the period of greatest U-boat action in the Atlantic as "The Hinge of Fate," because it represented the turn of the Allied situation from almost uninterrupted disaster to success. As shown in Figure 4, the Atlantic became a graveyard of Allied shipping in less than one year.

---

[7] Ragnar Ragnarsson, "Phantom of the Fjords: Northrop's N-3PB Flying Viking," published in *Wings*, A Sentry Magazine, by Sentry Books, Granada Hills, CA 91344, February 1981, Vol.11, No. 1.

[8] Loc. Cit., Vol. IV, *The Hinge of Fate*, Chapter 7.

[9] Loc. Cit., Vol. V, *The Closing of the Ring*, p. 6.

[10] Admiral Karl Doenitz, *Memoirs: Ten Years and Twenty Days*, translated by R. H. Stevens in collaboration with David Woodward (Cleveland and New York: The World Publishing Company, 1959) p. 490. Doenitz had been Commander in Chief of the German Navy's U-boat arm since its beginning in July 1935 and became Commander in Chief of the entire German Navy in January 1943. On May 1, 1945 he succeeded Hitler, by the latter's appointment on April 30, as Head of the German Government.

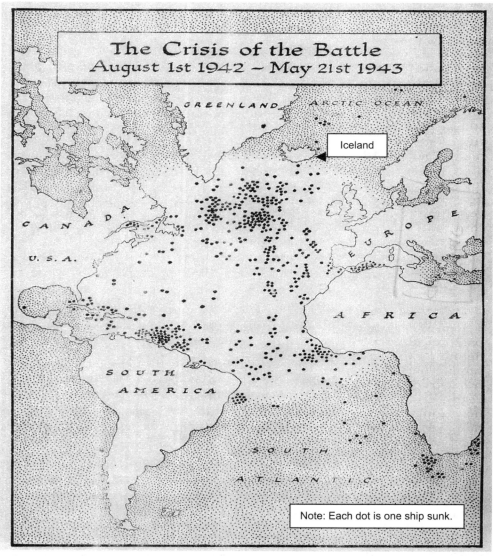

The Crisis of the Battle
August 1st 1942 – May 21st 1943

GREENLAND ARCTIC OCEAN

Iceland

CANADA

U.S.A.

EUROPE

AFRICA

SOUTH AMERICA

SOUTH ATLANTIC

Note: Each dot is one ship sunk.

Figure 4. At the peak of The Battle of the Atlantic, 185 U-boats operated 24 hours a day in that ocean and in the Greenland and Norwegian Seas to attack Allied convoys headed for Russia and Britain, sinking almost 4 million tons of shipping in 10 months. (Map from Winston S. Churchill, The Second World War, Vol. IV, The Hinge of Fate, p.128.)

Of course the Icelandic operations were not the only thing that turned the Battle of the Atlantic about. The threat to Italy and Southern Europe posed by the Allied successes in North Africa was pivotal among several other factors. The imminence of Allied invasions there prompted Doenitz, who was now Commander-in-Chief of German forces, to move many of his U-boats from the Atlantic to the Central Atlantic and Mediterranean Theater. This shift, however, did not have a lasting effect on the "Battle of the Atlantic," because it turned out to be a temporary tactic on the part of Doenitz to try to stopper the Mediterranean so as to deny a sea passage to Allied shipping preparing for the Allied invasion of North Africa.

Taking a lesson from the Germans, the Allies also were exploiting the covert advantages of the submarine, for when Lt. Gen. Mark Clark of the U.S. Army met secretly with French officers in Algeria in November 1942 to plan the Allied invasion of Algeria and Tunisia as a predecessory step for invading Italy, he did so in a submarine. The ship surfaced near the beach at night so Clark could take a raft to shore, confer, and return for departure before daybreak.

Doenitz knew by October 1942, when the Panzer Tank Corps of Rommel, the Desert Fox, was driven out of El Alamein, Egypt, for the second time, that the Mediterranean had to be secured to prevent North Africa from being used as an invasion base by the Allies and also to prevent the Suez Canal from being used to supply Russia's southern front against German attack. Accordingly, a major shift of the U-boat fleet began in November 1942 from the North Atlantic to the Mediterranean and concurrently the German army stepped up its southern attack on Russia, so as to compel the Allies to re-direct convoys through the Mediterranean where the U-boats would be waiting. The allies, meanwhile, were planning to take the pressure off Russia and in the process end "The Battle of the Atlantic" by attacking southern Europe through Italy, putting the Italian fleet (which the Italians had supplemented with French ships) out of action.

Despite the shifting of U-boats, by May 12, 1943 both Algeria and Tunisia had been occupied by the Allies. On September 3, 1943, with Mussolini having been forced to resign by the King of Italy on July 25, the new Italian government entered into a secret armistice with the Allies and on October 13, 1943 declared war against Germany, now the sole Fascist power, but still fighting to hold northern Italy.

As early as February 1943, the U-boats were back in strength on the North Atlantic convoy route and from that time forward some of the most fierce and fatal convoy battles of the war occurred. This phase of the "Battle of the Atlantic" constituted a U-boat campaign that some historians, including Roskill, say was won by the Allies by the narrowest of margins.[11] As Figure 4 indicates, there were two principal pathways across the Atlantic: one north around Iceland through Denmark Strait and the other south, in the Atlantic..

This review of "The Battle of the Atlantic" and its decline is pertinent because that battle was the arena in which the N-3PB seaplane discovered its mission and demonstrated its prowess. The N-3PB had been designed to reconnoiter the enormous coastline of Norway with its thousands of small islands, bays, and narrow fjords, with

---

[11] Captain Stephen Roskill of the British Royal Navy is a much read and quoted authority on the sea war of WWII. His book, *The War at Sea,* became the basis of a highly praised television series of the same name narrated by the British actor, Richard Burton. Even Doenitz quotes Roskill numerous times.

sheer cliffs dropping straight into the sea, but with relatively smooth waters. A seaplane was required because Norway had only a few, widely separated airfields and, to be effective in its reconnaissance mission, the airplane had to set down wherever there was something to be investigated; water landings on relatively smooth inlets therefore were a routine expectation.[12] In the Icelandic operations, a longer-range flying boat was called for, but few were available in this period. When they did become available, they replaced the N-3PB. In the interim, because the Northrop design had so much performance capability in speed and fair range, it was relatively easy to configure it with anti-submarine and air defense armaments for sea patrol over the convoy routes during "The Battle of the Atlantic"; but it was never intended to be operated from rough seas and in the continually inclement weather encountered in the North Atlantic.

By the time the N-3PB squadron and its Norwegian crews were integrated with the Royal Air Force's Coastal Command in Iceland, the German U-boat threat to Allied and neutral merchant convoys was causing heavy losses. Thus, the reconfigured, single-engine Norwegian patrol bombers became a welcome addition to the Icelandic base of operations for convoy escort and protection far into the Atlantic and Arctic oceans in all directions.

The N-3PB provided both direct attack capability to reassure merchant seamen that they were being looked out for and also a form of psychological warfare on U-boat captains and crews. In the latter dimension, U-boats had to stay well submerged to keep from being seen from the air; and as they surfaced to periscope depth to prepare for and launch an attack they always had to deal with the thought that at any moment they might be bombed or torpedoed from the air. Thus the mere presence of the N-3PB during "The Battle of the Atlantic" was a deterrent.

The N-3PB flew anti-submarine patrol missions for the two peak years of "The Battle." The squadron literally wore itself out flying convoy duty, as there was only a minimum factory pipeline of spare parts maintained after the production contract was completed. The airplane was a familiar and welcome sight to those at sea and Icelanders at home.

Restoring one of the planes was an appropriate commemoration of an uncertain time of survival that was overcome by the ingenuity, tenacity, and dauntless durability that characterizes the West. The "hinge of fate" continued to swing, however, in materializing one of the planes to be restored. But once again it was not just fate that determined the outcome. It was the people who had the ingenuity, tenacity, and dauntless durability to finally answer the question, why? And it was from these people that the leadership arose to organize and motivate a team that made this "mission impossible" accomplishable.

Thus the history of the airplane and the subsequent leadership and organized teamwork to restore it forged a duty akin to that spoken of by St. Exupery. In the end it was not the airplane that was so important, as the duty to restore it. The history of the

---

[12] Loc. Cit., pp. 24-25, and 35.

airplane bespoke acts of heroism and of ingenuity, tenacity, and dauntless durability that themselves had to be restored as an example for the present world.

Fittingly, the leadership stepped forward in Iceland itself, in the person of Ragnar J. Ragnarsson. The people of Iceland have historically lived out of the mainstream of transit and communication between America and Europe, partly due to geographic location but mainly due to an inherent propensity and choice of the spirit. Nevertheless, being conveniently located as an intermediate port of landing and refuge to make the Atlantic crossing more manageable, if not safer, Iceland has acquired in particular a notable history of aviation since transatlantic flights began. For example, in 1933, Count Italo Balbo, an Italian military officer and Air Marshal assigned to promote and demonstrate Italy's air power, made Iceland a stopover point with his 24 aircraft. His many transatlantic flights promoted commercial aviation, as well as Italy's military aviation. Coincidentally, the Norwegians referred to a hangar built by Icelandic Airways in 1930 for its commercial aircraft as Balbo Hangar during WWII.[13] Ironically, Count Balbo was a leading Fascist in Italy noted for leading the Blackshirt militia in its October 1922 march on Rome. Mussolini made him General of Militia in 1923, Undersecretary of State for Air in 1926, Air Minister in 1926, and Air Marshal in 1933. But Balbo, while being a top salesman for Fascism, had two serious faults: he was pro-British and had a rising popularity that competed with Mussolini's. Mussolini removed him from the limelight by making him Governor of Libya. Shortly after, in June 1940, he was killed when his airplane was shot down by Italian anti-aircraft guns in Tobruk Harbor, Libya, after he apparently did not give the correct recognition signals on his approach for landing. That's how tyrants treat their buddies.

Ragnar was one of the founding members of the Icelandic Aviation Historical Society (IAHS) in June 1977.[14] As Ragnar has noted in response to questions asked for this book, the mission of IAHS is to preserve the broad history of aviation in Iceland, the flights of Count Balbo being one example. Military aviation, of both World War II and the ensuing Cold War and the following peacekeeping missions, is a special segment of interest for which he and the first IAHS president, Baldur Sveinsson, have been responsible for within the organization.

---

[13] The Norwegians, fighting to return to their homeland, no doubt wanted to be as transient in Iceland as the Count had been, and so humorously referred to this hangar, which they used for maintenance, as Balbo's. To the benefit of history, their choice of nickname for this hangar immortalized both their heroic fight to return home and the Count's early transcontinental flight in which he refueled in Iceland.

[14] Note that while "Ragnar" is a first name and the author may be considered unduly familiar in using it, he does so because the custom in Iceland is to use that name in addressing a person, since, by law, the first name of the father becomes the root for offspring. The syllable "son" is added for sons, as in Ragnarsson, whereas "dottir" is added for daughters, as in Ragnarsdottir. Women retain their patronymic surname after marriage. Thus whether male or female, one's family tree is readily traceable. In any society, this may be a quite useful control, both for behavior and demographic accountability. In Iceland, even the phone book is organized by first names. With a population of just under 300,000, Iceland's citizens are listed in the annually updated National Registry, a convenient form of census.

Ragnar got the idea for raising N-3PB No. 320 quite coincidentally. In 1972, he had been engaged by the Royal Air Force to guide a British team into the interior of Iceland to salvage a Fairey Battle bomber that in 1940 had made a forced landing on the great central lava plain near the Hofsjokull glacier. It was a difficult trek across heavily crevassed terrain surrounded by mountains rising to over 6,000 feet in elevation. On the way inland, he learned that the Fairey Battle bombers had preceded the Norwegian N-3PB seaplane and RAF Squadron 330(N), which of course had been staffed by Norwegians. Since Iceland had originally been discovered and settled by Norwegians, he decided he would check on the background of N-3PB operations during that great and recent war that had pushed Iceland onto the world stage, willing and ready or not. He was intrigued not only by Iceland's historic tie with Norway in terms of people, but by the heroic determination of the Norwegians who had escaped German occupation and come to Iceland to continue the fight for their country's freedom. It was the same persevering, dauntless, undefeatable, independent spirit as that of Icelanders.

His interest intensified when, going northward along the Thjorsa River to get to the Fairey Battle's crash site, he learned from farmers who were questioned about parts and shown pictures of the Fairey Battle that they knew also about a single-engine military seaplane that had crashed in the river. At one farm, the salvage team found parts, including some from the engine, from that plane, which the British identified as an N-3PB. Since it was a Norwegian airplane, the British, hunting for the Fairey Battle, were not interested in it and so, with Ragnar leading the way, they pushed on to the site of their aircraft, which was recovered and subsequently rebuilt for display in the RAF Museum in Hendon, England, where it is today.

Having seen what could be done to restore one's sense of historical awareness and presence in the world, Ragnar couldn't stop thinking about that N-3PB immersed somewhere in the Thjorsa River. It became not only an operational challenge to find, recover, and restore that airplane, it became a historical necessity – an ancestral duty, one that would commemorate the spirit of Iceland as well as its Norwegian forerunners who had fought to preserve the future of their homeland using Iceland as a base of operations. Finding and raising the N-3PB became the first major military aircraft restoration project of the IAHS and added impetus to Ragnar's participation in the formation and operation of that Society.

This book tells the story of how that N-3PB got buried in the Thjorsa River, how Ragnar succeeded in bringing it to the surface again, and how it got restored by Northrop Corporation to commemorate Jack Northrop's 85th birthday and then became a permanent aviation museum exhibit in Norway, the country that had made it possible in the beginning.

Inseparable from this story, however, is another one. It is first of all a story involving four nations and over 500 people, many of whom contributed a large measure of their time, effort, and ingenuity over a two-year period without pay. It is in the larger, less physical sense, a story of a restoration of a past duty well-performed: a duty of the nation that had an urgent mission need for an airplane of certain capabilities during a time when its survival was in jeopardy; of the men and women of the company that designed and built it; of the men who flew and supported it; and finally of the men and women who brought it to life again. That's what this book is about: teams of people working individually at their best toward a common goal that synthesizes their contributions into something yet greater that restores what it meant individually and as a team.

The N-3PB restoration spans the history of the 20th Century in the context of aviation and the impact of aviation as an industry that was dominated by innovative, risktaking individuals and yet required teams of people to develop, produce, and operate aircraft. Though the N-3PB entered on this history just before mid-century, its genesis began with the Wright Brothers and a man known worldwide as Jack Northrop. While the Wright Brothers proved that man could fly, Jack Northrop is known for having made the airplane adaptable to the multiple missions in use today. Northrop was successful, because he had the vision and the essential team spirit that great visions require to be materialized. He was the right man, in the right place, at the right time, as were the people who were members of his team; and as were the people and the nations who succeeded because of the aircraft his team supplied them.

This restoration is not a one-time story. Great restorations are iterative, because at their most fundamental level, they are of the spirit. These are the classic restorations that, over time, assume mythical dimensions as feats transition to legends and legends to myth. Even Icarus, the classic example of the person whose spirited reach misfortunately exceeded his grasp, can be restored; and in the process, we learn and benefit from, together, the great lesson Icarus learned.

In the end, we learn that a true restoration is not of the past, but of a new, higher – even transcending – level of being in the future. The N-3PB exemplifies one such classic restoration. Its story tells of one restoration leading to another. Norwegians, by fighting back as a team with everything available, restored their nation. Today, Norwegians are helping other nations restore themselves through teamwork. Similarly, Northrop, Britain, and Iceland continue to restore themselves. Thus the story of restoration, in any form or level, is an important lesson for the world today and the future.

CHAPTER 2 - SNOWSTORM, FLYING BLIND, CRASHING: SETTING UP THE RESTORATION

While the background of World War II puts the N-3PB military seaplane into its historical perspective and shows how and why it came into being and use, the story of its restoration begins where the airplane's mission life ended. By 1943, the Battle of the Atlantic was changing character and in the course of fighting that battle, the N-3PB had fulfilled its unintended assignment well. Inevitably, however, newer and better aircraft for the mission were becoming available and were replacing the N-3PB. It was the forced crash-landing of one of the N-3PB's being replaced that made the restoration possible and that brought about the circumstances leading to the airplane's recovery from the crash site.

By November 1942, the RAF had decided to transfer Squadron 330(N) to Scotland and re-equip it with Short Sunderland's.[15] By then, the convoy patrol operational requirement had resolved into two separate missions: convoy protection and fighter operations against recce aircraft. For example, German reconnaissance aircraft, operating out of Norway, were flying over the Denmark Strait between Iceland and Greenland, the North Atlantic to the south of Iceland, and the Norwegian Sea between Iceland and the Shetland Islands north of Scotland. This change in the Icelandic mission mode from pure convoy protection to recce interception took place as the German Command temporarily shifted many U-boats to the Mediterranean to counter the buildup of Allied shipping logistically supporting invasion forces there. The Luftwaffe deployed an increased number of reconnaissance aircraft in the Iceland area to assist the subs in their mission and to watch for convoys bound for Russia. In short, the Germans needed more air reconnaissance of the North Atlantic and Arctic convoy routes so as to focus the attack of the U-boats. The RAF in turn was bringing in newer, faster, more mission compatible aircraft to fight this kind of multimode, air and surface, battle engagement.

After January 1943 all that remained of the N-3PB operations was C-Flight under the command of Lt. Wsevolod W. ("Sevi") Bulukin.[16] Lt. Bulukin had become second-in-command of C-Flight on September 29, 1942 and took full command on February 20,

---

[15] The Short Sunderland S.25 had been in use by the British since 1937 for general reconnaissance but, as its war mission progressed, became well armed to ward off air and surface attack while dropping bombs and depth charges on surface ships or U-boats. Crews who had flown the N-3PB welcomed the relative comfort of the Sunderland, which had efficient interior heating. The plane was so well armed with nose, dorsal, tail gun turrets and gun hatches in the aft fuselage, plus hand-held guns fired by crew members, that one survived attack by eight Ju 88s, shooting down three of them. Because it literally bristled with guns, the Germans allegedly nicknamed the Sunderland the "Flying Porcupine."

[16] Lt. Bulukin's full name was Wsevolod Walentinovich Bulukin. The first two names were shortened to "Sevi" by those who knew him.

1943.   Previously, he had been Deputy Technical Officer of Squadron 330(N). He had specifically requested to be transferred to C-Flight, where he knew he would fly on patrol missions over the most active sealanes between Iceland and the Faeroe Islands (northeast of the Shetlands) where the North Atlantic meets the Norwegian Sea – an area known as the Northern Passage Route to U-boats entering the Atlantic in search of Allied convoys. Another motivating factor was that at the time of his transfer, C-Flight – and also B-Flight out of Akureyri on the north coast – had been given the additional mission of flying fighter patrols to intercept German recce aircraft serving as convoy spotters for the U-boats; but "Sevi" wanted C-Flight, because it flew into the Norwegian Sea toward his homeland, whereas B-Flight flew westward into the Denmark Strait.

Although he had not flown the N-3PB in combat until the transfer to C-Flight, he was an experienced fighter pilot. In just eight months he logged 174 hours in the N-3PB while serving concurrently as first, deputy commander and then commander. He flew the airplane on convoy patrol against U-boats and in air attacks against the increasing number of German recce aircraft. Though some sources anecdotally related that he had attacked a U-boat he caught surfaced and bombed as it crash-dived, he later disavowed such an attack.[17] In air combat against Focke Wolfe Condor reconnaissance aircraft – which were fast and heavily armed – in one engagement he silenced the rear gunner and caused the aircraft to head home and in another he was saved when the N-3PB's propeller stopped an incoming tracer (signifying a stream of bullets) aimed directly at him. Including this one, Sevi recorded three air combat engagements in his personal logbook. Such engagements, in general, had become more frequent as the Battle of the Atlantic progressed and the U-boat fleet became increasingly coordinated for convoy attacks by German recce aircraft.

So when Lt. "Sevi" Bulukin and his radio operator, Warrant Officer Leif Dag Rustad, climbed into their respective cockpits of N-3PB Serial No. 320 on the afternoon of April 18, 1943, to fly inland across Iceland rather than out to sea, they anticipated an uneventful – even short, by mission standards – flight. Their flight plan this time was to fly to Reykjavik on the southwest coast to turn the airplane in for scrapping, since C-Flight operations had been officially terminated as of the end of March. While he had flown this type of airplane many times out over the North Atlantic for the convoy patrol missions between Iceland and the Faeroe Islands, now it was to be a routine flight inland, covering the 250-mile distance between Budareyri and Reykjavik in under two hours, one-third the duration of a regular patrol mission over the open sea.

As shown in Figure 5, the terrain between the two bases is characteristic of Iceland's virtually inaccessible, uninhabited interior, consisting of large volcanic mountain cones

---

[17] Ragnar J. Ragnarsson, a historian of U-boat operations in Icelandic waters, has compiled a detailed record of U-boats sunk and confirms that Bulukin never attacked or sank a U-boat in his N-3PB missions. See Chapter 13, page 292, for Bulukin's direct statement on this subject. Perhaps due to the fervor of the war spirit, other reports of N-3PB attacks on U-boats and even the battleship Bismarck turned out to be unfounded assumptions, rumors, or mistaken. Some got published in newspapers in the local Northrop Aircraft community.

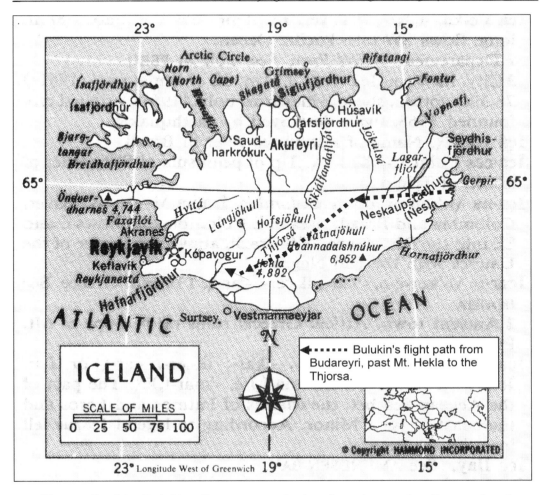

Figure 5. Lt. Bulukin flew over glacier-ringed, semi-active volcanic mountain ranges in a blinding snowstorm, attempting to return N-3PB SN 320 from C-Flight's port on the east to Reykjavik on the southwest coast of Iceland.

and interconnecting ridges interspersed with rivers running generally in a southwest direction.

As they took off from the fishing village port at Budareyri, the weather was relatively clear for Iceland and Bulukin later said that the forecast from the RAF's Meteorological Office in Reykjavik was that the weather would hold for the entire flight. This was good news for several reasons: for one, the trip was somewhat nostalgic, because this was probably one of the last times he and Leif Rustad, would be flying as crewmembers together in an N-3PB airplane; second, it was also probably one of the last flights of the N-3PB aircraft series in Iceland; and third, they needed good weather to make the trip safely.

Since weather was a key factor in what was about to happen, Ragnar Ragnarsson, in researching the last flight of N-3PB Serial No. 320 reached the conclusion that the RAF forecast would not have deviated from that of the Icelandic Meteorological Bureau, since both worked from the same data. From Ragnar's review of the historical data it was evident that the presence of an approaching front ought to have been known to both agencies and made known to anyone inquiring about flying conditions. For instance, at 1 p.m. local weather stations in the vicinity of Bulukin's forced landing reported freezing drizzle or rain during the past hour, visibility of 20-30 km (12 to 19 miles), temperature of 2 degrees centigrade, cloud ceiling of 200-300 meters (approximately 650-1,000 feet), and an eastsoutheast wind of Force 2 (4-7 mph). But even knowing this, Bulukin and Rustad may not have been too concerned, since they usually flew away from the island rather than across it and were aware that the weather inland changed by the minute.

From Bulukin's and Rustad's view, the trip was somewhat nostalgic, because Squadron 330(N) members, like themselves, had spent hundreds of cold, droning hours, strapped in their lone cockpit stations, on patrol over the ocean, out of sight of land; and the plane had served them well – had proved itself in combat and returned them to base alive mission after mission with minimal maintenance in the face of the urgent mission need the airplane had to fulfill. It was this last factor that made clear weather so important, for N-3PB Serial No. 320 was likely not only on its last flight, but was on its last wing-and-a-prayer as a viable aircraft for any kind of extended flight. In fact, the airplane had been returned on March 30 after a two-week major inspection by the maintenance section at Balbo Hangar in Reykjavik, where it was granted a limited flight extension of 30 hours, but not to be used for operational missions. Bulukin stated later that several flight instruments did not work well.

So, in general, Bulukin and Rustad felt a sense of sentimental introspection as the airplane lifted from the fjord and turned onto its course. The flight plan, as shown by the map, was to fly a westsouthwest heading of 260 degrees directly to the seabase at the port in Reykjavik, the capitol of Iceland. This was the shortest route and would take them just south of the 4,790-foot Trolladyngja peak and north of the 6,562-foot Vatnajokull glacier. Beyond these glaciers, by staying about a mile high they could fly all the way to their destination and maintain visual contact to spot landmarks in the changing topography of the rugged, desolate terrain along the way.

But one hour and over 100 miles into the flight, as they approached a ridge over which they must pass, a gray overcast began forming and Bulukin had to descend to stay in visual contact with the terrain. Above were high cirrus clouds and as they proceeded on course the ceiling got continually lower, a combination warning any flyer that they were approaching a front.

Skimming over the ridge to get to the west side of the range, he was forced still lower to stay below the overcast. They were being forced slightly northwest in order to stay over lower ground and beneath the overcast. In that direction the plain dropped in altitude to around 1,500 feet and they could maintain ground contact beneath the lowering, thickening overcast.

Had they turned directly northwest and stayed on a visual course they would have been able to go north around the Langjokull glacier sitting in the center of the island, and then head southwest to their destination. But the approaching weather front, directly in front of them and riding on a 20-knot wind blowing directly at their plane, blocked that option. Bulukin, thinking they had a 10-to-20-knot tailwind, was trying to maintain his direct heading to Reykjavik. He was looking for the Hvita River, a landmark he knew would lead them to the coastline he could then follow to Reykjavik. Since between the point where the Hvita discharges into the sea about 30 miles southeast of Reykjavik and his destination there is a 1,800-foot mountain range he could not have crossed given the weather conditions, his only choice was to follow the coastline around the Reykjanes Peninsula to Reykjavik; that is exactly what he intended to do, as he told Ragnar J. Ragnarsson in an interview 36 years later at the recovery site. But his intentions and the indifferent forces of the weather were two independent variables, the latter beyond his control.

As they let down on the west side of the range, Bulukin saw in the distance that the weatherfront was massing lower still. Ahead, this still lower formation of clouds was dark and ominous. But his assurance returned quickly, because he could now make out the glint of a river underneath this formation. With this river (which, due to their tailwind, he assumed was the Hvita) as his anticipated checkpoint, he felt confident that they were on course.

However, flying to the east of the river and following it south a few minutes under the lower clouds, it became evident something was wrong: the river appeared to curve suddenly west and the valley did not widen out into a plain, as it should have if he was where he thought he was. And now, the clouds were pressing him still lower and lower. As so often happens when trouble occurs, the situation was compounded suddenly and dramatically when it started to snow. Visibility was soon reduced to 200 meters forward.

He had to turn west to keep the river in sight. Now it was curving back to its southwest flow. It was evident they would soon be flying blind in snow. There was no alternative but to land; as he descended directly toward the leg of the river beneath them he saw behind them that the ridge they had just flown over was engulfed in dense clouds to ground level; their path of retreat was cut off. In a minute the river would no longer be visible, as the snowstorm closed about them, blanketing his view. Like all pilots caught in similar situations, he prepared to land, instinctively seeking refuge in procedure.

They were descending over a slope that ended in a river with bends and twists he had not expected. There was no time or room to set up a landing pattern. All he could do was throttle back the big 1,200-horsepower Wright Cyclone engine and feel for the water while staying ready to maneuver immediately in response to any sudden bend, twist, or obstacle that might suddenly appear as the river unfolded in front of him.

He was well aware and apprehensive of the numerous landing hazards unseen in a glacial river: sandbars; rocks; ice; shallow pools; and here, the sudden change of direction – but there were no other choices left. Nature had trapped them where they were and they and the plane had to deal with the situation confronting them.

Bulukin eased the plane's descent toward the snow-enshrouded, uncertain landing strip of water under a powerglide at 80 knots, the snow squall seeming to intensify its pummeling of the plane as Bulukin slowed it. The floats smacked the water once and the aircraft lifted and flew just above the surface for a few seconds before Bulukin chopped the power all the way to let it settle in. Simultaneously, out of the swirling snow, a dark mass of land loomed directly ahead. He kicked full right rudder and lowered the right wing in a desperate effort to turn, but the right float struck water and, with the aircraft in a right skid, the side loads on the float proved too much; the float pedestal crumpled and the float tore loose as the aircraft continued forward a short distance before settling in the water.

Unbuckling their seat harnesses, Bulukin and Rustad scrambled over the cockpit railing onto the port wing, unsure as to what the plane might do next, sink under their feet or float; but they were sure of their emergency procedure. Bulukin quickly took his flight boots off and stuffed them in his jacket. He advised Rustad to do the same, but Rustad, turning the dire event into a moment humorously out of place, refused on the grounds that he had on new boots and didn't want to lose them.[18]

Sliding off the wing they entered the water and began stroking and kicking cumbersomely toward the nearest shore, feeling for bottom as they went. Within minutes they could see that the current was sweeping them southwest toward shore, which was now directly ahead of them. If they could stay afloat, they would be carried to shore.

The temperature transition was immediate and a shock. Like many Icelandic rivers, this one was glacial and the temperature of the water went from freezing at its source, to the low 40F's as the water fed in rivulets into the river, and then to the high 40F's as the river flowed on downstream to the North Atlantic where, in winter, the water temperature hovered in the mid-50F's. But instinctively seeking to escape to safety from sudden danger, the wet coldness energized them for maximum effort. At this time of year, the river was making its transition from the subzero, instantly freezing temperatures of winter to spring, when the water was perhaps 10 degrees above freezing at most.

Shore, about 50 yards to the portside of the plane, was fortunately the direction in which the river was flowing and was reached after a relatively short swim. The last few feet they were able to walk. On shore, they hesitated only long enough for Bulukin to put his boots on. It was still daylight, but snowing heavily. To pause meant hypothermia, getting sleepy, passing out, and freezing.

Soaked to the skin, they moved on up the sloping beach onto a lava field and headed cross-country, moving generally west, directly away from the river, clambering up the hill. Coming suddenly on to a road, they proceeded along it and came to a farmhouse. Within the hour they were wrapped in blankets and their clothes were being dried before the fire.

---

[18] As noted later by Sevi in Chapter 13, Rustad somehow lost his new boots. One can imagine the uncertainty the two men felt, staring into the whiteout of an arctic snowstorm, being swept along by a river of unknown size and destination at near freezing temperature, their only orientation of stability themselves and what they clung to.

They had by luck or instinct reached a farm called Asolfsstadir, where Ragnar Ragnarsson, the leader of the recovery of the N-3PB, would learn of the crashed aircraft's existence 29 years later.

Their host, Farmer Asolfur Palsson of the Farm Asolfsstadir, explained to the two flyers where they were and told them of the treacherous section of the river where they had crashed. They had actually come down on the Thjorsa River, not the Hvita they had been looking for. The curvature in the river was where it flowed almost due west around Mt. Burfell. The Hvita River was 25 miles away, due west. Now it was clear what had happened, how and why.

As shown in Figure 6, in the blinding snowstorm, they had unknowingly tried to land at a sharp bend in the river where its southerly course turns abruptly west for about one-half mile.

If the plane had been forced down closer to the east bank they would have ended up on the opposite shore (the east shore, instead of the west) where there were no farms; and there they would have soon perished in the snowstorm. If they had to be forced down and crash it was the best place and time to do it, for in April the water is rising and flowing faster due to the spring melting of snow and ice. The 5-knot current, flowing southwest and picking up speed as it rounded the curve that had blocked their landing, had fortuitously swept them rapidly to the west bank.[19]

From the farm, Bulukin phoned the Reykjavik flight base of Squadron 330(N) and reported the forced landing and their situation. By air, they were over 55 miles from their intended destination. They were lucky they had been in an airplane with floats. Once again the N-3PB had delivered them to safety. Though the plane had crashed and was no longer usable, its flying days were over anyway.

One has to wonder at the coincidence. Training, talent, and instinct had saved them, with a degree of luck added. They weren't killed or injured and this farm, while not the only one in the area that they could have reached within their survival limits, was the closest. Besides Asolfsstadir, there were several others within walking distance, but all in a line running generally north-south. If they had continued westward, they would have trekked through mountainous terrain for miles before reaching another farm. Sevi, later relating that he had first caught sight of a light from the Farm Asolfsstadir when about 200 yards away, admitted it was a close call.

N-3PB, Serial No. 320, seemingly had performed this last mission in lieu of being scrapped. Minus the right float, it settled slowly into the sand and silt of the Thjorsa River, which became its bed for the next 36 years. The crash, in effect, had become the prerequisite for its recovery and restoration.

---

[19] The seasonal change in the current flow of the river was a factor that had to be considered and dealt with in the recovery of the airplane from its eventual resting place in the riverbed southwest of where it was forced down. So while the current aided Bulukin and Rustad in taking them to the west shore surely and quickly, it made it difficult for the recovery divers to stay in position while working to free the airplane from its burial site in the riverbed. Details of the extent of this problem and how it was resolved are presented in Part II.

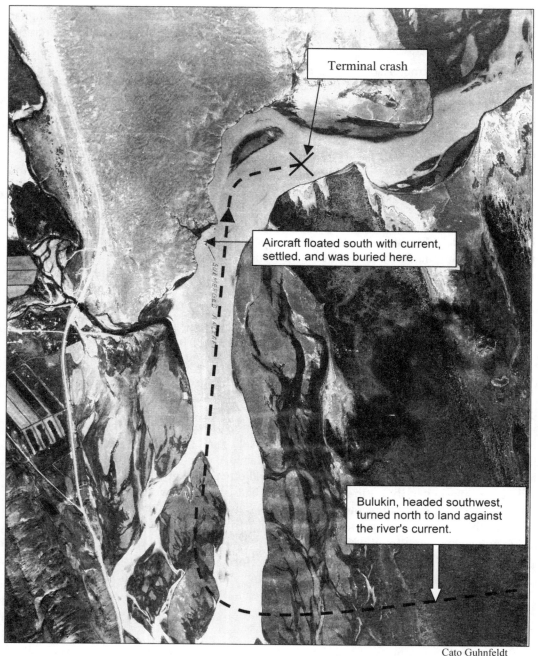

Terminal crash

Aircraft floated south with current, settled. and was buried here.

Bulukin, headed southwest, turned north to land against the river's current.

Cato Guhnfeldt

Figure 6. The Thjorsa River, where the plane was forced down in a snowstorm, flows southwest from the Hofsjokull and Vatnajokull glaciers and is the longest in Iceland. While circumstances had caused the crashlanding, they also saved the crew and, in the end, the airplane.

Had Bulukin been more familiar with Iceland's interior weather patterns and peculiarities, after crossing the first major ridge out of Budareyri he would have flown northwest around the central volcanic cone, where the terrain flattened out and was lower in altitude, and then headed southwest to Reykjavik. It would have been a longer flight, but the low-altitude threat of the weather front would have been largely avoided. But, as normal duty required, his flight time and experience had been over the open Atlantic and the Norwegian Sea, away from Iceland, where the weather, though harsh, was more predictable.

Bulukin took the Figure 7 picture a day after the forced landing. The plane had tilted to the left, because the right wing, without the weight of its pontoon, lifted toward the surface with the rushing current of the river. This tilted posture of the plane was to have a serious impact on the way it interacted with the river and humans over the years of its entrapment and set the stage for a potential fatality years later.

Sevi Bulukin

Figure 7. N-3PB SN 320 settled onto its remaining (left-side) float immediately after its forced landing in the Thjorsa River, about 120 feet offshore, in 12 feet of water. Its tail section would gradually disappear below the surface over the next two decades.

Bulukin returned to the site 36 years later to coordinate the participation of Norway as an international team member in the recovery and restoration of the plane. Directly at the recovery site, he also indoctrinated the international diving team in the configuration of the airplane that they could not see but were committed to raise from the riverbed. Once again he met Farmer Palsson, who had invited him and Rustad to his fireside to dry out on the day the plane hit the river and crashed.

A week after the crash, Bulukin and Rustad flew back to Budareyri in N-3PB Serial No. 318. Since C-Flight was no longer in operation, they returned to Reykjavik on May 17, after picking up remaining C-Flight gear. It was the last N-3PB flight to depart Budareyri.

Lt. Sevi Bulukin went on to other major wartime experiences and accomplishments. His son Jan, who lives in Norway, has written of him as follows:

He was born on March 11, 1913 in Oslo, as a son of Russian immigrants. The family being poor, his life was not easy, but he still managed to get an education as a pilot (even a stint learning soaring in Germany) as well as complete his studies at the university.

During the German invasion of Norway on April 9, 1940, he was grounded by his pro-German superior, not being allowed to fly his fighter plane against the invaders (the superior being imprisoned after the war for his actions). My father then fled north, and left the country in Narvik onboard a British warship, the H.M.S. Devonshire, which by chance also was carrying the Norwegian King and government fleeing the country. Via the UK, he came to Little Norway in Canada where he received training on the N-3PB. He was onboard the first ship bringing (the) Northrop's (N-3PB's) to Iceland and led the assembly of the planes on the beach in Reykjavik.

My father was readymade for wartime service. He was completely fearless, direct, fantastic in improvising, and he always went the extra mile. In 1945, he was posted to Germany. Due to his Russian ancestry, he organized and headed expeditions behind Russian lines to rescue Norwegians entrapped in German concentration camps. Only his ingenuity and bravery allowed him to penetrate the Russian lines with three separate expeditions, find what he wanted, and get out alive. He went eastwards through the Russian lines into East Germany under cover of bringing Czech POW's to Prague (which he even actually did).

He used German POW's as drivers to find the way, then zigzagged his way westwards freeing and picking up Norwegians. He threatened, lied, bribed, forged documents and drank vodka with the Russians, all to accomplish his urgent goal. He even managed to bluff three of his staff out of Russian capture, after they had been arrested as spies and set up for interrogation in Moscow with probable subsequent execution.

In total, he brought some 1,100 Norwegians out, military and civilians alike. The ones he could not find quickly ended up in Siberia as slave labor and disappeared.[20]

With the deactivation of C-Flight, Lt. Sevi Bulukin was transferred to the deHavilland factory in England as a technical officer, where he was stationed until the end of the war was apparent. His contribution in this aircraft technical field of endeavor

---

[20] E-mail from Jan Bulukin, Norway, on April 23, 2001.

was deemed as valuable to the Allied success in the war as his contributions to the requirements of Squadron 330(N) in his technical, operations command, and aviator's roles.

Postwar, back in Norway, he became a Lt. Colonel in the Royal Norwegian Air Force. Lt. Bulukin had put a lot into the flying business, but he took more out. His experience with the N-3PB was a classic case of man and his machine against that ancient threat, the enemy and nature; and the man and his machine were not vanquished.

Leif Dag Rustad, his radio operator, was killed less than six months after the N-3PB crash-landed, on October 12, 1943, when flying as a crewmember of Norwegian Squadron 330(N) on a training flight aboard a Sunderland flying boat that crashed in the sea near Alness (Invergordon), Scotland. The entire 11-man crew was killed. His body was not among the five recovered.

As the story of the N-3PB unfolded, Sevi Bulukin continued to play an important role. The recovery and restoration of the plane continually restored the meaning and the significance of his life to him, as he moved on to perform as a member of the recovery team. Though he continued to rise in rank as an officer, he remained familiarly and fondly known in aviation circles as "Sevi."

Meanwhile, the N-3PB was to become so lost in the Thjorsa River that even its true "Serial No." identity was to become mistaken. But as events unfolded, it was to be found that a very special bond existed between pilot and plane – a form of team in itself.

CHAPTER 3 - THE SEALANE PATROL MISSION & THE FASTEST SEAPLANE

As World War II approached, the world itself was undergoing rapid change. After his son was kidnapped, Charles Lindbergh, having moved with his wife to Europe to escape the sensationalized news coverage of this tragedy, had reported in 1936, with some hint of admiration, the advances in aircraft design and mass production being achieved by the Germans.[21] From a military perspective, this report stimulated a change in the aircraft industry in the U.S. much as the Soviet's launch of Sputnik into orbit about the earth had done in 1957. But, already, commercial aviation had begun growing and the major aircraft companies that blossomed during the war and afterwards became the core of the new aerospace industry included, in the early 1930's: Curtiss, Ryan, Vultee, Vought, Grumman, Douglas, Lockheed, Boeing, and, of course, Northrop. Still earlier, mail delivery by air had begun concurrently in Europe and the U.S., after the First World War had demonstrated the reliability and performance capabilities of aircraft and pilots eager to continue flying were immediately available for employment. Lindbergh himself, too young for the first war, but fresh from flight duty with the army in 1924-25, became an airmail pilot in 1926, flying the mail between St. Louis, Missouri, and Chicago, Illinois. It was this job that introduced him to the group of St. Louis businessmen who financed his solo, 33.5-hour transatlantic flight on May 20-21, 1927 in the Ryan-built *Spirit of St. Louis*.

Seven years older than Lindbergh, Jack Northrop's career paralleled the former's, though concentrated on the design side of aircraft. From the time he first saw an airplane fly in 1911, at age 16, Northrop knew that the design of better-and-better aircraft was what he would devote his life to. It was five years later, after jobs as an auto mechanic and construction draftsman, that he saw his next airplane – a seaplane brought to Santa Barbara, California, where Northrop had grown up, by the Loughead brothers. In his spare time, Northrop hung around the brothers, who called him "Jack," helping with maintenance of the plane, which the brothers were paying for by giving sightseeing rides. When the brothers won a contract with the Navy to build two Curtiss-designed seaplanes, they started an aircraft factory locally and Northrop was one of the first employees. Having studied and performed stress analysis as part of his job as draftsman at the construction company, he now applied the same skills to the seaplane, which the brothers were modifying to meet the Navy's specifications. After the war, the brothers decided to build a sports plane, the S-1, which Northrop designed as one of the first high-strength, lightweight, monocoque-fuselage aircraft. The plane couldn't compete pricewise, though,

---

[21] Lindbergh created further sensation in 1938 when he was awarded and accepted a decoration from the German government and then, on returning to the U.S. in late 1939, advocated that the U.S. remain neutral after the war had erupted in August of that year with the sudden invasion of Poland by Germany.

with all the surplus Army Air Corps bi-planes that suddenly flooded the market at $400 each when the war ended.[22] When the brothers were forced to close their plant, Northrop returned to his job with his father in the construction industry, which was now undergoing postwar expansion. Then in 1923, when Donald Douglas opened his aircraft company in Santa Monica, Northrop, wanting to get back to aircraft in any capacity, took a job as an assembler and three weeks later was designing fuel tanks for the historical "Round-the-World Cruiser."

In 1927 he returned to work with the Loughead brothers at their renamed Lockheed Company.[23] There he designed the famed Lockheed Vega. The record-breaking Vega, though still a high wing monoplane, was the most advanced airplane of its time, both structurally and aerodynamically. Early pilots of note such as Amelia Earhart, Art Goebel, Wiley Post, and Hubert Wilkins used the Vega in establishing their fame, in historic flights to faraway places. It was the design breakthrough achieved in this airplane that freed aircraft structural design from the previous classical mechanics of the cantilevered beam; and that prompted Claude Ryan to engage Jack Northrop to design the lightweight wing eventually required to make Lindbergh's *Spirit of St. Louis* feasible for the first solo crossing of the Atlantic.[24]

Northrop had still more advanced concepts envisioned, as shown in Figure 8. Having mastered conventional designs, he wanted to experiment with more radical solutions that promised still further advances in performance. In 1928 he and Kenneth Jay formed the two-man Avion Corporation to pioneer the development of the first all-metal, multicellular, stressed skin panel construction that finally became the standard for all aircraft wing design and manufacture. This breakthrough was an ingenious combination

---

[22] Even Lindbergh bought one of these, a Jenny, at Souther Field, Georgia, in April 1923, paying $500, partially funded by a note signed by his father and partially from money he had earned as a barnstormer doing parachute jumps and wing walks, during the summer and fall of 1922. He selected his Jenny from a large stock of surplus Army trainers stored on the now-deserted airfield that had been used to train Army pilots during the U.S.'s participation in the First World War. The $500 was only half the asking price, but all that Lindbergh had. For that amount, he got a completely refurbished airplane with a new Curtiss OX-5, 90-hp, water-cooled engine and a fresh coat of olive drab paint on all the fabric surfaces, plus an extra 20-gallon gasoline tank in the fuselage. With only 8 hours non-solo flight time in a Standard and 35 minutes in a Jenny, he almost crashed on takeoff. His first solo flight is described thusly in *The Last Hero: Charles A. Lindbergh*, by Walter S. Ross: "Lindbergh thought he'd try out the plane on the ground by taxing back and forth across the huge field. He taxied downwind to the opposite corner of the field. So far, so good. Then he headed back, into the wind. This time the Jenny began acting strangely. He tried to straighten it out, but before he knew it, he was airborne. Seeing the ground departing, he cut the throttle, came down too fast, gunned the engine, went up with one wing low, closed the throttle, yanked back on the stick, and luckily hit the ground on one wheel and wing skid." His problem may have been the change in cg caused by that extra gas tank. When he finally flew the plane with a qualified pilot accompanying him, it performed according to expectations.
[23] Since "Loughead" was pronounced "Lockheed" the new board of directors quickly voted to make the spelling agree with the pronunciation.
[24] Cf., John H. Northrop's Foreword, p. ix.

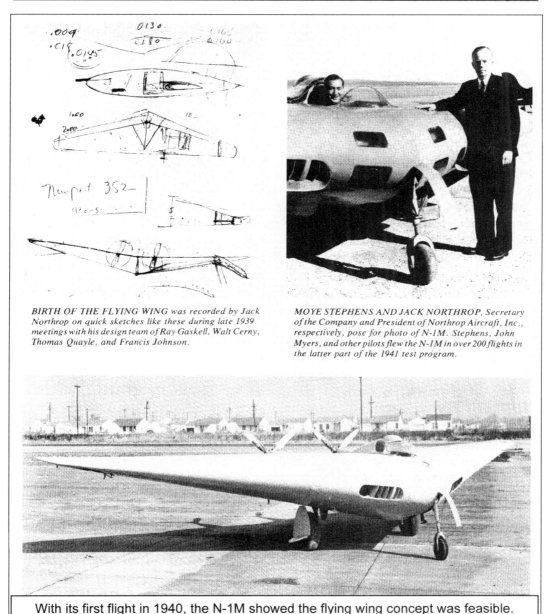

BIRTH OF THE FLYING WING was recorded by Jack Northrop on quick sketches like these during late 1939 meetings with his design team of Ray Gaskell, Walt Cerny, Thomas Quayle, and Francis Johnson.

MOYE STEPHENS AND JACK NORTHROP, Secretary of the Company and President of Northrop Aircraft, Inc., respectively, pose for photo of N-1M. Stephens, John Myers, and other pilots flew the N-1M in over 200 flights in the latter part of the 1941 test program.

With its first flight in 1940, the N-1M showed the flying wing concept was feasible.

Northrop, An Aeronautical History

Figure 8. Jack Northrop's ultimate design concept for using lightweight structure to maximize aircraft payload capabilities is expressed in the flying wing, a concept reducing weight and drag penalties by integrating the fuselage in the wing itself, as shown above by the N-1M prototype.

of design innovation and new materials technology. His ultimate vision for this synthesis of design and technology was an all-wing airplane.

The strategy behind Avion was for it to serve as an aircraft design and technology development center that would farm out the actual production work under license. This strategy would leave Northrop free to concentrate on his advanced aircraft configurations. At Avion, he materialized his first all-wing design, the M-1, as the feasibility model later built in flyable prototype form as the N1-M shown in Figure 8. Northrop's ingenious concept of synthesizing monocoque design of the fuselage with a lightweight, high-strength approach to wing design attracted the attention of the Boeing Company and Avion soon became part of a new organization called Northrop Aircraft, which though independently organized, was actually controlled by Boeing. By achieving high-strength with lightweight in both the fuselage and wing, Northrop had arrived at the way to optimize the entire airframe and maximize the amount of payload that an airplane could carry. This approach to payload maximization was the key to both commercial and military air superiority, and Bill Boeing wanted access to it.

The new company produced two exceptionally fine aircraft, called the Alpha and the Beta, which introduced the low-wing monoplane. Despite this breakthrough in higher speed and lighter weight design, the Great Depression was deepening into the 1930's and sales languished. Boeing wanted the company to move to Kansas and merge with the Stearman Company, also owned by Boeing. Jack Northrop, now recognized by almost everyone as the technology leader of the aircraft industry – the fastest growing segment of the transportation sector of the economy, instead left Boeing and rejoined Douglas to form, in 1932, yet another new "Northrop." He wanted maximum freedom to innovate, though still having to work for someone else. Also he wanted to stay in Southern California, where his genius had taken root and blossomed.

Douglas was pleased to win back Northrop from his competitor Boeing and gave him development latitude to produce such outstanding aircraft as the Northrop Gamma, the followon to the Alpha and Beta. The Army Air Corps bought the Gamma and numerous commercial models were sold to leading pilots of the day as well as to TWA for airline use. Northrop also produced the BT-1 Navy dive-bomber, the Army's A-17A attack aircraft, and the Northrop 2E multimission attack/patrol/dive bomber. The Northrop 2E was to be the last plane he designed before departing Douglas in 1938.[25] His reason this time was that his company, now known as Northrop Corporation, was, for financial reasons, to be merged as part of the El Segundo Division of Douglas Aircraft Company. Northrop departed even though the N-2E design and all other assets of his company were

---

[25] Northrop officially resigned as head of the Northrop Aircraft Division of Douglas Aircraft, Inc., on December 31, 1937, after Donald Douglas previously, on April 5, had bought Northrop's shares in Northrop Aircraft Corporation and converted the corporation to a division. Douglas then redesignated the N-2E as the Douglas 8-A, which subsequently went through five dash-numbered configurations for export. Douglas's drive to replace the Northrop designations with his own and reduce Northrop to employee status no doubt added to Northrop's desire to form his own company. In a bit of irony for Douglas, the N-2E, in being redesignated the 8-A, led to Norway's purchase of the N-3 seaplane.

taken over by Douglas in the new organization. Douglas immediately designated the N-2E as the Douglas 8-A attack-bomber, which was sold throughout the world.

Later, after Northrop was established as a competitor, Douglas acknowledged his historical role in the aircraft industry by saying, "Every major aircraft in the sky today has something of Jack Northrop in it." This was to become a perpetual tribute, because it is now well known that future aircraft will always have something of Jack Northrop in them. Conversely, however, if every airplane had a piece of Jack Northrop, so Jack Northrop had a piece of every airplane. It was his decision in late 1937 to combine and re-integrate these "pieces" under his exclusive control for the first time that led to the formation of Northrop Aircraft, Inc., in mid-1939. For the next 12 years, he had the freedom to fulfill his dream. These years, which he referred to later as "the golden years," would end when once again someone insisted on having a "piece" of him – the most valuable "piece" of all, the flying wing.

Northrop, though he stayed a short time with Douglas Aircraft after he was bought out and the company restructured, immediately on departing got together with La Motte T. Cohu, a financier from Chicago who was now on the West Coast looking for investment opportunities in this new industry and who was associated with other local investors. The two had just the right combination of interests and capabilities. Cohu was willing to operate behind the scenes as financier and let Northrop take the operational lead. With Cohu's financing resources, Jack Northrop was able to form, facilitate, and staff, in a short time, the third and final "Northrop" corporation. Known as Northrop Aircraft, Inc., through the 1950s, then Northrop Corporation as the aerospace industry emerged, today the company is called Northrop Grumman and is ranked among the top U.S. aerospace firms.

The baseline purpose of the new "Northrop" company was to concentrate on developing and exploiting Jack Northrop's flying wing aircraft as the ultimate solution to maximum cost-effectiveness for both commercial and military aircraft. The new management acknowledged, however, that it would be some time before this ultimate solution would be producible and that, in the meantime, other business would have to be found to sustain operations. Since an immediate solution was required, building conventional aircraft under subcontract to other companies became the obvious business objective, as a steady source of income had to be found. Contracts were soon obtained from Vultee Aircraft and Boeing to produce aircraft structural assemblies, as those companies were in need of outside help to meet new and ever-increasing production commitments as the war in Europe and U.S. preparedness mounted and converged.

Jack Northrop, as usual, was ahead of the plan. Before leaving Douglas, he had already advanced his N-2E design to incorporate retractable landing gear, getting rid of that ungainly source of drag. Since, on Northrop's departure, Donald Douglas, having bought the rights to the N-2E, redesignated it the Douglas 8-A, countries that had purchased the N-2E to modernize their air forces in the 1937-38 time frame were often delivered Douglas 8-A's instead. Norway, having ordered N-2E's in 1937, received 8-A's in Toronto, Canada in 1941, after being overrun.

What was happening to Jack Northrop is best seen within the context of what was going on in the world at that time. There was momentous change taking place in the still-developing U.S. aircraft industry in the mid-1930s, when political forces in Eastern and Western Europe began to take shape as Communism, Fascism, and Nazism. In fact, as Churchill points out, the rise of Communism following WWI stimulated the nationalistic reactions that produced, first, Fascism, and then its more intense, Teutonic form, Nazism.[26] Combined with the failure of the League of Nations and the consequent lack of enforcement of the Treaty of Versailles (under which Germany was never to rearm itself again) the rise of these conflicting political ideologies was given open military expression by the concurrent rise of Hitler to power in Germany, Mussolini in Italy, and Stalin in Russia. When Hitler reoccupied the Rhineland with troops on March 7, 1936 without even diplomatic resistance from the former Allies other than France and its "Little Entente" (Czechoslovakia, Yugoslavia, Rumania, Poland, and the Baltic States), an emotional shock wave was felt worldwide. For the first time the U.S. aviation industry began getting quantity orders for military aircraft from other countries.

This sudden appearance of a new international market is what prompted Donald Douglas to buy out Jack Northrop's shares in Douglas Aircraft Company and take over his military aircraft designs and redesignate them as Douglas models. Dramatic growth was about to occur in the industry both internationally and domestically – with the news every day reporting German and Italian military moves and aggressions – and Douglas was preparing his company to respond. But so was Jack Northrop, who, as noted, already had been approached by a group of financiers to form his own company so he could find fullout expression of his highly competitive aircraft designs – for the benefit of everyone: himself, his investors, and his country.

As shown in Figure 9, it was the series of aircraft designed by Jack Northrop from 1930 through 1938 that provided the immediate readiness and capability of the new company to produce the seaplane so urgently needed by Norway as war encroached on its neutrality increasingly during 1939. As this figure shows, the advance of aviation from biplanes to all-weather passenger and airmail transports is the result of the innovativeness and tenacity of Jack Northrop. Virtually every year, Jack Northrop added a new feature to advance human transport by aircraft.

The series of aircraft known as the Alpha, Beta, Gamma, and Delta manifests the classical order of this advance to progressively higher performance aircraft that enabled higher payload carrying capability through lower weight structure and sleeker, more conformal airframe configuration for low-drag aerodynamic performance. Out of this series came the modern passenger and cargo transport aircraft, as well as modern military aircraft.

Figure 9 merely highlights this progression. Every civilian and military aircraft prior to WWII had some feature of the basic N-1, N-2, and N-3 series of Jack Northrop generic baseline designs for aircraft; and these innovations continue in some form in today's aircraft. That Jack Northrop had just left Douglas with the basic design of the N-3 ready

---

[26] Loc. Cit., Vol. I, pp. 12-15.

(a) Northrop Alpha (1930): First all-metal stressed-skin, 7-passenger transport.

(b) Northrop Gamma (1933): First all-weather coast-to-coast passenger and mail transport.

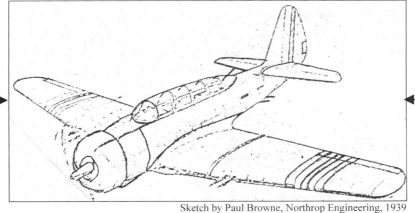

Sketch by Paul Browne, Northrop Engineering, 1939

(c) Northrop N-3 Attack Bomber – land version of N-3PB as specified to Norway in 1939.

(d) U.S. Army XA-17 Attack Aircraft (N-1) (e) U.S. Army/Navy 8-A Attack Bomber (N-2)

Figure 9. When Norway urgently needed to complement its military aircraft fleet with an advanced seaplane, Jack Northrop had a generational mission solution.

to produce was almost a mystic coincidence that continued to materialize in the form of the seaplane that Norway needed to resume its fight for freedom in an arena that was to become, as Churchill later admitted, his greatest fear of defeat for the Allies.[27]

Norway had been neutral in World War I and therefore did not participate in the rapid advancements in aircraft design and construction during and after that war. Not until 1938, when the European scene became threatening, did the Norwegian Air Force undertake to produce a limited number of in-country designed and constructed aircraft. It had became inescapably evident that there was an urgent need to increase the size of the Air Force at a rate that could not be met domestically.

As a result of its mounting needs for aircraft in the face of limited production capabilities, Norway in the mid-1930s purchased a number of Junkers JU-52's and JU-86 bombers as well as British Hawker Audex and Hornet reconnaissance and fighter aircraft. An order for Northrop 2E model attack bombers was also placed in the late-1930s. So the country was quite knowledgeable of Jack Northrop aircraft designs and their capabilities before its growth plans were cancelled by invasion.[28]

In early 1940, Cohu visited Norway in search of business for the new company. His wife was a prominent Norwegian with many high-level acquaintances and Jack Northrop was of English ancestry, with Norwegian on his mother's side. Cohu, through his wife, had the entrée, and, in Jack Northrop, the followup. Norway was looking for both land and seaplanes to upgrade its military posture as a neutral country, as the Germans made it clear that Poland was just the beginning of their territorial expansion.

Cohu took with him the specification for the Northrop N-3 airplane, establishing the baseline for the N-3 land-based configuration shown in Figure 9. As noted by Ragnar Ragnarsson, Norway's Army Air Force had already "...opted for the Douglas 8-A to replace its ancient Fokker CVs in the reconnaissance bomber role...."[29] However, Norway's requirements included, in addition, those for a fast single-engine seaplane that Cohu knew Northrop was prepared to fulfill as well, for Jack Northrop had already anticipated a replacement for the antiquated Norwegian MF-11 floatplane, using his N-3 derivative of the 8-A. It was then that Cohu alerted Jack Northrop that a seaplane derivative of his basic land-based design could be sold under immediate contract with Norway and to focus on that objective for acquisition of immediate business. Since Norway had been thinking in terms of an 8-A, the Jack Northrop N-3 would be an even more preferred solution, being the 8-A's latest design.

---

[27] See Chapter 4, p. 2.

[28] As reported in error in Robert McLarren's article "Norwegian Nemesis," in the April 1941 issue of *Model Airplane News,* the Model N-2E's were not delivered to the Norwegian government in exile in England as Douglas 8A-5's in 1940, but were delivered to "Little Norway" in Toronto, Canada, in 1941 and used for advanced training of Free Norwegian Air Force pilots. Douglas's pre-emption of the N-2E by the 8-A model designation clarifies this nomenclature confusion. The author notes this model re-designation to bridge the historical record between the McLarren article and the one by Ragnar Ragnarsson quoted below. Further clarification of this matter is provided in Chapter 4, p. 64.

[29] Loc. Cit., p. 25.

Although the U.S. Army Air Corps was phasing out its single-engine A-17 attack aircraft for the twin-engine A-20 attack bomber and its heavier payload and firepower capability, a viable export market still existed for single-engine aircraft, especially among smaller countries such as Norway. Thus to Cohu and Jack Northrop, a redesign of the Model 8-A designed by Northrop at Douglas seemed the quickest way to get a fullup aircraft production contract in the shortest time and thereby get the new company definitely established in business as a prime aircraft contractor.

It was on the basis of this business strategy that the N-3 derivative of the 8-A attack bomber (itself a derivative of the earlier N-1, as shown in Figure 9) came into existence at Northrop as a ready-to-produce design. Though a Norwegian design specification dated August 22, 1939 designated the 8-A as the model specified, the same specification dated February 7, 1940 and reviewed by Royal Norwegian Air Force Commander Kristian Ostby with Jack Northrop later in February specified the Model N-3 attack bomber. Surpassing the 8-A, the N-3 specification required improved performance and increased gross weight capability, along with provisions for ski- and water-type landing gear.

As a result of the meeting between Cmdr. Ostby and Jack Northrop, the N-3 specification was revised to call for a floatplane patrol bomber with a maximum speed of not less than 200 mph, an operational range of 935 miles in a patrol configuration or 625 miles carrying a torpedo, depth charge, or bomb load of 2,000 pounds. On March 7, 1940, this document was signed as the N-3PB seaplane specification. Ostby returned to Washington, D.C., to coordinate with his embassy and five days later, on March 12, as shown by Figure 10, the Norwegian Government entered into a contract with Northrop Aircraft, Inc., for the delivery of 24 of the specified N-3PB seaplane patrol bombers.

Then, overnight, the Norwegian plan for the airplane changed when Germany invaded on 8 April 1940. Ostby immediately returned to Northrop and the armament and ordnance requirements of the plane were changed to add a machine gun in a lower rear cockpit firing downward and to enlarge the space between the float pylons to carry additional bombs or depth charges without generating aerodynamic vortex.

The airplane would not be going to Norway for neutral-nation patrol flights in and out of the relatively calm water of the fjords there. Instead, it would be deployed as a primary weapon system for air-to-surface attack of U-boats and other German ships, plus, eventually, out of pragmatic need, air-to-air combat, in the patrol and protection of Allied convoys sailing their North Atlantic routes.

Once again, Jack Northrop was immediately ready and capable to respond to these new requirements. The specification and drawings were revised as required and released for production. While he personally handled the baseline design requirements, the outstanding engineering and manufacturing team he had assembled for his new company handled the major nonrecurring and recurring tasks and functions associated with final engineering design and production. Fred Baum, who had worked closely with him at other companies, was designated to be Chief Project Engineer for the N-3PB.

Commander K. Østby

Washington, D. C.
March 12, 1940

Northrop Aircraft, Inc.
Hawthorne
California

Gentlemen:

We have today completed our signing of the contract between
your company and the Royal Norwegian Navy Air Force, and are
returning one completely executed copy to you herewith.

In accordance with this contract's Article 22, we direct you

To make provision for installation of a gun in the
bottom of the fuselage on all 24 airplanes (sub-
paragraph 1), and

To furnish all 24 airplanes with Hamilton Standard
Hydromatic propellers and Constant Speed Governors
adapted for use in this airplane with the Wright
Cyclone Model GR-1820-G205B engine (sub-paragraph 3).

The installation of a Fairchild K-3C camera (sub-paragraph 2)
will be considered later.

In accordance with this additional cost, the total cost for
24 airplanes will be:

Item	Unit Price	Number	Total Cost
Basic airplane	$57,000	24	$1,368,000.00
Provision gun	325	24	7,800.00
Propeller	2,843.94	24	68,254.56
			$1,444,054.56

I have today issued instructions to have thirty percent (30%) of
this total sum paid in cash to the Northrop Aircraft, Inc. account
with The Chase National Bank of the City of New York, and the
balance, or seventy percent (70%), of this total sum laid down
in an Irrevocable Letter of Credit with the same bank, payable
in accordance with the regulations set forth in the contracts
Article 2.

Very truly yours,

K. Østby
Commander, Royal Norwegian Navy

KØ mcb

*Figure 10. The speed at which the specification and the final contract
were signed demonstrates that Jack Northrop was immediately prepared
to deliver a militarized seaplane called the N-3PB in a quantity of 24
aircraft, with the first unit to be delivered within 10 months of contract
signing. (From Jack Northrop Archives.)*

Over the years, Northrop himself had developed an outstanding people-oriented administrative talent. Although he was, by title, the company president, he functioned as Chief Engineer; and while he didn't like administrative duties, his management presence and style were felt all over the plant. He held frequent mass meetings with all employees to discuss openly the current status of the Company business, where he thought the Company was going, and to answer questions they might have about working conditions or their future.

As a company Liaison Engineer, the author himself was regularly in contact with Jack Northrop. The author at that time worked the night shift correcting and resolving manufacturing and engineering mistakes or questions on the production line. Northrop would often follow him on his rounds just to see what kind of things were going wrong or causing questions and what could be done to make permanent fixes and improve engineering drawings for more efficient and effective production. His synthesized design concept of aircraft, to achieve its intrinsic performance benefit in the operational craft, had to be translated into hardware with minimal – hopefully no – performance loss due to secondary re-interpretation between drafting board and production line.

Years later when it looked like the first big Flying Wing, the B-35, was about to make its first flight from the Hawthorne airport the General Manager of the Aircraft Division put out orders for everyone to stay at their job station and keep working. Naturally, everyone wanted to see it fly but with all the uncertainties associated with a project like that the GM didn't want everyone wasting time waiting for an event that could not be exactly scheduled. Consequently, when the big Wing finally did take off that day, Mr. Northrop was in his office complying with the order, penciling away diligently at his drafting board while many, if not most, of his employees were out on the side of the runway watching it take off. This personal integrity was to engender a loyalty to him and to the Company that was unprecedented in the industry and would be manifest in another incident when the contract for the huge Northrop Flying Wing was suddenly cancelled.

At this time there were several of the B-49's (jet version of the B-35) that were very near flying status but the Air Force ordered them all to be cut up. Over 1,200 employees signed up to finish one of them free of charge; however, the Air Force Secretary, Stuart Symington, was adamant and the Flying Wings were scrapped. The company spirit that motivated the workers to offer to work on the Flying Wing for free was the same spirit that drove the team that was assembled for the later restoration of the N-3PB. It was this same spirit that made the motto, "Northrop is a good place to work," unanimously accepted by all employees at Northrop throughout the war and the subsequent Cold War.

The specification agreed on between Cmdr. Ostby and Jack Northrop is shown in Table 1 and the three-view profile of the configuration is shown in Figure 11. Northrop had steadily advanced and refined the stressed-skin technology and the resulting N-3PB design was lightweight, strong, and very clean aerodynamically. As shown in Figure 12, the aircraft that resulted from this contract was a single-engine bomber featuring a fully cantilevered low wing, a semi-monocoque fuselage, and two wing-mounted pedestals to carry the two highly stable, but large, pontoon floats.

The wing had split trailing edge landing flaps. The crew compartment contained the pilot in the front cockpit, a gunner-observer in the rear cockpit, and, in between, a radio-gunner operator who moved to the lower rear section of the fuselage during attack modes. All flight control surfaces were fabric covered.

The normal armament arrangement included four 50-caliber machine guns in the leading edge of the outer wing panels, a flexible (freely aimable) machine gun at the upper gunner's station, and a flexible machine gun at the lower rear gunner's station. In addition, both internal and external bomb racks gave a wide selection of the type of bombs or depth charges that could be carried. Even torpedoes could be carried. The N-3PB was the most heavily armed single-engine military plane in existence.

The wing was constructed of a multicellular stressed-skin design originally developed and applied by Jack Northrop during the 1930s and used on most aircraft produced during the war. The complete wing panel was composed of five sections: a center section, two outer panels, and two removable tips. The wing had several shear webs or spars made of 24ST aluminum alloy sheet and this structure was covered with sheet aluminum of the same type. It was this Jack Northrop cellular design that made the flying wing feasible, but it was only with the advent of composite materials that this design found practical application. As with most innovative design solutions, it was a question of which came first, the means or the idea.

TABLE 1. THE N-3PB PERFORMANCE AND DESIGN SPECIFICATION

PARAMETER	REQUIREMENT
Airspeed (max.)	257 mph
Cruise speed	217 mph at 16,400 ft. altitude
Service ceiling	28,400 ft.
Rate of climb	2,600 ft./min.
Cruising range	1,400 mi. (average)
Landing speed	72 mph
Fuel qty.	320 gal.
Gross weight	10,600 lbs.
Fuselage length	38 ft. (overall)
Wing span	48 ft. 11 in.
Height	12 ft. (overall)
Wing area	376.8 sq. ft.
Wing loading	24.4 lbs./sq. ft.
Armament:	
50-caliber machine gun	Four, two per wing
30-caliber machine gun	Two, flexible aft-mounted (upper and lower)
Ordnance (center wing):	
Bombs	Up to five (2,200 lbs.)
Depth charges	Up to five (2,200 lbs.)
Torpedo	One (2,000 lbs.)

Note: All performance data measured during aircraft flight test with full fuel and weapons load, aircraft powered by 1,250-hp Wright R1820 Cyclone engine with 3-blade constant-speed prop.

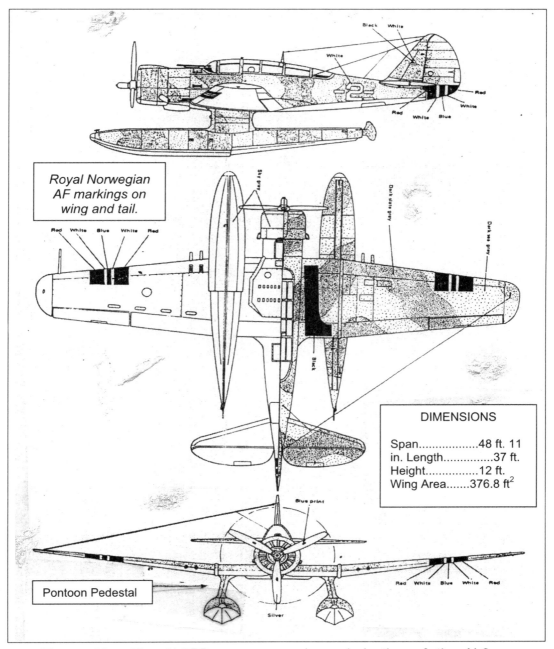

Figure 11. The N-3PB was a seaplane derivative of the N-3, an advancement over the Northrop-designed Douglas 8-A attack-bomber in use in 1940 by the U.S. Navy and Army Air Corps and by Norway. (Author compiled.)

The fuselage was fabricated in two halves divided along the horizontal centerline. The lower half was built integrally with the center section of the wing. Formed frames or rings were spaced periodically along the fuselage, which in turn supported longitudinal stringers of extruded aluminum, the whole framework then being covered with sheet aluminum. Heavy channel sections attached rigidly to the fuselage framework reinforced the cockpit and access door cutouts.

The engine mount was of welded chrome-molybdenum steel-tube structure attached to the front fuselage frame by four nickel-steel bolts through the firewall into the fuselage structure. These bolts permitted a complete engine removal once the electrical and fuel connections were unfastened. An NACA-type cowl enclosed the engine. The engine was a Wright Cyclone R-1820-G205A rated at 1,200 horsepower and turning a three-blade constant-speed propeller.

The pontoon floats (Edo Model 67-9000B) were designed by the Edo Corporation of Melville, New York, the same source for the huge Model 28 amphibious floats incorporated by Edo on the XC-47C (a late model C-47) for the U.S. Army during WWII. The ponderous Model 28 floats penalized the C-47 by adding 10% to the gross weight, making takeoff sluggish and limited to smooth water, and causing handling problems in aircraft performance once airborne. Consequently, the C-47 amphibian had limited use (in Alaska and the Southwest Pacific) and none appeared among the postwar conversions for civilian use of the C-47.[30]

By comparison, the integration of Edo floats on the much smaller N-3PB proved to have minimal impact on the plane's performance, as shown by its long patrol range, high speed, and effectiveness in air-to-air combat. As noted in Chapter 5, the only problem with the floats was in their maintenance, due to the tendency of the attachment brackets to develop cracks; and as described in that chapter, this deficiency became a main corrective action effort for Sevi Bulukin when he was Deputy Technical Director for Squadron 330(N). Though Sevi solved the operational problem, it may have been this very design factor that made the recovery of the airplane from the Thjorsa River possible in the time allotted. The floats also became a critical consideration in the final recovery phase, as described in Chapter 9. But even after the issue of the floats was resolved, the airplane still couldn't be recovered.

Figure 12 shows the production line station for final assembly. The first plane started down the production line in August 1940 and on December 13, 1940, only nine months and one day after contract signature, was rolled out at the factory in Hawthorne, California. The aircraft was then trucked to Lake Elsinore, California, for its first flight off water. Commander Kristian Ostby, formerly chief test pilot of the Royal Norwegian Naval Sea Factory, at Horten, Norway, who had helped develop the Norwegian specification requirements document, was designated the chief acceptance officer for all 24 aircraft.[31]

---

[30] Peter M. Bowers, "The DC-3 in Uniform," *Wings,* February 1981, Vol.11, No.1, P.8, published by Sentry Magazines, Granada Hills, California.
[31] Robert McLaren, "Norwegian Nemesis," Model Airplane News, 1941.

(a) Serial No. 320 is the fifth tail down the assembly line (or was it 318?).

(b) Only one person has coveralls and he's a former Douglas employee (just hired).

Figure 12. The production line ended at the final assembly station, where the engine, outboard wing panels and tips, flight control surfaces, and cockpit installations were done and the aircraft then painted, insignified, and serial-numbered for flight acceptance and delivery for Norwegian use. (Photos by Roy L. Wolford.)

Northrop's veteran test pilot, Vance Breese, conducted the first flight. Moye Stephens, well known for having flown Richard Halliburton, the writer-adventurer, around the world in the 1930's, conducted subsequent flight tests. Fred Baum was pleased to find and announce that no adjustments were required in the design either structurally or aerodynamically; the first airplane flew figuratively and literally perfectly. Maximum level flight speed was recorded as 257 miles per hour, which made it the fastest military seaplane in the world! With the first airplane performing successfully in continuing flight demonstrations at Lake Elsinore, production of the other 23 aircraft proceeded on schedule for delivery by February 1941 to whatever operational site the Free Norwegian Air Force might designate.

Since the first flight tests were conducted with the more powerful Wright GR-1820-G205A Cyclone engine – and the guaranteed performance requirements had been based on the smaller G205B engine – the aircraft's performance greatly exceeded each of the specified requirements. From the performance data obtained it could be shown that even with the smaller engine, the performance would have exceeded what had been specified by Ostby and committed to by Jack Northrop. The engine in Norway's Douglas 8-A's was the G205A and Jack Northrop, when he discovered this, had insisted on obtaining it.

Familiarization flights for pilots disclosed no difficulties not easily fixed; thus the airplane got very favorable comments and ratings from the pilots. Stick forces were found normal; stability satisfactory; maneuverability excellent; takeoff and landing characteristics good; stalls gentle; and, in general, the N-3PB was easy to take off, fly, land, and taxi. It proved an excellent aircraft in all maneuvers, except looping, which Ostby, before he completed acceptance of all the planes, personally demonstrated was inadvisable, as described in more detail in the next chapter.

Figures 13 and 14 show Jack Northrop conferring on the design, in the first with Walt Cerny and Tom Quayle on manufacturing requirements for the N-3PB. Cerny was the N-3PB chief design engineer and Quayle was in charge of manufacturing. Both Cerny and Quayle joined the new company in July 1939, before operational facilities had been built. With the other new employees they worked during the first few months out of the Hawthorne hotel, several blocks from the municipal airport where the main plant would be located. Most of the hotel's rooms were rented by the new company. Some rooms contained drafting tables for preparation and check of drawings and others were used as engineering and manufacturing offices. Cerny's next assignment was as chief engineer on the N-M1 flying wing prototype. Quayle later became manager of quality control.

Figure 14 shows La Motte Cohu and Jack Northrop at the full-scale mockup of the center fuselage section of the N-3PB. While most of the configuration was a straightforward adaptation of the N-3, the three-man cockpit section of the fuselage was mocked up to verify its human engineering compatibility for the crew.

Figure 15 shows Norway's resident inspector for acceptance of the N-3PB aircraft, Cmdr. Kristian Ostby, and the Norwegian government team that flew in from London and Washington, D.C., to observe the flight test of N-3PB Serial Number 301, the first production unit. As the faces show, all were pleased with the performance and mission readiness of their new seaplane, the first since 1932.

Roy L. Wolford

Figure 13. Jack Northrop confers on N-3PB manufacturing requirements with Walt Cerny, chief design engineer, and Thomas Quayle, head of manufacturing.

Roy L. Wolford

Figure 14. Jack Northrop shows the N-3PB cockpit design features to Northrop General Manager La Motte Cohu. Crew quarters for the N-3 seaplane adaptation presented the few special requirements differing from the baseline design, so a full-scale mockup was built to prove compliance.

Roy L. Wolford

Figure 15. The importance of the N-3PB for Norwegians in exile at the start of WWII is shown by the inspection team on-site at Lake Elsinore. From left, Free Norwegian Air Force Lt. Gunnar Haugen, mechanical engineer; 2nd Lt. Jens Riser, instructor pilot; Lt. Kaare Kjos, instructor pilot; Tom Fidjeland, flight chief; Hans Strandrud, flight chief; 2nd Lt. Harald Kruse, instructor pilot; Cmdr. Kristian Ostby, air attaché; Helge Torgersen, student pilot; Capt. Hans Bugge, instructor pilot; Lt. Erik Bjornebye, instructor pilot; Lt. Asen, radio officer; and Lt. August Standsberg, instructor pilot.

The first aircraft delivered for Norway's acceptance is shown in Figure 16 awaiting flight acceptance test at Lake Elsinore, California, about 80 miles southeast of the Northrop plant in Hawthorne. Though a seaplane, this aircraft signifies a turning point in the history of modern aircraft design. The N-3 model, whether with retractable gear in a land-based configuration or with pontoons for amphibious operations, represents the culmination of the design evolution achieved by Jack Northrop over the previous decade.

Roy L. Wolford

Figure 16. Ready to enter the water and take off, the first N-3PB beat schedule by more than one month and met all specification requirements at a unit price of $57,325 – almost $5,000 below the contract price: a product of the team spirit that was to make it a lasting memorial to freedom.

The N-3 was both a culmination and a new beginning for the refinement of that design approach in airframes that would eventually evolve to the B-2 bomber and the Space Shuttle. It signified the past and the future and became a link between nations and the symbol and instrument of restoring mankind on the path of unity as a team. His design approach to lightweight, high-strength airframes had made Lindbergh's solo crossing of the Atlantic possible, bridging the Western Hemisphere by air.

After Cmdr. Ostby accepted all 24 of the N-3PB's following flight test, they were disassembled for shipping. The first six aircraft were delivered to the Free Norwegian Air Force at Vancouver, Canada, in February 1941 for training. The remaining 18 were sent to Iceland in May 1941.

By June 2, 1941 the first aircraft had been re-assembled and test flown at the operational base at Reykjavik, Iceland, and on June 24 the squadron made its first operational flight when Serial No. 318 escorted a convoy through the North Atlantic south of Iceland. Besides being the first operational flight of Norwegian-RAF Squadron 330(N) and of the Northrop N-3PB, it was the first operational flight of the Free Norwegian Air Force.

Within six months of the delivery of all shipsets of the N-3PB, the U.S. was at war on two fronts globally as the strongest and lead member of what Churchill called "The Grand Alliance."[32]

Now there was no question about the company's survival. Besides acquiring major subcontracts to produce subassemblies of the B-17 bomber and other military aircraft, Jack Northrop won the prime contract for design and production of the P-61 Black Widow night fighter, a long-range, high-speed reconnaissance aircraft with night-time air-to-air- and air-to-ground attack capability. The P-61 was the first of the modern radar-equipped night fighters. It was followed after the war's end (in 1948) by the F-89 fighter.

And of course, throughout the war Jack Northrop was working diligently on his concept of the ultimate stealth attack weapon system, the flying wing; but the "hot" war was to end before the flying wing became operational and it was the follow-on Cold War that brought the wing forward as the culminating strategic weapon known as the B-2 bomber, two decades later.

Freed of being the main design force behind the Douglas production line and now head of his own engineering team at a company that was operationally and financially sustained by such programs as the N-3PB and the P-61 (of which over 650 were produced during the war), Jack Northrop was at last able to get to work on a flying wing in which the fuselage-wing synthesis would become a pure lifting body, with no external fixtures blocking the aerodynamic flow and detracting from lift, payload, and range by imposing drag. At the new "Northrop" he designated this design the N-1M.[33] Since the N-3PB design only required adapting the existing N-3 land-based design to the seaplane configuration, he had time during 1939 to finalize and build the N-1M.

Through 1941, Vance Breese, Moye Stephens, John Myers, and other test pilots flew the N-1M in over 200 flights to collect aerodynamic and structural data.

By 1942, he had hired Dr. William R. Sears as chief aerodynamicist for the flying wing development program. Dr. Sears had been an assistant to Dr. Theodore von Karman, Director of the Guggenheim School of Aeronautics at the California Institute of

---

[32] Ibid., Vol. III.

[33] Northrop to this day designates its aircraft projects with an "N" prefix and sequence number. The N-1M, for example (see Figure 8), is the first prototype of a "pure" flying wing and remains on display at the Smithsonian Institute in Washington, D.C. This aircraft also was the first new design of the new company. The N-3 was the third design within the lineage of conventional military aircraft designed by Northrop beginning with the A-17. Soon after the new company began business the N-3 was to have the letters "PB" (for "Patrol Bomber") added, to become Norway's N-3PB seaplane.

Technology, who also served as a design consultant on the program. Dr. Sears made such valuable contributions to the conceptual design of the flying wing that he was identified as a co-inventor with Northrop on the patent issued September 27, 1947. Jack Northrop made similar patent applications worldwide.

The Second World War, while providing business and design opportunity for Northrop, also presented challenging requirements in developing personnel resources. The nation was suffering manpowerwise, because all eligible males were subject to the military draft.

Jack Northrop immediately saw the solution. While hiring women as production line workers as did other companies – most of whom were now absorbed in defense work – Northrop established and operated the Northrop Institute of Technology. NIT overnight became a resource base for training both production and technical personnel for the entire aircraft industry. The Northrop Institute of Technology continues to operate fulltime today as Northrop Rice Aviation Institute of Technology, in Inglewood, California, just 10 miles north of the original Northrop Corporation next to Northrop Field in Hawthorne, California. Of course today the school offers not only hands-on aircraft manufacture and maintenance training, but computer-based training at home and in the classroom.

While names change, as in the case of Northrop Institute, the team spirit that went into the company known as, "Northrop, a good place to work," took off and flew with the N-3PB and became unified with the international spirit of Norway, Iceland, England, and the U.S. – in general, the Allied spirit that teamed to win the war for freedom with unity.

Figure 17 shows Jack Northrop being honored at an NIT Symposium awards dinner by other legendary industry executives, among them Alan Lockheed, who gave Jack his first serious job in aircraft design, Donald Douglas, who got a big "piece" of him, and Claude Ryan, who enlisted his aid to solve the key design problem for the *Spirit of St. Louis.*

By then he had been retired 15 years from the corporation he had founded and which was undergoing change in directions away from the team approach he had instilled; but this change was typical of all the aerospace companies, now held captive by robotic "management systems" in place of human team spirit.

After the fighting was over in WWII, with the Cold War keeping military preparations at a high level of government spending, NIT became a magnet school for returning veterans to attend in preparation for a career path in this new industry that was now the dominant one for commercial and military aircraft. When the Soviets launched Sputnik in the fall of 1957, the industry overnight became the "Aerospace Industry" and has not looked back since.

When the Figure 17 photo was taken, Jack Northrop had been retired 15 years and was 72 years old. In the interim, he had developed numerous patents in vital fields other than aircraft, including human-engineered prosthesises for war veterans suffering limb or extremity losses in combat; in addition, he developed special methods for the blind to hold jobs in manufacturing operations.

However, it still seems one of those inexplicable tragedies of greatness that after leaving Northrop Aircraft, Inc., he never again led an aircraft company, even though his original lightweight designs have continued to be the basic concept for aircraft structure, whether made of metal or composite materials. The styles change, but the basics remain the same.

Roy L. Wolford

Figure 17. Jack Northrop being honored by guests at an NIT awards dinner in 1968 (from left, Alan Lockheed, Jack Northrop, TV Celebrity Clete Roberts (serving as master of ceremonies), Donald Douglas, Sr., and Claude Ryan.

This photo is poetically historic, for in it are perhaps the four premier aviation executives who not only made the industry take off, but who founded or greatly influenced the companies that dominate the industry today. Three of them owe much of their success to the fourth, who was the guest of honor. That they were there to honor him bespeaks the quality of their own characters. In 1952, Jack Northrop walked away from it all to maintain his integrity as a human the same way he had maintained the integrity of modern man's ability to fly. While there was a piece of him in every plane flying, he remained integrally whole. Yet, most poetically, a final restoration was awaiting him, and it was to occur concomitantly with the restoration of one of the Northrop's.

CHAPTER 4 - ACTIVATION AND OPERATIONS OF SQUADRON 330(N)

That Iceland is in a strategic location militarily and commercially as an air transit center is shown by the fact that it is midway in the Atlantic between Greenland, Norway, and England. Sitting just below the Arctic Circle, Iceland is equidistant from New York, Moscow, and Europe. Directly over the Arctic cap are Japan, Korea, and China. Any ship sailing across the Atlantic to Russia, Scandinavia, England, or the European seaboard can use Iceland as a convenient port of call. So it was most appropriate that the Norwegians who would fly the N-3PB's out of Iceland chose as their motto for 330(N) Squadron, the expression "Trygg Havet," which is Norse for "Secure the Ocean."[34] Not only would their airborne role involve that very mission, but during WWII there wasn't a better place to operate from to perform it.[35]

Due to its strategic location, the British viewed Iceland much as Shakespeare said of England: "This precious stone set in the silver sea."[36] The importance of this 40,000-square-mile island (almost 2.5 times the size of its pre-WWII ruler, Denmark), at the outset of the war, was twofold. First its location in the North Atlantic between the American continent and the British Isles made it ideally situated as a base of operations for protecting ship convoys headed for Britain, which historically was dependent on sea commerce for survival. One of the reasons Hitler put so much emphasis on U-boat construction and operations was his strategy to isolate Britain from its shipping sources around the world by literally putting it under siege by sea; in fact the Tripartite Agreement between Germany, Italy, and Japan on September 27, 1940 had, as a major aim, shutting off Britain from Asia and the Mediterranean and was so important that Hitler did not consult or include Russia – an omission that eventually led to Russia's joining with the Allies to defeat the Axis powers.[37]

Second, however, Iceland was important to Britain as a pawn in getting the U.S. – which was trying to maintain its neutrality – to back it with war materials. Even Germany desired Iceland as a base of operations to compromise or even neutralize U.S.

---

[34] The subtlety of this expression has to be appreciated, for national security for countries surrounded so closely by the sea, as in Scandinavia, begins with securing the sea. England is a classis example. Churchill's primary concern during the war was to keep the sealanes open so that the logistics link required to sustain England would not be broken by German interdiction in any form.

[35] The strategic military importance of Iceland continues today. The island was a charter member in the formation of NATO in 1947. Its importance during the Cold War was evident, with the NATO base at Keflavik situated midway on the Great Circle route between Washington, D.C., and Moscow.

[36] William Shakespeare, *Richard the Second*, Act II, Scene I, Line 46.

[37] Winston S. Churchill, *Their Finest Hour*, Vol. II of The Second World War (Boston: Houghton Mifflin Company, 1950) p. 523.

support to Britain and eventually to attack the U.S. mainland preparatory to further conquest. It was Karl Haushofer, a retired major general in the German army and military advisor to Hitler's staff, who made the statement that Churchill quoted, without attribution, in saying that Iceland was a loaded pistol aimed at Britain and North America. The British had learned in early 1940 that Hitler actually had a plan for the invasion of Iceland called *"Fall Ikarus"* which translates to "Case of Icarus"as well as literally to the "Fall of Icarus." Interesting how Churchill uses the same term, as though Iceland would determine the fall or success for England:

> In view of the bad reports from the Faeroes about aircraft or seaplane bases and the fact we must reckon with the Germans all along the Norwegian coast, it seems indispensable that we have a base in Iceland for our flying boats and for oiling the ships on the Northern Patrol. Let a case (author's underline) be prepared for submission to the Foreign Office. The sooner we let the Icelanders know that this is what we require the better.[38]

As Churchill notes subsequently, when Denmark was overrun in April 1940, it was to forestall a possible invasion of Denmark's protectorate that Britain, on May 10, occupied Iceland.[39] Whether England fell, as did Icarus, seemed to depend in part on who controlled Iceland.

Haushofer, who had dedicated himself to the regeneration of Germany between the two world wars as director of the Institute of Geopolitics at the University of Munich, had a major influence on Hitler's geopolitical approach to and concept of world domination, but his life ended tragically. Having married years before the war a woman of Jewish descent, he was increasingly shunned professionally as the war progressed; and then his son, who was professor of geopolitics at the University of Berlin, discovered to be active in the underground against Hitler, was executed by the Gestapo. The effects of this personal loss and being investigated for alleged war crimes after German's defeat so depressed him and his wife that they committed suicide on March 13, 1946 – the end of a most worthy social philosopher.

Mussolini considered Iceland important, too. Though Lufthansa had tried to get an agreement to establish a German airbase there just before the war, Count Balbo had been sent to the Island in 1933 to establish a base for transatlantic flights of the Italian air force. As air travel grew during the 1930s, Iceland was particularly open to such ventures, especially in setting up an air terminal on the Island as a source of economic growth for its people in the commercial field. What Iceland didn't want was to lose its neutrality; so it shied away from military alliances.[40] But to make clear its interest in serving as a base for transoceanic flights, Iceland did build a hangar near the beach in

---

[38] Ibid, Vol. I, *The Gathering Storm*, p. 756.

[39] Ibid, Vol. III, *The Grand Alliance*, p. 138.

[40] Even today, when the island is used as a base by the U.S. for the Iceland Defense Force (IDF) and Iceland is a charter member of NATO, the island technically remains neutral and has no military forces.

Reykjavik and its subsequent use by the Count resulted in its being known as Balbo Hangar.

Two factors were at work to get the U.S. actively engaged in supporting Britain in its war effort. After Winston Churchill became British Prime Minister on May 10, 1940, he used every ploy to get the U.S. aggressively engaged in this support. Not coincidentally, on the same day he became Prime Minister, British troops were debarking at Reykjavik. While Churchill claims the Danish government, then in exile in London, had concurred in this action, the government of Iceland had not been told; and so there was considerable consternation of Icelanders for sometime at this unannounced takeover without prior, direct consultation. For months, Churchill, after becoming Prime Minister, tried to get the U.S. to provide aging, reconditioned destroyers, small patrol boats, and flying boats, to fill the gap in England's sea and land defenses until British production began turning out ships and aircraft; but President Franklin Roosevelt was dealing with a highly pacifist populace and congress. Isolationist sentiment was at high pitch in the U.S. To provide some rationale for transferring military equipment from a neutral to an at-war nation, Roosevelt initially suggested that the requested equipment be traded in return for bases in the West Indian islands and Bermuda, reasoning this would keep up an appearance of neutrality sufficient to satisfy all critics, including the Axis powers.

What convinced Roosevelt to take more aggressive action in support of Britain was Churchill's letter of December 8, 1940 in which he tabulated the weekly shipping losses to U-boats for just the first six-month period of his government, beginning May 27 and ending December 1. During that period the total British, Allied, and Neutral country losses he tabulated at 583 ships and 2,458,287 gross tons sunk. Of these totals, 66 percent of the ships and 70 percent of the tonnage were British. After the war, for his epic history, *The Second World War*, he had these figures retabulated from a more complete database, showing that 745 ships amounting to 3,319,190 tons were sunk, the same percentages British.[41] On December 13, 1940, Churchill wrote to Roosevelt:

> North Atlantic transport remains the prime anxiety. Undoubtedly, Hitler will augment his U-boat and air attack on shipping and operate ever farther into the ocean. . . . We have so far only been able to bring a very few of our fifty destroyers into action on account of the many defects which they naturally develop when exposed to Atlantic weather after having been laid up so long.[42]

Churchill later admitted that the only thing that ever frightened him during the war was the U-boat peril. He said he was even more anxious about the U-boat battle than "the glorious air fight called the Battle of Britain." He wondered how much the U-boat warfare would reduce Britain's imports and shipping. "Would it," he wrote, "ever reach the point where our life would be destroyed?"[43] The U-boat loomed as a sinister, submerged foe, striking in stealth against defenseless merchant ships.

---

[41] Ibid., Vol. II, *Their Finest Hour*, p. 714, Appendix B, Tables I and II.
[42] Loc. Cit., p. 606.
[43] Loc. Cit., p. 598.

Roosevelt of course was considering every way to come to the aid of Britain, but he had to keep the Japanese at bay, as well as the pacifists. The U.S., extending from Atlantic to Pacific, had two potential fronts to cover. Although Japan had signed the Tripartite Pact with Germany and Italy, a conservative premier, Prince Konoye, had maneuvered into office with the support of the Emperor and was trying to restrain the military leaders who felt that Japan's historic moment of conquest and expansion had come. When Hitler did not invade Britain in 1940 as he had insisted during the signing of the Pact that he would, indicating to the Japanese a certain weakness in Germany's war machine, Konoye began building a consensus on the policy that Japan should settle outstanding issues with the U.S. before taking any military action in Asia. By April 1941 his cabinet agreed to open conversations with the U.S. concerning peaceful settlement of all issues between the two nations. Even General Tojo, Army Minister, supported this policy and silenced all other protests.

The ensuing question historians have tried to answer is the extent to which Roosevelt knew about this policy and wanted to see it succeed, for it would have eliminated his concern about the vulnerability of the U.S. on the Pacific front. It appears that even if he believed in it (and there is every reason to think he was actively pursuing it, since ambassadorial communications were in process) he was persuaded by Churchill to put a reverse siege on Japan and bring it to its knees economically, so it couldn't even mount a war in Asia under the Tripartite Pact. Consequently, on July 30, 1941, the U.S., Britain, and Holland enforced economic embargoes on Japan that cut off all sources of its import of oil. This deprivation of fuel and lubricant resources would not only wipe out Japan's war capability but its domestic economy. Now Prince Konoye and his coalition were forced to forego their peace policy and get the embargo lifted without giving up any of the territorial advances Japan had already made in Indo-China and China itself. The Japanese army and navy were ready to fight rather than give back what they had already gained and, in addition, to have to agree to cease in their quest of further territorial expansion. Autarkic self-sufficiency was the tie that bound each of the Axis Powers.

As usual, Churchill was thinking only of England. ("I would negotiate with the Devil to save England," he was quoted as having said.) He had not been shy in making it clear that his position was to get Japan to fight, because it would force the U.S. out of its neutrality and into the war. He vitally wanted U.S. participation, because Britain had no other means of defending the Dutch East Indies or other elements of the British Empire in the East, including Australia, yet alone fighting a European war and keeping the sea-lanes to Britain open. Britain, he knew, had a 360-degree front of military needs that had to be met to stay alive. Having the U.S. in the war, Churchill reasoned, also would be an enticement for Russia to join the Allies against the Axis powers.[44]

Roosevelt, despite the pacifists and those who argued for neutrality, felt the same way and knew that Japan would not accept the economic sanctions, but would fight. His one failure as a most popular, three-term leader of the U.S. is to not have alerted the Pacific Fleet to be prepared for attack. But even in this apparent oversight he may have

---

[44] Loc. Cit., page 586-588.

been playing the psychological card he knew was needed to get the nation converted overnight to a war sentiment. What he did instead of negotiating with Japan was to turn the nation's attention to the Atlantic, using the data on ships sunk provided by Churchill as the more imminent and serious crisis due to its nearness, reality, and adverse impact economically and militarily.

For the Atlantic he had devised a gradual plan of war entry that would first provide aid to Britain without arousing the nation's isolationist sentiment, by obtaining in return for 50 destroyers new offshore bases that would further insulate the U.S. from direct attack. As early as September 1939, he had declared American coastal waters a security zone 500 miles into the Atlantic and "neutrality patrols" were then initiated by U.S. warships to prevent belligerent nations from entering the security zone. When German ships were discovered in or out of the zone, the British navy was to be notified of their location so they could be attacked.

After Churchill sent him the December 8, 1940 letter detailing massive shipping losses in just six months, Roosevelt tore the Figure 18 map from the National Geographic and with a pen drew the line around Iceland and down the Atlantic between 20 and 30 degrees longitude, demarcating the commitment of the U.S. to protect all shipping west of that line, leaving Britain to take over patrol east of it. Harry Hopkins, who in the meantime had devised the Lend-Lease Program as the way to circumvent the U.S.'s neutrality position and still help Britain (and other Allies such as soon-to-be-Ally Russia), took this map to London and presented it to Churchill.

On March 11, 1941, Congress passed the Lend-Lease Act, granting Britain unlimited and free American aid in ships and war materials, plus services. (Subsequently, following the Roosevelt-Churchill Atlantic Charter Agreement in August 1941, Lend-Lease was extended to Russia. This extension of Lend-Lease to Russia further rigidified the Japanese resolve to fight the Allies. Under cover of the Lend-Lease Program concept, the U.S. would be able to provide military equipment and even advisory personnel without declaring war on Germany; thus, in effect, the U.S. would be serving as a logistics support depot for British and Russian military needs without being subject to the risk of military attack by the Axis Powers.

Following the introduction of Lend-Lease it was projected that by April 1, 1941 the U.S. would take over the duty of escorting convoys with its own warships. Since Britain was to make available the bases from which the U.S. would operate, Roosevelt sent his son, Captain Elliott Roosevelt, to Iceland in May with a group of military advisors in four PBY's to survey its capabilities as a base for control of the North Atlantic convoy routes. Finally, on July 7, 1941, U.S. neutrality forces landed in Iceland, invited by Prime Minister Jonasson. Although Iceland too was neutral and wanted neither the British nor the Americans there, Jonasson conceded to the American presence in return for support from the U.S. in getting its independence from Denmark.

Initially, to maintain the appearance of neutrality, the U.S. sent only career Marine Corps troops, who were concentrated at Hvalfjordur, about 30 miles north of the capital, where the British had established a naval base. This initial U.S. deployment was intended to supplement, not supplant, the British and Canadian troops already in Iceland.

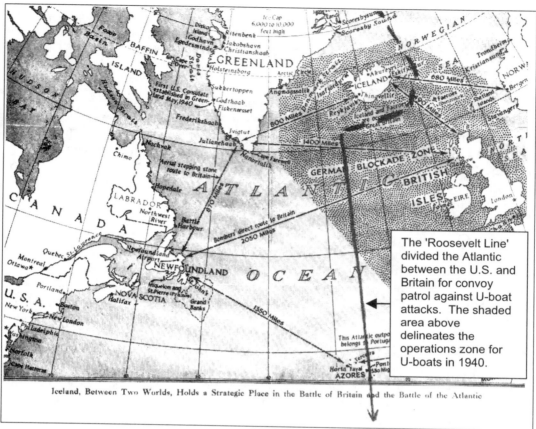

The 'Roosevelt Line' divided the Atlantic between the U.S. and Britain for convoy patrol against U-boat attacks. The shaded area above delineates the operations zone for U-boats in 1940.

Iceland, Between Two Worlds, Holds a Strategic Place in the Battle of Britain and the Battle of the Atlantic

Figure 18. The 5-month loss of 745 ships and 3,139,190 tons of shipping in the North Atlantic in 1940 prompted Roosevelt to initiate Lend-Lease as a strategy for maintaining neutrality while helping Britain and Russia with free military equipment and convoy patrol services. Iceland was to serve as base of operations and dividing line for convoy handoff between U.S. and British navies and air forces. (Source: The American Heritage Picture History of World War II, p. 193 (New York: Simon and Schuster, Inc., 1966.)

From this initial deployment, IDF developed as a joint U.S.-Icelandic operation and continues today, with Iceland providing neutral civilians for administrative functions. While the U.S. provided ground forces stationed in Iceland, its primary convoy patrol operations involved U.S. Navy ships and aircraft operating out of Newfoundland and Iceland. The British Royal Air Force's Coastal Command continued to provide air patrol from Iceland, with Hudson's, Wellington's, and Sunderland's operating out of Reykjavik.

Churchill was elated! And it was against this background of Allied and Axis Power geopolitical maneuvering for superior strategic position – centered on Iceland – that the operations of N-3PB 330(N) Squadron began. As far as Japan was concerned, Roosevelt reasoned that, as long as the U.S. focused on the Atlantic, Japan would feel secure and not attack in the Pacific. Thus for Roosevelt, concentrating attention on the Atlantic was a form of deterrence against having to fight on two fronts. Nevertheless, Churchill would be further gratified when Japan struck the U.S. from behind.

Though the N-3PB had not been intended for use in Iceland, it would soon be welcomed there by the British, because airfields for land-based airplanes were not yet ready to support squadron-level operations.[45] On April 9, 1940, when less than a month from the signing of the N-3PB contract with Northrop, Norway was invaded by Germany, uncertainty clouded the destiny of the N-3PB. The Norwegian Chief Staff Officers with their Army and Navy forces, though ill-equipped, outmanned, and caught by surprise by the attack, fought until the last minute at the initial invasion site at Oslo. But, as Churchill noted, the surprise, ruthlessness, and precision with which the Germans struck "upon innocent and naked Norway" made for swift victory. The German's attacked concurrently at Oslo and Trondheim with initial landing forces of only 2,000 men and "within 48 hours all the main ports of Norway were in the German grip." On the seventh of April, British air reconnaissance reported a German fleet had been sighted going to Narvik, the most militarily valuable northerly port on Norway's Atlantic coast, next to the port of Tromso in the Lofoten Isles. Norway's king, royal family, and government officials were immediately forced north to Tromso to escape capture. Churchill's reaction was that Norway's policy of neutrality and Britain's "respect for it have made it impossible to prevent this ruthless coup"[46] – a neat rationalization.

Avoiding capture at the invasion of Oslo, about 50 Norwegian naval air force personnel made their way from their base at Horten (just south of Oslo) to England. This was the initial cadre of escapees. They were determined to continue the fight to free their country and within a few days were joined by the royal family and government officials in London, as arranged by Churchill. Norway's two air services were re-organized to come under a unified command headquartered in London.

Prior to being invaded by Germany, Norway had tried quickly to increase the size and capabilities of its small and antiquated air force, in both its army and navy divisions. Having been able to remain neutral in the First World War, Norway nevertheless had realized the strategic importance of aircraft both for national security and economic development. Accordingly, it had initiated organization and development of an air force as early as 1915, by building a Navy Aircraft Factory at Horten, the main seaport in southeast Norway on the west bank of the Oslo fjord. It was here in the first week of April 1940, as the Germans began invading, that the Norwegian navy made its stand and

---

[45] The following account of how the N-3PB's got to Iceland and their operational performance there is based on an article titled "Phantom of the Fjords: Northrop's N-3PB Flying Viking," by Ragnar Ragnarsson, published in the February 1981 issue of *Wings* magazine, Vol. 11, No. 1 (Sentry Books, Inc., Granada Hills, California). Cato Guhnfeldt, who represented the Norwegian Aviation Historical Society at the recovery of the N-3PB and is a published author as well as journalist for Aftenpost, a major Norwegian newspaper, provided valuable supplementary data on Norwegian aviation resources and operations in WWII.

[46] Loc. Cit., Vol. I, *The Gathering Storm*, p. 600.

sank some German transports using shore-launched torpedoes and also damaged the cruiser *Emden.*

But until the German threat to its neutrality became apparent in 1938, Norway's chief complement of military aircraft had been those designed and built in-country at its two Navy and Army "Aeroplane Factories." In 1938, as Germany, Italy, and Russia began maneuvering militarily to form and activate as the Axis Powers, Norway quickly tried to strengthen its air forces and neutral stance by procuring aircraft from Germany, England, and the United States. Nevertheless, by June 1940, three months after being invaded, Norway's Army and Navy air forces were wiped out in the battle of Narvik (located on the Atlantic coast over 400 miles north northeast of the major seaport of Trondheim). It was at Narvik, where the country narrows down to within 25 miles of the Swedish border and access to plentiful iron ore, that the remaining Norwegian forces had joined with the British from May 28 to June 9, 1940 to try to stop the advancing German army and keep the northern leg of the country free; but, as Churchill conceded, with some admiration, even the British couldn't match the highly trained and disciplined, well-equipped Wehrmacht, which even the snow and mud of the mountainous Norwegian terrain couldn't stop or slow down in its determination to occupy the entire country.

As the British retreated from Narvik and escaped to their ships and returned home, King Haaken VII and his royal family and retinue left with them on the cruiser *Devonshire*, from Tromso, the remaining government administrative center about 100 miles further north. The king's staff of key army, navy, and air force personnel accompanied him. Other Norwegians escaped overland, by sea, or even by air.

As noted in Chapter 3, Commander Kristian Ostby was at the same moment in the U.S. coordinating procurement of the N-3PB and also the Douglas 8A-5 attack bomber (the Douglas Aircraft derivative of Jack Northrop's N-2E, from which the N-3PB was derived via Northrop's N-3 advanced version of the N-2E). Cmdr. Ostby subsequently served during most of the war as deputy and then air attaché in Washington, D.C., for the Provisional Norwegian Government in London. Before the war ended he became head of the Norwegian Aviation Mission in London and afterwards was appointed Norway's postwar air minister.[47] Thus out of the fall of Norway arose a modernized, stronger air force staffed by Norwegians adamantly resolved to free their nation from foreign occupation. In fact, this group became known as the Free Norwegian Air Force.

After Norway fell to the Germans, the Provisional Government, at the urging of Churchill, who wanted to supplement British forces which were direly stretched numerically to cover all the British empire's war theater deployments adequately, initiated negotiations with French authorities for a Norwegian training and operations

---

[47] This account of Norway's post-invasion efforts to regroup its military airpower is a summary of background documentation, including Winston Churchill's The Second World War, Vol. I, *The Gathering Storm*, p. 653; Robert McLarren's, "Norwegian Nemesis," published in *Model Airplane News*, 1941; and Ted Coleman's "The Northrop World War II History," published by Northrop Aircraft, Inc., as the Cole-Facts quarterly, May 1960; Ragnar Ragnarsson's article in *Wings* magazine; and information provided from Norwegian national archives by Cato Guhnfeldt.

base to be established on the Mediterranean coast of south France. But as the German forces continued to advance on the Continent in the spring and summer of 1940, those plans came to an abrupt end. Since the British, at the invasion of Norway, had immediately occupied Iceland in April, establishing a base of air operations there became the obvious and optimum alternative for putting the Norwegians to the most beneficial use; furthermore, the Norwegians, being the primary forerunners of the Icelanders, would be accepted more readily than the uninvited British – and they were going to be flying a seaplane.

There were no immediate bases ready in Iceland, so an agreement was reached with the Canadian Government for the establishment of a Norwegian training camp there. This alternative also satisfied Churchill's objectives, in that with the Norwegians in Iceland, the Canadian forces planned for location there would be freed to join British forces for the direct defense of England.

So this is the way Norwegian Squadron 330(N) got established in Iceland under the RAF and how the Northrop N-3PB attack-bomber seaplane got put to use in a much more demanding mission role than it had been designed to perform. The enthusiasm with which the Norwegians viewed the aircraft and the opportunity it gave them to fight back and put their patriotism to use effectively is shown by the "Trygg Havet" (Secure the Ocean) motto they chose for their new squadron. For two years, during the most demanding period of the Battle of the Atlantic, the squadron was to fulfill this motto in every dimension of its meaning.

During the first days of August the first Norwegians, 120 officers and men of the Army and Navy air forces, arrived in Toronto to start construction of a camp at Island Airport, Toronto. This installation grew into such a completely self-sustaining complex that it became known as "Little Norway." Figure 19 gives some idea of the formal level of training activities conducted there. As shown, even the five-year-old Prince Harald visited, of course representing his grandfather, King Haakon VII. The Norwegians staffing "Little Norway" were among those who had escaped their homeland either with the royal family or by using their wits and daring to exit over various convoluted land routes, by sea in small boats, or by air in last-second flights of Norwegian or even, in one case, a stolen German aircraft. Some traveled from around the world to join their fellow Norwegians in Little Norway.

At Toronto, operating out of the headquarters of Little Norway, the Norwegian airmen were given flight and ground crew training while they awaited delivery of the N-3PB's from Northrop in the U.S. On February 5, 1941, the first N-3PB was received and by the end of the month a total of six aircraft had been shipped by Northrop in California to Patricia Bay, near Vancouver, British Columbia, where training of former naval airmen would be possible during the winter.

Meanwhile, new recruits were receiving their elementary flight training in Tiger Moths and Fleet Finch aircraft at the Toronto Flying Club. Later in the year, basic training shifted west in Canada to places with such exotic Indian names as Muskoka, Medicine Hat, and Moose Jaw. Little Norway then became dedicated to advanced training using several of the Douglas 8A land-based patrol bombers that had been ordered by Norway (as N-2E's) just before the war. These aircraft were shipped direct by Douglas Aircraft in the U.S. to Little Norway in 1941. The personnel trained in them subsequently were assigned for operational service in either Iceland or England. Training operations continued at Little Norway until a phased transfer of personnel was made to Winkleigh, Devon, England, between the winter of 1944 and early spring 1945. The Douglas 8A's were sold back to the U.S. and some were resold to South American countries after the war. A listing of all the aircraft models used by the Free Norwegian Air Force during the war is shown in Appendix C.[48]

On February 21, 1941, less than three weeks after training had begun at Patricia Bay, the first accident occurred when an N-3PB crashed on landing there. Both crewmembers, the pilot and the radioman-observer, were killed. A few weeks later, on March 18, the second N-3PB was lost when it crashed into the sea, killing two of the three crewmembers (this time the rear gunner was onboard).

Both these accidents were attributed to pilot unfamiliarity with the high wing loadings and attendant fast stalling characteristics of the advanced low-wing monoplane designs like the N-3. Being accustomed to flying the much lighter, slower and more maneuverable biplanes of the pre-war era, such as the old bi-wing MF-11 reconnaissance floatplane that had been flown in Norway since 1932, the Norwegian airmen did not at first fully appreciate the more reactive performance characteristics of their new equipment.

Following these two tragic accidents, the Norwegians viewed the Northrop floatplane with somewhat mixed feelings, and rumors soon reached Toronto that "the Northrop's," as the N-3PB was to become known among the Norwegians, were unsafe. This, of course, was a premature conclusion, for once the pilots learned to upgrade their flight experience to the higher capabilities and performance demands of the N-3PB, "the Northrop's" were to prove themselves many times over under the most adverse conditions, such as those both man and plane were to endure in Iceland.

Because it would be flying pontoon-equipped "floatplanes," Norwegian Squadron 330(N) was to be assigned for deployment and activation in Iceland in coordination with the British RAF Coastal Command already operating there. In March 1941, an agreement had been reached between Norwegian and British governments for the placement in Iceland of one maritime squadron equipped with the Northrop seaplane patrol bombers for convoy escort and antisubmarine operations.

The number "330" was assigned by the RAF, since the 300-series of numbers were not being used for British air units. The squadron would be manned by Norwegian personnel but be under the operational coordination of the RAF's Coastal Command, which had begun establishing land and seaplane bases in Iceland immediately following "the occupation" by British Forces on May 10, 1940.

---

[48] This summary of training operations conducted by the Free Norwegian Air Force in Canada during WWII and the aircraft used was provided to the author by Cato Guhnfeldt, Norwegian author and journalist who participated in the recovery and restoration of the N-3PB as a representative of the Norwegian Aviation Historical Society.

General Major Einar Tufte-Johnsen (left) and Major Ole Reistad (right) review the training fleet.

Thorleif Nodeland watches the others land.

Oluf Reed-Olsen, second from right, awaits his wings.

New arrivals via Karachi, India.

Prince Harald, 5-year-old son of Crownprince Olav and Crownprincess Maertha, inspects the cockpit readiness of Cadet Johan Wilhelm Garben, later a Spitfire pilot.

Ground school precedes flight training. Alf E. Bjercke, left, became war consul for Tunisia after the war.

Figure 19.   Fighting to return home, Norwegians formed a "Little Norway" in Toronto, Canada.   Through early spring 1945, airmen trained here for Iceland and England duty. (Photos, "Little Norway" brochure; identities, Cato Guhnfeldt.)

As Cato Guhnfeldt reported to the author concerning this relationship between the two air forces:

> 330 Squadron was an independent squadron.... The squadron leaders of 330 were in constant communication with other Coast Command Units in Iceland as part of a normal coordinating process and when advised to assist other units, they naturally did so. During the first weeks the Norwegians were grateful for all help and advice from other units to broaden their knowledge of the waters in which they operated, but 330 was not...controlled by other squadrons.[49]

The four remaining Northrop's of the first batch were flown from the initial Patricia Bay training site near Vancouver to Toronto in the spring of 1941, in preparation for their eventual delivery to Iceland. N-3PB training continued in Toronto over the next year until the spring of 1942, when the three remaining aircraft were shipped to Iceland as reinforcements for 330(N) squadron. In the interim, a third Northrop had been lost on June 20, 1941, when it crashed into a ferry while taking off from Toronto Bay, killing the two crewmembers aboard. So by the spring of 1942, 21 of the original 24 N-3PB's had been transferred to Iceland for mission operations by Norwegian crews under Coastal Command, whose mission requirements were becoming increasingly urgent.

By the spring of 1941, U-boats were operating far out into the Atlantic, beyond the 1940 zone of operations shown in Figure 18 and well beyond the effective reach of Allied surface and air escort for merchant convoys. Allied and neutral merchant ship losses were already passing unprecedented figures, and Coastal Command was hard pressed for aircraft to counter the U-boat threat, since priority for all new long-range bombers was still being given to the buildup of an offensive bomber force to strike back at the enemy targets in Germany. Thus, a maritime squadron of the single-engine Northrop patrol bombers, however unsuited they might be to the task facing them, was a welcome addition to the Command's meager force, for there were many uses to which this versatile, durable, efficient airplane could be put.

The Northrop's were to replace a squadron of Fairey Battles that had been stationed in Iceland since the preceding summer when the RAF had begun operations. Now equipped with the Northrop's, a squadron of Lockheed Hudson's, and another of Sunderland flying boats, Iceland was shortly to become the base of a small but highly specialized and skillful maritime air force. The N-3PB was still the lightweight member of this force; for it must be remembered that it was originally designed to operate from Norway's coastline, which has thousands of small, somewhat hidden and remote, but well-protected bays and fjords, thus making water landings a routine requirement. Iceland, on the other hand, is literally a group of volcanic mountains jutting from the Atlantic, open to the sea currents and with few good harbors or seaplane anchorages. Also, fully exposed in mid-Atlantic, Iceland experiences weather that is far more severe and volatile; and, with few safe harbors or inlets, is not well suited for regular operations of single-engine aircraft, which require a great many alternate landing sites to choose

---

[49] E-mail from Cato Guhnfeldt, dated January 25, 2002.

from in a sudden storm or emergency, as Lt. Sevi Bulukin's story in Chapter 2 so well relates.

The first 15 Norwegians to arrive in Iceland in the spring of 1941 were volunteers who had enlisted in the Free Norwegian Air Forces after escaping Norway via the Lofoten islands in 1940. They were among the many who escaped following the British commando raid in May 1940 on Narvik, Norway, where, as their last objective before leaving the country in German hands, the British wanted to (and did) destroy the port to prevent German access to iron ore shipments.[50] Led by Lt. Cmdr. Roald J. Thommessen, this select band of volunteers arrived in Iceland on April 12, 1941 and immediately began establishing a base for receiving the N-3PB aircraft. A constant flow of reinforcements continued during the next weeks, made up of men who had escaped German-occupied Norway, sometimes traveling, under the most trying conditions, nearly halfway around the world. Others included survivors of torpedoed merchantmen and officers and enlisted men of the regular services dispatched from England or from Little Norway in Canada.

The report from Cato Guhnfeldt to the author on January 25, 2002 provides further historical background on the sources and mix of personnel staffing the new squadron:

> 330 Squadron was staffed primarily by officers of the Norwegian Navy Air Force, although there might have been one or two from the Army side. The ground personnel were a very mixed bunch indeed, some ground trainees from the Toronto camp, many of whom were sailors who had gone ashore from Norway's merchant fleet and the whaling fleet, both of which returned to Europe from Antarctica in the spring of 1940 (to find their country occupied). Some were sent up from England, again a mixture of trained ground crews and newly recruited men, many of whom had fled from Norway, not having any technical background except a short recruiting school in London. In general, escapees went to the Army Air Force while former sailors went to the Navy Air Force.
>
> (Not all) the men who went to Toronto to train became 330 Squadron. In Toronto both pilots and ground crews of both the Navy and Army air forces were trained. When 330 Squadron was formed, only a small part of the personnel at Toronto training camp (primarily Navy personnel) were dispatched off to Iceland to form the new squadron.[51]

According to Ragnar, one young Norwegian, Warrant Officer Oluf Reed-Olsen (see Figures 19 and 20), escaped Norway six months after the German occupation of the country by crossing to England in an 18-foot sailboat. After training to fly the N-3PB in Canada, he joined Squadron 330(N) in Iceland. As reported to the author by Cato Guhnfeldt on February 5, 2002, Oluf Reed-Olsen was still alive and living in Norway.

---

[50] Hitler's interest in Norway was part of his geopolitical strategy by which to control the North Atlantic sealanes to contain the British Isles and concurrently assure access to abundant natural resources to wage war and make the Third Reich self-sufficient above all other nations. Iceland, of course, was part of this strategy.

[51] E-mail from Cato Guhnfeldt, dated January 25, 2002.

Like Sevi Bulukin, later during the war he was an intelligence agent working behind the lines and underground to free Norwegians held by the enemy as well as to free his homeland. After the war, he wrote about his experiences in books titled *We Shall Return* and *Two Eggs on My Plate* (made into a major film called *Contact*).

Squadron headquarters in Iceland was named "Corbett Camp" after the commanding officer of Squadron 701 of the RAF's Fleet Air Arm, Lt. Cmdr. J. W. S. Corbett, R.N., who had originally established the camp. This squadron had initially established operations in Iceland with the Supermarine Walrus flying boat, which was antiquated but still indispensably useful given the crucial air patrol mission requirements that had to be met in the North Atlantic. The base consisted of a dozen Nissen huts scattered about a "mud hole" along Fossvogur Bay, on the outskirts of an airfield being constructed by the British south of Reykjavik, the capital of Iceland on the southwest side of the island. Fossvogur Bay and Corbett Camp lay one mile from Reykjavik. The base is shown in Figure 21 after activation by Squadron 330(N). While the "mud hole" was in places sloppy, it provided the waterway ingress needed to beach or bring the aircraft close to shore for service. Today, the Reykjavik airport is located between the bay and the capital where the British had previously had their airfield.

On April 24, 1941 the commanding officer, Cmdr. Hans A. Bugge, arrived at the base and on the following day No. 330(N) squadron was officially established in Iceland, to become the first operational squadron of the Free Norwegian Air Force. It was a historical event, one that set a precedent for Norway's squadron numbering that continues today, with Squadron 330 finally performing the mission originally intended, flying search and rescue patrol along the Norwegian coast. But now the squadron flies in Westland Sea King amphibious hull-type helicopters with two engines and heated cabins – a most worthy destiny and memorial for the original squadron that fought arduously above the open sea in the single-engine Northrop's to free that coastline from the enemy.

By early May everything was ready for the first aircraft's arrival, and on the 19th of that month, much to everyone's relief, the Norwegian steamer SS *Fjordheim* sailed into Reykjavik's outer harbor with the squadron's complement of 18 Northrop N-3PB's, including spares, ammunition and bombs. The month of May saw a sharp rise in merchant ship losses to enemy U-boats, and it would hardly have taken more than a single torpedo to send the *Fjordheim,* loaded with the squadron's store of high explosives, to the bottom of the Atlantic, thus putting a premature end to the N-3PB's story. Fortunately, it was not to be the fate of the *Fjordheim* to fall prey to one of Germany's U-boats, and three days after its arrival the crated aircraft were being unloaded at Reykjavik's small and, by then, congested port.

Trucked through the streets of Reykjavik, the Northrop's were assembled at the historic Balbo Hangar on the outskirts of Reykjavik, a few miles away from the squadron's operational base and headquarters at Corbett Camp on Fossvogur Bay. The hangar had gotten its name after the famed Italian aviator, Count Balbo, who, in 1933, had staged through Iceland with a formation of 24 amphibious aircraft on his flight across the Atlantic to promote Italian aviation and tourism.

Oluf Reed-Olsen

Figure 20. Oluf Reed-Olsen, Squadron 330(N) N-3PB pilot, exemplified the bravery and determination of Norwegians fighting to free their homeland.

Oluf Reed-Olsen

Figure 21. Squadron 330(N) operations base at Fossvogur Bay with the "mud hole" on the beach and the capital city Reykjavik a mile away.

The hangar was to serve as the squadron's technical and maintenance center throughout its deployment in Iceland, while Fossvogur Bay, offering better takeoff and landing conditions, was used for operations. Of historical interest, this hangar had been constructed by the well-known German aircraft manufacturer, Junkers, as part of Iceland's second attempt to establish domestic air services as a means for economic growth. As reported to the author by Fridthor Eydal of the Icelandic Defense Force (IDF):

> ...the hangar was built by an Icelandic company commonly known as Icelandair No. 2 that was established in 1928 and operated in the summers of 1928-30 with single-engine Junkers F-13w floatplanes leased from Lufthansa. The company was bankrupt in 1930 and the hangar was used for storage, etc. until the next attempt at establishing Icelandic domestic aviation service in the late 1930's. The hangar was made available for the famous Count Balbo Flight to America in 1933 and apparently as a result the British military that occupied Iceland in 1940 began referring to the hangar as the Balbo Hangar and the beach next to it as Balbo's Beach. It is my thought that the name may very well have first appeared in either pre-war or early-war British Foreign Office or War Office intelligence reports describing conditions in Iceland. With the arrival of the N-3PB in the spring of 1941, the Norwegian Squadron, 33rd, took the hangar for its use for assembly of the crated airframes and major repair work. Their base of operations in Reykjavik was on the opposite side (south side) of the small peninsula that the city is built on and next to the British built airfield.[52]

Figure 22 shows one of the few photos ever taken of this hangar, which after the war was dismantled and moved to another part of the Island where it serves as a museum. By the time the U.S. landed at Balbo Beach, Squadron 330(N) had already assembled its N-3PB's and moved them over to Fossvogur Bay on the other side of the Reykjavik peninsula. But the landing of U.S. marines in Stuart light tanks was such a major departure from the U.S.'s avowed neutrality (two months before Pearl Harbor) that American newsmen landed concurrently to film the event (the long shadows in Figure 22 are cast by camera crews filming the scene from behind the lone photographer in the foreground).

Balbo Hangar was used by Squadron 330(N) for major maintenance of the N-3PB's until the squadron departed in the spring of 1943, taking the remaining Northrop's with them. As reported by Fridthor Eydal, Deputy Public Affairs Officer of the Icelandic Defense Force, the hangar was used solely by the Norwegians, never by the British or the U.S. for their respective seaplanes. After the war, the hangar was disassembled and put in storage. Then three years ago (1998-99) it was restored as part of the Icelandic historical museum in Patreksfjordur in northwestern Iceland, and is on display there today as a retrospective of the country's early entrance into aviation.[53]

---

[52] E-mail from Fridthor Eydal, dated February 11, 2001.
[53] E-mail from Fridthor Eydal, dated November 27, 2001.

U.S. National Archives II

Figure 22. On October 10, 1941, the U.S. Marines landed at Balbo Beach (hangar to left), carrying through with the Roosevelt-Churchill agreement for the U.S. to relieve British troops for duty in the European theater. With the establishment of the U.S.-led Icelandic Defense Force, Iceland was permanently freed of its tie to Denmark and became an independent nation (photo provided by Fridthor Eydal, IDF's Deputy Public Affairs Officer).

Figure 23 shows the respective locations of the maintenance center at Balbo Hangar and the flight operations center at Corbett Camp in Fossvogur Bay. As shown, the hangar was located on the northside of the peninsula and flight operations on the south. Due to the exceptionally long mission duration capability of the N-3PB, flights rotated daily and preflight inspections and refueling were conducted on a continuous schedule at Fossvogur Bay.

As Figure 24 shows, aircraft ready for mission sorties were moored at floating docks offshore while aircraft being given preflight inspections and refueled were beached. Beaching gear was kept on the mooring docks for installation prior to beaching; an airplane was taxied from the dock to the shore and onto the beach without having to stop. Maintenance and servicing was performed in all-weather conditions, on the mud-hole

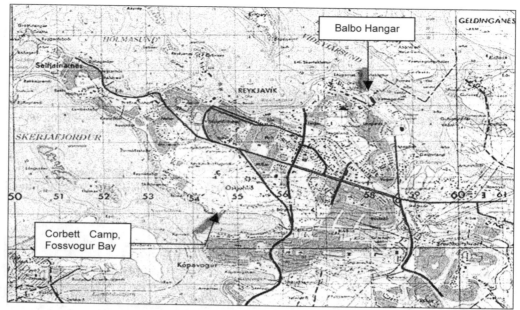

Balbo Hangar

GELDINGANES

SKERJAFJORDUR

Corbett Camp,
Fossvogur Bay

Fridthor Eydal

Figure 23. Located across Reykjavik peninsula from each other, Corbett Camp provided direct access to the sea while Balbo Hangar provided a sheltered cove for major maintenance activity.

beach or dockside. Bombs and depth charges were the anti-sub ordnance carried between the pontoons.

The Norwegians were eager to get into the fight with Germany so they worked 24 hours a day, seven days a week, to get their aircraft into the air. By June 2nd the first of the Northrop's was flight tested and flown to Corbett Camp, followed by another 11 aircraft during the next three weeks.

Meanwhile, the squadron's CO and flight commanders were busy acquainting themselves with the RAF's operational procedures and bringing the highly motivated squadron to operational status.

Other Norwegian airmen were being taken on familiarization flights in Sunderland flying boats of RAF Coastal Command's Squadron No. 201, which had been operating in Iceland since mid-1940.

Shortly after arrival of the first of the Northrop's at Corbett Camp, operational training of aircrew commenced. None of the Norwegian airmen had been through formal training at a standard Operational Training Unit (OTU) and although the regular officers of the pre-war Naval Air Force were all experienced airmen, most of the newly trained arrivals from Canada were green recruits. Thus 330(N) squadron became not only an operational unit at Corbett Camp, but an OTU for its pilots and other air and ground crewmen.

Figure 24. All-weather arctic maintenance and servicing kept the planes flying and the U-boat commanders on alert. (Photos by Oluf Reed-Olsen.)

This dual usage of aircraft initially limited the number available for operations and put a heavy workload on the ground crews, who often toiled through the night to keep the Northrop's serviceable. Their job was not made easier by the fact that all servicing of the aircraft had to be made in the usually freezing open air except for major repairs and scheduled maintenance inspections and overhauls performed at Balbo Hangar. Much of the credit for the noteworthy flight hours record of the squadron is due to this team of men who, despite arctic gales and subzero temperatures, carried out their task with unswerving commitment and good-humored complaint, and who are to be commended directly for the squadron's excellent serviceability record.

While minor problems were to delay aircrew training somewhat in the beginning, a chronic deficiency in the aircraft's magnetic compasses was to be cause for grave concern. The N-3PB's were equipped with a Kollsman Direction Indicator, which was not designed for high-latitude application where magnetic forces are incredibly strong. With the 65-degree latitude parallel running through the center of Iceland, the island is within 25 degrees of the North Pole. Uncompensated for this high northern latitude in their design, the compasses were found to be extremely sluggish and unreliable once the aircraft were operating in Iceland.

The resulting navigational inaccuracy was a serious matter once the aircraft were out of sight of land and even close in if fog and bad weather demanded reliable instruments to return safely to base. The ground crews tried relocating the compass above the instrument panel to minimize deviation and air-swung them some 60 miles at sea, away from land, using an astro-compass as benchmark; however, the compass problem was not definitely eliminated until several aircraft came close to being lost after nearly or completely missing the island on their return flights. One aircraft was well on its way to Greenland, which is over 150 miles from Iceland on the shortest heading, before the crew discovered the navigational error and turned back, landing at Fossvogur Bay with the fuel gage indicating empty. The Kollsman compasses were then replaced by British models specially calibrated and tested for high-latitude application.[54]

One inherent design shortcoming of the N-3PB in particular was to harass the maintenance crews throughout the aircraft's operational life. This problem was due to the number of magnesium fittings Jack Northrop had incorporated to reduce weight, but which required frequent inspection and anti-corrosion treatment. Having pioneered the use of magnesium in aircraft construction, Jack Northrop had used it for a number of N-3PB parts, in particular control wire pulley brackets, bomb racks and other fittings, to gain the low-weight and high-strength benefits of this corrosion-prone metal. Although acceptable for land planes, it was not an ideal application for seaplanes constantly exposed to the worst imaginable corrosion conditions from wind-whipped saltwater and rime ice. A fresh-water wash down and inspection of the magnesium fittings was to

---

[54] The problem of magnetic compass usage in the Iceland and Arctic region was not peculiar to the N-3PB. As reported by Doenitz (Loc. Cit., Appendix 3) U-boats had similar difficulty; and in particular magnetic detonators used on German torpedoes failed to operate properly until launch procedures were changed to compensate for the magnetic deviation anomaly peculiar to Arctic latitudes.

become part of the daily maintenance routine, and every three days the bomb racks had to be removed, cleaned and treated against corrosion.

Other technical problems experienced included the cracking of the float pedestal brackets, which was quickly remedied by a field design improvisation to the bracket attachments; also the poor serviceability of the Lear radio equipment was to cause many abandoned missions. To keep these radios operational, wireless operators were taught to make in-flight repairs, and even though the standing order was to return to base should the radios fail during flight, as time passed, the airmen largely disobeyed that directive.

Despite problems which initially delayed the squadron becoming fully mission effective, the N-3PB's first operational flight took place on June 23, 1941, when the squadron was requested by RAF headquarters in Iceland to put up two aircraft to escort a merchant convoy passing south of Iceland. Taking off from Fossvogur Bay at 2225 hours, this inaugural flight of the squadron met the convoy off the Reykjanes peninsula, the southwest tip of the island. Typically, the escort pattern was to fly a series of concentric circles of increasing radius about the center of a convoy, flying low enough to spot conning towers, underwater shadows, or the unusual swell pattern submarines cruising underwater cause at the sea surface. The first flight escorted the convoy for about two hours before the aircraft were recalled because of deteriorating weather. The two Northrop's making the squadron's debut landed at Fossvogur Bay after a flight of two hours and fifty minutes, relatively short for the norm eventually established. Due to continuing bad weather the relieving flight was subsequently cancelled also.

Figure 25 shows typical mission operations. Flight crews were on standby at their assigned aircraft waiting for weather fronts to clear or aloft in flights of one or two aircraft. Missions typically ran five to seven hours in duration and covered a thousand miles of ocean roundtrip. Due to the arctic weather and Spartan air-conditioning provisions of the N-3PB, the crew had to wear their warmest flight gear on every mission.

Due mainly to the compass problem, the British were skeptical as to the capability of the single-engine Northrop's to fly antisubmarine patrols far out at sea, and so at first were reluctant to assign operational tasks to the squadron. Consequently, during the month of July its aircraft made only three operational flights. The Army, on the other hand, showed considerably more interest in this latest addition to the island's defenses. During the first months of its existence, the squadron enjoyed spirited and close cooperation with the Army, making dummy attacks on Army installations and towing targets for its antiaircraft artillery, for training purposes.

On becoming operational, the squadron was divided into three Flight Groups, of three to six aircraft each. A-Flight with six aircraft was based at Reykjavik; B-Flight with three aircraft was based at the town of Akureyri on Iceland's north coast; and C-Flight, also with three aircraft, was based at the fishing village of Budareyri, located in a small fjord surrounded by high mountains, on the island's east coast. The remaining six aircraft were stored and kept in reserve at Balbo Hangar. In June and July, advance parties were sent to Akureyri and Budareyri, and by July 20th, B-Flight received its three Northrop's, followed by C-Flight with its three on September 11th.

Figure 25. The Northrop's flew two years from three strategic sealane bases. (Photos by Oluf Reed-Olsen.)

As Figures 24 and 25 indicate, it was a cold, snowy landscape most of the year and even in the summer the days were chilly.[55]

During the month of August 1941 a large concentration of German U-boats was detected in the waters south and southeast of Iceland. In its effort to provide maximum air coverage over the probable U-boat area, Coastal Command's aircraft based in Iceland and the British Isles flew intensive antisubmarine patrols between Iceland and Ireland, attacking eighteen U-boats, sinking one and capturing another during the course of the month. The Norwegians, eager to see some action, persuaded the British to employ them on the hunt, with the result that out of ten sorties flown during August 26-29, the squadron's Northrop's delivered four attacks on German U-boats sighted off Iceland's south coast. From then on the squadron's capability was firmly acknowledged and during the next eighteen months its Northrop's were to play an active role in World War II's most crucial battle of all: "The Battle of the Atlantic."

The squadron's first encounter with the enemy during that period came on August 27, 1941, when one of three N-3PB's, out on a U-boat strike, sighted a submarine's conning tower a short distance ahead. Diving from 900 to 50 feet, the Northrop's three depth charges failed to release and by the time the aircraft came in for its second attack the U-boat had already submerged. Greatly disappointed by the failure of his attack, the pilot, Quartermaster Conrad Helgesen, proceeded to carry out a square search of the area in the vicinity of the attack, and only 29 minutes after the first sighting, a U-boat's periscope was spotted half a mile ahead. Diving from 750 feet the aircraft opened fire with its wing-mounted machine guns and the three 350-pound depth charges were released manually but slightly ahead of the point where the periscope was last seen. However, the sea was quite rough and no evidence of damage to the U-boat was observed. The aircraft remained in the vicinity for another 50 minutes then dropped a sea marker and returned to base. Helgesen, for security purposes after the war, changed his name to Skjoldhammer and became an airline pilot with Braathens South American & Far East Airlines.

The Norwegians put up three Northrop's early next morning to follow up on the previous day's attack. Having been airborne for one hour and forty minutes, Quartermaster Hans Olai Holdo, piloting one of the three Northrop's aloft on a strike mission, sighted a British destroyer, four antisubmarine trawlers, and a surfaced U-boat at close range. Believing that the U-boat was about to deliver an attack on the naval vessels, Holdo dived his "Northrop" for an immediate attack, releasing two of the aircraft's three depth charges which exploded about 50 feet to each side of the U-boat's hull, practically lifting it clear of the surface. While climbing out from the attack, Holdo received a signal from the destroyer saying the U-boat had surrendered and was being taken care of. Unknown to the Northrop's crew, the U-boat had already surfaced the previous day and surrendered to an Iceland-based Hudson aircraft of No. 269 squadron RAF, and now

---

[55] The average air temperature at sea level is about 5C (41F) and for six months is freezing. On the western side of the Island it snows about 100 days of the year and on the east about 40. Rainfall averages 45 inches annually. On clear days the wind hums constantly, vortexing off the ocean.

awaited only a naval boarding party. Much to everyone's relief, this otherwise well-executed attack did not cause any damage to the U-boat, which subsequently was towed to Iceland and eventually, ironically, entered service with the Royal Navy as the HMS Graph; but not before it had provided the British with valuable information on German submarine technology and construction.

Holdo resumed his patrol and some 45 minutes later sighted the conning tower of another U-boat, which he attacked with machine-gun fire and the aircraft's one remaining depth charge, but no damage was inflicted as far as could be observed. While trying to return to base, the aircraft was lead astray by its deficient Kollsman compass, and was already halfway to Greenland by the time the crew realized the error. Holdo and crew barely managed to reach a small fishing village on Iceland's west coast before the aircraft ran out of fuel. They had been airborne for 7 hours and 20 minutes though the Northrop's estimated maximum endurance was only 7 hours!

During the following months, the Northrop's of A-Flight were to continue on convoy escort and antisubmarine operations to the south and southwest of Iceland without engaging the enemy but once, with inconclusive results. Meanwhile, following Germany's attack on Russia in June 1941, the Allies had initiated the arctic convoy route, and it was soon to become the task of Squadron 330(N)'s Northrop's to provide escort to the convoys carrying Russia's vital military supplies. These convoys assembled in Iceland and were escorted by A-Flight along Iceland's west coast and through the Denmark Strait, where B-Flight's aircraft took over. B-Flight then escorted the convoys hundreds of miles north of the Arctic Circle; but the final 500 miles to Murmansk could not be covered by Allied aircraft in 1942 and the convoys were on their own once they left Jan Mayen Island behind them.

Although assigned officially to convoy escort and antisubmarine missions, the Northrop's of Squadron 330(N) were diverted often to other urgent tasks, such as army logistics transport and airborne ambulance services, air-sea rescue, ice reconnaissance, and, in fact, any task for which a seaplane could be used; and since there were few airfields in Iceland, the N-3PB's were the first to be called upon when some emergency service was required. Many military and civilian patients owed their lives to the airplane's virtuosity in landing and taking off anywhere there was suitable water.

The Northrop's of B-Flight at Akureyri flew long hours patrolling the Denmark Strait for enemy surface raiders attempting to break out into the Atlantic, while C-Flight's aircraft at Budareyri patrolled the Northern Passage Route used by new U-boats coming from Germany's Baltic ports to enter the Atlantic. As the Battle of the Atlantic progressed, the Northern Passage airspace became an air combat arena for C-Flight as the number of German recce aircraft supporting Wolf Pack deployment of U-boats against Allied convoys increased.

Once the Allied convoys started sailing from Iceland to northern ports in Russia, the frequency of German reconnaissance flights to Iceland increased rapidly. Operating from bases within occupied Norway, the German reconnaissance aircraft, consisting of such types as the Focke-Wulf 200 Condor, Junker 88 and Bv 138, would make landfall on Iceland's east coast, and it was soon to become the task of B- and C-Flight's Northrop's to put up fighter patrols to counter this latest threat. Armed with its four 50-caliber fixed guns and two 30-caliber flexible guns, the Northrop possessed a formidable array of firepower about its entire airborne envelope, but it lacked the speed to follow up after initiating an attack on the faster Luftwaffe aircraft. On several occasions, however, the N-3PB got in close enough to register hits on the intruders, but none of these engagements were to be rewarded with a definite "kill".

On July 24, 1941, the squadron's first operational accident occurred when an A-Flight N-3PB overturned on landing and sank at Fossvogur Bay. The aircraft's two occupants escaped with only slight injury. Damaged beyond repair, the aircraft was later recovered and cannibalized for spares. Only six days later the squadron's first fatality occurred when a plane on a navigational training flight disappeared without a trace, taking with it its crew of three. Altogether the squadron was to loose eleven of its Northrop's in Iceland for various reasons, but the most tragic accident of all came on the squadron's first anniversary, when Cmdr. Bugge, the squadron's commanding officer, failed to return from an antisubmarine sweep. No trace of his aircraft was ever found, despite an intensive search.

Operating a single-engine aircraft such as the N-3PB on prolonged open ocean flights in arctic regions, without even such safety devices as de-icing equipment, can barely be called hazardous; for, in more normal times it would have been considered foolhardy. Even a seaplane had little chance of making a successful forced landing on the high swells of the North Atlantic. It is a tribute to the Wright "Cyclone" engine that none of the squadron's aircraft, with the possible exception of the two that disappeared for reasons still unknown, were lost due to engine failure; and for the two that didn't return, the engine probably stopped from lack of fuel. That the Norwegian crews, confronted by some of the world's worst flying weather, never failed to take on the challenge of these long, daunting patrols, is a tribute partly to the courage of these young and gallant descendents of Vikings, but also to their intense commitment to free their homeland.

In the summer of 1942, A-Flight was re-equipped with the Mk Ill "Catalina" (PBY-5A) amphibians; and, after August of that year, A-Flight operated its Northrop's exclusively for designated convoy patrol in the Denmark Strait. B- and C-Flights, however, continued flying the N-3PB on intra-island operations as well as sealane patrol.

Then in December 1942, A- and B-Flights were disbanded. The squadron, except for C-Flight at Budareyri and the maintenance section at Balbo Hangar, was transferred to Scotland in January 1943. C-Flight alone was to continue fighter patrol, escort and antisubmarine operations under the command of Lt. Sevi Bulukin off Iceland's east coast through the spring of 1943, when it also was disbanded to join the squadron's main body, now operating Sunderland flying boats from the Shetland Islands.

As there no longer existed an operational requirement for the already aging Northrop floatplanes, and the assembly line had long since closed down, the remaining aircraft were ordered scrapped. The Norwegians, however, probably for sentimental and historical reasons, retained two of the Northrop's, both of which managed to reach Norway at war's end, only to be sold for salvage during the post-war years. Necessarily, the wartime Norwegian Air Force was more preservation-conscious than its postwar counterpart.

In the fighter role the Northrop's of Norway's Squadron 330(N) engaged in combat with German reconnaissance aircraft on eight occasions, and although none of the intruders was confirmed as being destroyed, they almost certainly suffered some damage, as hits were observed on all but one of the aircraft attacked. Furthermore, since most of the encounters took place at sea far from Germany's mainland bases in Norway, it is reasonable to assume that some of the German aircraft damaged by the N-3PB's in air-to-air combat never returned to their base.

To summarize the amazing military role of this supposedly miscast airplane, from June 23, 1941, to March 30, 1943, Squadron 330(N) carried out 1,412 operational sorties totaling 3,512 hours and 52 minutes flying time. Of these missions, 991 were specifically strike missions against U-boats and 421 were convoy patrols. Eight attacks on German U-boats were delivered, and although not rewarded with conclusive results, it should be remembered that, in principle, the antisubmarine aircraft's greatest contribution to the maritime warfare of World War II was not accounted for by the number of submarines damaged or destroyed, but by the number of merchantmen saved from U-boat attacks by the aircraft's deterrent presence above and around the merchant convoys. During its convoy patrols not one ship was lost to a U-boat. It can be confidently said that this airplane, originally designed for peacetime patrol of Norway's 1,500-mile coastline serrated with thousands of fjords and offshore islands, was definitely a psychological "pistol" held to the head of every U-boat commander operating in the Icelandic region.

The most suitable ending to this account of the aircraft's service with the 330(N) squadron can best be expressed in the words of Norway's Cmdr. Kristian Ostby, the technical and contractual coordinator who got the airplane produced by Northrop and was the acceptance officer following flight checkout of each aircraft. Cmdr. Ostby, who was head of the Norwegian Aviation Mission to the U.S. and had over 4,000 hours flying a large variety of aircraft, expressed this evalution of the plane: "I'm of the opinion that the N-3PB is the very finest aircraft I've ever flown." Ostby was not an unqualified judge; he was an experienced test pilot and a graduate of the Massachusetts Institute of Technology, with a degree in aeronautical engineering.

Ostby, shown on the wing in Figure 26, was the first and only pilot to try looping the airplane. Roy Wolford, the photographer Jack Northrop had assigned to record the production acceptance flight tests at Lake Elsinore, California, verified Ostby's attempt; he was seated right behind Ostby in the radio-operator-observer crew station. Ostby asked him through the intercom if he'd like to try a loop. Wolford, normally somewhat taciturn, smiled (inwardly skeptical) at Ostby in the latter's rearview mirror and gave him a thumbs-up. Ostby smiled back, returning the thumbs-up as acknowledgement.

At about 3,000 feet above the lake, Ostby put the plane in a shallow dive and, on reaching 250 mph indicated airspeed, pulled the airplane up smoothly to near vertical and then applying full throttle, pulled the stick all the way back. Almost over the top, the plane stalled upside-down and went into a flat spin. Ostby immediately put the stick

Roy L. Wolford

Figure 26. Norway's Cmdr. Kristian Ostby and Northrop flight test photographer Roy Wolford before attempting to loop the N-3PB at Lake Elsinore, California, during the flight test program in December 1940.

forward, cleared the throttle and then opened it all the way, concurrently kicking right rudder to roll the plane out to its normal horizon. Ostby smiled back again, signaling a thumbs-down. "Too much weight in the wrong place," he shouted over the intercom. Wolford nodded in assent and looked out the canopy.

"Wow," he thought, "we lost a lot of altitude."

They had gone from 3,000 to 400 feet in what seemed like seconds. For Ostby, a gymnast who could do a one-handed headstand on request, even fully suited with coat and tie, trying to loop the pontoon-laden airplane was a natural impulse, given the plane's power, speed, and agility.

The key milestone life history of each of the 24 N-3PB's is shown in Appendix A, as recorded in Squadron 330(N) records in Reykjavik in 1943. It is noteworthy that Serial No. 318 was listed as the one that crashed in the Thjorsa River. This bookkeeping error was to provide much welcomed comic relief years later at the moment of greatest tension during recovery of the crashed airplane from the river.

Among the many testaments to the value of the N-3PB during WWII are two that are likely to get overlooked in the global drama of the war. Many Icelanders, especially those who lived in and about the coastal fishing villages where the airplane landed, moored, refueled and took off again, were at first skeptical about this unusual airborne intrusion in their lives, being people of the sea. It was only after they saw the resilience and resourcefulness of the plane in carrying out its meaningful mission and the audacity and relentlessness of the Norwegian aviators in flying it under such environmental adversity, that they came to not only accept the plane in their presence but to admire and welcome it. They concluded rightly that the plane was there because Iceland was an important place for it to operate from; and that Iceland, through the plane, was taking its rightful place in the world.

The second testament is that of Cmdr. Ostby himself. Though it was only on the merit of Jack Northrop's reputation and his paper design that Ostby could base his procurement decision in the spring of 1940, three years later the correctness of his judgment had become well demonstrated by the operational record of the airplane. As a highly qualified pilot and engineer, his singling out of the N-3PB as the finest aircraft he'd ever flown was unquestionably the highest praise that could be bestowed. After the N-3PB contract was fulfilled, Ostby remained in the U.S. as air attaché for the Norwegian refugee government in Washington, D.C. Like most of the Norwegians who escaped their homeland to fight Fascism, he did not see his wife or children until after Germany was defeated and did not even hear from them until 1942. After the war, he became the air minister for Norway.

What Ostby had foreseen in the N-3PB, perhaps intuitively, was that the transition from Jack Northrop's visionary concept to a mission-reliable airplane would produce the very means Norway was looking for "to secure and safeguard the ocean." As it should, the plane proved the motto, *Trygg Havet.*

So while the Northrop's ceased operating in Iceland by May 1943, Squadron 330(N) continued flying sea patrol missions using other aircraft. There were other Norwegian squadrons operating similarly, such as 331(N) and 332(N) Squadrons, which had been formed as part of RAF's Fighter Command stationed in Yorkshire, England. When the war ended, the Norwegians had five squadrons in the 330 series. All moved to Norway and have kept their 330-series numbers to this day.

The 330-series was established first of all, because the Norwegian authorities in London during WWII did not want their forces to be absorbed namelessly into the British forces. The Norwegian government, though provisional, wanted to organize and operate genuine Norwegian units that were staffed and run by Norwegians. One reason for preserving identity was that the government thought that the Germans would get spread too thin as the war progressed and they would be able to invade and oust the Germans within a short time. Also, the government believed that by having pure, distinctly identifiable Norwegian units the morale and unity of the dispersed nation would be kept strong and the military units would provide an existing and experienced organizational structure for securing and rebuilding the country quickly after the war.

Though 330(N) Squadron was augmented with six Catalina flying boats in the spring of 1942, by the end of that year, 10 of the Northrop's and two of the Catalina's had been lost. Since by then the Northrop's were beginning to wear out and spare parts were no longer available, the squadron was reassigned to Oban, on the west of Scotland, to train in Sunderland IIIs. In July 1943, the squadron was stationed at Sullom Voe in the Shetland Islands, 160 miles north of Scotland. Now the squadron, relatively cozy in the spacious, well-heated Sunderland's, was patrolling west to Iceland as far as the Denmark Strait off Greenland, covering the entire North Atlantic gap where U-boats operated in packs. In 1944, the squadron was switched to patrol off its homeland coastline.

When the war ended in May 1945, the squadron continued to operate out of Sullom Voe, because Coastal Command still had cleanup work to do in the North Atlantic and there was no base set up as yet for the squadron in Norway. But on November 21, 1945, Squadron 330(N) finally flew home, landing at its new base at Stavanger on the southwest tip of Norway. Its assignment, at last, was to patrol the Norwegian coastline. Though decommissioned a couple of times by budgetary constraints in the postwar years, Squadron 330 has been in continuous operation since the early 1970s performing its standard mission of safeguarding the Norwegian thousand-mile coastline.

Despite not being credited with sinking any U-boats while flying the Northrop's, the squadron did sink two of them while flying the Sunderland's out of Sullom Voe. Despite its lack of known "kills," the N-3PB, in its tour of duty, had sustained the team spirit that made the return to homeland possible. The Northrop's, reaching out on their long flights over the North Atlantic, served as a bridge to Norway.

Today, Squadron 330 – no longer requiring the (N) add-on that distinguished the Norwegians from the British during WWII – safeguards the sea along Norway's coast, from fives bases: Sola AFB outside Stavanger on the southwest end of the country; Bodo AFB, mid-country south of Narvik; Banak AFB on the northern end; Orland west of Trondheim; and Rygge AFB south of Oslo on the eastside of Oslo fjord. The specific mission of the squadron is search and rescue along the Norwegian coast, as intended in the beginning.[56]

---

[56] Information on the operations and deployment of Squadron 330(N) was provided by Cato Guhnfeldt in e-mails dated November 21, 2001 and June 7, 2002, updated from a book written by him published originally in 1981. He has been working on an English edition of this book titled, *Northrop N-3PB at War*.

Part II – The Recovery

CHAPTER 5 - RESTORATION ZEN: INTUITION OF A BURIED AIRPLANE

As the 5th Century BC Greek philosopher Heraclitus said, "You never step in the same river twice." Like most sage sayings, this has a figurative meaning as well as a literal one. Literally, since rivers flow from high elevations to the sea, the water at any one spot is constantly changing, so one never steps in the same water twice. Figuratively, however, the meaning has a larger, more universal sense, in that life is a process of change; one never experiences exactly the same thing twice and one is never exactly the same twice. In fact, according to the Second Law of Thermodynamics, the universe itself is undergoing constant change from an energy state of high order to chaos. So, for example, even though Hemingway said, "The sun also rises," it is never the same sun.

It was reasonable to assume that time and the river also changed the N-3PB seaplane, Serial No. 320 that had been forced down in a blinding snowstorm that April day in 1943. Gradually, the airplane had disappeared. Initially, though, for the first decade, portions of it could be seen above water as the depth where it was pinned by the remaining pontoon to the riverbed varied by six feet from springtime snowmelt to winter freeze. During the next decade it disappeared from view as its weight and the current plunged it deeper into the finely ground lava sand of the riverbed. The Thjorsa River and the nature of glacial flows at the Arctic Circle is what had to be dealt with now.

Where the forced crash had occurred was in a complex, curved configuration of the river from west to east and then north again. Hydrodynamic forces grind away at such locations. Here, the Thjorsa is subject to similar forces as a meandering river, except that meandering rivers are located in softer terrain and less inclement meteorological conditions. But it was the force of the river that had carved out the bluff that suddenly loomed out of the snowstorm and forced Sevi Bulukin to do a spinout on water.

The disappearance was abetted by human factors as well. Farmer Bjorn Johannsson, who lived near the crash site at the Farm Skridufell, reported to Ragnar Ragnarsson in 1972 that for some years after the crash the upper fuselage surfaces and tail section had extended above the river's surface, listing, in general, forward and to the left. This general listing attitude was the same just after the crash, as shown by the photo in Figure 7 of Chapter 2.

Two major incidents occurred near the end of the first decade that critically altered the plane's relationship with the river, both the result of human intervention. One can imagine the intriguing sight this airplane must have posed for Farmer Johannsson over the years as it sat fixated in the riverbed, pinioned by its one pontoon, with the seasonal rise and fall of the water level coyly revealing more or less of its fuselage. To an innovative, adventurous spirit such as an Icelandic farmer must possess, it became a challenge to free the plane from its earthbound entrapment. Farmer Johannsson confirmed to Ragnar that in about 1950 he and his brother had attempted to pull the aircraft from the river. They had tied a steel rope around the aircraft's propeller shaft and with the other end hooked to a GMC 6-by-6 surplus army truck tried to pull the aircraft to shore. The aircraft, however, remained firmly entrenched in the riverbed and the engine broke loose from its mountings at the firewall; and so the engine and the accessory section forward of the firewall got pulled to shore, less the engine cowling, which apparently had come loose in the process and sank in the river or floated or drifted off with the current.

About two years later another attempt was made to free the aircraft, this time by pulling on the tail section. It is believed that this was the blow that accelerated the complete submergence of the airplane in the riverbed. With the aircraft situated fore and aft with the current flow – much as though the water represented an airstream – any attempt to pull on the tail from shore would impose a tremendous overload at a right angle to the fuselage, the weakest angle for a load vector. The person responsible for this attempt said he aborted this approach when he saw that the aircraft would not budge; and he claimed that no visible damage to the tail section resulted from this ill-conceived attempt. The only other cause of the damage subsequently discovered could have been ice flow, but the ice would have had to be impossibly thick.

Ragnar was aware of both attempts and they made him wonder how much if anything was left of the airplane. After all, coupled with the destructive forces in the river and the recurring ice of all the past winters, nothing might remain. Farmer Johansson hadn't seen the airplane for the past 15 or so years; and as he was fond of saying, "What the Thjorsa takes, it never gives back."

But what Ragnar hoped had happened in this last attempt of the farmers to wrench the airplane free from the riverbed is that the remaining pontoon pedestal was severely fractured and that this allowed the airplane to stay in place, though sink from sight.

Ragnar tells of a relevant incident concerning the sensitivity of the pontoon suspension system to torsion loads. The pontoons of course carry the weight of the airplane when it's sitting on water, plus the side-, vertical-, and torsional-force loadings when the airplane is taxiing and turning in being positioned for takeoff and for mooring after landing. These loads are compounded by the g-loads imposed by choppy seas or rivers and by the drag induced by water flow on takeoff and landing. Once airborne, the cumbersomely large pontoons hang in the ambient airstream at an average 150-mph airspeed; and, in addition to normal aerodynamic drag, any yawing induced by maneuvers or winds aloft generate extensive sideloads. So the pontoons in general pose a demanding, complex load environment for the designer to meet with an appropriate structural system. The problem focuses on the pedestals to which the pontoons are mounted and that in turn attach to the wing, transferring the loads ultimately to the main airframe.

Jack Northrop addressed this design problem in his usual ingenious way, by using a design integration of fuselage/wing/pedestal that provided a synthesized load path for transmitting and absorbing the loads felt by the pontoons to and in the primary structure provided by the large, beefed-up structural section of the center wing box. This section was designed and manufactured as an integral part of the fuselage, so loads transmitted directly to it were in turn distributed for dissipation throughout the fuselage. The pontoon pedestals mated directly with the "mainplanes" (thick, specially heat-treated wing ribs) to which the wings attached. These "mainplanes" in effect constituted secondary keels outboard of the center keel of the fuselage. Thus loads from the pontoons were effectively absorbed in two stages, first at the mainplanes and then at the fuselage. As the recovery operation found later, however, this path for the normal distribution of loads – which the airplane designer has to meet by a factor of 1.5 times the maximum load – can be completely defeated if eccentric loads are applied transversely to the fuselage. These are the kinds of loads that nature doesn't impose on an airplane, designers thankfully acknowledge. But the recovery later showed as described above that men who don't know the nature of airplanes can take ill-informed actions when they want to move one.

Returning to Ragnar's story about the pontoons, Lt. "Sevi" Bulukin had a special problem to deal with on the pontoons when he was serving as Deputy Technical Director of Squadron 330(N):

The N-3PB's airframe was pretty sound and held up well under the hard conditions it was subjected to in Iceland. Apart from the corrosion problem with the magnesium parts, which was eventually resolved, there was a problem with the pontoon brackets. These brackets held the huge pontoons to their pedestals, four to each pontoon/pedestal assembly (another four held the pedestal to the wing). The brackets came under tremendous strain as you can imagine, in choppy seas, hard landings, etc., and in about July 1941 the squadron received a message from the Norwegian training base, Toronto, Canada, that cracks had been detected in the brackets of one of the N-3PB trainers they had there at the time. Shortly thereafter cracks were being detected on planes in Iceland as well. Bulukin, who had a degree in mechanical engineering, had an understanding of metallurgy in which he found an alloy he though might cure the problem. . . .

With his book and a sample bracket in hand, Bulukin visited a blacksmith in Reykjavik who had a small foundry in the corner of his shop. Bulukin explained to him the problem and told him what he needed. Now, alloying is not a simple science. To achieve a certain chemical composition in a finished product one has to add the metals to the furnace in altogether different proportions because their characteristics change during the smelting process. Bulukin watched as the old man went about his work and was amazed to notice that he never once consulted any written tables or other written references while preparing the alloy. He just took a little bit of this and a little bit of that, weighed it, and added (it) to the furnace. Whether the finished product turned out to have his desired chemical composition or not, Bulukin never knew, but the squadron never experienced any problems with the pontoon brackets after that! The moral of that story is that experience is the best education you can ever obtain (the author notes that as a wag once said about the value of experience to education, "It should be better, for what it costs!").[57]

The "old blacksmith's" alchemy may have been the reason both pontoons eventually separated from Serial No. 320, not at the pedestal interface, but at the wing mainplane.

By the mid-1960's the remaining airframe had sunk from sight and was no longer seen even during the winter when the river was six feet less in depth due to the glacial freeze of the water source. While the manmade forces contributing to the airplane's disappearance were intermittent and sporadic, nature bore down relentlessly. The constant environmental grinding to which the plane was subjected by nature is indicated by the seasonal changes it had to endure year after year, as shown in Table 2.

TABLE 2. SEASONAL CHANGES OF MAJOR ENVIRONMENTAL FACTORS IN ICELAND*

ENVIRONMENTAL FACTOR	SUMMER	WINTER	CHANGE
a. Thjorsa River depth.	8 ft.	12 ft.	50%
b. Current velocity.	5 mph	3 mph	-40%
c. Water temperature.	8C	0C	-100%
d. Water makeup.	Sandy, milky	Ice	100%
e. Air temperature.	11C	-1C	-109%
f. Wind velocity.	10 mph	15 mph	50%
g. Rainfall (Reykjavik).	1.9 in./mon.	3.5 in./mon.	84%
h. Snow frequency (days).	20	50	150%
*As measured at N-3PB recovery site, except as noted. Percent change from winter to summer. All figures are averages.			

By the early 1960's the airplane remained beneath the surface of the river throughout the year, unseen to passersby or those who lived and farmed in the area. It was in 1972 that the Zen of recovery – what might be called the first phase of restoration – began to work its way to the surface of man's consciousness. In that year, Ragnar Ragnarsson was retained by the RAF to lead an aircraft recovery expedition into the undeveloped, rugged, glacial and volcanic interior of Iceland to recover a Fairey Battle, a light, single-engine bomber with a three-man crew, that had crash-landed there during the war while on a transport flight to Akureyri on the north coast. The way led along the remote road used by the sparse, scattered farms to access the coast – a road that ran parallel to the Thjorsa River and past the site where the N-3PB had been seen last. Ragnar, by then an aviation enthusiast and pilot, had heard that Farmer Johansson had parts from a crashed aircraft

---

[57] E-mail from Ragnar J. Ragnarsson, dated May 3, 2001.

stored on his farm and so stopped there so the expedition could examine the parts to see if they might be from the Fairey Battle aircraft.

It was at this juncture that Ragnar first learned of the invisible, crashed N-3PB, for the parts in Farmer Johansson's yard and barn proved to be from it. After successfully completing his mission with the RAF, Ragnar couldn't keep the thought of the N-3PB from recurring. Often he wondered about it. Was it still there? Was anything left? He saw the airplane as a part of Icelandic legend, in particular as the role of Iceland in the air missions of the Battle of the Atlantic had become more legendary and he and associates organized specifically to document the history of that legend in every possible form, if they could.

Ragnar was curious whether this object was the N-3PB or just some rusty old car that had ended up in the river. His discovery of this report of the detection incident immediately connected with his recurring meditations on the lost N-3PB seaplane that he had heard about from Farmer Johansson. He was suddenly enthused as to the possibility of locating the plane and recovering it. It was the kind of mission impossible that made living in Iceland an adventure few had access to and could enjoy. Further, it was part of the Icelandic legend arising from WWII, when the N-3PB itself had engaged in a mission impossible and succeeded. The more he learned about the exploits of the N-3PB and the crash landing of Serial No. 320 and the years it had endured the onslaught of man and nature to remain, in some sense, aloft, the more he wanted to find and recover it for restoration, if, indeed, it were still there and could be located. Due to his meditations on that airplane, the Zen of restoration was filling him.

While other airplanes had served the Allied cause in Iceland and moved on to other bases of operation, this airplane remained a part of Iceland on a seemingly irretrievable basis. And the plane would have remained forever out of sight and eventually forgotten entirely were it not for other manmade forces at work. Even as Iceland had been courted before the war by Germany to serve as a base for air operations and then again had been involuntarily recruited for such services during WWII, so after the war it was a natural progression for aviation to become Iceland's major interface with the world. That spirit of the peoples who had settled there was ever urged aloft, to harken to the wind that ever blows across its glacial face, lifting with the northern course of the Gulf Stream.

Locating, recovering, and restoring the lost N-3PB became Ragnar's first priority, when in June 1977, with the participation of other Icelandic aviation enthusiasts, he helped form the Icelandic Aviation Historical Society (IAHS). A short time later, with his inspired urging, the group decided to try and find and recover the Northrop N-3PB that Lt. Sevi Bulukin had been forced to crash-land under whiteout conditions 34 years previously. The project was to be directed by Ragnar, who was the newly formed society's vice-president and who, in thinking about and studying this particular historical incident over the past several years, had established contact with the Norwegian Aviation Historical Society, which was also enthusiastic about the idea of recovering one of Norway's most memorable WWII aircraft. Subconsciously, he was thinking too of his place of birth, the U.S. It would be neat to put together the same international team that had originated the airplane and made its operation possible during the war.

Ragnar set the project in motion immediately, with the IAHS now ready to proceed. An initial surveillance of the site was made on June 11, 1977, by a team that included Ragnar, Baldur Sveinsson, Jon K. Snorrason, Einar Gunnarsson, and Sigurdur P. Hardarson, all from the IAHS. The team also visited Farmer Bjorn Johannsson at his nearby farm, Skridufell, where they were briefed on the background of the airplane from the time of the forced crash until it sank from view. Was it still there? He was betting on a positive answer. He was encouraged when Farmer Johansson confirmed the report of Lt. Bulukin that there had been no external damage other than the missing pontoon, the absence of which caused the airplane to list forward and to the left side. He also confirmed the progressive submergence of the plane slowly over the years into the riverbed, until it was no longer visible and eventually completely immersed in the riverbed.

Although Farmer Johannsson indicated that the plane had been left untouched, the following parts from the aircraft were found at the farm Skridufell:

- All three propeller blades (heavily bent and corroded).

- The forward engine casing with crankshaft and piston rods (badly rusted).

- The propeller hub (in fair condition).

- Parts of engine mountings.

- Parts of canopy framing. (The sliding parts of the cockpit canopy had been removed and used as glass panes for a ram's shed.)

- A pontoon rudder – removed from the pontoon that broke off (in excellent condition).

- An Aldis lamp (modified to take a 12-volt current).

Farmer Johannsson recalled seeing the pontoon that broke off the aircraft half ashore on the west bank of the river just north of where the airplane came to rest, and he showed a photograph of the pontoon in which it was without the pedestal. The pontoon, being lighter and buoyant, had floated to shore north of the airplane and then spent the next winter iced-in on the riverbank. When the spring thaw came it had been swept south, past the airplane, with the rising water and current.

After being shown the approximate location of the wreck off the sandy beach where the tail of the plane had gradually disappeared beneath the surface over the years, Sigurdur Hardarsson made several diving attempts to survey the site and establish the problems and conditions for a possible recovery operation. The basic conditions were also the worst problem; namely, the visibility under water was zero and compounding the difficulty of this blacked out environment was the strong current which threw the diver continually out of control with every movement and swept him from the area. This adversity was particularly discouraging because it increased the probability that the aircraft had broken up and washed to sea. Further attempts were aborted and it was decided to postpone a definitive survey until the river's water level and current subsided in the autumn as winter came on. There was some discouragement, but the recovered parts gave hope that the seaplane could be located.

Ragnar remained resolute, however, and immediately set about planning, organizing, and preparing for a search and survey expedition for September and October of 1977. It was evident from the previous, initial foray into the river that the site of the airplane had to be found and specifically circumscribed and that provisions for holding divers on location in the river current at that site had to be devised. The first requirement Ragnar knew could be met by using an electronic detection device, copying what the U.S. Navy was already doing to locate metallic objects (such as mines) underwater. Once the site was known and a perimeter established a rope network could be overlaid to provide handholds for the divers as they moved over the site or worked in place.

Because the job was going to require a range of expertise and specialized equipment, coordination was initiated with the joint U.S. and Icelandic Defense Council (which oversees the Iceland Defense Force) to get its advice and participation in meeting the recovery requirements. In addition to the various equipment required, such as 600 meters of nylon rope, an inflatable powered boat, a four-wheel drive vehicle, arrangements were made through the Council for the Iceland Defense Force (IDF) to provide the metal detection equipment for use in locating the aircraft. The request was granted by the Commander of the IDF, and in addition to the required equipment, the U.S. Navy staffed and assigned an Explosive Ordnance Disposal Group (EOD GRP) of five men especially trained in diving under the most difficult sea conditions to operate the metal detection equipment. This expert team also came equipped with the requested four-wheel drive vehicle and inflatable outboard-powered boat.

In the meantime, the Icelandic Life Saving Association's Rescue Team, "Albert", was also approached with a request to provide safety and rescue specialists and equipment. The association immediately provided a team equipped with a Volvo Laplander four-wheel drive, an inflatable outboard powerboat and all necessary first-aid and safety equipment.

A local producer of ropes, Hampidjan Ltd., contributed 600 meters of marine nylon line; and Hotel Lofileidir provided, free-of-charge, a picnic lunch for the U.S. Navy's EOD unit, showing the hotel's appreciation for having benefited form the U.S. presence over the years. Other participants provided their own food. Other miscellaneous items, such as stakes, fencing poles, and buoys were purchased locally by the IAHS with its funds.

The plan, coordinated with and agreed to by all participants, was to locate the aircraft or object by means of the metal detector and then dive and survey its layout on the riverbed; and then plan in detail the next step. In the aerospace world of systems management this is known as the rolling wave approach to program planning. In that system, a program is divided into phases consisting of the major unknowns that have to be defined before cost-effective progress can be made (i.e., progress at the lowest cost in the shortest time). Then the process is iterated from phase to phase, learning, defining, and implementing a progressively more detailed, advanced plan, as though building a bridge into the future. Once the airplane was located, the situation from which it had to be recovered had to be thoroughly known, as the first step. A detailed survey of the aircraft's site situation and condition had to be made before the plan for its recovery could be definitized with confidence in the cost and schedule of the operation. Though of smaller scope and magnitude, the task approximated in uncertainty man's first launch into space, because of all the unknowns to be discovered and resolved.

The project, as it proceeded, was to reach a scope and magnitude that would require its being divided into discrete phases. Ragnar had organized and kicked off what was to be Phase I. This was the verification phase that would turn intuition into realization and feasibility. Though not by design, an ad hoc organization was at work as shown in Figure 27.

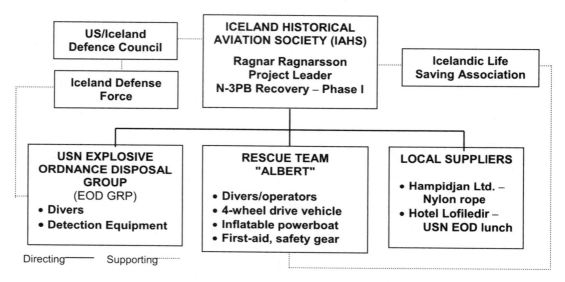

Figure 27. The Phase I organization, though ad hoc, was the beginning of a formally planned and implemented aircraft recovery and restoration effort.

Because the Thjorsa is a glacial river, its water level varies considerably depending on the season of the year. During the summer months when the glacier thaws its water flow increases by up to 400%, carrying an enormous amount of rocks, clay and sand, crushed by the movement of the winter icecap. Consequently, the visibility in the water, which has a milky color when viewed from above the surface, is restricted to practically zero beneath the surface. For this reason it was decided to mount the detailed search-and-survey expedition in September and October, as the summer runoff lessened and the river would be at its lowest, but before the ice set in. "Search" would be the first phase of the program.

On October 9, 1977, all participants were briefed on the overall strategic concept and program plan, and the launch date set for October 15.

At 0700 hours, Saturday, on the designated day, the project group departed from Reykjavik and arrived at the site about two hours later around 0900 hours. Weather conditions were most favorable: calm, bright, and warm. The season was at its most favorable for their current expedition. The river was at its lowest level of the year, following a dry spell over the past fortnight.

The "Albert" team handled transport of equipment to the riverbank and their 4-wheel-drive Volvo Laplander utility vehicle proved to be a most versatile asset for transporting the heavier equipment to the site and over the last couple of hundred meters of lava field to get from the road to the beach where operations were centered.

At 0930 hours, two of the USN's EOD group divers entered the river with their sonar-type detector, and although a return signal indicated on their monitoring instrumentation shortly afterwards, the current was so strong they couldn't hold the detector in position long enough to take a bearing on the signal. The current was so swift and the riverbed so mushy with lava sand they couldn't get a foothold to set up.

The divers agreed that the only way to operate was from the surface, not below where the water was so dark and moving so swiftly over the slippery, unstable bottom that they couldn't get a foothold to orient themselves and secure a position from which to work the equipment. The outboard-powered inflatable boat had been brought for this very purpose, as a backup should direct entry be infeasible. Since the sonar system required a submerged water environment in which to operate, it wouldn't work on the surface from inside a boat. An electromagnetic detector had been brought along for this purpose, as backup. It could be operated from the boat as it moved about over the riverbed site where the airplane was possibly buried.

The main difficulty to deal with in this mode of operation was how to hold the boat in position over the site in the stream of the current. The outboard motor could be used to power against the current with the boat headed upstream to maintain a steadystate position, but only in one spot at a time. That, however, would be too tedious and time consuming. Each time the boat fell off its upstream heading the current would sweep it away and minutes would be consumed bringing it back into position; and even then there would be no way of easily setting up a series of known positions from which to record a reliable database of readings with the detector.

The solution was to hold the boat in position from a line secured on land, so the boat could power back and forth in a known arc like a pendulum. The 700-foot length of nylon line had been brought precisely for this purpose. As shown in Figure 28, about 450 feet north of the operations site, where the river curved eastward, there was a sandspit that appears at this time of year, because the water level was getting lower as the glacial sources of the river froze. In Figure 29, which shows a direct view eastward at the bend, the sandspit can be seen as the dark band in the water. Here the river was about twice as wide as at the site of recovery operations and a line could be run from the spit to hold the boat in position in the current. Accordingly, the boat stationed a two-man team on the sandspit to play out and secure the nylon line attached to the boat. With this line holding it, the boat could stay in one location or move back and forth over the site broadside to the current, and take carefully plotted readings of the electronic signals. Since the exact location of the plane was not yet known, with the sandspit as center, the boat could swing back and forth in an arc into the river and back to shore, for the widest search pattern.

Cato Guhnfeldt

Figure 28. The Thjorsa River operations area provided beach entry to the burial site and access to an upstream sandspit from which the powerboat could be tethered broadside to the current. The magnetic sensor system was then maneuvered systematically over the site by the boat to locate the buried airplane. But was it the N-3PB? The sensor couldn't tell.

Secured in this manner against the current, the boat crew maneuvered transversely, cross-current, in controlled increments using the outboard engine, with the line length constant, or longitudinally, up- or down-stream, by shortening or lengthening the line. Now precise measurements could be made of the signal strength revealing the location and depth of any object detected.

The sweep was directed by the shore party, which maintained continuous radio contact with the men on the sandspit and in the boat. Procedurally, technically, and practically this approach worked well and at approximately 1230 hours, just as the first transverse sweep was nearing completion, a signal was received on the detection equipment that a magnetic object was below the boat. IT HAD TO BE THE N-3PB!!

But was it? Despite the nodding of heads and smiles, there was still uncertainty. Glacial rivers collect a lot of debris over the years. The bend in the river set up a natural depository on this side, where the current was diverted south again and the hydrodynamic

Cato Guhnfeldt

Leifur Thorsteinsson

Figure 29. Two project members were stationed on the sandspit (showing mid-river in the top photo) to tether the powerboat (below) for electronic sensor surveys to identify where the N-3PB seaplane was buried. It was October 15, 1977, 34-1/2 years after the crash landing. (Photos provided by Fridthor Eydal, IDF Deputy Public Affairs Officer.)

forces changed from laminar flow to an upward swirling vortex that in softer terrain caused meandering rivers. Here, the lava was ground into fine silt and objects foreign to the river were quickly buried by it, if not ground up and absorbed. All that could be concluded was that there was something metallic beneath the surface at this site. The sensor could detect but not say what it was.

Position fixes were immediately made from the shore and the divers prepared to enter the water. Two of the USN divers and Sigurdur P. Hardarson of the IAHS went in to see what was there. Within 20 minutes, at 1250 hours, it (the object) was located almost accidentally when one of the USN divers actually stumbled on a protruding portion while returning to shore for the lunch break.

The visibility underwater was 1-2 inches, so any detailed visual inspection, other than by feel, was impossible. The object, at its nearest wingtip proximity to shore, was about 100 feet out, where the water depth was about 5 feet.[58] The entire object appeared to be covered by clay and sand; and, although only a rudimentary inspection could be made, the indications were that it was an airframe of some type and was intact.

One of the divers removed the pitot tube from the left wing tip, along with a piece of aluminum skin. The pieces were quickly examined and verified. Now there was no doubt: they had found the resting spot of the N-3PB. The pitot tube was in remarkably good condition, but the piece of skin was badly worn and pitted on the external surface. Such surface wear was found to be the general condition of the aluminum skin surfaces that had been exposed to the riverbed or ice. Such exposed areas were found to be worn and damaged by the abrasive lava materials and drift ice carried by the river.

Before leaving the aircraft, the divers tied a line to it leading to shore, and a buoy was secured to one of the 50-caliber machineguns of the left (portside) wing. Floating on the surface, the buoy served as a marker as to the exact location of the plane. The shore party had already driven steel fencing poles into the beach opposite the plane. Thus three markers coordinated the plane's exact location: the buoy, the line coming to shore, and the poles on the beach. The fact of the airplane's existence and its location were now well known.

Although the airframe surface areas exposed to the current seemed to be in a worn, abraded condition, it was assumed that areas covered by clay and sand, which included most of the airframe, would be in a better condition. It was thought that the greatest damage would be caused by the hammering action of abrasive materials and drift ice carried by the river, and not corrosion, which would be practically non-existent in this water, which was fresh. The same reasoning would apply to structural members of the airframe which were covered on the outside by the aluminum skin of the airframe and on the inside by clay and sand and, therefore, provided with overall protection from the river's abrading materials and actions.

---

[58] Distances were measured to an accuracy of 0.39 inch or 10 millimeters (see Appendix M for conversion factors).

Since the diving environment permitted only a very brief, cursory inspection of the plane's situation and condition, it was not possible at this point to determine whether all structural members of the airframe were intact and present, or damaged.

Clearly, however, gradually and inevitably, change had buried the plane. As Heraclitus said, "One doesn't step into the same river twice," for both the person and the river – as well as objects in it – are subject to continual change. Surprisingly – and to the esteem of man – as was later to be discovered, many of the components of the plane continued to be functional, even after it buried itself, with the river's help.

The team was exuberant over their "find." Though they couldn't see it, they knew the plane was there. Ragnar could picture it, he had thought about it so much. The knowledge of its being there made its recovery a reality. After this successful first phase of the recovery program it was impossible to stop. Restoration Zen was firmly seated in the minds of all participants. The situation of the buried airplane was in dedicated hands. With the information gained in this phase, Ragnar's meditations about the airplane's recovery and restoration were taking on definitive form. The goal was no longer a dream, but a vision materializing. His intuition had been right, all along. History was waiting to be restored in the Thjorsa River.

Phase I showed also that the recovery and restoration was definitely a team effort. Just as a team had produced the airplane and a team had flown it, so a team would be required to bring it back to life. The team membership would vary as the successive phases of the recovery, restoration, and exhibit became active. But each phase would make possible the next and contribute to the overall excellence of the result. Each phase would constitute a restoration within the final restoration. The Zen of restoration would be shared and enjoyed equally by all, and the airplane would be not so much a thing in itself as a symbol of the spirit that inspired its origination, utilization, and restoration. The airplane in its restored state would signify and restore the origination, the utilization, and, again, the restoration itself.

Robert M. Pirsig described the same idea in his modern classic, *Zen and the Art of Motorcycle Maintenance*: "The real cycle you're working on is a cycle called yourself." And further:

> The study of the art of motorcycle maintenance is really a miniature study of the art of rationality itself. Working on a motorcycle, working well, caring, is to become part of a process, to achieve an inner peace of mind. The motorcycle is primarily a mental phenomenon.[59]

And so it was with the N-3PB, Serial No. 320: first the work and then the meditation to realize the work and the team that made it work. The restoration valorizes all, and is thus a form of Zen – which is the team of the spirit signified by the airplane restored.

---

[59] Robert M. Pirsig, *Zen and the Art of Motorcycle Maintenance; an Enquiry into Values*, a Bantam New Age Book, published by arrangement with William Morrow and Company, Inc. (New York: Bantam Books, Inc, 1983), Prolog, p. i.

CHAPTER 6 - ORGANIZING FOR RECOVERY:
THE INTERNATIONAL TEAM

The task facing the recovery team was demanding to the point of being confrontational. The presence of the airplane was now known, but not its precise situation or condition. All the team had after the initial survey was an electromagnetic signature provided by the detection device and the general perimeter within which that signal had been emitted. They knew the airplane was there; it had, in effect, acknowledged its presence by waving back electronically. What the team didn't know was what exactly was there and what condition it was in.

The recovery operation had now assumed the form of an archeological dig, but under conditions archeologists normally don't encounter. Divers were going to be submerged 12 feet in ice cold water so densely saturated with black lava sand they couldn't see a hand held directly up to their eyes; and further as they tried to orient themselves relative to a buried object they are trying to find and uncover, they would be struggling to keep from being swept away by a constant current flow of four knots (about 5 mph). Effectively they were going to be in a liquid black hole with nothing to orient them or hang onto, trying to do a job.

Figure 30 depicts the general cross-sectional view of the plane in the recovery area, looking upstream. At the beginning of Phase II it was not known at what angle it might be turned relative to the current flow or to the riverbed. All that was definitely known was that the right pontoon was missing as a result of the crash landing. As the figure indicates, it was a large, complex object that the river had undertaken to bury or, in its indifferent, hydrodynamic force field, rip to shreds.

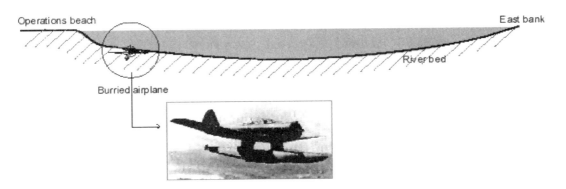

Figure 30. Phase II of the recovery would require precision measuring techniques, indifferent to the Thjorsa's adverse underwater environment, so the airplane's precise disposition in the riverbed could be known.

In the first phase (Chapter 5), the existence of the airplane was confirmed and it was tentatively located, by means of a powered, liferaft-type boat tethered over the site from a sandspit. With an electromagnetic detection device onboard, the boat had been run back and forth in the current to map the differences in the electronic signal strength reflected from the riverbed. For that phase, it had been accepted that the N-3PB airplane was the source of the change in signal, because (1) it was known from reliable witnesses that the airplane had disappeared in that general vicinity and (2) the signal response matched the general shape of the airframe viewed from above.

From this time forward, it appeared that the recovery task would require operating on the airplane, in the water, to first delineate its situation positionally and then to determine how to free it from the riverbed's quicksand grip. Where before, the "doctor" had scanned the "patient" from the surface in relatively open space, now the "doctor" would have to descend to the "patient's" entrapment through cold, rushing, and opaque water and operate directly on the patient at the site of entrapment with one hand while hanging on to the patient with the other. As all invasive operations pose the threat of further injury to the patient, the mitigation if not prevention of such collateral damage had to be conducted while concurrently struggling with the environment. The Thjorsa River suddenly seemed very covetous and unyielding in its possessiveness of its captive. The river began to loom as a very tricky opponent.

The question was how to operate in this dynamically hostile and visually impenetrable environment. After only the brief encounter with the river during Phase I, the recovery had almost at once become seen as a major challenge, maybe even a "mission impossible." More and more the project assumed the character of a perilous rescue than a methodical recovery. It would require not only careful planning, but the best professionals and equipment.

All along, Ragnar had known that eventually other team members would have to join the project, but now he realized specially equipped and expert teams would be needed to deal with plane in the river. Otherwise, the mission would indeed be impossible.

Phase I had clearly shown that the scope and magnitude of the project was beyond the capabilities of the IAHS alone. After all, the intent was to deliver an N-3PB to Norway in remembrance of the Norwegian's valiant defense of their nationhood and also in commemoration of the fact that having the plane in Iceland had done two historically significant things for the Island: (1) had freed Iceland for its own nationhood and (2) had "broken the ice" on Iceland's traditional reclusiveness from world relations. But the plane itself had involved the U.S. and England as well as Norway and Iceland.

Hence for Phase II of the recovery the IAHS organized an international team. The logical members besides Iceland were Norway, Britain, and the U.S. Having learned as a result of Phase I the rigor and expertise with which the recovery would have to be performed and knowing that after it was recovered it would have to be restored by equivalent expertise and commitment, Ragnar initiated coordination with the Norwegian Royal Air Force, the original owner and operator of the plane during WWII. In the U.S. he made contact with Northrop Corporation, the original designer and builder of the plane. The IAHS was now thinking beyond Phase II to Phase III, the restoration. The international team would be in a better position to plan, implement, and carry the project through to its final goal of putting the airplane on display and preserving it for the future. After all, it was the only representative of its kind and of the design ingenuity, technology, and courage it encompasses and represents.

Figure 31 shows the organization structure of the international team finally put together by Ragnar through the IAHS. But it wasn't as easy as the figure makes it appear. After 34 years, time and the river had changed others too.

In the latter part of October 1977, now confident that the aircraft's presence and location in the Thjorsa River had been confirmed, Ragnar first notified the Norwegian Aviation Historical Society (NAHS). The NAHS had a similar mission to that of the IAHS, in terms of preserving national aviation history. In turn, the NAHS forwarded the information to the Norwegian Defense Museum (Forsvarsmuseet), which would be the logical conservator for the airplane if restored.

Over the next year, the IAHS maintained contact with both parties, trying to firm up their intent to participate in recovering the aircraft, whose historical value was obviously most important to Norway, without whom the N-3PB series would never have existed. Adding impetus to the recovery was the fact that the last surviving N-3PB (Serial No. 322) had been scrapped in 1956. Although both repeatedly expressed interest, a firm commitment was not forthcoming. Ragnar waited expectantly through all of 1978.

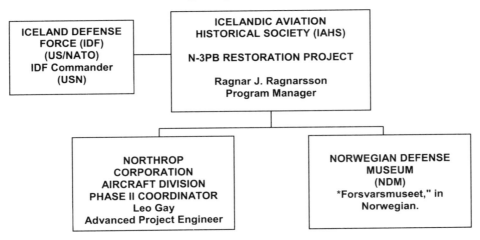

Figure 31. Compatible with the historical background of the N-3PB, the IAHS organized an international team to implement the recovery, restoration, and continuing exhibit of Serial No. 320.

To keep the momentum going on the project and concerned that the airplane had now endured yet another year of ravaging in the river, Ragnar decided as 1978 ended to contact the Northrop Corporation as a third-party strategy to spur Norwegian participation. With Northrop onboard to perform the actual restoration of the plane, he was sure the NAHS and the Defense Museum would decide to join the team. After all,

Northrop had produced Norway's first military airplane for WWII and continued to be a major military aircraft producer; and Norway had a whole fleet of Northrop F-5 lightweight fighters. Northrop, in effect, was just the right associate for Norway.

At Northrop, the January 1979 inquiry came at a most propitious time as the company was looking for historical highspots to include in the celebration of its 40th birthday, which was in March. Of course, there was no chance the N-3PB could be recovered and restored that year, but just the fact that there was an abundance of company spirit and historical reminiscence at this time made the project appealing.

Ragnar's letter first went to J. K. Corfield, company representative at Northrop's London Office, who sent it on to the Aircraft Division in Hawthorne, California. An affirmative answer was immediately prepared and sent to Ragnar by Donald G. Page, Director, Aircraft Division Public Affairs. In a quick exchange of followup letters, it was agreed that a Northrop representative would be sent to Iceland to coordinate the detail requirements for the company's participation. On February 2, 1979, Leo Gay, a Northrop Advanced Project engineer, flew to Iceland with authorization to conduct negotiations with the IAHS if the project looked feasible.

During a four-day stay in Iceland, Gay met with the IAHS N-3PB Recovery Project Group, civil engineers, and the USN staff at the IDF. An agreement was reached as to the role the IAHS would play in the recovery operation, and it was decided that Northrop would use its prestige and role in the N-3PB design and production to get the Norway parties onboard and also the British. A preliminary approach to the recovery operation was outlined to establish a timeline and an understanding was reached, in principle, that given the successful recovery of a restorable aircraft by the IAHS, Northrop would restore it to museum quality display condition, after which it would be displayed in the USA and Iceland prior to being transferred to Norway for permanent display.

With the gift of a restored N-3PB for museum display as bargaining chip, Gay next went to Norway to meet with Col. Nils Joergensen of the Royal Norwegian Air Force. With Col. Joergensen leading the way and Northrop's commitment to deliver on the N-3PB restoration phase of the project the Norwegian Defense Museum at last agreed to help. The Colonel also arranged for the Norwegian Air Force to provide air logistics support to return the airplane to Northrop for restoration once recovered.

Thus while Northrop at that time put only $3,000 cash directly into the IAHS budget the company became the main source for getting things done and eventually paid all the bills associated with its travel, time, and material to support the recovery, to receive and restore the aircraft, to host ceremonies at its rollout, and to attend the displays and museum installation ceremonies in Iceland and Norway. Showing how time impacts values, Northrop had sold the airplane in 1940 for less than $60,000 per unit. By comparison, it is estimated that the direct and indirect costs associated with the restoration of just the one airplane added up to more than $1,000,000. This figure excludes the recovery costs incurred or absorbed by the IAHS and Norway. Most significantly, this figure does not include the more than 150,000 free hours put into the restoration by Northrop employees and friends who volunteered their time and skills, or the free time and materials donated by Northrop suppliers.[60]

It was agreed by all parties that, due to the limited cash that initially could be committed for what might be construed as an extravaganza or even historical trivia by some, all phases would be conducted as much as possible on a volunteer and contribution basis. To ensure an authorized nonprofit interface for receiving the returned airplane in the U.S., it was agreed that the San Diego Aerospace Museum would act as legal custodian on behalf of the Northrop Aircraft Division. The agreement reached between all participants was that each would organize, staff, facilitate, implement, and fund those functions most suitable to their respective areas of expertise.

Ragnar wasn't waiting any longer for all the parties to reach a formal agreement. Two years had elapsed since the project began. As soon as he received Northrop's tentatively positive response to participate, he initiated Phase II.

What had become obvious as a result of the year-long coordination necessary to get just Northrop's concurrence was that more definitive information had to be obtained on the exact situation of the airplane in the riverbed. It was now clear that another phase of investigatory operations would have to be conducted as prerequisite to any attempt to actually raise the plane from the riverbed. Had it been just sitting on the bottom of the river, the approach to raising it would have been clear. But the scant evidence gathered so far indicated that the plane was deeply buried, hardly any portion not covered. To convince international team members that the project was feasible, more data as to the plane's actual situation in the river had to be obtained.

Since the experience in Phase I had shown that the river offered virtually zero visibility at full flow, that time of year was not conducive to using divers to determine the position of the plane; however, in dead winter, with the frozen river virtually inactive, the task changed to one that was relatively simple, given use of the right equipment to map the buried airplane. Since the airplane was metal, it could be mapped while the river was frozen over, by a crew working at its leisure atop the ice. Having attempted to work in the river at full flow, the project team would now eliminate the river as an uncontrollable variable and turn it instead into a useful, stable, work platform.

On February 3, 1979, less than one month after his initial letter to Northrop, Ragnar led a survey crew to the site, where the river now was covered by an ice sheet approximately two feet thick. The first objective was to verify that the location markers put in place in Phase I (over a year ago) were still there; and the second was to establish a precise position of the buried airplane both in its horizontal layout and depth in the riverbed.

This trip at the peak of the Icelandic winter was not a jaunt just to create work to hold people's attention and participation in Iceland: it was a carefully devised approach to map the precise position of the airplane in the riverbed. In particular, the IAHS recovery team wanted to know the direction the airplane was pointing and its attitude buried in the

---

[60] It is estimated that the total cost incurred by the international team in recovering, restoring, delivering, and displaying N-3PB Serial No. 320 was about $1.5 million; but beyond valuation.

riverbed. In other words, was it pointing north, east, south, or west or at some in-between heading; and was it horizontal or tilted? When last seen sticking out of the water (see Figure 7), it had been canted along its longitudinal axis, nosedown 10 degrees and tilted left 15 degrees, pointing north. Now the question was whether it had further changed heading and attitude. This was important information, because it would determine the scope and magnitude of the effort to free it from the riverbed, in particular where to begin the recovery operation in the riverbed (where to make that first incision) and specifically what method to use to bring it to the surface.

The timing of Phase II was ideal. Now that Phase I had located the airplane, the iced condition of the river in winter was ideal for the straightforward mapping objective that had been defined for the second phase. This time of year was the river's downtime from the summer runoff of glacial water to the sea. It was a time when the survey crew could work under highly stable conditions on top of a two-foot-thick sheet of ice and operate systematically without the physical and mental duress of being swept about in blacked-out water running over the riverbed at full current flow. With the layer of ice covering the site, a survey could be made from a stable platform in a deliberately planned, implemented, and recorded way, without having to rush or be constantly tossed about, continually disoriented, while lost in total blackout.

The ice would enable use of a special technique to identify the orientation of the airplane in all dimensions. Specifically, the plan was first to define the position of the plane through the ice with a sonar (acoustic) type metal detector. Then holes would be drilled in a numerically controlled grid pattern and the vertical distance measured to the point of contact with the metal of the airframe and the lateral distance measured from there to where there is no contact. By repeating these measurements a sufficient number of times, a pattern would begin to take shape tracing in general the outline of the airplane and its orientation in three-dimension space.

On February 3, 1979, the ice-cap approach was initiated with Leo Gay, the Northrop coordinator present. Figure 32(a) shows the survey team setting up and conducting initial survey operations at the iced-over site. Ironically, though the methodology was feasible, the sonar equipment did not function properly, possibly due to the extreme cold, and so did not detect anything. After numerous attempts at drilling holes blindly through the ice without making any contact with the plane, the effort was stopped. Since the problem was definitely the fault of the acoustic detector, whose sound wave propagation was probably attenuated by the thickness of the ice, it was decided to revert to the electromagnetic type metal detector that had been used with success in the Phase I survey.

The recovery team returned to Reykjavik and contacted the U.S. Navy's Iceland Defense Force agency to make arrangements for borrowing the electromagnetic detector once more, as in the first phase. Without hesitation, the USN/IDF provided the detector and, in addition, the two-man squad shown in Figure 32(b) to operate it. The survey team, newly equipped and staffed, returned to the site on February 10. Their objective now would be approached by electronically locating and demarcating the plane and then

(a) Initial survey with sonar.

Baldur Sveinsson

(b) IDF's electronic sensor squad:
Lt. Paul Netusil (l); Equipment Chief
Stuart Eanes, Jr. (r).

Baldur Sveinsson

(c) Drilling to make contact
with metal.

Baldur Sveinsson

Figure 32. February 10, 1979, the Phase II position survey: drilling on the ice-becalmed Thjorsa to map the layout of the airplane buried beneath. (Photos provided by Fridthor Eydal, IDF Deputy Public Affairs Officer, courtesy of IAHS.)

drilling to establish the specific depth of the structure and the type and thickness of the riverbed materials covering it. If the structure was tilted, the drilling process would reveal it by showing variations in depth to where the drill bit struck metal.

The Iceland Defense Force's background is itself historically interesting and relevant to the N-3PB seaplane, in that the IDF grew out of the friendly invasion that made it possible to station the N-3PB in Iceland during WWII. The IDF would not have been there had not the N-3PB preceded it, so the organization pitched in enthusiastically as the background and purpose of the recovery project became better known and it appeared that there was indeed an N-3PB there to recover for historic restoration. The IDF is the Iceland Defense Force currently operated by the U.S. Navy; but that wasn't always the case. The IDF has its roots in WWII under the British. Its beginning is dramatically told by the IDF's internet homepage:

"..., it was a rude surprise for the people of Reykjavik to awaken to the sight of a British invasion force on May 10, 1940. The country's strategic importance to the British was understood; what was annoying to Icelanders was the lack of consultation.

Iceland protested the use of military force by Britain but immediately accepted the *fait accompli*. Nothing could be accomplished by resisting. Newspaper accounts from that period suggest that there was a certain feeling of relief. Because of the historic links between Iceland and Britain, it was felt that if someone had to invade the country it was better to see the Allies come, and not the Axis.

Acceptance of the invasion, however, did not mean that nothing could be done about the situation. If it were true that the country needed "protecting," couldn't a neutral power provide that protection, thereby permitting a belligerent Britain to do its fighting elsewhere?[61]

This supplantation of the British by a neutral power gained strong support in Iceland as a solution to the nation's internationally coveted geographic location. Following talks between Churchill and Roosevelt in the spring of 1941, Iceland agreed to a tri-partite treaty under which the British would be relieved by the U.S. on the condition that all military forces would be withdrawn at the end of the war. Of course the British, represented by Churchill, eagerly agreed to this arrangement, because it would draw the U.S. closer to the war and require that the U.S. provide active support militarily while still neutral. Icelanders were also pleased, because their postwar independence was now assured.

---

[61] IDF Homepage www.nctsket.navy.mil/idf/, "IDF History," p. 1, accessed March 22, 2001. This site also notes that: "In 1939, with war imminent in Europe, the German Reich pressed for landing rights for Lufthansa's aircraft for alleged trans-Atlantic flights. The Icelandic government turned them down. A British request to establish bases in Iceland for the protection of the vital North Atlantic supply lines after German forces occupied Denmark and Norway in April 1940 also was turned down in accordance with the neutrality policy (agreed to with Denmark in 1918)."

Accordingly, the U.S. Marine Corps landed at Reykjavik, by invitation of Iceland, on 7 July 1941. The U.S. presence and military engagement increased rapidly thereafter, first due to the entry of the U.S. into the war following the Japanese attack on Pearl Harbor in December and then, at the end of the war, due to the phaseover of hostilities to the Cold War. Since the U.S. was still officially neutral in July 1941, Roosevelt landed the Marines because the Corps consisted only of career soldiers and the presence of draftees would have signified non-neutrality.

After the war, because of the strategic importance of the Island's position directly opposite the Soviet Union and Korea across the Arctic polar cap, Iceland, despite its zero military power, was made a charter member of NATO at its formation in 1949. When the Korean War broke out on 20 June 1950, it was agreed within NATO that the U.S. would assume responsibility for Iceland's defense. In line with this responsibility the U.S. and Iceland formalized the IDF on May 5, 1951 and it has continued to develop in importance as a forward base for the U.S. and, in addition, 24 other nation members of NATO.

While Iceland continues to be a neutral nation, the IDF adds to its national income by providing employment for several thousand civilian Icelanders at the main base at Keflavik outside the capital of Reykjavik. Because of the U.S.'s long-term role of protection and patronage in Iceland, the ready support provided by the IDF to the IAHS for its N-3PB recovery program was not unusual.

After confirming use of the magnetic detector, Ragnar set the date of the next three-dimensional survey effort for February 10, a Saturday. The plan, as agreed to by Lt. Paul Netusil, officer in charge of the USN detector squad (the EOD unit from Phase I), was to determine not only the depth and three-dimensional attitude of the airplane, but approximately how much of the airframe remained and what the composition and stratification was of the riverbed material entrapping the plane. Not as much drilling would have to be done with the electromagnetic detector, as with its accuracy of performance on metal (being actually a MK X Mine Detector, which performed precision detection of enemy and friendly submerged mines) it would be able to outline the buried airplane virtually by itself. Acquisition of the other data, as to the three-dimensional orientation of the plane about its longitudinal axis, would be attempted by drilling holes through the ice to measure distances to metal contact. Also, drilling would be used to determine the riverbed's material composition and the condition of the airframe.

The project group departed Reykjavik at 0800 hours on Saturday, February 10, and reached the recovery site on the Thjorsa River at approximately 1100 hours. In addition to Ragnar, the survey team included IAHS members Baldur Sveinsson, Einar Gunnarsson, and Sigurdur P. Hardarsson, along with other Icelandic participants, Gunnar P. Gunnarsson, Leifur Benediktsson (Civil Engineer), and Olafur Palsson (Civil Engineer). The U.S. Navy's EOD squad consisted of Lt. Paul Netusil and PRC Stuart E. Eanes, Jr.

The site was still covered by a layer of ice two feet thick. Weather conditions were fair with a light breeze, bright sunshine, and a temperature around 5-7 degrees F below freezing. The first task was to remove snow from the ice above the area of the riverbed to be searched, after which the airframe was located by means of the magnetic metal detector. The signal strength was weak in a number of places within the search area and holes drilled through the ice at those locations revealed only the riverbed.

After concentrated search and chipping, the buoy that had been attached during Phase I to the port wing 50-caliber machine gun was located frozen deep in the ice. Knowing the wing was below, Ragnar had detector sweeps concentrated in this area. After more weak signals and still more holes revealing nothing but the riverbed, a strong signal was suddenly received approximately 11.5 feet (3.5m) from the buoy, in the direction away from the river's bank. A hole drilled at this location revealed contact with metal at a depth of 11.82 feet (3.6m)from the river's surface. Detector sweeps around this area, however, resulted in no further significant magnetic responses.

Consultation among the site team concluded that the hole that had tested positively for metal might be directly over the wing center section, where the greatest mass of ferrous metal is located. However, the first run of holes drilled to each side of the contact hole struck riverbed. Then, finally, one hole (No. 17), a distance of 4.9 feet (1.5m) from the contact hole and in a direction away from the riverbank, resulted in contact with metal.

Disappointingly, the metal detector gave no indication as to the direction in which the airframe might be heading. It was decided, therefore, based on the consistent though limited pattern of contact holes at right angles to the riverbank, to proceed by drilling holes upstream from the first contact hole and at right angles to the river's bank. This decision produced immediate success and contact with metal was made in this direction over a distance of 10 feet (3m), at depths varying from 10.2 to 14.8 feet (3.1 to 4.5m). Concurrently, holes were drilled parallel to this line of contact holes to determine the position of the wing mainplanes. These were finally located approximately 23 feet upstream from the first contact hole. Altogether some 34 holes were drilled through the ice, out of which 14 (41%) resulted in contact with metal.

Figure 33 shows the pattern of contact holes.

A drilling survey of the buried airplane area showed that the riverbed was at a depth of 10 to 15 feet (3 to 4.5m), sloping downward toward midstream. The first layer of the riverbed, approximately 12 to 20 inches thick, consisted of glacier clay. This material was soft and easy to excavate. The second layer consisted of sand mixed with volcanic pumice and was considerably firmer. Twisting the measuring stakes while pressing on them produced only slight downward penetration. Without suitable tools, neither the thickness of this layer nor the distance to the solid lava river bottom could be measured.

At this time drilling was discontinued because the sun was setting and darkness was closing in on the site. It was not regarded necessary to continue the survey the next day, as Holes 32 and 34 had obviously located the two mainplanes at their specified separation distance of 7.39 feet (2.25 meters). With the mainplane locations and attitudes known, it was now concluded that the airplane was pointing upstream (north) and that it was lying transversely about the longitudinal axis of the plane approximately level, relative to the plane of riverbed. Comparing this information with that of Holes 2 and 33 – the extreme fore and aft contact holes – it was evident that the airplane also was lying relatively level

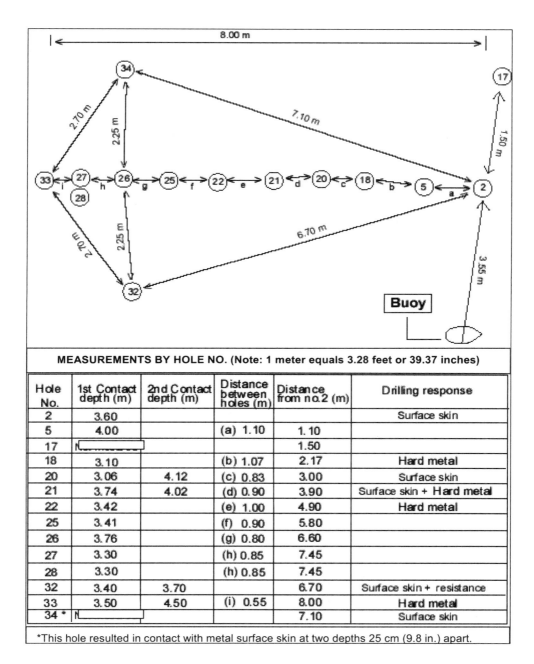

MEASUREMENTS BY HOLE NO. (Note: 1 meter equals 3.28 feet or 39.37 inches)

Hole No.	1st Contact depth (m)	2nd Contact depth (m)	Distance between holes (m)	Distance from no.2 (m)	Drilling response
2	3.60				Surface skin
5	4.00		(a) 1.10	1.10	
17	N			1.50	
18	3.10		(b) 1.07	2.17	Hard metal
20	3.06	4.12	(c) 0.83	3.00	Surface skin
21	3.74	4.02	(d) 0.90	3.90	Surface skin + Hard metal
22	3.42		(e) 1.00	4.90	Hard metal
25	3.41		(f) 0.90	5.80	
26	3.76		(g) 0.80	6.60	
27	3.30		(h) 0.85	7.45	
28	3.30		(h) 0.85	7.45	
32	3.40	3.70		6.70	Surface skin + resistance
33	3.50	4.50	(i) 0.55	8.00	Hard metal
34 *	N			7.10	Surface skin

*This hole resulted in contact with metal surface skin at two depths 25 cm (9.8 in.) apart.

Figure 33. Operating from the Thjorsa's frozen ice cap, the team scanned through the cap with an electromagnetic mine detector to locate the airplane and then drilled holes to outline the plane and measure its depth in the riverbed.

fore and aft along the longitudinal axis. Thus it was evident that the airplane was lying level with respect to the riverbed. No further measurements were necessary.

To pinpoint the geographic location of the contact holes shown in Figure 33, the two civil engineers participating in this phase of the project made a precise transit survey of the area. Now there was no question of exactly where the airplane was located and how it was dispositioned in the riverbed. The recovery team was now sufficiently informed to proceed with planning exactly how to accomplish the raising of the plane.

With Northrop having concurrently coordinated the successful formation of the international team for conducting the entire restoration project, it was now time to proceed with the final phase of recovery. Ragnar, in the interim, had made good use of the open time, so that as soon as the ice melted and the river was running free and could be entered, the way to approach the airplane would be specifically known.

A substantial amount of useful information had been gained through Ragnar's initiative. The fact that the airplane was lying level in the riverbed indicated that both floats might be missing. That it was facing upstream gave credence to that theory; for, if present, the floats probably would have turned the airplane sideways to the current flow and over the years caused it to be moved far downstream where it would be unlikely to be found; and if found, would likely be torn apart and scattered about in pieces.

Ragnar's leadership had verified that the airplane appeared to be sufficiently intact to be worth recovering. On this basis the new international team had a validated objective to apply itself to and meet. It was now clear that only by raising the airplane could the next question of whether to restore it be realistically answered.

The severe difficulties posed by having to work in the Thjorsa River, with its ice cold, powerful current and low visibility, required that a carefully thoughtout strategic plan be derived. Every contingency had to be identified and resolved if the capabilities of the international team were to be used efficiently.

There was a definite time window in which the airplane could be raised and yet that was the worst time to operate in the Thjorsa River. All of the present unknowns would have to be uncovered before proceeding and before a final approach to raising the airplane could be defined, scheduled, staffed, facilitated, and implemented. Much had to be done in the next three months.

While drilling holes could be done in ice, the plane would have to be raised in water. That was the crux of the situation facing the actual raising of the plane. As Ragnar said in retrospect, it was a mission impossible: the kind he liked. Again, technology and teamwork would be the key to making it possible. With an international team now ready to proceed, the only thing needed was a good plan by which to put the team capabilities to work; and here "good" meant both efficient and effective.

But, obviously the plane couldn't be raised through two feet of ice. So whatever plan was devised, it would have to be performed under the conditions imposed by the Thjorsa in its unfrozen state; but, as things turned out, the Thjorsa, even when thawed didn't want to yield its hold on the plane and had other means to keep what it had taken.

CHAPTER 7 - ASSESSING THE RECOVERY SITE AND SITUATION UNDERWATER

Even though it had been difficult enough just to prove the airplane was indeed there, the real problem lay ahead. The team had demonstrated that the upper surface of the plane was at an average depth of 10.5 feet in the Thjorsa River and that the entire plane was buried in the riverbed; but how to dig the plane out and how to do it when the river was flowing was the problem that had to be assessed next.

Digging blindly in the current-suspended lava silt of the flowing river, while trying to stay in position, would be impossible without some method of (1) remaining oriented with respect to the plane and (2) being securely restrained against the reactive forces of digging.

While Phases I and II had yielded the results sought, they also had revealed the hostility of the environment and the obstacles that had to be overcome. Serendipitously, what had finally worked in those phases was the help lent by nature. But compared to the task ahead, the objectives in those phases had been superficial, diagnostic. Now the real operation had to be performed, mainly by touch alone, without benefit of light and while holding on to the patient. The patient would survive, but would the doctor?

Phase I had answered the question of whether there was a reason to proceed. Yes, the airplane was there. Phase II had indicated that there was probably enough there to restore. Yes, a large, integral portion of airframe was contained within a rectangular volume 26.25 feet in length, 14.76 feet wide, and 3.28 feet thick. The question now was how to proceed; how to approach the actual raising of the airframe. Who would do what, when, where, and how? Answering these questions required assessing conditions at the site and the real situation of the plane in the riverbed.

The question of *why* they were doing this project apparently had been answered to everyone's satisfaction. Following confirmation from Northrop Corporation that it was ready to proceed a step further based on the positive results obtained in the Phase II survey, the Icelandic Aviation Historical Society decided to take advantage of the first seasonal window of opportunity to move the project closer to its ultimate goal. Though the question of why an international team was doing this project had been resolved, that of how it was going to be done remained open. Phase III would be devoted to answering that question.

During March 1979, the IAHS coordinated with the other team members (cf., Figure 31). Again Ragnar J. Ragnarsson was the point of contact. Now that it was known that a substantial portion of the airplane was intact, the principal issues were whether Northrop and Norway still wanted to proceed all the way, given the rigor of the recovery task that lay ahead, and what were their thoughts on the best approach to getting the job done in the time period now approaching when the river would be free of ice.

The recovery would have to begin in the next month, if it were to be done in the springtime. Because of the tightness of the schedule and the uncertainties still to be resolved, Northrop and Norway agreed that a detailed plan had to be prepared on just how the airplane was to be raised from the riverbed, before they committed resources. Northrop had proceeded thus far on the assumption that its job would be solely to restore the plane once raised and delivered. Leo Gay's initial report had been enthusiastically positive and the company was willing to proceed on the basis of having an N-3PB to present to Jack Northrop on what might be his last birthday. But as always in the world of aerospace, a detailed plan was needed, so everyone would know how it was going to be done in reality.

But moreover, Norway wanted the opinion of a known expert in underwater salvage, before committing resources to the final stages of recovery, restoration, and the logistics of bringing the airplane back to Norway for permanent exhibit. The Northrop N-3PB was a well-known instrumentality of Norway's fight for freedom and the restored aircraft had to be worthy of memorializing that history. A mere replica wouldn't do.

It was clear, from these different outside perspectives, that the project was still perceived as questionable. So much time had passed since the initial introduction of the project and so far no specific progress had been made to establish a definite plan of accomplishment, yet alone to determine the mere feasibility of being able to recover the plane from an icy, fast-flowing, glacial river just below the Arctic Circle. The idea seemed great, but the reality seemed intangibly far away.

Northrop was favorably disposed toward the project, if an airplane were delivered to it for restoration. Of course the word "airplane" had a definite connotation to everyone at Northrop. Everyone had seen pictures of this airplane and many people had worked on it. It would be simple to clean up the plane, replace damaged parts, and paint it. Even though it was obvious the plane couldn't be ready in time to exhibit for Northrop Corporation's 40th anniversary, in the current year, it could be the centerpiece for celebrating Jack Northrop's 85th birthday in 1980. But no one – even Leo Gay – had any real idea of what lay buried in the Thjorsa's riverbed.

Just that Northrop was willing to proceed was encouraging to Norway, because it was confident the company would deliver an airplane worth exhibiting if it took on the responsibility of restoring it; but Norway still wasn't sure the airplane was worth the effort if it couldn't be salvaged in a restorable condition.

To resolve this final uncertainty, a highly expert opinion was needed. Enthusiasm was great, but one must have something tangible to make a decision on and then to work with. The significance of the airplane was too great to recover something that was not truly restorable. The restoration had to be more than a replica.

Ragnar knew the project was in a difficult stage and at a pivotal decision point. He had to come up with a plan that would convince the other team members that the plane could actually be recovered in a viable condition for restoration. A detailed, step-by-step approach had to be documented, based on the realities of the site and the situation and condition of the plane. Northrop's Leo Gay would be there at the site and would know whether the plan would be likely to work and whether it was optimum for the time and resources likely to be available. Ragnar knew the burden of proof was on him, so he wanted the best people he could get on the team.

While he personally assumed responsibility, he knew also that it was Iceland's role in the international team to recover the airplane. In fact, his coordination with the two other team members had shown him that, in Norway's view, if Iceland recovered the airplane, Norway would see that it got delivered to Northrop; and, in Northrop's view, if the plane were delivered to it, the plane would be restored.

But underlying this cause-and-effect sequence was the determination that the airplane after 35 years was "restorable." So the project at this stage was truly Iceland's "mission impossible" and Ragnar's moment of truth. He felt he must succeed, because he was still an American citizen with dual citizenship and wanted to bring this airplane back to America as a token of his esteem.

Ragnar's first activity was to coordinate with the other two international members to make sure he had their ideas on how to proceed. Regarding the approach to raising the airplane, it was agreed by the international members that an Icelandic team must proceed immediately to get specific information at the site as to the actual condition and situation of the plane and what would be required to raise it from the riverbed, but only if visibility in the river was good enough and the plane were accessible.

Accordingly, a followon diving expedition was scheduled for the next month, April, by which time the river, though still ice cold, would be free of ice and lower in depth, because the glacial thaw would not have started yet. Given these conditions, the visibility in the water would be better than at any other time of the year that it could be entered and the airplane would be in relatively shallow water where it could be inspected and a detailed recovery procedure determined.

It was agreed also that as part of this inspection, the airframe and the riverbed would be examined as closely as possible in order to assess the probability of being able to recover enough of the aircraft for a viable restoration. "Viability" would be that condition of the airplane which would enable its original manufactured form (that is, its original structural configuration) to be restored to a nonflying status. With that probability determined to be acceptable, a detailed approach to raising the airplane would be defined. This "site, situation, and condition" assessment would provide the basis for a formal detailed planning phase, the third but final one of the recovery project.

Although the IAHS could draw experienced divers from its own ranks for this detailed inspection and assessment, as well as from the Icelandic Coast Guard (ICG), it was realized that a highly experienced, internationally recognized salvage diver was essential at this stage to remove all doubt. This diver would make an expert inspection and assessment of the conditions and situation from which the airframe must be recovered and whether the airplane was still sufficiently intact and structurally able to withstand recovery.

Ragnar began a search for just the right person to make this probability determination. It had to be someone with an established reputation for professional expertise in the field of marine archeology. His search led to Peter J. Cornish of the British Sub-Aqua Club (BSAC) as the most highly recommended and qualified candidate.

An experienced salvage diver who had the recovery of a number of aircraft and ships from sea- and lake-beds to his credit, Cornish was contacted and accepted the offer. Fortunately, immediately available, he was able to arrive in Iceland the next week on April 26 to take part in the diving operations scheduled for the weekend of April 29-30. Cornish would provide the necessary expertise and corroborate, as an outside, impersonal, professional inspector, the exact condition of the airplane, the probability of success in recovering it, and exactly how to proceed.

Due to the technically expert survey and documentation he made of the plane's underwater situation and condition, Cornish was to have a singular impact on the final approach to recovery. He was a highly experienced and regarded salvage diver, experienced in working under varying underwater conditions with the type of equipment used in such operations. He had been especially sought after by the Iceland Aviation Historical Society because, as a result of the previous two surveys, it was now evident that difficulties known and unknown would have to be met in recovering the airplane and an experienced salvage diver, such as he, would be able to minimize the unknowns and maximize the probability of success, as well as the speed of the recovery. But above all, he would know whether the plane was salvageable for restoration.

Since Phase III was still exploratory and would require only two days of his time, Cornish agreed to participate. Besides, as an archeological diver, he was impressed by the historical background of this particular airplane.

One can quickly see, by reading Cornish's final report on his underwater survey of the N-3PB site and the airplane itself, that the project had finally obtained just the right person to assess the condition and situation of the plane in its underwater encryptment and to recommend precisely how the plane ought to be approached in first excavating it and then raising it to the surface. Cornish was basically an archeologist who has chosen the marine world as his realm of exploration and discovery in place of dry land. Being British, he had the sporting, daring spirit for rugged, pristine environments that explorers innately possess. His vocation was his avocation, so he was completely at home and relaxed operating under submerged conditions that the average person would find intolerable.

Cornish, in fact, was a key member of the renowned British Sub-Aqua Club, which today has 45,000 members worldwide. Prince Charles is the President, having succeeded his father Prince Phillip in 1974. The club was formed in 1953 to promote underwater exploration and science and, in particular, to develop, promulgate, and teach diving technology and methods so that the scope and magnitude of underwater exploration can be expanded much like outer space is explored today. To be a member of BSAC is to be recognized without question as a certified diving expert anywhere in the world.

There are currently over 200 BSAC schools formally offering a curriculum in underwater exploration and diving practices around the world. Schools and regional diving clubs are located throughout Europe and in the Middle East, Asia, Southeast Asia, and the U.S. The headquarters is located in England, where there are 14 branch offices and clubs throughout the kingdom. Major BSAC franchises operate in Japan and Korea. The organization has a large headquarters facility in Ellesmere Port, northwest England, and contracts with *Dive* magazine as its journal for publishing articles on all aspects of diving as a sport and profession.

As a leading member of BSAC, Peter J. Cornish had a year-round schedule of underwater explorations, so his participation in the eventual recovery of the N-3PB would have to be precisely scheduled in advance and even then might be tentative, in the event something still more historical or life-threatening might suddenly surface. Fortunately, for the current requirements of performing a quick survey he was available; and the project would benefit greatly from the renewed enthusiasm that his final technical report provided in making clear the feasibility of recovering the plane.

The principal items of equipment obtained for this phase included a large tent, spare diving bottles and an air compressor. The local Icelandic Lions Club "Freyr" provided the tent, the ICG and the Rescue Team Albert provided the spare diving bottles, and the ICG provided the air compressor. As before, EOD Group 2 of the U.S. Navy's Icelandic Defense Force at Keflavik was asked to take part in the diving operation, but they had an inspection schedule conflict and were unable to participate. In case the group had to stay overnight at the site, accommodations were arranged at the nearby Burfell mountain hydroelectric powerplant, where there was also available a three-phase power supply for an air compressor, if required.

In addition to Peter Cornish, the IAHS diver Sigurdur P. Hardarsson (who had participated in Phase II) and ICG diver Hermann Sigurdsson volunteered. Thus there would be three divers, two of whom had been at the site previously and the third who had experienced virtually every type of underwater situation involving salvage of aircraft and ships.

To cover every contingency, Ragnar had arranged for Northrop to provide the latest aerospace technology in underwater communications equipment, used in training astronauts in simulated space environment.

Now the international team took on the organizational form shown in Figure 34. It was designated Phase III of the overall survey.

The most experienced and expert divers were there, along with the most reliable life-support equipment and operators. The divers were to make a comprehensive, detailed inspection of the accessibility and condition of the aircraft and the riverbed over, around, and under it. From the data obtained, a detailed approach and plan would be defined for the recovery, if Cornish determined the plane to be salvageably restorable.

It had been assumed from the beginning of the project that the eventual raising of the plane would have to proceed in stages, due to the buried situation of the airplane and the difficulty of working blindly in the strong current. This assumption, unverified by actual underwater survey, is all the guidance given Cornish to begin with; but it was something he was asked to verify; for another major question still to be answered, once the issue of

Iceland Coast Guard (ICG)	ICELAND AVIATION HISTORICAL SOCIETY (IAHS)	Iceland Life Saving Association
• Diver, air bottles and compressor	Baldur Sveinsson President	• 4-wheel drive Laplander • Inflatable powerboat • Air bottles

British Sub-Aqua Club (BSAC)	Ragnar J. Ragnarsson Vice President & Phase III Recovery Project Leader	Iceland Lion's Club (Freyr)
• Diver		• Tent (Supplier)

NORTHROP CORPORATION AIRCRAFT DIVISION	NORWEGIAN DEFENSE MUSEUM (NDM)*	DIVERS
Leo Gay Advanced Project Engineer • Underwater communication system	Note: The NDM was in coordination by telephone, awaiting the survey's outcome. *Forsvarsmusett	• Sigurdur P. Hardarsson (IAHS) • Hermann Sigurdsson (ICG) • Peter J. Cornish (BSAC)

Figure 34. In Phase III of the recovery operation, diving in the early spring thaw, before the Thjorsa River reached peak current and sediment-saturated blackout flow, was the key to defining the final strategy and approach for raising the buried N-3PB Serial No. 320.

feasibility was resolved, was how long would a site team have to stay at the remote river location once the recovery effort was actually underway?

Cornish therefore saw his task as twofold: to resolve the issue of feasibility and to estimate how quickly a recovery could be accomplished. Once in the water, he kept these objectives as his principal orientation in seeking out the airplane, distinguishing it from the riverbed, and determining what to look for. Should the visibility in the water not be sufficient for a visual inspection, he planned a purely tactile inspection. While the other divers were communicating with the shore by means of the underwater voice-communication equipment provided by Northrop, Cornish knew it was best for him to work alone and proceed hand-over-hand, face-mask-to-riverbed, moving slowly, deftly over the site as he mentally recorded what he could see, feel, and imagine.

The Phase III group departed Reykjavik at 0800 hours, Saturday, April 28, 1979, and arrived at the site at approximately 1100 hours. The weather was unfavorable, with a 25-to-30-knot wind causing a high chill factor, in an ambient air temperature of between +2C and -3C; but the condition of the river was at its best, with the water level low and clarity providing visibility of about 20 inches, the same distance from which a surgeon views his patient, but incredibly good visibility for the Thjorsa. The team had the rest of the day and the weekend to complete its work.

"Albert's" 4-wheel-drive Laplander again proved its value in transporting all the equipment and the shore party. The shore personnel erected the 5-meter-diameter circular operations tent while the divers prepared their equipment for an immediate descent.

Each functional squad had a lead member. Sigurdur P. Hardarsson, the IAHS Project Treasurer and host diver (trained by the Icelandic Coast Guard), was appointed squad leader of the divers, who set up coordinated safety measures: lifelines were made available for immediate shooting into the river; and the inflatable powerboat was set up and crew assignments made so that it would be constantly manned on the river while diving operations were in process. That afternoon, the three divers made four 15-to-20-minute dives each for a total diving time of around 3.5 hours. The current in the wreck area was not a problem, but the water temperature of just above freezing (2 to 4 degrees Centigrade) limited the duration of each dive, due to the diver's hypothermia threshold, despite the longer duration of the air supply. Even though the divers were enthusiastic about staying submerged, the policy was to limit dives to a maximum of 20 minutes.

The first objective was to get an overview of the aircraft's situation. Overall inspection showed that it was buried in the riverbed, except for the partial exposure of the cockpit section where the 3-man crew sat in tandem and a section of vertical fin aft of the cockpit area. Blowing compressed air to remove sand and silt from around the upper portion of the airframe enabled closer inspection of the airframe. At the aft end, the fuselage was found to be broken in two pieces, with the break located about 20 centimeters (8 inches) forward of the vertical fin's leading edge. The tail section was lying on its side, buried, with the right stabilizer and elevator missing, a sign of severe transverse loading.

Since both fuselage sections were still adjacent, it was thought that they might still be attached to one another by means of the control cables. If this were the case, then the missing right horizontal surfaces and the vertical surfaces, which were missing from the tail section, might still be attached to the airframe but buried further down below the tail section. The left horizontal stabilizer and elevator were found intact, almost entirely buried, but in good condition given the environment they had been in for 36 years, at least 20 completely buried. Even the fabric covering of the elevator did not seem to have deteriorated during the 36 years spent in the river.

At the front end of the plane, consistent with Farmer Johansson's story of trying to pull the airplane from the river by tying onto the engine, the fuselage terminated at the firewall. The lower part of the firewall had come loose and was brought ashore. This part, which is attached to the fuselage by machine screws, is of stainless steel, and was found in virtually original condition. The primer paint had worn off, but the metal was as bright as a mirror. Attached to the lower firewall was a cable to which a manifold pressure gauge was attached. The glass on the gauge was broken and the gauge was covered with underwater growth. The manifold pressure registered by the gauge was 21.5 inches. Perfect! Somehow it seemed that the airplane, on crashing that April day in 1943, had, out of its natural element, the air, immediately entered a state of suspended animation as it entered the water.

The top fuselage skin aft of the firewall and up to the pilot's instrument panel was found to be missing, although the bulkheads and longerons appeared to be intact. It was concluded that the skin had been torn off when the engine was yanked from the firewall. The pilot's instrument panel was not intact; where it had been, only fractured pieces of metal remained. It appeared that the instrument panel had been pried from its station in the forward cockpit at some time before the aircraft sank in the riverbed.

In the cockpit area, the divers were able to remove some of the sand to expose the control column and the hand fuel pump or hydraulic hand pump handle. Also the engine fire extinguisher handle was seen and the inscription on the instruction plate could be easily read. The upper part of the pilot's seat was also in place.

The left side of the fuselage along the pilot's cockpit was damaged about 25 centimeters back from the instrument panel. This damage also had probably been caused when the engine was pulled off the firewall, especially if the line of pull, as estimated, had been at an angle of 45 degrees to the fuselage's centerline. In this area the pilot's electrical switch panel was dangling from the electrical cables. These were cut by the diver and the switch panel brought ashore. A few switches were missing, but the ones still in place worked perfectly. Even the rheostat knobs could be turned freely. Finally, a vibrator inverter that was removed from the cockpit area and brought ashore was found to be in relatively good condition.

All the cockpit framing was gone, but the steel runners for the sliding canopy sections were still in place on their respective sides of the fuselage. The deck beneath the pilot's and the navigator's cockpits was still in place. The navigator's cockpit at the rear of the 3-man cockpit was so buried in sand it was not inspectable at this time. However, the aft curvature of the rear cockpit could be seen clearly, but extended only about halfway before ending in fractured metal where the fuselage was broken in half.

The center wing section was buried to the upper skin in sand and clay, even with the riverbed, and was easily cleaned off to reveal various inspection panels. One of these covered a fuel cap from which, when removed, fuel squirmed upward to the surface of the water. The gasoline fumes could be clearly smelled by the shore party.

The left and right joints of the outer wing panel were located but both fairings were missing. The bolts were in place and did not seem to be distorted. The left wing was followed to the tip, which was partly buried and the skin crumpled. The outer wing panel was distorted. The two 0.50- inch machine guns in that panel were in position, but not in alignment. It appeared that someone had made an attempt to remove the guns or use them to pull the airplane free and, in being subjected to a heavy pulling force they came out of alignment and distorted the outer panel.

The right wing could be followed for only a short distance before it disappeared into a steep underwater sandbank. By clearing away sand and clay, the right wing could be followed just beyond the place where the two 0.50-inch machine guns should have been. The guns were missing and only a hole in the leading edge of the right outer wing panel remained.

The steep underwater sandbank to the right of the aircraft accounted for the way the aircraft listed to the left, without the weight of the missing right pontoon to offset the river's action. A quarter mile or more upstream, the river curved abruptly to the right (eastward), at the point where Sevi Bulukin had tried to land the plane. The southward flowing current came around this curve and slanted toward the beach, forcing sand under the right wing and building up a sandbank on that side of the plane.

The pontoons and their wing pedestals would be major impediments to raising the plane easily, because they would anchor the plane in the riverbed; therefore a major effort was made to locate the pontoon pedestals under the wings to verify their presence and, in particular, the presence of the left pontoon; but the pedestals couldn't be reached, mainly because the riverbed backfilled sand and gravel faster than it could be scooped away. This backfilling was seen as a major problem to be dealt with in the final raising of the plane.

That the plane was tilted downward on the lee side portended a further problem; that was the side the remaining pontoon would be on, if it was still attached to the wing. The lee side of the airframe was almost completely buried in sand and clay, while the side facing the river's current was exposed about one meter down from the fuselage upper surface, because of the sandbank that kept the right side higher. Surfaces exposed to the abrasive action of the river were found to be both bent and worn, while surfaces covered by sand or clay were found to be in almost original condition.

The broken fuselage was the area most severely damaged. So completely torn apart were the two sections it was concluded that this damage was the result of human and not natural forces. On closer examination it was found that the vertical fin's trailing edge, for about 75 centimeters (about 30 inches), was bent back at an angle of 90 degrees, a condition indicating that the vertical tail surfaces (the rudder and spar) had been broken off by a heavy force. This condition apparently occurred when the reported attempt was made to pull the aircraft free from the riverbed by means of a steel cable tied around the tail section. On being pulled, this cable would have broken the right horizontal and vertical tail surfaces off the tail section, and then the entire tail section would have followed.

Assuming that the left pontoon was still attached, Cornish drew the sketch shown in Figure 35 to depict where the tail broke off and the extreme displacement of these two major sections of the fuselage. This sketch satisfied Ragnar's requirement for evidence that enough of the plane was there for restoration.

Cornish, acknowledged worldwide as the leading expert on recovering aircraft from water, defined his participation in this phase as helping in the technical appraisal of the potential for recovering the aircraft.[62] Detailing the approach by which to raise the plane would take further study and analysis. Cornish, as was his usual practice, said he would submit a written report on his findings and recommendations. This report became a major influence on the approach and strategy for raising the airplane from the riverbed in the final phase of recovery.

The airframe, though mostly buried, was pointing northwest, with the current sweeping south over it; thus the plane was pointing toward shore at an angle of about 45

---

[62] Peter J. Cornish, *Survey of the Underwater Wreckage of a Northrop N-3PB*, report to IAHS dated May 5, 1979.

degrees relative to the near bank (to the left or west). The plane was measured as being about 20 meters (66 feet) from the west bank, but this distance would vary seasonally according to the depth of the water. For example, in the Phase I survey, which was performed in October 1977, the plane had been measured to be about 30 meters (82 feet) from shore.[63]

While the riverbed sloped gradually downward to its greatest depth in the center of the river, the airplane had remained virtually level, due to the sandbank that had built up under the right wing away from the bank. This accounted for the measurements made in Phase II that indicated the airplane was lying flat in the riverbed.

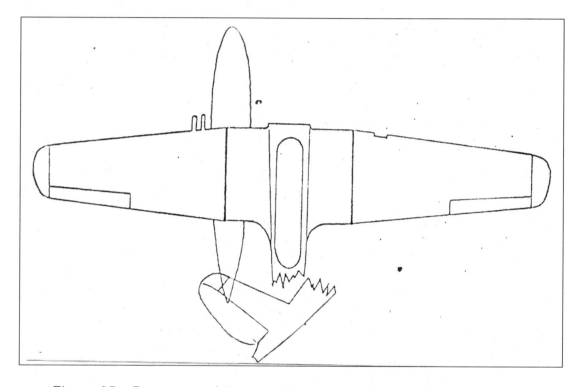

Figure 35. By means of the detailed examination made possible under the favorable underwater conditions of Phase III, this diagram of the apparent configuration of the buried airplane was drawn. Human forces, not natural, had caused the greater damage.

---

[63] As the glaciers melted during the summer months, the water depth at the site could increase from 6 to 12 feet and the river width could increase to 230 meters (about 250 yards) as the water level rose (cf., Table 2, Chapter 5).

Although the missing parts were a disappointment, the aircraft as a structural assembly was still intact overall and certainly worth recovering for restoration. It was the only remaining one of its kind and had such a distinctive mission history for the Allied team effort during WWII that it would be a treasured technological history for aviation in general and Northrop in particular, while standing as a monument to Norway's spirited fight to remain a free nation.

The environmental conditions in the water had been so favorable for the Phase III detailed examination of the underwater site that the three divers, knowing exactly what they were doing, completed their work in one day. It was now known that a massive amount of silt and clay would have to be removed from around the airframe to expose it sufficiently for flotation to the surface by means of airbags. Use of flotation bags was the recommendation of Cornish, the highly experienced British diver, and that method was thought by all to be the most straightforward and efficient way to raise the airplane. Later in the year, when the current was swifter and the water still low in visibility, the current itself could be beneficially used to carry off the silt and sand that would be blasted away by a pressurized air hose to excavate the plane. Furthermore, deeper water would be needed and available for the airbags to bring the plane to the surface.

The team personnel at the site and the international team members were encouraged, knowing that definite evidence had been obtained to show that the airplane was sufficiently intact to restore. Given the success with which the detailed examination had proceeded – and knowing that the results would be well received by the international team members – there was a sense that nature itself, the original cause of the airplane's crash landing, would this time be a major beneficial factor in its recovery. The divers were convinced that underwater recovery technology was more than adequate to handle the raising of this relatively lightweight vehicle. In fact, everyone suddenly realized that later in the year, the same favorable environmental conditions would occur in reverse as winter came on. There would be plenty of time over the intervening months to plan, organize, staff, and equip the final phase of recovery, which would include the logistics phaseover and delivery of the airplane to Northrop for restoration in the next year, 1980 – Jack Northrop's 85th birthday.

Ragnar was pleased that he had a sound basis on which to proceed. The pressure of proving the project was doable was somewhat lifted, because now he had data to back him and witnesses who shared his confidence. He could proceed at once with preparation of the detailed plan for recovery of the plane. Cornish had promised his report by early May.

He was proud of his Icelandic team. He was confident Northrop would get its plane to restore and that Norway would receive it in due time for permanent exhibit. It would be good to see a real N-3PB, after two years probing almost blindly in the river. His world was opening up. Being suspended midway, in nationality, between America and Iceland he could now bridge the two nations with Norway in their original historical teaming. The Thjorsa would be denied what it had tried to take; and though it might take a "mission impossible" to do it, he was ready to proceed.

CHAPTER 8 - DEFINING THE RECOVERY MISSION AS DETAILED PLAN

Peter J. Cornish had done his work well. His detailed report on the situation and condition of the airplane – in what he called its "grave" – graphically and clinically described the plight of the airplane and of those who would recover it. It was clear that no longer could the team expect just to jump in the water and lift out this airplane. It was going to be a difficult job and would require not only expert and well-equipped divers, but a well-thought-out, methodically planned and executed approach. For despite the thoroughness with which he had examined the plane, the riverbed, and the general underwater environment – and despite the methodical approach he had already outlined for recovering the plane – there were still doubts as to what lay below the silt, clay, and pumice that entombed most of the structure and clamped it in place as though held in concrete. As he had written, "Eighty percent of its structure is there in the river – bent, torn, and now very friable."[64] For a metal object, "friable" connotes a condition of terminal decay. More graphically, it means a former resilient material that is likely to crumble if you touch it. One can picture Cornish, underwater, gliding about the airplane's site, touching visible metal surfaces here and there, clearing silt from others just beneath the river bottom, and, based on his expertise, appraising the condition of the overall plane after so many years submerged under such conditions. What Cornish's report conveyed and portended was that although the plane was mostly still intact, it would require very careful handling to extract it from what was – other than for those who treasured it – its "grave." The Thjorsa was busy 24 hours a day making the plane friable.

Offsetting this gloomy prospectus, however, is his conclusion that the airplane could be recovered if done quickly by a team of dedicated divers and helpers.

Phase III had confirmed for those watching from the beach that not only was the airplane there, but in the form of almost a complete airframe. It was easy to imagine a striking airplane such as the N-3PB buried there and awaiting only the prowess of those who wanted it back before them, to come forth from what otherwise would indeed be its grave. Consequently, with its mission objective, the N-3PB, tangibly established in a known arena of operations, the international team now was ready and eager to proceed with the fastest possible recovery. As Ragnar J. Ragnarsson had concluded in his Phase III progress report to the team:

> Although the parts found missing from the airframe give reason to some disappointment, the aircraft is still found very worthy of recovery, considering it is the only remaining aircraft of the type known to be available for recovery. It is left to others to decide whether this particular aircraft can be restored to display

---

[64] Peter J. Cornish, Loc. Cit., p. 5

condition, but purely on a subjective assessment it is not thought to be an impossible task.[65]

It is clear from Ragnar's careful wording of this paragraph that he himself had reservations about the practicality of proceeding and was leaving it "to others to decide whether this particular aircraft can be restored...." Cornish had expressed the same conclusion, saying in his report dated May 9, 1979, "Essentially others will have to make an assessment as to whether the wrecked aircraft is worthy of recovery for future refurbishing." He had capped his conclusion by noting that, "Technically the recovery would be difficult – indeed one of the most difficult in view of the conditions involved but it does provide a challenge for a dedicated team." [66]

These two viewpoints are interesting in that while Ragnar's is intrinsically contradictory, espousing the worthiness of the recovery while shunning the decision as a risk others will have to take, Cornish leaves no doubt that the plane can be recovered, hinging the decision solely on worthiness. So in Cornish's view, if, as Ragnar says, the aircraft is worthy of recovery, it is also refurbishable; that is, it all comes down to the worthiness of the recovery, for obviously no one would recover mere junk. Cornish's conclusion is the important one, because he bases it on having personally examined the aircraft, in situ, underwater; and he decided it was refurbishable if worthy of recovery.

To the IAHS, it was urgent to move ahead so as to keep its N-3PB recovery crew intact. Furthermore, it wanted to complete this historical task that was becoming almost as challenging as the original mission of the aircraft. Norway was eager to support the effort to raise and deliver the plane to Northrop for restoration and subsequent delivery to its air museum. At Northrop, those who had worked either with Jack Northrop or were there when his character and personality still dominated the management spirit of the company were especially motivated to proceed, in that something uniquely special would be available to celebrate his 85th birthday. The N-3PB seaplane would be in effect a form of restoration for him, in that it would take him back to his 45th year when he had just started Northrop Corporation and this very airplane, though a sudden, unforeseen contractual opportunity, had been the first he designed there and the first that corporation produced. During a 12-year period at his new company, Jack Northrop's genius was expressed in a family of aircraft that constitutes a cross-section of modern aviation. These were years that included such followon aircraft to the N-3PB as the P-61 night-attack fighter-bomber and its photo-recon offshoot, the F-15; the F-89 fighter; the B-35 and –49 series of flying-wing bombers; the C-125 tri-motor transport; the MX rocket wing; the JB-1 power bomb; the JB-10 jet bomb; and the SM-62 intercontinental guided missile. The common characteristic of these aircraft was their mission-based functional design. As shown in Figure 36, the N-3PB, the first aircraft produced by Northrop Corporation, led to a series of missionized aircraft introducing the mission approach used in the design of all aircraft today.

---

[65] Ragnar J. Ragnarsson, *The Northrop Recovery Project*, "Phase III – Progress Report," dated May 1979, p.6.
[66] Peter J. Cornish, Loc. Cit., pp. 5 and 6.

Northrop Archives

Figure 36. Highlights of Northrop's missionized aircraft lineage (L to R from top): N-3PB (1940), P-61 Night Fighter (1943), XP-56 Wing Fighter (1944), F-89 Fighter (1951), SM-62 Intercontinental Missile (1952), X-4 Transonic Fighter (1946), F-18 Navy Air Combat Fighter (1976), B-2 Stealth Bomber (1982).

So once again, the N-3PB was serving as the centerpiece for an allied team effort. Whereas in the war years the team had banded together for military purposes and joint mission operations, now the key nations – Iceland, Norway, Britain, and the United States – were, due to the success of that Allied teaming, once more securely independent and working together voluntarily to recover and restore, by means of this aircraft, that sense of unity and purpose that the war had necessitated and instilled for sake of survival.

WWII forged a unity among those nations through numerous challenges and successes that ultimately resulted in peace and prosperity. For the individual, it marked a distinctive change point in time to look back on, somewhat like the point at which a person is "grown up," before which certain things just happened and after which all events are measured for their significance and value to further growth. The war was a team effort and a period to look back on with both nostalgia and pride; it had been a time when growth seemed suspended and yet greatest maturity was achieved. The nostalgia was a synthesis of being very mature all at once but not very old; the remembrance dwells on not just battles won by the Allied nations but the many accomplishments of the civilian sector: the thousands of airplanes produced, the scrap metal drives, the war bonds sold and purchased, the material and food sacrifices, and the all-out patriotism.

It is unfortunate that it takes war to unify man in such tightly bound, sacrificial commitments that seemingly no other form of competition can bring about. The recurrence of this teaming for survival seems to indicate a general principle. Is it not that when any effort reaches such an intensity of purpose that high levels of unity are achieved between individuals and groups, it is because the means used to achieve a certain end and the end itself have become synthesized: in effect, to win requires total commitment of not just individuals but of groups, for while individual capabilities vary, the group synthesis equilibrates and harmonizes all differences and enables the group as a team to proceed toward a goal not sought or achievable individually.

It is through this synthesis of the group as team that a synergy of output is reached that surpasses what would normally be expected. This is a synergy generated by willingly contributed, freely given commitments of time, effort, and sacrifice. War is the familiar, common ground for such synergy, but being so extreme tends to hide or obscure the fact that a principle is at work that affects the most normal, peacetime activities. This principle resides in all efforts that require exacting forms of detail planning for achieving quality results in the shortest time at the lowest cost. Such efforts replicate, in essence, the same common ground as war; in effect, all states of intense competition are smaller forms of war that differ only in the degree of discipline, capability, commitment, and sacrifice required and, in the extreme, the potential for injury, bloodshed, and mortality.

The unity underlying great team efforts, though sometimes spontaneous if the members are of equally high capability, is usually the product of detail planning. As Churchill showed in his management of Britain during WWII, a central, encompassing plan was required not just to save England, but the world. It was Churchill's constant planning and coordination of planning that resulted in the formation of that supreme example of team effort Churchill called "The Grand Alliance." It is through such planning that the synergistic multiple is achieved, a multiple that surpasses the capability and contribution of any individual or single group. Of course any plan must be configured and managed to respond to change, as rigidity can be as self-defeating as having no plan at all.

The team members understood this and, wanting to produce a plan that would result in successful results in the shortest time and with the small budget available, took time for detailed planning before proceeding with the final phase of recovery. In fact, a separate phase was set aside just to define the detailed plan for the final recovery effort. Such planning phases have become a standard policy and procedure of the aerospace industry. The urgency of meeting the mission needs of space and military forces with the latest technology, in systems that cost billions of dollars to design, develop, manufacture, and logistically support once fielded, requires it. Otherwise, due to the incessant newness of advancing technology, unknowns would inevitably surface to cause costly, time-consuming correction of mistakes and oversights.

Such planning first defines the objective and then the major steps that lead to it. These steps may be major phases or stages of task activity or the tasks themselves. In any event, the planning, to be detailed, is defined to the lowest level of separately schedulable and budgetable tasks. It is at this level that the program is managed and controlled.

Once the tasks are defined, their work content is assessed for the capabilities required and the assets available to perform them. This assessment leads to the staffing of the tasks with the available, appropriately qualified personnel and the provisioning of equipment and facilities required for them to do their work in accordance with the tasks in the time allotted. The time and budget constraints on the performance of tasks determines the number of personnel and the proficiency of equipment required. Time and cost are major factors in the tradeoffs used to optimize the staffing, facilitation, and scheduling of the detail plan. Such tradeoffs are known in general as cost-effectiveness analysis of program planning. Today in the aerospace industry such analysis is performed daily as a computerized methodology called the Cost/Schedule Control System (C/SCS or C^2S^2).

At Northrop Corporation such sophisticated planning had long been in use by the time Phase IV of the N-3PB Restoration Program was ready for implementation. In fact, Jack Northrop, in his hands-on, "I'm a team member" approach to constant improvement in the management of Northrop to produce aircraft of highest quality and lowest cost, had already anticipated these systems, which were to reach ultimate sophistication in the realtime management and control made possible by computer networks, as currently in use.

This principle of management for synergy through unity of team effort was applied to the final phase of recovery, in the detailed plan for raising the N-3PB from the riverbed and getting it to Northrop for restoration. The fact that three site survey phases had already been performed to establish the feasibility of recovering the N-3PB shows that this goal was naturally a candidate for detailed planning, to enable the effort to proceed quickly and preclude further damage to a "friable" aircraft, as Peter J. Cornish had so well stated the requirement.

Immediately after completing the detailed physical assessment of the condition of the airplane in April 1979, Ragnar J. Ragnarsson began a three-month detail planning activity to define the scope and magnitude of effort for the final phase of the recovery project and to organize, staff, facilitate, and schedule it for implementation. Referred to as Phase IV, this detailed planning and strategizing activity would be followed by the implementation of the plan as Phase V of the overall recovery effort. The final recovery would be divided into the most efficiently and effectively manageable steps, which would become the basis for staffing, facilitating, scheduling, and budgeting the overall effort according to the detailed tasks to be performed in each step. To coordinate the plan among the international team members, the following people were designated:

1. Ragnar as Project Manager of the recovery operations, acting on behalf of the IAHS.

2. Sevi Bulukin as Team Leader for Norway's personnel, equipment, and functional responsibilities.

3. Leo Gay as Team Leader for Northrop's equipment and functional responsibilities.

At Northrop, the effort to raise the N-3PB was now known as "Project Northrop," the name used to designate something very special, and not yet widely known, for Jack Northrop's upcoming birthday. Donald G. Page, Manager of Public Affairs at the Aircraft Division, was once again actively supporting the project now that the airplane appeared to be definitely a feasible candidate for inclusion in the birthday party. He had been the initial stateside contact for Northrop in 1977 when the existence of the airplane first surfaced. Leo Gay, reporting to Page, continued as the direct liaison for Northrop with the IAHS and would be present at the site for the final phase of recovery.

Norway's Sevi Bulukin was back in action in Iceland after a 36-year career in Scandinavian aerospace. During those years, with a master's degree in mechanical engineering, he had worked as a design engineer and executive for the deHavilland Aircraft Company in Britain and Norway. Just a month into his 30th birthday at the time of the crash-landing into the Thjorsa River, Sevi was now 66, had retired from the Norwegian Air Force with the rank of colonel, and had a son, Jan, who was 20 and in the Norwegian Navy. Ragnar had contacted Sevi immediately after the plane's presence in the riverbed was verified in 1977 and requested that he serve as coordinator of the recovery project with the Norwegian Aviation Historical Society and the Norwegian Air Force. The participation of these agencies was consolidated for coordination through the Norwegian Defense Museum. It was Sevi's background in Norwegian aviation and his direct experience with the N-3PB that got these agencies interested in and organized for participation in the recovery.

Once the decision was made to raise the airplane, Sevi used his influence with the Norwegian Navy to get Jan assigned to the project. Jan Bulukin was a scuba diver by avocation. To permit his participation in the raising, the Navy temporarily assigned him to the Norwegian Maritime Museum (NMM) as one of the four Norwegian divers eventually assigned to the project. As additional backup support, Sevi signed up three other veterans of the original Squadron 330(N) in which Sevi and the airplane had served. During the final raising of the airplane, Sevi was in charge of the Norwegian personnel at the site, a total of nine including himself. So it was that Jan Bulukin was recruited by his own father to assist in recovering the father's WWII airplane; and so the team spirit of The Grand Alliance passed from father to son.

Northrop would become the major leader and operations center during the final phase of actually restoring the airplane. During Phase V of the recovery phase, Northrop would provide communications equipment, a key requirement at the operations site, particularly considering the number of personnel to be involved and coordinated. This equipment (listed in Appendix E) was specifically selected for underwater communications between the divers and the control center on the shore. Northrop actually exported the equipment to Iceland. Since Sigurdur Hardarsson, the IAHS project diver trained by the Iceland Coast Guard, wanted the equipment for subsequent use in other underwater operations, he shared the cost with Northrop for one set and also purchased a second from Northrop.

Because of Iceland's central role as the major participant for the raising of the plane, overall administrative control during Phase V was assigned to an IAHS Project Committee. This committee was responsible for policies and final review and approval of the plan for final recovery operations. Because of the experience and familiarity of the Icelandic personnel with the environment and climatology of the operational site and the situation and condition of the aircraft, the committee was particularly concerned with the detailed tasks to be performed in raising the plane and their logical organization, staffing, and facilitation relative to the task requirements and the environmental conditions under which they would have to be performed.

The committee was composed of:

1. Ragnar J. Ragnarsson as chairman.
2. Baldur Sveinsson as secretary.
3. Sigurdur P. Hardarsson as treasurer.
4. Einar Gunnarsson as member.
5. Jon K. Snorrason as member.

These are all recognizable as historical Icelandic names. So, clearly, the committee was composed to make sure that Iceland's role as host nation was properly represented and carried out. Each member was a specialist selected to ensure that all contingencies were thought of and prepared for in advance for a fault-free raising and delivery of the aircraft. All had worked in previous phases of the recovery.

To implement operations in accordance with the policies and procedural constraints of the committee, the functions to be performed were identified and organized in the following major categories:

1. Diving: Underwater operations as necessary to clear the aircraft for its raising from the riverbed.
2. Diving Support Services: Servicing and maintenance of compressed air bottles for use by the divers; operation and maintenance of the air

compressor for use in filling the air bottles; operation and maintenance of two inflatable outboard-powered boats.

3. <u>Communications</u>: Operation and readiness of long-range high-frequency transceivers, with standard telephone interface, for emergency and rescue requirements; and operation and readiness of fixed and portable, short-range citizenband transceivers for communications within the recovery site; plus local farm telephone backup.

4. <u>Photographic Recording</u>: Photographers equipped with still and cinematographic cameras.

5. <u>First Aid and Rescue</u>: First-aid technicians operating from tented equipment area; catapult-launched lifelines with buoys attached ready for deployment on beach; and 4-wheel-drive ambulance.

6. <u>Transportation</u>: Personnel and equipment for transport operations for commute from site to city for all personnel and equipment; for two 4-wheel drive vehicles with power winches for use in pulling the aircraft from the water; for a semitrailer-tractor vehicle for transport of the aircraft to Keflavik International Airport near Reykjavik; and for air transport of the aircraft on request to the U.S.

7. <u>Housing</u>: Three Swedish-type army tents with folding chairs and tables for 16 people per tent, plus folding type sleeping berths for up to 44 people, who will provide their own sleeping bags.

8. <u>Food</u>: Food services for breakfast, lunch, dinner, and coffee break for personnel directly assigned to the project, with other non-direct personnel required to provide their own meals.

9. <u>Lavatories</u>: Sanitary facilities to be provided adjacent to the operations area, backed by natural hot water swimming pool approximately 15 minutes away.

With these functional requirements specified as the basic organizational structure for personnel assignments, the key personnel organization shown in Figure 37 was established by the committee to manage and control implementation of the functions. These personnel constituted the key members who would be responsible for implementing the functions of the detailed plan for raising the airplane from the riverbed and transporting it to Iceland's international airport at Keflavik for delivery to Northrop. As backup, 10 to 15 additional workers were scheduled to participate for the first three days to set up the housing and equipment at the operational site.

Of course, the three original international team members (the Iceland Aviation Historical Society, the Norwegian Defense Museum, and Northrop Corporation) were still the primary participants and organizers. Operationally, however four organizations were selected to implement the Phase V Recovery Plan, because of the expertise, personnel capabilities, and equipment now known to be absolutely necessary. Still leading the recovery operations was the originator of the project, the Icelandic Aviation Historical Society (IAHS).

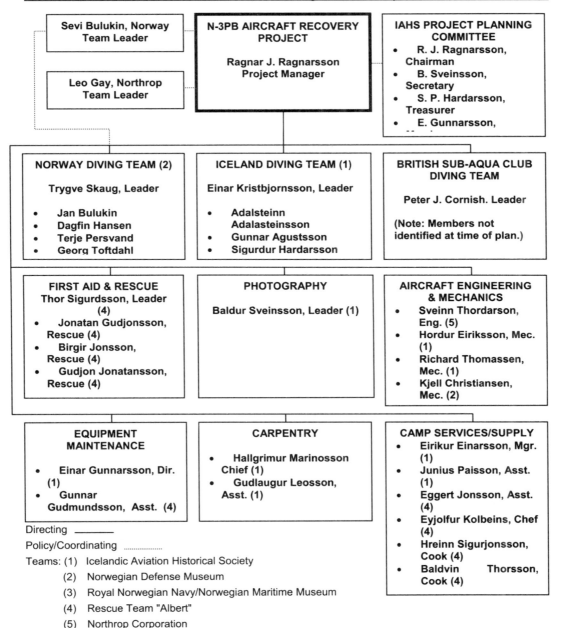

Figure 37. Through detailed planning of the final recovery phase, the international team organized and staffed a comprehensive functional organization capable of expert and fast response to every task.

Now, with Sevi onboard to represent Norway's interest and capabilities, the plan was for most of the diving expertise to be provided by the Royal Norwegian Navy (RNN) and the Norwegian Maritime Museum (NMM), with the IAHS's Sigurdur P. Hardarsson (trained by the Icelandic Coast Guard) providing direct site experience to share with the new divers. In addition, it was planned that Peter J. Cornish, who had so thoroughly assessed and documented the plane's situation in Phase III and outlined the basic approach for recovering it, would be present as a key diver, along with other members of the British Sub-Aqua Club.

Thus, as planned, the final phase would have the dedicated team of divers and helpers that Cornish had noted would be necessary to recover the airplane quickly, in the face of a moving and quickly refilling riverbed, and to do so skillfully so as to preclude further damaging the already "friable" structure.

The Iceland Life Saving Association's highly experienced and ready Rescue Team "Albert" (RTA) volunteered to provide first-aid and rescue services, plus cooking for the on-site personnel, and also to assist in camp management services. The remainder of the on-site functions were performed by IAHS personnel. Northrop's Sveinn Thordarson, a native Icelander and Northrop structural research engineer, was loaned by Northrop to provide on-site consultation regarding any engineering questions about the airplane during the recovery operation.

In all, the on-site recovery team now added up to 35 personnel, backed by 68 individuals and companies who contributed manpower, equipment, material, and food to support operations for the estimated 10-day period of operations.

Deciding on the time of year to perform the recovery was the principal requirement and the factor that drove all other considerations for detailed planning. Ragnar knew that this was the one-time chance for success in raising the buried airplane. If the effort failed this time, the team would become disinterested and disband. After all, two years and four site surveys had gone by and the plane was as deeply encased in the riverbed as ever, if not more. There was no way to gage whether the plane was sinking further or had stabilized in its descent.

The Thjorsa River was the chief competitor for the plane. As Farmer Johannsson, smiling, had told Ragnar in 1972 when asked about the chances for salvaging anything in that part of the river, "Everyone in these parts knows that what the Thjorsa River takes, she never returns."

The Thjorsa, 237 kilometers (147.3 miles) in length, is the longest river in Iceland; and, next to the Olfusa, the second most powerful in hydrodynamic flow rate (330 cubic meters per second compared to 400 for the Olfusa, on average). It flows from the approximate center of the island in a southwesterly direction, draining two of the four major glaciers, the Vatnajokull and the Hofsjokull, as shown in Figure 38. The flow rate peaks in July and early August at about 500 cubic meters per second.

In 1965, a dam was built across the river north of Mt. Burfell and Mt. Samstadamuli to service a 270-megawatt hydroelectric powerplant that today supplies almost one-third of Iceland's electricity from hydroelectric sources. Known as the Burfellsvirkjun

www.homestead.com

Figure 38. The Thjorsa River, the longest in Iceland, flowing southwest from the center of the island to drain the Hofsjokull and Vatnajokull glaciers, had the airplane trapped in its bed where it hooks westward, briefly, 34 miles from the ocean.

Hydropower Plant, it generates electricity by means of a tunnel that directs the Thjorsa's flow from the dam through the two mountains to hydroelectric turbines at the southern base of Mt. Burfell, where the water returns to the Thjorsa near the spot the N-3PB seaplane crash-landed in the spring of 1943.

Still more fascinating about this river is that it has a total of five hydroelectric powerplants along its length. These plants generate 845 megawatts of electricity, 82 percent of Iceland's total hydroelectric power. An enormous resource.[67]

As Cornish had observed in his Phase III report, the Thjorsa River presented four major impediments to the recovery:

---

[67] Hakon Adalsteinsson, Project Manager of Iceland's Hydropower and Environmental Resources Agency, provided the data on which this description of the Thjorsa's contribution to electrical power generation for the nation is based. Hakon also noted that an additional 180 megawatts of electricity is supplied from purely geothermal sources (a source as renewable as the Earth itself).

1. Freezing or near freezing water.
2. Swift current flow, increasing as water channel deepens.
3. Near zero visibility, decreasing as current increases.
4. Soft, silty, gritty, moving, self-filling bottom, with underlying compaction.

The fourth was a combination of the fast current flow and lava ash and pumice sand overlaid on a clay bottom. In fact, the airplane was kept from moving with the swift current because it was stuck deeply in the clay bottom. Pinned in this way, the entire fuselage was buried in about six feet of finely ground volcanic ash and lava. As one attempted to dig deeper in the riverbed, the material became denser, more compacted, and more resistant to removal.

The plane, in effect, had buried itself. The material covering it would have to be removed so as to free it for raising. The task of removing this material, however, was more complex than it seemed. The plane was caught in a Catch 22 situation, because the finely ground nature of the ash and sand caused any depression or hole to be immediately filled; hence as ash and sand were removed, the fast current flow would replace it almost immediately with more of the same. As Cornish had noted in his report on the Phase III survey:

> The riverbed moves and so the hole needed to expose the plane would have to be large enough to accommodate the refill. The digging effort will need to be more or less constantly mounted to keep back the expected refill…. Hopefully, efforts could be made to provide a bulwark against more of the river-borne material coming over the site…. In the river at full flood, it runs at 5-7 knots.[68]

As Cornish further noted, the airplane would have to be raised when the river was at its deepest flow of two to three meters (six to ten feet), so as to provide adequate flotation clearance for the airplane with its portside float still attached to the wing mounting pedestal. This depth requirement, however, occurs when (1) the river is widest and running at its highest flowrate; and (2) the airplane is at its greatest distance of almost 100 feet from shore. Ideally, the airplane would be closest to shore, to make it easier to beach; and ideally there would be at least 10 feet of liquid water from surface to riverbed: but, as usual, what is ideal is not always realistic. Given these conflicting conditions, Cornish concluded that:

> Technically, the recovery would be difficult – indeed one of the most difficult in view of the conditions involved, but it does provide a challenge for a dedicated team.[69]

To establish the optimum time period for the recovery, the hydrographic flowrate data recorded for the Thjorsa during the 10-year period from 1968 through 1977 were compiled. Figure 39(a) shows the flowrate for the river every other year for that period.

---

[68] Peter J. Cornish, Survey *of the Underwater Wreckage of a Northrop N-3PB*, report submitted to the IAHS on completion of Phase III survey, dated May 9, 1979.
[69] Ibid.

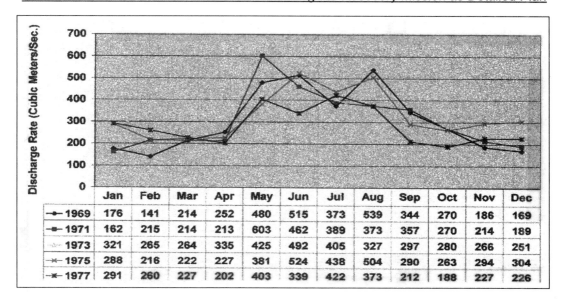

(a) The 10-year historical record for discharge flowrate indicated a continuing decrease that would favor August as the best month to conduct final recovery.

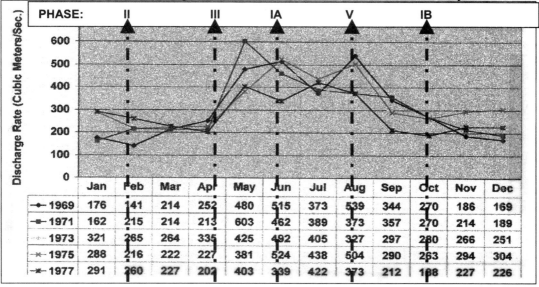

(b) Survey Phases I-III had explored the spectrum of annual flowrates. The final Phase V would be selected for optimum current flow versus visibility, as Figure 40 shows.

Figure 39. In the Phase IV planning period (May-July 1979) the Thjorsa's historical flowrate was used as a planning model to select the optimum date for the final recovery operation on N-3PB SN320 in Phase V.

139

The flow pattern follows the anticipated seasonal changes: the time of highest flow rate is during the spring-summer-and-fall months (April-September) when the glacier surface ice thaws, and the time of lowest flow rate is during the winter months (October-March) when the melting of the glaciers slows and the river develops an ice cap. The higher flow rate would be accompanied by greater water depth, faster current, and lower visibility, whereas the lower flow rate would be accompanied by lower water depth river, slower current, higher visibility, and a 2-foot-thick ice cap. At the operational site, the width of the river from summer to winter would decrease about 30 percent from around 250 yards to 175 and the water depth over the plane would decrease from about 15 feet (4.6 meters) to 11.5 (3.5 meters). However, at the lower water depth, 2 feet of the water depth would be ice cap, presenting an impossible condition under which to raise the plane.

The best time to raise the airplane, according to Cornish, would be when the water was still deep enough to float the plane with its one pontoon still attached and there was enough visibility to see the plane underwater closeup, where the removal of sand and clay from around the fuselage and wings could be seen as it was accomplished. Obviously this would be a time when there was no ice cap, therefore ruling out the winter months. Since visibility was worst during peak flow rate, the choice narrowed down to either spring, when the ice cap liquefied, or fall, when the glaciers started freezing up. Since flowrate increased rapidly in the spring and visibility decreased correspondingly, the optimum choice was clearly fall.

As Figure 39(a) shows, in the Fall there is over a month (August-September) during which there is a consistent but more gradual slowdown in the flowrate, meaning that as the visibility increases with decreasing flowrate, there is a relatively long period over which the water depth decreases. Since the detailed plan showed that the plane could be raised in 10 days, mid-August, the beginning of the changeover from summer to winter, was selected as the time of optimum tradeoff between water depth and visibility. Based on the hydrographic data plotted in Figure 39(a) for the two most recent years (1975 and 1977), it was concluded that the year 1979 itself ought to have an optimally slow rate of change for this tradeoff, with both the optimum visibility and the optimum depth of water prolonged from mid-August to mid-September. A spell of charmed existence arose in the key planning personnel, for nature seemed to be joining into the team effort to ensure success.

The decision as to the optimum time period for the final effort to raise the airplane was further supported by the information shown in Figure 39(b). Thus far, the airplane had been approached and surveyed at its burial site four times. June 11, 1977 had been the first time that the site was surveyed. The first phase had been initiated when Farmer Johansson was interviewed as to whether the plane even had gone down in the Thjorsa at the suspected location and whether it still was in the river, had drifted away, or had become too deeply buried to be verified as existing and salvageable. At that time, as Figure 39(b) shows, it was mid-June at the peak flowrate. It was no surprise to learn later why Sigurdur Hardarsson, in diving alone in this first survey of the site for evidence of the plane, had been unable to see his hand before his mask, because of the extremely low visibility that coincides with peak flowrate. Thus the first attempt to find the airplane had demonstrated that summer would not be the best time for a fully staffed and facilitated recovery operation.

The next attempt had been made four months later in 1977 on October 15, which as Figure 39(b) shows, is the beginning of winter and the time of lowest flowrate but, as nature would have it, the lowest water depth and the beginning of icecap formation. At that year and time, due to a recent dry spell, the water depth had been only about 5 feet (1.5 meter) and it was thought the airplane was discovered when one of the divers inadvertently stumbled on a protruding piece of metal on walking back to shore.

So in 1977, in the first two attempts to verify the existence and location of the plane, the two worst times to try to raise the airplane also were experienced. But these experiences also taught a positive lesson in that it was now clear that operating from the icecap would provide the kind of stable platform necessary at least to locate the airplane and delineate its overall airframe identity by precise drilling. This conclusion led in February 1979 to the Phase II icecap drilling survey in which the airplane was verified as definitely still there in some substantial form; and two months later, on 28-29 April, to Phase III, which showed that the airplane was sufficiently intact and complete enough to be restored (though, as Cornish had noted, in "friable" condition).

Phase III, while performed at a time of year when the increasing flowrate still allowed underwater visibility of about 20 inches, nevertheless also showed that sufficient water depth would not be reached to float the plane out of its burial crypt in the riverbed before visibility became impossibly low to uncover the airplane. Consequently, the experience of this phase, given those of the preceding phases, pointed again to the selection of the August timeframe as the optimum choice.

All doubt had been erased by a process of elimination, by the survey team efforts spread over all other potential times of the year, as shown in Figure 39(b). Nature, having preserved the airplane, had reserved August as the best time to recover it. At that time, ice would be absent, the temperature would be at its highest, and underwater visibility would be maximum. The tradeoff between flowrate and visibility, based on the 1979 forecast, is shown in Figure 40.

With close to 100 people involved in the program – many from other nations – the IAHS Project Planning Committee (Figure 37) issued policies governing travel to and from the site. To keep the number of personnel at the site to a minimum, access was limited to vehicles assigned to the project or as specially permitted. To ensure direct communications inside and outside Iceland, a mobile, vehicle-installed, high-frequency radio was obtained for use at the site. This radio enabled the team to contact Iceland Radio – the Island's radio station – in case of an urgent requirement or emergency; and also, through Iceland Radio, provided access to any telephone number in the world. As backup, arrangements were made for accessing a telephone at a local farm within five minutes driving time of the site.

In general, the personnel support policy and plan was that permission to be resident at the site would be limited to the 35 people who had been assigned tasks requiring their on-

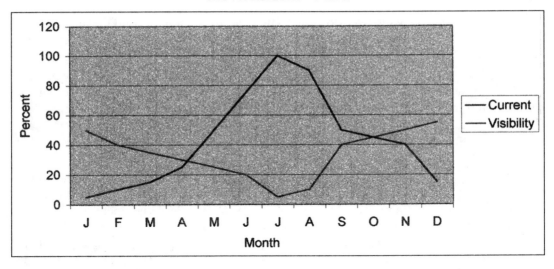

Figure 40. The fact that visibility in the Thjorsa River increased with decreasing flowrate provided a convenient tradeoff between those two factors in selecting the warmest temperature time of year to raise the airplane from its burial site in glacier-ground lava sand and ash.

site presence to perform. The on-site personnel logistics plan was tailored accordingly for a 10-day period. To accommodate these personnel with sleeping quarters and a messhall, Norway provided four 16-man Army tents and 32 folding cots for sleeping.

So that all personnel would know distances and travel conditions to the site and be prepared accordingly (particularly those flying into the Keflavik International Airport), the map shown in Figure 41 was sent to all participants. Surface travel to the vicinity of the site was over paved roads, except for gravel roads the last 27 miles. Once opposite the operations beach on the main road in, a distance of about 1,000 yards had to be traveled over open terrain to get to the beach. A standard passenger vehicle could be driven the first 765 yards (700 meters), but only a 4-wheel-drive vehicle could cross the rutted and faulted lava field extending the last 220 yards (200 meters).

From Keflavik to the city of Selfoss southeast of the capitol Reykjavik, Highway 1 (known as the Coastal Ring Road that circuited the entire island) the road was a primary, hard-surfaced thoroughfare running 64 miles (104 kilometers). From Selfoss, Road I-30 continued as hard surface another 10 miles (16 kilometers) approximately due east, before changing to gravel for the next 13 miles (21 kilometers) to the intersection with I-32. This road, also gravel, then ran northeast for 14 miles (22 kilometers) where it came to within one-half mile (900 meters) of the operations site on the westbank of the Thjorsa, and then continued northward parallel to the river. This road and the ingress to the beach would later play an important role in the final raising of the airplane.

The general operational concept was to have fixed installations on the beach at the recovery site and a barge anchored offshore. The onshore facilities were to centralize the

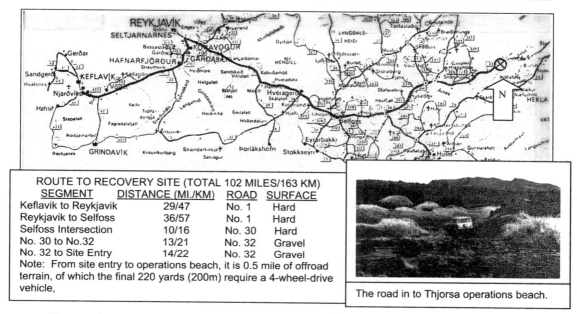

ROUTE TO RECOVERY SITE (TOTAL 102 MILES/163 KM)			
SEGMENT	DISTANCE (MI./KM)	ROAD	SURFACE
Keflavik to Reykjavik	29/47	No. 1	Hard
Reykjavik to Selfoss	36/57	No. 1	Hard
Selfoss Intersection	10/16	No. 30	Hard
No. 30 to No.32	13/21	No. 32	Gravel
No. 32 to Site Entry	14/22	No. 32	Gravel

Note: From site entry to operations beach, it is 0.5 mile of offroad terrain, of which the final 220 yards (200m) require a 4-wheel-drive vehicle,

The road in to Thjorsa operations beach.

Figure 41. Detailed travel directions and conditions were issued to all participants to ensure safe and efficient use of time in getting to the site.

command and control of the operation and to provide accommodations for resting and eating, while the offshore facility would provide a platform for divers, their diving equipment, with space also for direct support personnel. A thermal tent was located on shore for the divers to use in warming themselves and working on their gear between dives.

The approach recommended by Cornish to uncover the airplane from its buried position in the riverbed was for the divers first to use a suction hose to vacuum the overburden layer of lava silt, sand, and pumice from around the airframe. Suction was the only feasible approach, he said, because pressure might damage the structure further, particularly the aluminum skins. With the overburden (the relatively loose aggregate making up the top layer of the riverbed) removed, then crowbars and pressure jets could then be used to break up the compacted bed of the river which began, on average, about one foot beneath the overburden layer. Finally, the broken up compacted material would be suctioned up.[70]

Suctioning was the preferred method of removing materials from in and around the plane to prevent damage to the structure, but also because any small, loose parts could be recovered by screening the suctioned materials. The suction equipment would be located on the offshore barge and work in conjunction with a floating-type "sifter" also anchored offshore further from the recovery area. This sifter unit was a floating screen through which all materials sucked from the riverbed would be filtered to trap any parts which

---

[70] Peter J. Cornish, Loc. Cit., p. 5.

might have become separated from the airframe and buried in the riverbed during its entrapped years or which might become separated during the recovery itself.

In his report, Cornish expressed particular concern about the infill propensity of the river. His personal observations underwater, in what he referred to as the excellent viewing conditions prevailing in the month of April, with the ice not yet fully melted and the current at half the rate to be encountered at full flow, showed that the infilling material returned as soon as suctioning ceased. He noted that areas cleared of overburden were fully covered again within 45 minutes (and this was during a time of year when the river was near its slowest flow rates and visibility was at its best). Due to this quick fill-in character of the riverbed, he recommended that a large deep bowl area of the riverbed be removed from around the entire airframe, so that the airframe could be lifted and a sledge put underneath and pulled to shore with the airframe on top. Cornish specifically noted lifting the plane by an overhead means once it was cleared of riverbed materials.[71] This particular strategy for raising the airplane from the riverbed and getting it to shore became a crucial omission that threatened to abort the recovery of the plane in Phase V.

To make this strategy work, Cornish also thought that some type of upstream bulwark or deflector would be required to keep the bowl relatively free of the infilling material throughout the shaping of the bowl and the lifting, floating, and winching of the plane to shore. Cornish was particularly concerned about this situation, because he figured that the left pontoon was embedded in clay as far as 10 feet down in the riverbed. As he saw the situation, a bowl-shaped depression 10 feet deep in the middle would have to be suctioned from around the airplane to free the float and allow the airplane to be sledged to shore.

With so many detailed requirements to be met by the August deadline, the Planning Committee decided to wait and see, under the actual operating conditions found in August, whether the riverbed would fill in faster than material could be removed, when attempting to sustain the necessary cleared area for freeing the airplane. The problem had been discussed with Sevi Bulukin, who was arranging for Norway to supply both high-volume suction and pressure pumps. In these discussions, infilling was treated as a separate issue from the initial requirement to suction the overburden layer from around the plane so as to recover any loose parts.

A two-phase concept was defined. To counter the infilling material after the initial screening, it was thought that by dispersing all suctioned material far enough away from the site, the current would carry it away. With the offshore sifter unit already located away from the recovery site, dispersal would be accomplished by means of a high-pressure hose and nozzle attached on the output side of the sifter screen to create a vortex directing the sand laterally away from the site to be carried away by the river current. It was thought that this combination of suction and pressure dispersal would more than offset the ability of the riverbed to infill itself at the rate it normally occurred, by denying it the material removed.

---

[71] Ibid.

144

As a backup contingency plan, however, Sevi, having been maintenance director of Squadron 330(N) during its WWII operations and being particularly knowledgeable about the pontoon floats (as recounted by his experience with the Icelandic alchemist in Chapter 5), had in mind detaching the airplane from the remaining float if necessary to free it from the float encumbrance for raising. Separating the float would greatly reduce the amount of material to be removed initially and, commensurately, the amount of infill. Cornish's upstream bulwark might not be necessary.

In fact, in a letter to Northrop's Leo Gay on July 8, 1979, Ragnar J. Ragnarsson said:

(I) believe we shall have to detach (the) remaining float from (the) mainplane before lifting (the) airframe. If not possible (to) remove the four brackets (Sevi's area of expertise) securing the float pedestal to the mainplane, propose that this be cut with an oxygen fed underwater cutting device. Have asked the Norwegians to provide this. The float can then be worked on afterwards. Trying to free float while still attached to airframe exposes divers to considerable danger and causes too many difficulties in freeing the airframe from the riverbed.

So Sevi had anticipated this problem and would be arriving at the site with the necessary equipment and knowledge to do something about it. Not having to deal with the float as part of the airplane would greatly simplify digging it out of its riverbed grave. As part of this backup plan, Ragnar requested Leo Gay to bring the tools required to unbolt the brackets holding the float pedestal to the wing mainplane. Gay also provided the wing contour dimensions for two sledges to be made, one for each wing, on which the airplane would rest so it could be winched to shore as Cornish had recommended. Sevi added these sledges to the list of items Norway would supply.

A survey was made of the recovery area on July 12, 1979, and the following conditions recorded: average water level at airframe depth was approximately 5.5 feet (1.70 meters), water temperature +10 Centigrade, airframe completely covered by sand and clay, negligible current in wreck area, visibility zero. Subsequently, the river's discharge was reported to have reduced further.[72] It was felt that only an exceptionally heavy rainfall prior to the recovery operation would have any serious effect on the river's condition from that recorded. So planning was defined accordingly.

At this point of the planning the conditions for recovery were considered to be favorable, and quite exceptional for that time of year. The team figured that a slower current over the wreck would contribute considerably to the ease of the diving operation, and it was not thought necessary to erect a barrier or use special pumping to divert the river's current away from the recovery area.

---

[72] As already noted, a hydroelectric plant had been in operation since 1965, upstream of the site and around the bend in the river, where the Mt. Burfell Hydropower Plant was located. To what extent the Thjorsa's flowrate might have been affected by maintenance of the throughput tunnel for this plant is not known. The flowrate data shown in Figure 39(a), covering a 10-year operational span that begins almost with the activation of the plant, does not indicate any particular pattern attributable to either periodic or corrective maintenance.

The recovery team was scheduled to depart Reykjavik at 1800 hours, Friday, 3 August. Erection of the camp and the various facilities required would commence on arrival at the site. It was anticipated that operations could begin at 1200 hours, Saturday, 4 August, and continue for up to 10 days.

The approach defined in the detailed plan for the recovery operation was to proceed in four evolutionary stages. Though broadly defined, it was thought best to outline the approach and be prepared to adjust it as the stages proceeded, meeting unforeseen situations with solutions as encountered. The team was prepared to improvise, responding to each of the improvisations offered by the river. The recovery of the airframe and its components was projected to take place in the following four stages:

- STAGE I: The tail plane, now detached from the main fuselage section, would be recovered before exposing the wings and fuselage center section. It would be necessary to inspect control cables and make a search for the missing vertical and right horizontal tail surfaces, prior to recovery of the tail-plane, as these might be buried in the riverbed under, or adjacent to, the tail plane.

  It was planned that suction, rather than pressure, be used for exposing the tail plane from the riverbed, in order to trap small objects which might have come loose from the airframe and buried themselves in the riverbed. Having exposed the tail plane from the riverbed, it could be lifted to the surface by means of air-filled drums, and winched ashore.

- STAGE II: The left pontoon, believed to be still attached to the wing center section, and the right pontoon pedestal, possibly also still attached, should be detached prior to an attempt to lift the airframe, in order to avoid as much as possible a prolonged pumping operation, with an unknown quantity of riverbed infill. Should it be intended to expose the airframe with the pontoon attached, the divers would be exposed to considerable danger while working under the airframe to expose the pontoon. The team did not think this was acceptable due to the possibility of the airframe collapsing during the operation and/or a sudden infill of riverbed material should there be a sudden change in the current over the wreck area.

  Suction pumps would be used for removal of sand and clay from within the fuselage, and possibly also from within the wings, should these be found to contain riverbed material. It was also suggested that suction rather than pressure, be applied as much as possible, while exposing the airframe from the riverbed, again in order to trap small objects which might have become detached from the airframe.

  Following its uncovering from the riverbed, the airframe would be lifted to the surface by means of airbags placed under the wing center section and outer panels. The airframe would then be winched ashore strapped to a specially designed sledge placed under the fuselage section.

- STAGE III: Following successful execution of the second stage, an attempt then would be made to uncover the remaining float and the two pedestals (now assumed to be resting separately 5 feet [1.60 meters] below the riverbed). This task would be the most difficult of the entire recovery, because it was expected that the infill of riverbed material would be rapid once trying to extract material below the level of the riverbed. Further, it was likely that sand and clay would have to be removed from within the float, prolonging the operation such that riverbed material would have time to infill again.

- STAGE IV: Following success in Stages I-III, the recovery area would be swept by a magnetic metal detector to locate any objects that might have become detached from the airframe and buried themselves in the riverbed. This task would require availability of both the men and the equipment to be provided by the U.S. Navy's EOD Group, as in Phase II.

- POST-RECOVERY LOGISTICS: Once ashore the wing outer panels would be detached from the wing center section. All parts of the airframe would be placed in wooden supports and taken across the lava field to a point accessible by truck. It was planned that the U.S. Air Force in Iceland would provide helicopter-lifting facilities for transport of the airframe over the stretch of lava terrain covering approximately 200 meters. If not, earthmoving equipment would be required to prepare a track to the site, through the lava field

With these recovery stages planned and for the most part facilitated and ready to implement, the team felt confident success was at hand. Mankind had done its part, now it was up to nature and man's innovative spirit to implement the plan. Basically the team had done what had made Northrop "a good place to work." But at Northrop the starting point was the synergy brought about by the spirit and character of Jack Northrop. Usually working overtime, Northrop didn't eat his meals alone. He used mealtime as a means to break bread and converse with the production line workers in the company cafeteria. He didn't sit back in his office and wonder if everything was working as it should. He wasn't the classic manager who waited for something to go wrong – a simpleminded management technique known as "management by exception." His standard was not "if it works don't try to fix it." His attitude was to look constantly for ways to improve operations, to make things work more efficiently and effectively; in other words, to maximize the synergy so that the airplane as manufactured was at least as good if not better than the aircraft as designed.

Jack Northrop's instinctive management approach, like his design of aircraft, was a precursor of things to come. Today, the aerospace industry manages its multibillion-dollar space and weapon system design, development, test, and manufacturing programs by means of the principle of "management by prediction," not "management by exception." The lesson has been learned that if you don't manage by prediction, you'll be inundated by "exceptions," even as the N-3PB SN320 had gotten trapped by an exception in the weather.

Quite clearly, it is people like Jack Northrop who brought mankind out of the cave into the sunlight of history; and who continue to do so. It was his missionized approach to the aircraft design (such as those shown in Figure 22) that led in the early 1960's to the functional analysis approach to design specified by the U.S. Department of Defense.

Today that approach has been refined into what is known as the mission need analysis approach to design of systems, an approach used by both DOD and NASA. Jack Northrop was a team player; and through his team attitude and practice, made his company a good place to work for years after his retirement. The team would get the results it had planned by putting into effect this same spirit of teamwork.

But somehow in all this formally setaside planning period, the specifics of exactly how the airplane would be lifted once uncovered were still vague. The use of airbags beneath the wings, as planned in Stage II, seemed to conflict with the idea of using an underwing sledge on which to rest the plane and pull it to shore. Cornish had suggested in his Phase III report that what he called a U.S. Air Force "Jolly Green Giant" helicopter be on hand to lift the plane so it could be put on a sledge and winched to shore. Alternatively, Ragnar thought perhaps a crane could be borrowed from the Mt. Burfell Hydropower Plant. But, even assuming a crane could be borrowed, getting it over the last 220-yard stretch of lava bed to the beach would be a major task in itself. The use of airbags, in the manner described, seemed to omit a lot of variables not so easily dismissed.

At this juncture the plan suddenly entered the region of the unknown. There was still too much to be learned about the actual, detailed situation of the plane in its encryptment in the frigid, obfuscated, fast-flowing Thjorsa River, to determine, ahead of the actual event, just how the recovery scenario might play out and how it might end.

CHAPTER 9 - PERFORMING THE RECOVERY MISSION TO PLAN

The detailed plan, once completed, benefited from and summed up the experience of the past two years that, in sequential surveys of the Thjorsa River crash site, had first verified the plane was there; then, that it was in recoverable condition; and finally how it was situated in the riverbed. The plan had been prepared in a special fourth phase of coordination, analysis, and definition that had been specially set aside for that purpose. But would the plan work? As the Scottish poet once said, "The best laid plans of mice and men gang aft agley."[73] But, after all, what is a plan but a beginning, a roadmap to the unknown; and something to be filled in with details as the way unfolds and becomes clear? As noted previously, in the aerospace industry, this approach to detail planning is known as the "rolling wave" concept.

As the date approached to begin operations under the plan, the first problem suddenly loomed: getting a sufficient number of divers. Having the necessary expertise for this function was of primary importance, because of the known and still unknown, yet to be discovered, difficulties posed by the actual underwater situation of the airplane and the river environment, and what might happen when the burial site was disturbed. Divers experienced in working in a strong current flow, low visibility, and near-freezing water, while manipulating suction and pressure hoses in precise directions amidst sharp-edged wreckage, were essential to the success of the recovery.

Ragnar already knew that divers from the U.S. Navy's Explosive Ordnance Disposal (EOD) Group at Keflavik would not be able to participate due to previously scheduled military mission operations. The first major blow to the plan, however, came in early July when Peter J. Cornish wrote Ragnar that he would not be available for the August operation, because he had a commercial salvage contract to fulfill at that time. Cornish was the diver from the British Sub-Aqua Club who had performed the April recovery survey, in which the actual disposition of the airplane in the riverbed had been fully examined and recorded and the feasibility of recovery determined. It was Cornish's timely May 9, 1979 report and recommendations that had made it possible to decide on the final approach to the recovery in terms of all basic requirements and strategy for the approach to the recovery and for personnel, equipment, and, ironically, the best time of year to proceed. As Ragnar reported to the author later:

> Peter's letter informing me that he wouldn't be able to participate...came as a tremendous blow. A commercial operation involving the raising of a fishing trawler off the coast of Scotland had come up and there was no way he was going to make it to Iceland until that was over. Peter Cornish was considered the world's leading expert on recovering aircraft from water, having been involved in

---

[73] Robert Burns, poem titled "To a Mouse; on Turning Her Up in Her Nest with the Plough, November 1785."

the raising of six aircraft and two submarines, all successfully accomplished. Not only had he been appointed the recovery project's diving team leader, but he had also recruited some three or four of his fellow divers from the British Sub-Aqua Club to join the operation in Iceland, all on a volunteer basis. At this point I seriously considered postponing the operation, but quickly came to the conclusion that if I did, that would be the end of it. We'd come too far and if we lost momentum now, all would be lost. Would Northrop even be interested, if the plane couldn't be restored in time for Jack Northrop's 85th birthday, I also had to ask myself.

But as would happen time and again during the recovery operation, it was almost as if the course of the "Northrop Project" was being directed by a mystic force over which I had no control. Several days after receiving Peter's disappointing letter, I received a telephone call from Einar Kristbjornsson, president of the Icelandic Divers Association and himself the owner...of Kofunarthjonustan, an Iceland-based construction and salvage diving company founded by his father. He'd heard about the upcoming recovery project and now offered us the volunteer participation of two divers, himself and Gunnar J. Agustsson, both experienced construction and salvage divers (later, Einar's brother-in-law, Adalsteinn Adalsteinsson would also join the diving team). Einar, a horse of a man, had worked as a construction diver in different parts of the world, including the frigid waters of Greenland. But most importantly for the recovery project, he had an intimate knowledge of the Thjorsa River, having worked on the river on the Burfell hydropower plant, further upstream (from the recovery site), during its construction some 10 years earlier; and, ever since, on the underwater maintenance of the plant, including the regular inspection and cleaning of the plant's penstock. His offer to join the team was a Godsend, if there ever was one. Should I be asked to single out one person to whom the success of the N-3PB recovery is owed, he would have to be the one.[74]

Einar and his divers would make up for Peter Cornish and his divers. The Zen of Restoration was definitely at work in the Icelandic spirit. Ragnar was determined now to proceed and, in fact, had little choice, in that all agreements and arrangements had been concluded with the other international team members for the necessary personnel and equipment, including airlift of the recovered plane to Northrop's facility in the U.S. by the Royal Norwegian Air Force. If the schedule were to be changed now, the project likely would be dropped.

Fortunately, Ragnar had Sevi Bulukin to back his determination. Sevi had been appointed by the Royal Norwegian Air Force to support the recovery project with the best resources available in Norway. This included divers, for whom Norway, a seafaring nation, was noted. Earlier, when Ragnar had been unable to get divers from the U.S. Navy's EOD Group, which had participated in the Phase II and III site surveys but was now committed to Cold War missions, Sevi had gotten two additional divers assigned

---

[74] Ragnar Ragnarsson, The Restoration, Part 3, Review Commentary, dated October 22, 2001.

from the Norwegian Navy, for a total of four. When Einar Kristbjornsson mystically joined the team to take the place of Peter Cornish and his divers, Ragnar's plan was fulfilled to have at least eight divers operating in pairs throughout the day in uncovering the airplane from its burial site in the riverbed of the unrelinquishing Thjorsa.

The two groups of divers now were the Icelanders and the Norwegians, as shown in Figure 37. While both spoke English as a second language, it was natural in the rush and dynamics of the diving operation for the two groups to revert to their native tongues. It was not like two language groups being aboard the Space Shuttle, where everyone is working in the same open area and routine tasks are being performed without environmental duress and all participants have the relative leisure to speak English. The two diving teams had separate underwater areas assigned and used different suctioning equipment; thus the two groups tended to converse in their native tongues within their respective groups. Not only the dynamics of the underwater environment, but the exactness of communication required under such conditions to preclude mistakes in understanding that might adversely impact personal safety further encouraged each group to use its native tongue. As Jan Bulukin reported to the author, as the recovery project proceeded and underwater problems mounted, this tendency to communicate separately increased. This tendency became predominant as the number of Icelandic divers increased from two to four and the area of the riverbed to be sustained against refilling increased in size. As Jan also noted, however, there wasn't much to communicate of a practical nature, considering the zero visibility underwater. The critical mode of communication was the standard international distress code for underwater operations, and all the divers knew that, as their lives depended on it.[75] Nevertheless, international teaming can pose problems due to language when the common task to be performed is dangerous. In Ragnar's situation, however, he had to proceed with the diving personnel available and trust to their expertise and professionalism to get the job done efficiently and safely.

With Norway to provide four divers and a pump support specialist, plus diving equipment and other recovery and personnel support equipment, the Norwegian Air Force's commitment and the Norwegian diving team provided under Sevi were now an essential part of the operations and overall project plan. The Norwegians were to arrive on 1 August and bring with them 15 tons of equipment. In addition to the sleeping accommodation facilities noted previously, the following equipment was brought:

- Suction and pressure pumps to clear the riverbed from around the airplane.
- Air bags capable of being inflated to pontoon the airplane from the riverbed.
- Lifting straps for helicopter transport of recovered aircraft parts over the lava field to a flatbed truck for transport to the Keflavik International Airport.
- An air compressor for filling the diver's air bottles, plus spare bottles.

---

[75] This interesting description of the impact of native language differences on one-time projects involving hazards to personnel safety during their performance was reported to the author by Jan Bulukin in an e-mail dated November 16, 2001.

- A 6-kilowatt, gasoline-engine-powered generator for electrical supply at the site.

- An underwater cutting torch for use in separating parts from the airframe if necessary to free it for flotation.

On Friday, 3 August 1979, the entire 35-man recovery team assembled on the bank of the Thjorsa River, ready to put the recovery plan in operation. The various teams shown in the organization chart (Figure 37) of Chapter 8 went immediately to work on their assignments. The diving team launched its offshore barge with the pumping equipment aboard. The camp services and supply team put up the tents, lighting and electrical generator. Each person was assigned a sleeping cot. Each team checked out its equipment for satisfactory operation. Everyone was ready to begin the recovery at sunrise. Including transportation personnel and observers, over 40 people were present.

Back in July, when Ragnar learned that Peter Cornish would not be able to join the expedition with his diving team, Einar Kristbjornsson – Cornish's mystically appearing replacement – with his customary energy and initiative had reviewed the planned recovery approach and, knowing from experience, the nature and characteristics of the Thjorsa River, particularly in the recovery area, had discovered that the approach did not address the river's principal threats and challenges to the success of the operation. At the increased river depth, faster flow rate, and lower visibility conditions to be encountered in the month of August, a much more powerful device was needed to suction the riverbed up at rates faster than the river could infill. This device not only had to have a high-volume rate of material throughput, but it had to be able to apply enough suction to cut through the loose overburden layer quickly and, without pause, both break up and suction up the compacted secondary layer of the riverbed – all in one step. In effect, the river had to be challenged on its own terms, or else it would never give back what it was taking.

Einar's device, depicted with the purely mechanical pump in Figure 42, operated on a basic principle of physics known as hydrodynamic pressure differential, which requires only a differential flow of air pressure to generate a force capable of lifting a material mass underwater. The suction pumps to be provided by Norway were electromechanically driven to generate suction while submerged. Whereas Einar's device could be designed to suction large quantities of material simply by sizing the diameter of the pipe and the air volume to produce the required performance, the mechanical pumps depended on gear ratios and generally smaller throughputs of suctioned materials to preclude jamming. The Norwegian pumps would be adequate for suctioning the loose overburden layer of the riverbed, which, as Cornish had observed, at most averaged about a foot in depth, but would tend to bog down when entering the primary compacted layer, where if pressed too hard, they would likely jam. Once jammed these pumps would have to be shut down and brought to the surface for cleaning – a process that could take up to two hours. Under such performance restrictions, hollowing out the riverbed into the bowl-shape recommended by Cornish for floating the airplane for lifting would be extremely time consuming if not impossible. The plane could only be freed by means of fast, sustained, multilayer suctioning capability, given the underwater conditions imposed by the Thjorsa.

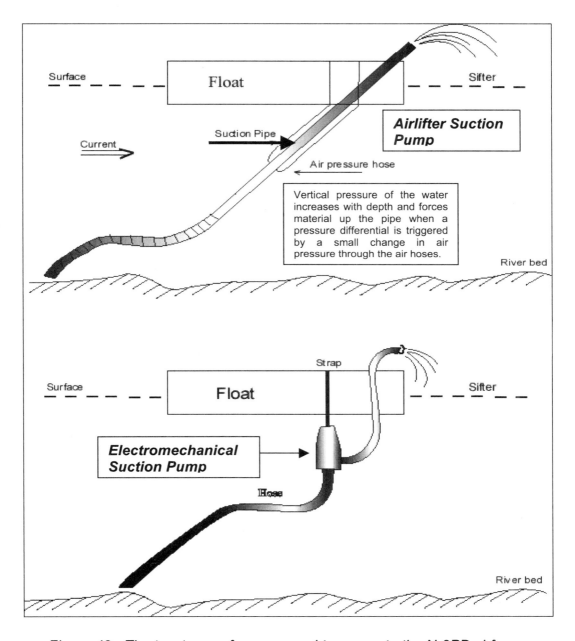

Figure 42. The two types of pumps used to excavate the N-3PB airframe provided a complementary capability for fast high-volume and slower, but more precise low-volume excavation of the riverbed and infilling materials, in the Airlifter and Electromechanical pumps, respectively.

Einar knew how to do this by means of a simple tube device he called the "Airlifter." The physical principle on which this device operates is that as one goes deeper in a fluid, the pressure increase due to the weight of the fluid; for example, the pressure of the earth's atmosphere is 14.7 psi at sea level, but decreases with altitude until above 15,000 feet the air is noticeably thinner and getting enough air when moving is difficult for the average person. In water, the pressure differential is much greater, increasing at the rate of 62.4 pounds for every cubic foot of depth. Einar's device, sticking vertically in the river at a depth of 10 feet, experienced a differential water pressure of 624 pounds per square foot at the submerged end. By applying enough air volume within the pipe near its bottom end to evacuate the water column within the pipe, the pressure differential sought immediate release up and through the pipe. Any material in the path of the inrushing water would be carried along, exiting at the upper end. Objects weighing over 120 pounds could be sucked up if small enough to enter the pipe. Since silt, sand, and broken pieces of compacted riverbed were the objects sought, massive amounts of riverbed could be sucked up in the continuous flow of water from the bottom of the river to the top. The extremely beneficial ingenuity of this device is that it had no moving parts to get clogged, as did the electromechanical type pump.

The principle applied is the same as that which makes a straw work. Einar applied this suction principle in a tube with large enough diameter and length – and integrated functionally with high enough air volume – such that large volumes of material could be sucked up and dispersed into a sifter screen, where any small airplane parts were separated before the material was returned to the river and carried off by the current away from the site. The design concept was elegant! With enough air pressure, the device could continuously erode the compacted primary layer of the riverbed and exhaust it out through the pipe. This device was called the "Airlifter" to set it apart from the standard, mechanically limited, centrifugal type electromechanical suction pumps requested from and supplied by Norway.

The suctioning power that "Airlifter" provided for the recovery is indicated by its size. The tube, made of aluminum pipe with ¼-inch wall thickness, was 20 feet in length and 6 inches in diameter. Air pressure differential was generated inside the pipe at two stages, with the initiating stage two feet from the suction end of the pipe and a boost stage at three feet. Installed on the barge anchored directly above the airframe, the pipe was long enough and rugged enough that it could reach the deeper offshore side of the recovery site, in water that was 12-15 feet deep, or the shallower shoreward side in 10 feet of water, and still provide enough length projecting to direct the output for sifting. With a flexible hose attached at the submerged end, the diver could move about the riverbed to excavate a large area during one dive.

The two types of suction pumps were, in applicational use at the site, complementary, especially at the outset of the excavation process. The electromechanical pump was effective on the loose overburden layer of the riverbed in exposing the airframe and cleaning out the recesses, cavities, and compartments where silt and sand seeped in and gathered recurringly. The "Airlifter" was the big gun and took over where large volumes of material had to be moved fast. Use of the more powerful device occurred almost always where the loose overburden gave way to the compacted primary layer of the riverbed.

As the excavation proceeded steps were taken to increase the material removal capacity of both types of pumps, to stay up with the increased amount of impacted material required to be removed and, as the site hollowed out, to keep the river from infilling. Excavation began with the "Airlifter" using a 300-cubic-foot, high-pressure air compressor that was loaned by the Burfell hydroelectric powerplant where Einar worked as maintenance diver periodically. A 380-cubic-foot compressor loaned by a Reykjavik-based construction company soon supplemented this compressor. By the fourth day it was necessary to replace the initial compressor with a 600-cubic-foot unit and bring the total high-pressure volume to 980 cubic feet, to meet the accelerating rate of excavation required to hollow the site and fight infilling. A similar increase in capability was sought for the mechanical pumps, both to enable them to process the compacted material and cleanout infilling material faster.

The divers and their equipment were fighting not only the river, but the airframe itself, which, through its years of gradual submergence and eventual burial, had become infilled in every crevice, cavity, and compartment into which silt and sand could seep. Though never measured, it was estimated by those working with the airframe at the site that it had gained perhaps an additional three tons of weight over its original weight of two tons, over the 36 years the Thjorsa had tried to lay claim to it. With the added overburden and compacted layers of riverbed, the airplane, as buried, may have added up to 10 tons of material. It would have been impossible to lift the plane by any means than to rid it of this extra weight by first excavating it down to its basic structure, just as though it were an archeological specimen. As Cornish had noted in his Phase III survey report about the condition of the airframe: "Eighty percent of its structure is there in the river – bent, torn and now very friable."[76] Jan Bulukin, in correspondence with the author, expressed the same thought, that if an attempt were made to lift the airframe without first excavating it clear of the riverbed and the overburden of sand and silt, it would break into pieces.[77] Jan's "break into pieces" is obviously what Cornish meant by the word "friable."

Both Peter Cornish and Jan Bulukin may be viewed as qualified witnesses of the condition of the plane, because both were highly experienced salvage divers and had many hours of contact underwater with the N-3PB at its burial site in the Thjorsa. Over a three-day period at the end of April, Cornish had spent about 10 hours underwater at the site, uncovering the plane of overburden, examining it, and sizing up its general underwater layout and situation, all under what he called superb conditions of visibility. At the same site in what was now August, Jan Bulukin would make an average of eight dives per day over a six-day period, accumulating 24 hours underwater. While he would never see the plane, by examining it by touch and by the feel about him of the dense, gritty harshness of the water constantly flowing past – combined with the gradual, but

---

[76] Peter J. Cornish, Loc. Cit., p. 5.
[77] Jan Bulukin, e-mail dated June 21, 2001

relentless shifting compaction of the sand and silt integrating the sundered structure as part of the riverbed – he could sense that the plane was in a critically fragile state.

The plane had come to rest in the riverbed about ¼-mile from where it had crashed, to the north, where the river bends abruptly eastward for another fourth mile, then north again. Its final resting place was fortunate in one respect and a drawback in another. On the positive side, the location was in a slightly recessed area of the shore where the current had built up a sandy beach that sloped gradually into the water. This area provided a most suitable location for the recovery operations to be supported with tents for sleeping and eating and for parking the vehicles and setting up the area lighting, generators, and air compressors. The general layout of what came to be known as "Camp Northrop" is shown in Figure 43. A similarly accommodating location was not available any where else along the contiguous west shore, most of which consisted of sharply ridged lava blocks and lava flow angling abruptly or sloping jaggedly into the river. In the operations area, the river was within about one-half mile of the main road and utility vehicles could make it to the operations beach by crossing the 220-yard lava flow that marked the terminal part of the terrain between road and beach.

But while the location was fortunate from an operational command and control aspect, it was all the more troublesome for the divers and the excavation process. With the east-west bend in the river just a quarter mile above the operations beach, the current tended to sweep harder along the west shore as it flowed southerly again coming off the bend, bringing with it a heavier load of silt and sand that accelerated infill as well as obscured visibility underwater. Cornish had reported that in the preceding April, visibility underwater was about 1.5 feet, "superbly clear" he said for a river like the Thjorsa, but, taking into account the time of year, a condition not likely to prevail as the ice thawed and the current increased along with the depth of the water.[78] By the August timeframe, Cornish forecast that the visibility would reduce to zero as the current flow doubled to over 5 mph.

Jan Bulukin verified these conditions; saying in his report to the author that the divers worked utterly blind in water so "milky" you couldn't see your hand before your mask. A flashlight was useless. Every task and action underwater had to be done solely by feel and a diver had to be constantly reminding himself where he was relative to the airframe so as not to cut himself or his suit or airline on jagged pieces of metal or get tangled in the numerous lines ascending from the airframe to floats on the surface or attached airbags. Once the diver was submerged in the fluid invisibility of the river and hanging onto a rope or piece of protruding airframe to keep from being swept away by the current, he became so disoriented that it was difficult to confer with the other divers about the location where he had worked. Each diver had to devise his own touch-and-go system to get back to where he had previously been excavating.[79]

At the recovery site, this condition of zero visibility was probably at its worst due (1) to the overburden of silt and sand laid down on the west shore by the sweeping current

---

[78] Peter Cornish, Loc. Cit., p. 1.
[79] Jan Bulukin, Loc. Cit.

Cato Guhnfeldt

Ragnar J. Ragnarsson

Figure 43. Camp Northrop, showing the layout of equipment at the recovery site on the Thjorsa: Top, the barge float tethered off the north point in full current flow; Bottom, on the beach, looking east, across the river, from the lava flow. The water, higher than in the April survey, ripples along at 5 mph.

157

and (2) the increased flow rate for August, which lifted the overburdens looser, lighter particles and kept them suspended in the water. Conversely, where Cornish had experienced a slower flow rate and some close-in visibility, the divers on the final recovery operation experienced a faster flow rate and zero visibility.

However, there was another converse relationship between the April and August time periods that proved of some advantage to the divers on the final recovery operations. Whereas Cornish had experienced immediate infilling of those areas of the site excavated to examine the condition and layout of the airframe, infilling in the August operation, though still a problem, was not nearly so fast. As Ragnar said, in commenting on the author's early draft of this book:

> While infill did present a problem, it did not present a major obstacle. The infill was relatively light (in weight) and uncompacted material that did not present much added weight to the airframe in the water. It was a cause for some delays, because each morning a couple of hours had to be spent pumping out the material that had filled in during the night before, so that "digging" further down could be resumed. As the hole grew larger and deeper, the current in the area increased and so did the infill. To overcome this, we moved startup time in the morning forward by two hours, from 8 to 6 a.m. and at the same time replaced one of the two compressors with a larger one. The real problem lifting the plane was caused by the fact that the weight of the airframe was far greater than we had anticipated and in the shallow water the airbags lacked the buoyancy to successfully lift it from the bottom of the river. While much of the sand and silt had been removed from what remained of the fuselage interior, the wing center section and port outer wing panel were tightly packed with glacial clay. The only way to remove this was by removing the aluminum surface skin of the wing, but by doing so under the prevailing conditions in near-zero visibility would probably have caused untold damage to the wing structure. So it wasn't the infill creating the added weight. That could be removed. The problem was the material within the wing structure.[80]

Why, in August, was infilling no longer the problem Cornish had reported it to be in April? The reason was that the faster flow rate, in combination with the higher water level, kept the overburden in suspension longer. The water, in effect, now had more volume to contain suspended matter and more speed to keep it waterborne. In sum, these environmental factors taking place in the river due to the seasonally warmer weather gave the river increased capacity to sustain more particulate matter in suspension, thereby

---

[80] The author questioned Ragnar's attributing the weight problem to riverbed infill trapped in the airframe, in particular the wing, which on being opened by Northrop during the restoration revealed no infill; in fact, Harris Stone, who restored the wing, found a California lizard still inside from 1940 when the airplane was built. The wing portions still attached to the fuselage were well sealed and would not have been accessible for cleaning prior to their return to Northrop, unless disassembled in Iceland. As subsequently shown in this chapter, the author makes a case analytically that the weight attributed to infill was only apparent, the real source being the capillary force drawing the airframe to the riverbed.

actually aiding the divers to contend with their relentlessly recurrent, toilsome problem, infill. However, as subsequent events would show, while the rate of infilling was slower in the Thjorsa's August current, the difference from April was actually a change in deposition rate of infill over time; thus if a given amount of infill took one minute in April, in August it might take one hour. What the divers discovered is that what they had excavated during the day was to a large extent filled in again overnight, so that each morning the day began by having to clean out excavated areas before new digging could be accomplished. When Cornish surveyed the wreck in Phase III, complete infilling had occurred within 45 minutes. Now, though slower, the amount would be greater.

Fortunately, due to Einar's design innovativeness and Trygve Skaug's archeological knowledge and experience, the divers were well-equipped and staffed to suction the riverbed at high rates of excavation. Now, with the river itself helping to hold suspended matter in its waterborne state over longer periods of time, Einar's mass-volume "airlifter," working in partnership with the mechanical rotary pumps, would be able to reduce the infill problem to the early morning tidying up noted by Ragnar as necessary before the compacted primary bed of the river could be once more attacked during the remainder of each day. As the recovery moved ahead over its total of nine days, the teamwork between the two types of suctioning systems increased and became virtually like an orchestrated drill; Einar's big gun "Airlifter" moved in advance breaking up the compacted riverbed and suctioning up the larger pieces of material as the smaller capacity Norwegian pumps followed to enlarge the bowl in a cleanup sweep.

Thus, through teaming between man and nature, was the methodology for excavating the airframe perfected. Again it was the combination of teamwork between man, his machines, and nature that made a mission impossible achievable. As Ragnar indicated earlier, it was almost mystical the way "time and again during the recovery operation" forces greater than his own stepped in to solve the seemingly unsolvable problems. As throughout, the Zen of Restoration was at work, bringing man into his natural teaming relationship with his nature and that of nature itself – in this case the Thjorsa acting as nature's agency in not only giving up what it was noted for taking, but helping to do so. What a team!

But the actual implementation of the recovery would not proceed without problems. There were many unknowns yet to be uncovered. While the equipment and the people would remain the same, the plan would have to be updated and changed virtually daily. Even as the river flowed past relentlessly, changes below, where the airframe was trapped, were as relentless. As would be found, the excavation concept would have to be changed twice from its original formulation and eventually abandoned for a more radical alternative. This revision and eventual total rewrite of the plan came about as the Thjorsa showed how resisting it could be in giving up what it had tried to take. In essence, the problem of infill was more complex than had been thought, simply because the river worked at its "taking" 24 hours a day, while man had to rest.

In Einar's demonstration of the capabilities of the "Airlifter" on the first day, it was at once evident that this device would set the pace and strategy for excavating the plane. Accordingly, the divers were in agreement immediately that Einar was to be the expedition's overall diving team leader, as the IAHS Planning Committee had planned when Einar joined the project team. The highly experienced salvage and archeological diver, Trygve Skaug, of Norway, was to be the Norwegian team leader. As a member of the Norwegian Maritime Museum, Trygve Skaug had many years of experience on a variety of underwater recovery projects involving recovery of historical ships, including the raising of a 1,000-year-old Viking ship. He participated in at least two underwater recovery projects each year.

The offshore platform was the central base for the excavation operations of the divers. Known as the "barge," it was both a necessary offshore base camp for the divers and point of deployment for the pumps and the material sifter. The barge is shown in Figure 44, at its offshore anchorage, with Ragnar J. Ragnarsson, the project director, and Sevi Bulukin, Norway's team leader conferring in the foreground. The barge was made by attaching a wooden platform to an 8- by 25-foot skiff (combination sail and rowboat) with Styrofoam blocks as outriggers. The barge was then moored directly over the buried airplane by lines running to anchors set in the riverbed. The mooring lines served also as handholds for the divers as they moved about in the current over the burial site.

Leo Gay

Figure 44. Ragnar J. Ragnarsson (left) and Sevi Bulukin on 4 August 1979, the first day of the final recovery of N-3PB Serial No. 320, discussing the approach to raising the airplane with the left pontoon still attached. Offshore is the diver's platform barge.

There were two air compressors and one generator located on shore. From the latter, a line was run to the barge to power area lighting for night operations from the barge. The two air compressor sets provided compressed air to operate the Norwegian rotary suction pump and Einar's "airlifter." The 20-foot "Airlifter" suction tube was operated from the barge, while the Norwegian pump was a submersible that could be located on the riverbed with a suction hose for the diver to move about with and apply in specific suctioning tasks. The high-volume "Airlifter" was steered on its suctioning pathway by a diver stationed at the submerged end, while suctioned materials exhausted at the barge flowed into a sifter that separated any aircraft pieces and parts prior to dispersal of the screened material into the river current away from the site. The mechanical pump similarly dispersed its suctioned material away from the site, while the suction unit was submersed on the riverbed.

As scheduled, Sevi had arrived in Iceland on Wednesday with his nine-man team, flying from Norway in a Royal Norwegian Air Force C-130 Hercules transport. Besides the five-man diving team headed by Trygve Skaug, he brought three of his former teammates of Squadron 330(N), one who had flown the N-3PB and two, Kjell Christiansen and Richard Thomassen, who had worked as mechanics when Sevi was Deputy technical director of the squadron. Richard, according to Ragnar, was obviously there, as a benign gesture on Sevi's part, being quite frail healthwise and dependent on a handcarried life-support system of medicine that he regularly took from a portable medicine chest. While skeptical of Richard's capability to endure the rigors of a week's campout on a remote section of the Thjorsa River and, as project director, concerned about Richard's safety and the possible emergency that his health might cause in the midst of an expedition, Ragnar finally relented. He already faced uncertainties analogous to those of a commando foray into enemy territory, but he accepted this veteran's participation when he realized, after discussing the matter with Richard, that Richard's just being there again in Iceland, after 36 years, was a form of restoration for another human being. After that, Ragnar, couldn't shake his empathetic feeling for this man who was so joyous at being back where he had once been as a member of a more important expeditionary force – one in which he had fought for the restoration of his homeland. It turned out that Ragnar's decision was no mistake, for Richard, having been an expert mechanic on the N-3PB's of Squadron 330(N) throughout its operational tour in Iceland, knew every detail part of the airplane by name if not by part number.

Ragnar's empathy with and compassion for Richard is revealed in his own recounting of Richard's valuable presence in the midst of the recovery project that, for Richard, was a form of restoration of himself:

> Not to disturb team members during the night when every couple of hours he had to get up to take his medicine, Richard had brought his own little tent along. This he put up in the sand dunes beyond the ridge above the main camp, a small Norwegian flag flying from its forward pole. This was immediately dubbed "Little Norway." At no time was Richard a burden to me or anyone else on the team. On the contrary he turned out to be quite a valuable asset. When the divers started bringing up parts of the aircraft from the river, these were placed in

a fenced off area on the beach. Here Richard would handle them with compassion, his eyes gleaming with joy, and without the slightest hesitation, identify even the most obscure bits and pieces no one else could. He knew the N-3PB like the fingers of his hand, and I think he could have done it blindfolded. What a guy! Shortly after he returned to Norway, Richard passed away, the happier for the time he spent at the Thjorsa River. I'm sorry that he never got to see the plane after it was restored. That would really have made his day.[81]

It's clear that Richard Thomassen shared the same feelings for the restoration effort that were evident in Ragnar and the rest of the team. For him the airplane remained as fully assembled and operationally ready in his mind as on the days during WWII when he had watched it take off from Fossvogur Bay and then waited, listening for its return hours later for him to ready it for the next flight. Often the fight for freedom is more memorable than the victory.

The weather was cool for August, averaging 40-to-50F during the day and dropping to just above freezing at night. Water for drinking and cooking was drawn by hand from a stream nearby by the husband and wife team that operated the kitchen. Both were chefs at Reykjavik's most posh hotel, the Hotel Saga, and always had food, hot tea and coffee, and mess kits ready at mealtime, breakfast, lunch, and dinner for the usually famished team. The food services were remembered for their quality by all team members ever afterwards, and observers were not joking when they asked if there was something they could sign up for to stay at the site and enjoy the fare. The work- and weather-whetted appetites of all participants were more than satisfied throughout the recovery operation.

All food was donated by some 20 local foodstuff distributors and processing companies. Between 3 and 4 a.m. each day, the camp manager sent one of his people to the nearby town of Selfoss to get milk and dairy products set aside especially for the expedition by the local diary, after which a stop would be made at the local bakery to pick up freshly baked bread and other baked goods. The kitchen at the site, a fully mobile unit mounted on the chassis of a British Bedford 4x4 army vehicle, was loaned by Arena Tours, a safari tour company based in Reykjavik. The unit was humorously dubbed the "Kwitcherbitchenkitchen."

In general, the recovery of the "Northrop" was receiving a lot of attention on the Island. As shown in Appendix D, over 50 individuals and 100 businesses contributed time, material, and logistical support. Many got involved because of the newspaper accounts of the return to Iceland of Sevi Bulukin and three Royal Norwegian Air Force crewmembers of the acclaimed Squadron 330(N). Newspapers had noted them flying into Reykjavik airport on an RNoAF C-130 with an expert diving team aboard, just for the recovery project. As Ragnar related to the author:

> There was hardly a person in the country who didn't know what was taking place at the Thjorsa River. Cato Guhnfeldt, a reporter from Norway's leading evening newspaper, *Aftenposten*, and a member of the Norwegian Aviation

---

[81] Ragnar J. Ragnarsson, Loc. Cit.

Historical Society, was already at the site and reporting back to Norway, as were representatives of international news agencies such as Reuters, etc. ....[82]

Two years later, in 1981, a book about the N-3PB and its mission operations in Iceland would be published in the Norwegian language with Cato Guhnfeldt as author.[83]

A week before the recovery operation was formally scheduled to begin, Ragnar had a construction crew at the operations site, to build the sledge that Cornish had recommended as the way to bring the airframe to shore without further damage. The sledge was designed to fit under the airbag-elevated airframe like a pair of skis and then be winched to shore with the airframe attached piggyback. By the time the entire recovery team arrived at the site on the starting date, everything was ready to set up so operations could begin the next morning.

Operationally, the plan was to excavate the airframe clear of the riverbed and then lift it by attaching airbags to its upper surface, but only after both float pedestals had been separated from the wing mainplates. Due to the potential for infilling of a large hollowed out bowl around the plane, Ragnar had decided that Cornish's idea of raising the plane with the left float intact would be too time consuming and probably not even feasible. By separating the float pedestals at the wing, the airframe would be unencumbered for lifting and a smaller area of the riverbed would have to be excavated. Then the pedestals and the left float could be excavated and recovered separately. The underwater cutting torch had been brought by the Norwegian team to separate the pedestals from the wing; and the 20-foot "Airlifter" had been designed and built specifically to suction through 10 feet of water to the riverbed and then another 10 feet if necessary to the bottom of the left float.

So with the excavation and infill requirements met by the combination of suction pumps, the first operational objective was to apply this equipment so as to expose the float pedestals. Because the condition of the float pedestals and the left float had not yet been established, even by Cornish's detailed underwater examination of the airframe's condition and layout in April, the initial excavation activity was aimed at this objective.

The first day of excavation, however, was devoted to checking out the effectiveness of the suction equipment in various locations over the entire site, so as to get generally oriented as to the best deployment of the equipment relative to the distribution of the airframe beneath the barge and the overburden of riverbed to be removed. While Einar's objective was to establish the best operational plan for the use of the "Airlifter" in coordination with the smaller-volume mechanical pump, Trygve's objective was to define an overall profile of the airframe's burial situation and site in the riverbed so that the excavation could be approached quite logically as an archeological dig. Just as the two suction systems were turning out to be complementary and able to work together as a team, so the two diving team leaders were finding that their respective areas of expertise

---

[82] Ragnar J. Ragnarsson, Loc. Cit.

[83] Cato also attended the Northrop rollout ceremony for the restored N-3PB at the Northrop Corporation plant in Hawthorne, California, in 1980. Representing the NAHS, he wrote a letter of appreciation to Northrop, addressed to Northrop's Darrell McNeal, who headed the restoration phase project. The letter, shown in Appendix J, is quoted in Chapter 13.

were complementary and could be unified to make the operation unfold effectively. Einar was an underwater construction and salvage diver and Trygve Skaug was a marine archeologist. The two professions found an ideal merger in tackling the Thjorsa to take back Norway's N-3PB seaplane as a trophy commemorating Squadron 330(N) and its homeland mission in Iceland during WWII.

Sevi had brought a scale model of the N-3PB with him from Norway for use in briefing all the personnel working directly on the recovery, particularly the divers, on what they were looking for in the silt-laden water and how the plane was situated and pointing in the riverbed. For the first time, by means of this model, everyone on the team could see what it was they were after and the complexity of the task posed by the N-3PB configuration. Sevi had used the model to brief his son, Jan, in Norway, and Jan had suggested that the model be taken with them to the site so that all the divers could be oriented in what the plane actually looked like.

Sevi described the remaining left-hand pontoon in detail, in particular how it was attached to the airplane by special brackets he had made in 1942. Clearing this pontoon – or detaching it from the airplane – was the first major objective. Getting it uncovered was the key to raising the wing and fuselage intact. He gave each diver instructions on how to proceed once the pontoon pedestal was cleared. Because the huge pontoon constituted a form of anchor, detaching it from the plane seemed the logical approach, so that the airframe could be raised without it. Then the pontoon could be raised separately; but keeping the attachment brackets free of infiltrating silt while removing them might be an impossible task, especially with only one diver at a time able to work in such close quarters and visibility near zero. Without sharing his thoughts and his memory of the brackets as a maintenance problem when he had been Deputy Technical Officer of Squadron 330(N), Sevi secretly wished that the brackets had failed over the years and the pontoon was no longer attached. He could picture the tremendous task ahead for the divers, based on his son's description of the underwater scene.

Though Sevi harbored hopes that the pontoon was not there, the British underwater salvage expert, Cornish, who had examined the airplane in detail the previous April, had reported that it appeared the pontoon was still in place. Cornish, Sevi thought, probably had reached this conclusion because of the airplane's portside list he had seen during his dives. The existence or nonexistence of this pontoon was something the team needed to know first, because that knowledge would greatly impact the scope and magnitude and hence the duration of the subsequent activity necessary to raise the plane.

As Cornish had noted in his report, he figured that if the pontoon were attached it would have to be over five feet deep in the riverbed. In other words, add five feet to the depth of the water and that's how far beneath the surface of the river the divers would have to be working, but only if the pontoon were still attached. The question concerning this pontoon was immensely important, because as Cornish had determined, one foot down on the left side of the airplane the riverbed entered a stratum of virtually solid clay and special tools would be needed to break it up. If it were necessary to dig out this pontoon, it would be a time-consuming and tedious process descending through four feet of clay with the river constantly backfilling as the divers fought their way downward struggling against the current in limited visibility – it was almost a nightmare to think about it; but, as always, if it was still there, a way would be found to free it.

Both Sevi and Ragnar felt that Cornish was probably right in assuming the pontoon was still attached to the airplane, because, after all, back in 1942, Sevi had had that Icelandic metallurgical alchemist mix a specially strong blend of metals for the brackets that held the pontoons to their pedestals and the pedestals to the wing. Since the pontoon had been attached the last time Sevi saw the airplane in 1943, right after the crash into the river, he felt it was reasonable to assume it was still there. The list of the airplane toward the shore seemed to indicate that the plane was more firmly anchored on the left side, where the pontoon would be, than on the right, where he knew there was no pontoon.

Site activation was the objective on August 3, the day of arrival at the site. Most of the team worked late into the night setting up the tents, lighting, and operations equipment and getting the barge ready to move to its anchorage in the river. By daybreak the next morning, the operations beach looked very much like the view shown earlier in Figure 27.

"D-Day" (Day One of the Recovery Plan) officially began at 9 a.m. on Saturday, August 4, 1979. The first schedule milestone of the day was to begin excavating the airframe at 12:00 noon. It was "high noon" of the "mission impossible."

The first morning task was anchoring the diver's barge over the excavation site, attaching the anchor lines to anchors positioned in the riverbed a week earlier, when the construction crew for the sledge went to the operations beach. Next, a diver's briefing was conducted by Einar to outline the objectives and tasks for the day. Excavating would begin by exploring three of the main target areas of the airframe: (1) the port wing on the beachside of the site, to determine whether the pontoon was still attached; (2) the detached tail section, to determine its disposition in the riverbed and integrity for lifting as an integral assembly; and (3) the fuselage crew compartment area, to begin the removal of silt and sand so as to lighten the integrated wing-fuselage assembly in preparation for lifting.

At 11:50 a.m. Einar entered the water, followed by the first shift of divers, and at 12:05 p.m., 15 minutes later, excavation pumping began. Mission impossible was already five minute behind schedule, but everyone on the beach and on the barge was elated when the compressors began loading up and the sight and sound of suctioning began. The team was functioning!

The Icelandic and Norwegian diving teams constituted two squads organized to maintain continuous excavation at two underwater locations. Such excavation activity can be dangerous under the best of underwater conditions for visibility, temperature, and current. When zero visibility, near freezing water, fast current, tangled ropes, and jagged edges of unseen metal are the normal conditions, such excavation can be extremely dangerous, even in relatively shallow water. To maximize diver safety, no more than two divers were allowed underwater at one time and each was assigned to separately controllable, nonadjacent excavation areas. Each was connected by a cord at the waist that ran back to shore where a second diver monitored the cord for any signal that the diver in the water was in distress. For this reason, all the divers had to know the standard international diving distress signals that constitute a form of sign language communicating the distress situation. If a distress signal was received, a third diver on standby (already suited up and having only to throw on air bottles and a lead weightbelt) would immediately enter the water and follow the signal cord to the diver in distress.

Jan Bulukin reported that at this particular site, it was fortunate that no one got into any really serious situations requiring rescue, because with the current, the signal cord continuously got tangled in the wreckage and transmitting interpretable signals would have been difficult and, if the line was snagged, impossible. The main hazard for a diver underwater at the site was getting tangled in the many ropes ascending from the airframe and the site, some connecting airbags to lift the airframe and others running from anchors to the barge. In getting untangled a diver might cut himself or pierce his diving suit on jagged pieces of the fuselage extending as much as three feet above the riverbed as the overburden was removed. As Jan pointed out, "It was imperative to keep your head cool. Any combination of getting stuck, together with panic or equipment failure (for instance, an air regulator) under such conditions would surely result in immediate disaster."[84]

The signal cord was used also use by a diver when normally coming out of the water, so that the standby diver could enter and follow the cord to the excavation location and take over the suction pump, that way minimizing any delay in suctioning that might allow infilling to negate what had already been accomplished. Thus, in total, three divers were working as an excavation team at any one time, one in the water, one monitoring the signal cord, and one on standby for the next shift in the water or to respond to any signal of distress. As a diver left the water and his standby entered, the monitoring diver became the standby diver and the fourth backup diver took over as monitor. The diver who has just left the water then was "off-duty" to rest for awhile, but then went back to work on any of a number of chores: operating the compressor for breathing air and filling air bottles, maintaining the suction compressor and hose, mending diving suits.

Typically, the Icelandic divers used a diving helmet and air-filled dry suit whereas the Norwegians wore scuba gear. The air-filled dry gear is more comfortable, but more cumbersome and more difficult to manage if punctured, because then the suit fills with water and a buoyancy compensator has to be activated to maintain stability of air pressure inside the suit so the diver does not lose orientation control (perhaps turning upside down). But the air-filled gear was appropriate for underwater operations with the "Airlifter" suction system because the diver could operate at a distance from the suction target, whereas with the mechanical pumps the Norwegians had to work close in to the suction target. The larger-volume "Airlifter" was more suited for broad area suctioning, whereas the mechanical system was for detail areas.

After lunch at the Kwitcherbitchinkitchen on Day One of excavating, while the diving teams continued working toward their first assigned objectives, Ragnar, Leo Gay, Jan Bulukin, Orn Hardarson, and Photographer Baldur Sveinsson, accompanied Sevi Bulukin to the farm Asolfsstadir where he and Leif Rustad had found help on that fateful

---

[84] Jan Bulukin, Loc. Cit.

spring day in 1943. Farmer Asolfur Palsson greeted Sevi on the same front door steps the two had met on 36 years earlier, following Sevi's and Rustad's two-mile walk to get there. It was a historical moment. After an instinctive embrace, they stood at arms length smiling silently at one another in worthy appreciation of the original event that had introduced them to each other, the years that had elapsed, and the opportunity that life had given them to meet again. Again the Zen of Restoration was at work. It had been a mission impossible before on a world scale and now had zoomed in on the recovery project on the Thjorsa. Ragnar's sense of the mystic force embracing and overseeing the project, linking past and present in a transcending restoration, was instantly recharged. Later, Sevi took Cato Guhnfeldt to the farm to meet Farmer Palsson and to provide Cato background for the book he was to write.

By 2:30 p.m. they had returned to the operations beach. Just as they arrived, the divers excavating the cockpit area brought up the first parts from the river. These were treasure everyone had to see. In one of his many feats of recall, Richard Thomassen immediately stepped forward to identify them as a cockpit heater valve and its solenoid switch.

Prior to this, the problem that Einar had anticipated with the mechanical pumps had made itself evident. The Norwegian team had trouble excavating the tail section, which as Cornish had reported was buried at a cocked angle descending downward through the overburden and into the compacted primary layer of the riverbed. Working around the section, the Norwegians had cleared away a substantial portion of the overburden, but on entering the compacted layer, their pump jammed, not able to process the larger chunks into which the compacted material tended to break.

Taken to the surface, the pump was inspected by Trygve Skaug, who determined that the pressure pump was not powerful enough to break up the compacted riverbed material for suctioning and dispersal into the current flow. Trygve recommended to Einar that a more powerful pump be obtained, possibly from a local fire department, and that in the meantime, now that the pump had been unclogged, to use the unit in the overburden area only, where the riverbed was less compacted. In conferring with Einar, Trygve also recommended that the powerful "Airlifter" be concentrated on the tail section, as, from an archeological standpoint, that section, being downstream of the wing-fuselage assembly in the current flow, ought to be raised from the river first to keep it from being further damaged from excavation activity upstream of it.

Accordingly, with the mechanical pump ready to go back in action, Einar reassigned excavation operations with the "Airlifter" from the port wing task of locating the pontoon, to the uncovering of the tail section for removal from the river; and assigned the Norwegians to the fuselage, where the material in the cockpit was a loose, smaller aggregate that the mechanical pump was capable of handling at its present level of throughput pressure. Discussing the proposed solution with Ragnar, Einar was able to get Sigurdur P. Hardarson, the expedition's resourceful procurement officer, dispatched to locate a more powerful pump for the mechanical unit. Sigurdur first tried the fire department in the nearby town of Selfoss and, having no luck there, finally went to the director of the Icelandic Coast Guard, who arranged for a high-pressure pump to be borrowed off a coast guard vessel in port.

With all this shifting around of excavation plans and major problem-solving with a major piece of excavating equipment – on the very first day of operations, Ragnar was beginning to lose some of his mystical optimism as to the invulnerability of the project to the unknown. With all the surveying and planning that had gone into the project before beginning the final recovery, he had felt highly confident that every exigency had been thought of and accounted for. His thoughts at the end of the first day were expressed as follows:

> At this point I was starting to feel uneasy that months of careful planning were coming apart at the seams. What next? But this is exactly the kind of situation in which the typical Icelander is at his best; improvising – solving the problems as they come along.[85]

By the next day, his optimism returned, for Einar, concentrating on getting the tail section out of the path of the debris flow coming from excavation activity upstream on the main airframe, succeeded in making the first recovery of a major airframe section. Most of the first day, after moving the "Airlifter" to the tail section, Einar had probed the riverbed around the tail section and finally found that it was lying inverted, with the vertical fin (stabilizer) dug into the compacted layer of the riverbed. By the end of the first day, Einar had decided that not all this compacted material would have to be removed, because most of the fin was missing. By excavating increasingly deeper around the tail section with air bags attached, it would eventually free itself, he was sure.

At 8 a.m. the next day, Sunday, August 5, Einar began attaching an airbag cable assembly to the exposed right elevator at the hinge, and then worked until 1 p.m. to remove riverbed material from around the tail section. In doing so, he discovered the tip of the vertical stabilizer in the riverbed behind the tail section. At 2 p.m. he brought the tip to shore. On examination it was found to be in good condition, with the aluminum grade mark clearly visible on the frame. When the tail section was finally raised, it was found that this tip piece and the root piece still attached to the tail section were the only parts of the vertical stabilizer and rudder that the Thjorsa was going to return.

By 5 p.m. sufficient material had been removed from around the tail section to attempt lifting it free by means of airbags. Accordingly, four airbags were attached to the airbag-lifter cable assembly. As the bags were filled and applied upward lift, the elevator hinge broke. Further investigation by means of the suction hose revealed that the tail section was effectively chained to the riverbed by its rudder and elevator flight-control cables, which were still attached to the buried fuselage section. These were cut and another airbag was added, which broke loose when its attachment rope was cut on the sharp, protruding edges of torn metal. Removal of additional riverbed revealed still more wires restraining the section, this time trim tab cables. As with the other control cables these were marked for identification purposes and cut. Finally, at 10:30 p.m., as riverbed

---

[85] Ragnar J. Ragnarsson, Loc. Cit.

material continued to be removed, the tail section suddenly pulled free and shot to the surface. Einar's crew then pulled it to shore.

Everyone had been watching the progress of the tail section excavation because while it was considered the simplest part of the plane to recover, success in getting it out of the river's grasp was the positive sign everyone had awaited. It provided confidence that the other parts of the plane could be recovered and in the amount of time allotted. Figure 45 shows the tail section lying on the beach in its as recovered condition, showing in physical terms what Cornish had meant by "friable."

Leo Gay

Figure 45. The tail section, which had been torn off the fuselage in an attempt by local farmers to pull the aircraft to shore years before, was the first piece recovered, the left horizontal stabilizer and elevator still attached. Northrop's Sveinn Thordarson cleans out silt from riverbed.

In parallel, Jan Bulukin had continued to work on determining the status of the left-hand pontoon, at the center wing section. As Cornish had reported, the airplane was canted left on its longitudinal axis 10 to 15 degrees such that the left wing was flat with but covered thinly by the riverbed, whereas the outer right wing was exposed for about three feet along the leading edge past its joint with the center wing box. However, due to this cant, there was one-half less of the loose sand and lava mix covering the clay stratum of the riverbed on the left side of the fuselage than on the right. While this was of some advantage in getting down to the clay level faster, it didn't help remedy the overall problem, which was quickly found to be the almost immediate infilling of the top loose stratum as it was removed. From the left side of the airplane to the right, the water depth went from about six feet to ten. The crew on the tail section had not had to contend with a sloping riverbed.

Jan Bulukin reported after the recovery was completed that only one diver could work at one place at a time around the wing and fuselage. The current required holding on with one hand while working with the other and too much commotion in one area stirred up the riverbed and reduced visibility drastically. The loose aggregate nature of the upper lava-sand stratum of the riverbed made the sand swirl when disturbed, blocking out what little visibility there was through the normally milky water. Because of the low visibility, current, and threat posed by jagged metal, a diver could get trapped and run out of air or even have his air hose cut or severed. For this reason, a standby diver was on watch on shore at all times, ready to enter the water at once in case of an emergency. While there was visibility of about one foot when working above the floor of the riverbed, once the loose stratum was disturbed and then the clay substratum broken up with crowbars, the visibility dropped to zero. Thus as the day proceeded, the water about the mostly buried airplane descended in layers from milkiness, to murkiness, to total brownout. After dark, underwater flashlights and other lighting glowed eerily and divers had to move in close to their work areas to see what they were doing.

Despite these difficulties, on the first day, after 15 continuous hours of diver relays working at the left pontoon station, the determination as to the pontoon's status was finally made. To everyone's initial relief, it was not there! Mostly by repeated suctioning, probing and feeling under the left wing it was determined that there was no pedestal there; therefore the pontoon had somehow detached itself or become detached years before the plane buried itself in the riverbed.

This was good news, because, given the adverse conditions under water, the absence of the pontoon would simplify the recovery of the main airframe portion still intact. Of course this still raised the question of where the pedestal and float were and what had torn them off, as Sevi knew they were still there and still attached when he crashed. Jan Bulukin, who had been given special instructions by Sevi on what to look for, had reported the discovery first and then Sigurdur Hardarsson of the IAHS went down to verify it. The pedestal, which connected the pontoon to the wing, was gone.

While there was still major work ahead, the team was exhilarated. The recovery would be completed faster than it had appeared earlier, based on the time and effort the tail section had taken. The hours it had taken just to verify that the pontoon was no longer attached proved how difficult it would have been to clear away a swimming-pool-size hole from beneath the plane so it could be airbag-lifted free with the ponderous length of the pontoon attached; and if the pontoon were filled with sand, its weight would have been massive.

But to Leo Gay and Ragnar, the absence of the one remaining pontoon raised a still bigger issue, for at least one pontoon was needed for a successful restoration. A seaplane couldn't be restored without pontoons! The pontoons, being unique to the N-3PB and nonstandard, were not available anywhere. Since they were mirror images of each other, with at least one of them available the other could be duplicated. Despite its ultimate criticality, they decided to postpone dealing with this issue for the time being, because the immediate priority was to get the plane out of the riverbed; if that couldn't be done, the pontoon wouldn't be needed anyway.

So without further delay the plan to lift the plane out of the riverbed by airbags, as the tail section had been done, was put into effect. With only one to two feet of the first riverbed stratum to be removed, the task ahead seemed relatively simple. The first step now was to attach the airbags to the airframe by their mooring straps and fill them with air from the offshore compressor. With 21 airbags tied to the airframe, the work area beneath the river surface became a tangle of ropes, with additional lines running from anchors to the barge overhead.

The idea now was to emulate Einar's raising of the tail section by having the airbags lift the airframe free from the riverbed as the divers suctioned riverbed material to unbury it. For four days the divers worked 16 hours a day trying to help the airframe lift itself free. Suspended from airbags that altogether applied an upward force vector of over five tons, it was still stuck fast. Jan Bulukin estimated that each diver averaged four hours each day underwater during this most intensive period of the excavation operations. Einar's success with the tail section convinced everyone that use of the airbags to lift the plane was the right approach. So while Einar's diving crew excavated over and around the airframe, the Norwegian crew excavated infilling material and cleaned out the cavities, compartments, and crew stations of the three-man cockpit area of the fuselage.

Back on Day Three, an opportunity presented itself for Ragnar to give the U.S. Navy's EOD Group an excuse to come to the site and do some work. The Group had wanted to participate, but was constrained by its regular Cold War operations schedule. There was, however, a loophole, in that the Group, as a member of the Icelandic Defense Force, had a commitment to de-fuse any ordnance items found as leftovers from use of the Island by the British and the U.S. during WWII. Normally, the EOD Group operated on military sea missions out of the naval airbase at Keflavik, near Reykjavik, the capitol, about 85 miles west of the recovery site, and seldom had any assignments inland. The Group had continued to be interested in the recovery project – and some of its staff wanted to continue to participate in the final diving tasks. After all, the Group had been largely responsible for the plane being located in the second survey in 1977, when an organized team made the first serious attempt to determine whether the plane was, as a whole, actually in the river or whether only small fragments were all that remained after the Thjorsa made its claim. That survey had taken place in October 1977, when visibility in the river was down to one inch and the plane had been detected by means of an electromagnetic sensor (cf., Chapter 7).

On the third day of the present full-scale recovery effort, the opportunity to get the EOD Group out to the site arose, when the divers excavating the cockpit uncovered a package of signal flares. Though probably inoperative after 36 years in the water, the flares did represent a form of ordnance and since the mission of the EOD Group was to dispose of ordnance items, they were the qualified and authorized agency to deal with these items. The flare powder inside was completely dry, as shown in Figure 46. Ragnar had awaited some instance in which his contacts at the EOD Group could be given an

Leo Gay

Figure 46. Signal flares stored onboard the plane still contained dry powder and, though probably inert after so many years, provided the excuse needed by the U.S. Navy's Explosive Ordnance Disposal Group to visit the site.

excuse for coming to the site, if only to see the recovery in process. As he reported to the author:

> These (flares) were potentially dangerous and needed to be made harmless. The proper authorities were now contacted and asked specifically to arrange for the dispatch of the American EOD team to the site to deactivate the flares and render them harmless. This request was immediately granted, even if the Icelandic Coast Guard had men quite capable of carrying out the task, and the following day members of the EOD team arrived at the site and deactivated the flares. It was a happy reunion and I was pleased we'd managed to pull this off so they at least could have a small part in the recovery itself. The following weekend, one of the EOD team members, Stuart Earnes, would arrive on the site with his family and full diving gear, including a Mark IX metal detector, to carry out post-recovery sweep of the general underwater site area.[86]

Once again the mystic spirit of the restoration made its appearance on behalf of Ragnar's mission impossible. But was this spirit also having its fun by taking even as it gave? In any event, it was demanding the most from the team, perhaps even testing its

---

[86] Ragnar J. Ragnarsson, Loc Cit.

will, strength, and faith in itself. While there was continual noise from the air compressors and generators running onshore, the beach scene was relatively paradisiacal compared to the scene below the surface of the water, where the divers moved about blindly, oriented only by sense of touch and feel of the current flow. The difficulty and danger of the diving environment was graphically described by Jan Bulukin:

> Imagine the combination of continuous current; absolutely zero visibility, the sharp wreckage parts, the tangled and swaying ropes and airbags, plus getting your suit punctured. Add to that from time to time getting stuck underwater without buoyancy compensators and without being able to see what is holding you, and you get a picture of what I mean by "not without risk." Any combination of getting stuck in the wreckage, together with the threat of panic or equipment (for instance an air regulator) failure under such conditions would surely result in immediate disaster.[87]

The "Airlifter" had a large-diameter hose attached that the Icelandic divers used like a giant vacuum to sweep up the riverbed around the periphery of the airframe. The silt would be drawn up the tube, passed over on the right hand side of the barge into the sifter sieve where small parts could be picked out. But soon it became obvious that the strategy, recommended by Cornish, of lifting the plane clear of the riverbed by suctioning out a large bowl-shaped depression around the entire perimeter of the airframe was not going to work. Again, the problem was that the first stratum of the riverbed, being finely ground lava pumice, would infill after awhile, the rate of infill increasing as the digging got deeper; in effect, the riverbed was constantly shifting to maintain the laminar configuration that the current insisted on flowing over. Any artificial pockets would soon be filled. The Norwegian dive team began to focus its efforts on just keeping those portions uncovered by the "Airlifter" from being infilled and covered again, as the higher-volume unit moved on to free new areas.

The water about the area was a milky yellow. The divers could see nothing. It was blind flying, this time in liquid soup. Each diver soon learned to orient himself relative to the different feel and location of the mooring lines to the barge and to the airbags and the direction and strength of the current; after a few hours under water, a diver could sense where he was relative to the left or right side of the airplane by the difference in the strength of the current, which was less powerful on the left, shoreward, than on the right, where the river was deeper. Though blinded by the environment, the divers were still able to orient themselves by the clues and signals in that environment.

Day Five, at mid-day, diver Gunnar J. Agustsson suddenly reached a depth in a location to the left of the fuselage and forward of the wing, where the "Airlifter" struck a large metal object. Further clearing of the riverbed around this object revealed that it was the long-sought left pontoon. Gunnar had uncovered only the forward end, which was angled upward, ahead of the wing leading edge, with the aft section angling downward, buried yet further in the riverbed. In general, the pontoon was in its original parallel alignment relative to the fuselage. Excavating further down along the length of the

---

[87] Jan Bulukin e-mail dated May 15, 2001.

pontoon revealed that the pedestal was facing down and the bottom of the pontoon was facing up. Somehow the entire pontoon-pedestal assembly had torn loose from the wing and inverted itself, the aft portion for some reason burrowing deeper into the riverbed than the forward end. Since the entire assembly was intact and clear of the airframe, as well, and out of the way of the area of operations for the present objective, Gunnar was told not to proceed further in uncovering the assembly at this time.

After the fifth day of operations under these conditions, it was evident to the team that an entirely different approach would have to be used. The plane had been uncovered and cleaned out to such an extent that it now seemed to be rocking loose on the bottom; but despite the installation of the 21 airbags with their cumulative lifting force of over five tons, it refused to follow the pattern of the tail section and lift free. And if the plane were indeed free of the bottom and "rocking", the five mile-per-hour current should have rocked it on down the river as Cornish had warned in his survey report. Something other than the Thjorsa seemed to be holding it down.

There were some smaller victories. Finding individual parts was relatively easy. These were brought to the surface as discovered. The first major part to be brought up was the right-hand horizontal stabilizer. Next, after the tail section was recovered, a piece of the lower rudder about 18 inches in length was found. These are shown in Figure 47.

Photos by Leo Gay

Figure 47. Major parts such as the rudder base (left) and the left horizontal stabilizer were recovered separately. Northrop's Sveinn Thordarson cleans.

Common sense said that the "real" problem keeping the main airframe on the riverbed was the excessive weight it had gained as the Thjorsa fed it silt and sand over the 36 years of its gradual assimilation. Since the whole mission-ready airplane, with fuel, weighed only slightly more than 5 tons in its operational days, the remains of the airframe alone – less crew, engine, pontoons and pedestals, ordnance, the tail section, and one outer wing panel – should have weighed far less than the constant 5-ton upward lift being applied by the airbags. But reason concluded that, filled with silt, sand, and lava pumice, the remnant airframe had to weigh far more than the lift capacity available from the 21 airbags. Furthermore, reason concluded that despite all the effort already expended, there was no way of cleaning out this packed in riverbed material without stripping the skins off the wings and fuselage. But this would only accomplish what the Thjorsa had so far been unable to do. Then, too, why go to this extreme when the 21 airbags, inflated to their lift capacity, did not have sufficient displacement room, at the depth the airframe sat, to be fully effective. That the airframe seemed to sit bouncing on the riverbed indicated that it and the airbags were at a standoff, the lift capability of the latter just matching the weight of the other. It was a standoff between the overweight of the airframe on the one hand and the incapacity of the airbags on the other. Conclusively, it was obvious at this juncture that the airbag lift approach was not going to work.

The option of using the sledge to pull the airframe out of the river was considered but there was still insufficient clearance beneath the airframe to put the sledge under it and hollowing the area deeper would only compound the daily task of removing infilling material. So at this point in the project, it was beginning to look like man's planned approach had been defeated by the nature of the Thjorsa River itself; that is, the Thjorsa's relentless effort to redeem its riverbed. Though the project had been held back waiting for the spring thaw and maximum water depth in the recovery area, it seemed the river still was winning by filling the plane to an overweight condition.

At the end of Day Five, all the team leaders went off in different directions for a moment to recover from their own frustration. Holding a conference after dinner, someone (it could have been Sevi, who might have used the same idea during his aircraft maintenance days at Fossvogur Bay) said, almost in jest, trying to instill some humor to offset the group's dour attitude, "Why don't we just jack it up?" The idea instantly got the group's attention. It had two immediate advantages. First, some of the divers thought that the airframe was so close to coming up that it was literally bouncing on the bottom. They even speculated that it might be generating some aberrant, fluctuating lift from the current flow over the wings. Second, no further digging out of the entire area around the airframe would be required, with the attendant cleaning out of an increasing amount of daily infill.

The idea of using jacking airbags rather than lifting airbags seemed the most effective all-around compromise. The idea had in common with the first approach the concept of lifting by airbags. But the new way of applying them would be more effective, because (1) a much greater lifting force could be applied; and (2) the additional area to be excavated and maintained free of infill was delimited to just the size of the bag.

The kind of airbag to be used in this alternative approach was of the type used by airport fire departments when an airplane had to land on its belly or if the landing gear of a plane collapsed, leaving the plane flat on the ground in much the same position the airframe under recovery was in. A phone call to the Reykjavik airport fire department showed they had three of these airbags, each capable of lifting 12 tons. What a margin for comfort! Over two times the weight to be lifted. Knowing about the recovery project, the fire chief said that the department would be glad to loan all three bags if needed to get the job done. Sigurdur P. Hardarson and Gisli Sigurdsson, the latter an employee of the Reykjavik Airport besides being a member of the IAHS, were immediately dispatched with a pickup truck to obtain the bags. Ragnar wasn't taking any chances at this stage; all three bags would be brought to the site, so there would be plenty of backup should one fail. The two men returned to the site at 5 a.m. the next morning, Thursday, just as the camp was getting up to have breakfast and start the day.

In parallel with the trip to get the lifting bags, Einar spent the night modifying the "Airlifter" at the workshop of the Burfell hydroelectric powerplant, where he often did work supporting his underwater maintenance and construction operations for the plant. Now he was actually decreasing the suction hose diameter of the "Airlifter" to work at its best efficiency and effectiveness on excavating the hole for containing one of the 12-ton lifting bags beneath the center wing section of the airframe. By its size, shape, and location, this hole posed a hazardous excavating task for the diver. The person who could perform this excavation task had to meet at least four qualifications: (1) he had to thoroughly experienced in working with the "Airlifter"; (2) he had to be a professionally capable and experienced diver who, as Jan Bulukin said, would not panic if something went awry in the hole; (3) he had to be accustomed to the blind, fast moving current conditions of the Thjorsa at this season; and (4) he had to be of medium size and in top physical form. As a final judge, Einar was to be the one who decided whether the person met these qualifications and of course that would have to be someone he knew personally was an expert diver. Only one person at the site could meet all these qualifications and the last one too: Gunnar Agustsson of Iceland. Gunnar was the person Einar knew and trusted best to perform the task. The two of them had often worked together under the most adverse underwater and seasonal weather conditions. Gunnar also was the diver who had performed the difficult excavation task to locate and determine the situation of the left pontoon and pedestal. In that excavation he had already opened up an entryway and cavity under the left center wing section under conditions almost identical to those to be encountered in excavating the lifting bag hole – "almost identical" because in the lifting bag hole he would be working directly under the center wing section with the 5-ton weight of the airframe above him.

The hole that Gunnar was to excavate would be 5 feet wide (parallel to the wing), 4 feet long (parallel to the fuselage), and 3 feet deep, all dimensions directly under the wing center section. One of the 12-ton bags would be placed in this hole from the front of the airframe. Gunnar would then crawl back in the hole and tie ropes (previously connected to tiedown points on the airframe outside the hole) to the grommets of the bag so as to hold it in place under the airframe as it inflated with air from a compressor onshore. The front grommets were to be connected by Gunnar after he left the hole. Thus the rear and the two sidewalls of the hole constrained the bag in those directions, while the front of the bag was held in place by the grommet tiedowns and the pressure of the river current alone.

A critical precautionary procedure, one that Cornish had noted in his report suggesting how to raise the plane, already had been implemented from the beginning of excavation activity; namely, the requirement to safeguard the airframe from being swept away by the river, by securing it to moorings.[88] In fact, the same anchors that secured the barge steadily in place in the river against the flow of current had been in use all along as moorings for the airframe.

For this excavation task, Gunnar wore the dry diving suit and air helmet that were standard gear for the Icelandic divers. With the helmet supplied with air from a compressor on shore instead of an air bottle carried by the diver, Gunnar was assured of a continuing flow of air for the duration of his underwater stay. Both this assurance of external air supply and the protection of the steel helmet, along with the capabilities of the modified "airlifter," were to save him and the expedition from a fatal disaster.

The dismembered condition of the airframe, its heavy weight, and its position in the stream of the Thjorsa posed an anomaly for the normal sedimentary flow and deposition of the river; in more technical terms, the presence of the airframe in the river interfered with its normal hydrodynamics. The airframe, in effect, constituted a vortex generator that swirled the current about in turbulent directions that caused the riverbed in the vicinity of the beach to change its normal configuration complying with the hydrodynamics of the river and to build up unstable sandbanks on the river (starboard) side of the airframe. It was this hydrodynamic anomaly that caused what Cornish had reported as a 15-degree list of the airframe about its longitudinal axis, toward shore, as though the plane were banking for a gradual turn. What caused this list was the buildup of an anomalous sandbank around and under the right wing facing toward the river.

What happened to nearly seriously injure or possibly kill Gunnar was that as he excavated beneath the center wing section and removed a 20-square-foot area on which the main load of the airframe pressed, virtually the full weight of the airframe was transferred to the anomalous sandbank under the right wing. The sandbank all at once collapsed and the airframe dropped, closing up his access hole and pinning his helmet between the bottom of the center wing section and the riverbed. This was one of those situations where, as Jan Bulukin had noted, an experienced diver told himself immediately, "Don't panic." Though the dry diving suit Gunnar was wearing had a voice communications system built in, he knew that it would take a long time before he could be rescued, given that a major shift in the riverbed had occurred and he had the immediately available high volume suction device with him. Nevertheless, as safety procedures required, he notified Einar that he appeared to be trapped due to a cave-in of the hole, but that his air feed was still working. In fact, according to Ragnar, Gunnar's

---

[88] Peter Cornish, Loc. Cit., p. 5, where Cornish says, quite colorfully, "Once afloat the buoyant aircraft needs to be anchored to stop it (from) rocketing down the river."

exact words, stated calmly, were, "The plane just collapsed on me and I'm trapped."[89] Einar, disciplined by experience in how to handle such a situation, talked with Gunnar, getting more information to assess the severity of his situation.

Finding out Gunnar was pinned, Einar shouted to Jan Bulukin to go in the water immediately with the mechanical pump and start opening up the access hole to where Gunnar was working. As he directed Jan to proceed, Einar began suiting up in scuba gear to examine the situation firsthand. Before entering the water he alerted the RTA rescue divers to stand by ready to assist if he called them. As Jan reported to the author, by the time he got to the underwater location where Gunnar had been excavating, Gunnar had already freed himself.[90]

While Einar and Jan were reacting to his situation, Gunnar was taking direct action. Checking his degree of freedom, Gunnar was relieved to find that his body below the pinned helmet and his arms and legs were free. Feeling around, exploring to see just how his helmet was pinned, he found that he could clear the riverbed from under the helmet by directing the "Airlifter" suction nozzle in that direction. Within a few seconds he was completely free to move, though in a cramped quarters. Having maintained his orientation relative to the front of the hole, he opened that area up with the "Airlifter" and crawled out, continuing to crawl on the riverbed toward shore until he could stand in waist deep water.

Before Jan could reach Gunnar's site with the mechanical pump, Gunnar emerged, smiling. He had handled the situation so adroitly that most members of the expedition were unaware of his plight until informed later. After a cup of coffee, he went back to the hole and by evening had opened it up to the required dimensions for the airlift bag to be installed. The diving team waited attentively on shore as air was pumped into it; but rather than the plane rising, the bag abruptly popped out of the hole and shot to the surface. The procedure was repeated two more times, each taking almost two hours, but with the same results. Finally, at 11:30 p.m., Thursday night, further effort to make the lifting bag approach work was abandoned.

With representatives of international news agencies at the site making daily reports and signs of success getting bleak, the team leaders couldn't rest even though soon it was midnight and Friday arrived. The expedition had been in the field one week and still the Thjorsa wouldn't let go of what it had taken!

The team leaders met and conferred for a couple more hours about the situation and alternatives for continuing. The original plan now appeared to be unworkable. Leo Gay, having spent a lot of time and effort on the project from the Northrop side of the international team since January 1977, wouldn't consider the possibility that this airplane couldn't be lifted out of relatively shallow water so close to shore. Success meant a lot to him, because he had been instrumental in getting Northrop to invest company time, equipment, and travel money in the project and make the commitment in writing to restore the airframe to N-3PB configuration form at its home plant. Northrop personnel

---

[89] Ragnar J. Ragnarsson, Loc. Cit.
[90] Jan Bulukin, Loc. Cit.

at home were looking forward to meeting this commitment. People would be disappointed if the plane didn't return to its original producer and be restored for Jack Northrop's 85th birthday celebration. Leo had sold them on the idea. He personally was such a dedicated Northrop employee and aircraft design, production, and marketing professional that he couldn't conceive of not bringing this relatively lightweight military seaplane to the surface and taking it back home to be restored. For him, the task was not a mission impossible, except in terms of using that expression as a goad to make sure you didn't fail – to inspire you to excel past your normal limits. To him, that expression was used just to make you try harder. He knew that before the sun came up an entirely different approach was going to have to be thought of and then immediately facilitated in whatever way necessary.

So for Leo this moment of urgency was compounded by the fact that he personally didn't want to return home without the airplane. In considering that prospect, for a moment his thoughts sought refuge in the home plant and how airplanes were so efficiently produced. He thought of how major assemblies were progressively built up and then transferred by crane to the next station until finally an integrated airplane rolled off the line. Suddenly, he saw the golden solution. "Cranes!" he thought, picturing the entire process as to how the plane could be lifted from the riverbed. He almost stammered as he said, "Hey, look! The way to do this is with a crane. That's the way aircraft are lifted when they're get built. From the top, not the bottom!"

Ragnar doesn't remember who came up with the idea of using a crane, but the author gives credit for that to Leo Gay, the Northrop coordinator for the international team. Here's why the author thinks Leo came up with the final solution. The author worked at Northrop in association with Leo Gay from the beginning of the restoration project concept in January 1977, when the IAHS proposal to recover the N-3PB Serial No 320 arrived and was reviewed. Leo was a project engineer in the Advanced Aircraft Systems organization and, having recovered and restored other vintage military aircraft, he was immediately a dedicated advocate for restoring the Northrop N-3PB that Iceland proposed to recover. He was a total aircraft enthusiast, from advanced design concepts to historical restorations ranging from a Japanese Zero (which he recovered from the ocean) to a Martin B-26 he recovered in Alaska, plus small antique aircraft. His presentations to the Northrop staff about the virtues and benefits of restoring the N-3PB, before the airplane was even recovered or thought recoverable, projected a glowing view of a full-up airplane just waiting on the river bottom to be pulled to shore. He confided to the author later that he didn't want to let this opportunity get vetoed at Northrop just because the company had so many other projects to fund, so he had deliberately presented the most positive picture he could to make it look like a simple, straightforward project that would cost little and provide multiple benefits. In retrospect, he was totally right. Leo's clincher for getting company support was that the plane would be the centerpiece for the company's 40th anniversary and for Jack Northrop's 85th birthday.

Subsequently, after the plane was indeed restored, Leo and the author were members of the Western Museum of flight that was formed as a result of the N-3PB restoration project that Leo had kept alive so that Northrop could and would restore it. Without any challenger, he is the one who brought the project home to its culmination in the actual restoration. In the 1977-79 period, Leo also had kept Ragnar moving ahead by providing encouragement and positive support during the series of site surveys leading to the final recovery decision, in the same way he was, in parallel, keeping Northrop interested and ready to proceed. The author remembers well when the airplane finally arrived in November 1979 at Northrop Field onboard a Norwegian C-130 that Leo shook his head knowingly and said, "David, it was a crane that delivered this baby."

The diving team had expended almost a week of 16-hour workdays trying the flotation approach, but ended by being utterly frustrated by the river, the riverbed, and the airplane itself. The plane's state of readiness to come up was so evident that some of the divers continued trying to make the lifting airbag work; but to no avail. Excavation equipment technology had done its part and now would have to team with mechanical overhead lifting technology to complete the job. The airplane literally would have to be plucked from the riverbed.

The crane approach brought forth by Gay was accepted by all with such immediate consensus that it was as if each person had thought of it themselves; and, actually, the idea had been hovering in the thinking of the other key personnel. It was so obvious that all the conditions at the site favored use of a crane, with the airframe now uncovered, in shallow water, and accessible from the beach, provided that a large enough crane could be found. Not a lot of serious thought was given to the idea, however, because transport of such heavy equipment was prohibited on the public road system, due to both size and weight. This restriction was so rigidly enforced that, several years earlier, when two electrical line transmission towers collapsed in a tumultuous North Atlantic storm and Reykjavik was left with a power shortage right at Christmas time, the National Power Company's request to move a crane via road to re-erect the towers and restore electricity to the city was denied outright by the Public Road Works bureau.

Gay initially had been exposed to the crane idea when one day during the recovery operation, seeking a break from standing around at the beach hour after hour with nothing taking place above water but the drone of equipment, he decided to take a walk. Needing diversion and exercise, he had walked up the nearby road to where the Mt. Burfell power plant was located. He was by nature a man of action, independent thinking, noted at Northrop for always being on his feet scouting around to see what was going on or engaging people in discussions and meetings about the various projects in advance engineering and prototyping; and for this reason, he was used extensively by the Marketing Department to travel and make presentations to customers. Seeing construction work going on up the road at the bend in the river, he decided to walk in that direction. Once there, he saw a towering crane with a 90-foot boom and a 7.5-ton capacity. This was a mobile crane used to lift mammoth turbogenerators and lower them into their generating stations. He had idly mused at the time that such a crane could reach right out over the recovery site, pick up the airframe, and deposit it on the beach in one action. But he had just as immediately dismissed the thought as farfetched considering the size of the crane and the difficulty it would have moving over the rough lava field to the beach. Besides, the approach already in process to raise the plane had been well defined, facilitated, and staffed and was making progress toward its fulfillment on schedule, with only minor exceptions that were being resolved as they occurred.

In retrospect, Gay could see that the mythic gods of good fortune had continued to look over the project as one after the other the planned approaches became self-defeating due to circumstances beyond the immediate control of the expedition. When the realization struck that only a crane could do the job in the time remaining, Gay asked if it would be possible to borrow the one up the road, since it was apparent that the entire Island was committed to assisting in every way necessary to make sure the project succeeded.

Ragnar, of course, had been aware that a large crane was in use at the hydroelectric plant, but had dismissed it as infeasible for use in the recovery due to the restrictive attitude of the Public Road Works bureau. But when the idea was put forth that only a crane could save the project in the time remaining, Ragnar immediately went into action to secure the one at the National Power Company; it was just the right size and there wasn't another one within a 50-mile range. While Ragnar realized that getting this crane bordered on the impossible, he too felt this was the only remaining alternative and that he had to make it happen. He was even more concerned than Leo Gay about the success of the project, because his reputation was under double jeopardy, being both a U.S. and Iceland citizen.

Ragnar sensed that the attention the project was drawing to Iceland in the Scandinavian and North American communities was a favorable factor and meeting with the right people in the right way might sway the PRW bureau to make an exception in this case. Putting the full weight of the IAHS behind the proposal, Ragnar chose Baldur Sveinsson, the IAHS president to join him and, to add international weight, Leo Gay. Besides presenting an international presence, Leo was an articulate, convincing presenter. Baldur was well known and respected in Iceland as the chairman and director of the mathematics and computer science department at the Reykjavik Business College (later Reykjavik University). His contribution to the project was already extraordinary, in that he had recruited over 65 Icelandic sponsors of the project, both individuals and companies, many run by his former students. Baldur and Ragnar had been founding members of the IAHS in 1977 and the society's first president and vice president, respectively.

Day 6: At 8 a.m. on Friday morning, Ragnar, Baldur, and Leo went directly to the Burfell hydroelectric power plant to meet with its manager, Steingrimur Dagbjartsson. Steingrimur already had been quite supportive of the expedition, having loaned the 300-cubic-foot air compressor used initially with the "Airlifter" Immediately it was clear the Steingrimur personally would do anything he could to help and would loan any equipment of a portable or transportable convenient nature, if under his administrative prerogative to do so, but that something like the crane, which would have to be disassembled for transportation, could not be so readily loaned. Of course Ragnar and the others knew about the precedent already established by the PRW bureau prohibiting the crane from using the public road. Now, however, with the recovery project well-known by everyone in Iceland, Ragnar felt that by contacting the key decisionmakers that prohibition probably could be lifted, especially to save the project. He reasoned that since the airframe was now ready to be lifted from the river after a week of effort excavating it and the distance to the site was just down the road, there was far more to be gained than risked. He could understand that as a rule you didn't want 35-ton cranes running up and down public roads that weren't built for that kind of width or loading. But this was an opportunity that justified an exception, given the short distance and the care that would be taken in good weather and open daylight to preclude any accident.

Steingrimur agreed with the rationale but still doubted the PRW bureau would make exceptions to its policy, though under the circumstances it was worth trying. When he offered the use of his office and phones to make the necessary contacts. Ragnar and Baldur went into action. They started at the top of the management hierarchy, knowing that any decision would eventually find its way there. Leo had already laid out the roadmap by asking, "Who are the decisionmakers? Those are the ones who have to be contacted." He knew that from experience, because that's the way the U.S. aerospace industry works. To get something approved, you start at or near the top of the decisionmaking tree.

The first call was to the director of the PRW. If he didn't waive the policy restricting transport of the crane on public roads, no further calls would be necessary. When the dilemma the expedition faced was explained to him, he cut in, saying, "I've been following the news, what can I do for you?" Told that the crane was the solution, he said, "No problem, you have our permission. Good luck."

Success had come with such ease that, for a moment, they couldn't release the intensity of the uncertain expectations they had built up. At that moment, Steingrimur returned to check on their progress and, learning of the positive outcome, said, combining congratulations with disbelief, "I'll be damn. And we were unable to do that when we needed the crane to restore transmission power to Reykjavik just before Christmas."

But getting Public Road Works approval was just the first step, for the National Power Company owned the crane. Getting permission to transport it was one thing, but getting permission to use it, along with a certified operator, was another.

Again the request was granted as though the director of the NPC had been awaiting the call eager to help out and be a part of what was now an Icelandic saga in the making, with the world as audience. There was still one condition that had to be met: getting the insurance company to extend the crane's policy to cover the recovery operation. Ragnar felt no qualms now, for he knew the director of the insurance company personally. The only remaining issue he was uncertain about was the insurance premium – how would it get paid? When the insurance company director said, "We'll take care of the insurance coverage and inform the National Power Company accordingly," and Ragnar noted that there were no funds to pay the premium, the director completed the sequence of success by replying, "Ragnar, did you hear me say anything about money?"

Finally the scope and magnitude of the team effort had become national. Governmental policy was suspended to ensure the recovery would go forward. As

Ragnar summed up the chain of successful networking that unwrapped so naturally at the moment of seeming impasse, so that everything necessary would be forthcoming:

At this point it is important to mention that the Icelanders have endured more than 1,100 years of facing the elements of nature. Tempestuous weather, earthquakes, volcanic eruptions and river flooding have all taken their toll on the country's populace through the centuries. Glacial rivers, such as the Thjorsa, had been a major obstacle for communications and travel in the country until four years earlier, in 1974, the last one had been bridged and a ring road circuiting the island finally completed. Living over 11 centuries on the fringe of the inhabitable world, the Icelanders have developed a "can do" attitude, a heritage that has been passed down through generations whose daily life involved facing and fighting the elements. Now the people wanted to see the river defeated, and at this point in time I think I could have mobilized the entire country to come to our assistance if needed.[91]

The next task was to get the crane down to the recovery site. Driving the crane down the road was easy compared with crossing the 220 yards of raw lava bed leading to the operations beach and then providing firm ground for it to stand on. The open terrain passage traversed by the agile four-wheel drive vehicles was impossible for the locomotive-size crane to cross. A road, no matter how temporary or improvised, would have to be built, leading down to the water's edge.

Now working together comfortably as an international negotiating unit, Ragnarsson, Baldur, and Gay proceeded to the town of Selfoss on the main highway 35 miles away to see about getting a bulldozer to improve the access road. New farmland was being cleared along the Thjorsa River and bulldozers were the main type of equipment in use. Good fortune still prevailing, an arrangement was quickly made with a construction company that operated a fleet of bulldozers. The three men simply went to a work site where the company had some bulldozer drivers working and got one who agreed to help.

One more thing was required: a truck to bring the bulldozer to the salvage site. Ragnar called GG Trucking in Reykjavik, the same firm that had transported the team's heavy equipment to the site. Since Friday afternoon was their busiest time of the week, they had no trucks immediately available, but the manager said, "Don't worry, Ragnar "We'll make sure you get the dozer this evening. Just make sure you get that plane out the river." A truck and driver were duly loaned to get the bulldozer to the site.

The three-man requisition team, Ragnar, Baldur, and Gay returned to the site around 6 p.m. The Icelandic divers, not willing to concede that a whole new approach to raising the airframe was necessary when it was literally bouncing on the bottom, ready to lift off, were making a last attempt with the 12-ton lifting bag. This time they were taking special care, by every possible means, to secure the bag in the hole beneath the center wing section. But to their consternation, once the bag was filled, its grommet eyelets

[91] Ragnar J. Ragnarsson, Loc Cit.

ripped loose and it shot to the surface as before, the airframe not moving an inch toward the surface.

By now, a week had passed and the project was at a standstill late on the Friday afternoon originally scheduled as the completion date. Most of the recovery team personnel had already made plans for the weekend in advance, thinking the project would be completed. Another crisis management factor was that many of the volunteers had taken vacation time to join the team and their time was running out. A team meeting quickly resolved this issue. All agreed that this project, though voluntary, took priority – such was the team spirit that had developed, reinforced by the team spirit that was now inspiring the local community. The commitment of the team members was without question; they were resolved to work day and night until the aircraft was freed from the river. What the Thjorsa had tried to take would be taken back, forget return. That Friday, 10 August, they worked all night. With a whole new approach now beginning – one that the entire Island was backing and the results of which the world was awaiting – it was as though the project itself were just beginning.

At 8:35 p.m. the promised bulldozer arrived and by 11 p.m. the roadway over the lava field to the beach was completed and named "Bulukin Boulevard." The crane, avoiding all possibility of conflicting traffic, arrived just as Bulukin Boulevard was opened to traffic and successfully made the crossing to the shore.

But now another problem loomed. The ground was too soft near the water to support the crane. Everyone was standing around voicing ideas on how to provide a firm support when the two truck drivers walked up who regularly stopped to check on the current status of the recovery. They were the same drivers who had transported much of the expedition's equipment to the site a week ago. Now they were returning to Reykjavik from Mt. Hekla (a volcano) where they regularly loaded up pumice stone to take to the port in Reykjavik for export to Germany for use in making prefabricated wall and floor panels for the building industry. This was a trip they made several times a week and each time they had stopped to see how the project was progressing. Again the Zen of Restoration was working overtime, for when the drivers saw the situation the crane was in they volunteered to dump their two truckloads of pumice as roadbed material, though it was 1 a.m.

As Ragnar reported on the situation at that moment:

Personally, I didn't think much of the idea, since the very light and porous pumice stone would probably be swept away by the river's current (this material is so light that it actually floats on water) once it entered the water. But what the heck, I thought, it can't hurt, so down to the beach they came and dumped their load at the edge of the water. The bulldozer immediately started pushing the pumice to make a jetty into the river and that is when a miracle took place. The mystic force guarding the "Northrop Project" had taken charge once again!

While normally the pumice would have gradually been taken away by the river, the weight of the bulldozer pressing down on it turned its porous quality into a sponge that instantly absorbed water from the muddy beach and left a thick layer of compressed glacial clay that was like concrete. Ragnar noted that when he returned to the site a month later the jetty formed by this material was still in place.

Seeing that the two loads were not going to be enough, with that amazing Icelandic spirit that no mission is impossible, the two drivers quickly volunteered to get another two loads of stone and promptly left to do so. Well, maybe not so promptly, for the bulldozer had to push them back up from the beach to Bulukin Boulevard because the approach was so steep.

By 2 a.m., the two men were back and dumped two more truckloads, bringing the total to 3,500 cubic feet of pumice. Since the crane still was not stabilized rigidly enough, Gudmundur Hermanniusson, the Burfell plant foreman, who had been supervising the building of the jetty, assembled some of his men and with their pickup trucks went back to the dam headquarters and obtained some wooden cable spools. When these were cut in two, they made excellent pads for the crane. Gudmundur had joined the recovery team full time with the delivery of the crane to the site.

When the two truck drivers prepared to return to Mt. Hekla to refill their trucks a third time for the trip into Reykjavik, Ragnar thanked them for their extraordinary effort in supporting the project at such sacrifice to their own schedule. The response was, "Well, you didn't think we were going to get our feet wet watching you lift the plane from the water, did you?"

By 4:20 a.m., the jetty was completed and tested as rigid enough to support the crane for its lifting operations from the beach. Like everything else of special purpose at the site, the jetty was given its special name, appropriately, in this case, Cape of Good Hope!

When the crane was driven into position and checked out as operationally ready at 5:00 a.m., the Cape of Good Hope was found to be a few yards short of putting the crane's 90-foot boom directly over the airframe at the required lift angle. This shortcoming was remedied by adding an extension jib to the boom.

While the shore preparations were being made, the divers had not been idle. They kept diving in two or three-hour shifts, continuing to move the riverbed silt and sand away from the wings and fuselage and bringing up many small parts. They would dive their turn, come up and warm themselves by the fire and then go in again. They repeated this cycle all night. As a final task they removed the airbags from the buried airplane and the mooring lines holding the barge in position in the current, so the crane could take over.

As a final step, the crane's lifting cable (a wire hawser) had to be connected to the airframe. In providing the sledge Cornish had recommended as the way the plane finally got lifted from the river, Sevi had brought from Norway a pair of heavy, contoured beams to place under the wing center section. Using the hole already excavated for the 12-ton capacity lifting bag, the divers put these two beams in place, one on each side of the fuselage. Cables at each end of the beams were then connected to the boom cable. Held thusly during the lift, the airframe would be supported and stabilized in place by a four-cable bridle running to the single lift cable of the crane. Thus as Leo Gay had indicated to the author, the plane was delivered as though by a stork.

With everything ready to proceed and the sun not yet risen, it was one of those rare moments of a tension filled experience when one could relax for a moment and look about with a sense of immense relief that what had been prepared for was as well done as it would ever be. As Ragnar reflected about that moment:

All was now ready to lift the plane from the river as soon as dawn arrived, and it was at this point that Gay, gazing into the dark sky above said: "Ragnar, I'm waiting to hear a voice from above saying 'Is there anything else I can do for you boys?'"

Jan Bulukin described the lifting of the airframe as one great snatch by the crane operator. He thought for a moment that the airframe had been snapped in two. But no, there it was hanging from the bridle that he and the other divers had installed. It was a moment of suspended reality, as in a dream, to see the main portion of the airplane appear suddenly above the river, water pouring from it, freed from its underwater crypt after so many years of disappearance. It appeared like magic. First there was only the taut cable reaching into the water and then the great winged assembly leaped out of the water like a great fish! The crane was obviously near its lifting capacity, as the operator, sensing the strain on the crane, offset the airframe's weight by surfing it across the surface of the river to shore. Carrying the airframe's full weight momentarily as it was lowered onto the beach, the boom's cable broke just as the airframe touched down. At least it was a three-point landing.

Everyone rushed forward to see what the crane had delivered, curious as to what the divers had been struggling with beneath the river's surface for a week. What they saw was the main forward remnant of the plane that matched the broken off tail section recovered four days ago. Before them was the center wing and fuselage section with the left wing and part of the right attached. It still contained silt and rocks from the riverbed and the crane men had to use double cables to lift it from the beach onto a drum platform for cleaning. They had estimated that this section, while still in the water, weighed more than the rated capacity of the crane. The crane operator had intentionally snatched the plane from the riverbed by alternating the tautness of the cable to load and unload the boom, thereby rocking the airframe and gaining lift momentum from the crane's structure concurrently. It was a basic operating technique, but dramatically suspenseful to watch.

The team eagerly clustered about their prize. As the crane lowered the aircraft, Cato Guhnfeldt, representing the Norwegian Aviation Historical Society (and also a reporter for Norway's largest evening newspaper, the *Aftenposten)* saw immediately by the numbers on the side of the fuselage that they did not match the serial number anticipated. Being a quick-witted newsman he knew that numbers are free, so he shouted, "It's the wrong aircraft, drop it back in the river!" Given the tension everyone had been under for over a week, it was a moment of great comic relief and everyone laughed, some adding their own uproarious comments. What had happened is that back in 1943 the flight records had been mixed up at Squadron 330(N) headquarters and Serial No. 318 had gotten reported in error as the plane that had crashed instead of Serial No. 320. The latter was the plane recovered from the river.

Sevi, in a moment of déjà vu, leaped into the cockpit and posed as pilot, as though the passage of 36 years had never occurred and the plane had never crashed or been buried. His mission impossible had been accomplished! Ragnar, usually quiet and composed, smiled, sharing the moment. It had been his mission impossible, too.

Cato Guhnfeldt, seeing this scene as a historic photo opportunity, snapped a picture of Sevi sitting in what was left of the pilot's compartment and later published in the *Aftenposten*. With the divers now examining the airframe for the first time in air, Baldur Sveinsson had them climb aboard so he could get the group picture shown in Figure 48.

Baldur Sveinsson

Figure 48. Sevi Bulukin surrounded by the team of Norwegian and Icelandic divers who recovered his "Grand Old Lady" from the grips of her unrequited lover, the Thjorsa River. (From left: George Toftdahl [standing], Gunnar J. Agustsson [seated], Col. Sevi Bulukin, Adalsteinn Adalasteinsson [seated front center], Jan Bulukin, Dagfin Hansen, Trygve Skaug, Einar Kristbjornsson [with diving helmet], missing, Sigurdur P. Hardarson.)

Looking about the cockpit area and seeing a piece of folded up paper, Sevi picked it up, wondering how it had gotten there. Opening it, he read: "Welcome back, Bulukin.

I've waited a long time for this. You should really do something about your landings! Your Grand Old Lady."

Sevi bent over with laughter. He had often over the years and recently at the recovery site referred to this airplane as his "Grand Old Lady." How the note got there was a mystery until the author surmised that one of the Norwegian divers had placed it in the cockpit just before the plane was lifted from the water. In correcting this illogic, Ragnar had to admit that he was the one who did it, wrapping the note in plastic to give it the appearance of having been there when the plane was raised from the riverbed. Since this book is intended as a comprehensive history of "Your Grand Old Lady," it's well that the story now has closure as to who wrote that letter!

The crane had been driven to the river's edge over a roadbed improvised on the spot by bulldozing the lava bed over which the recovery site was accessed. At the water's edge a jetty, constructed out of compressed pumice rock and discarded wooden wire spools from the nearby Burfell hydroelectric powerplant, extended the crane's roadbed into the river so the boom would reach directly above the submerged airframe. The airplane had been abruptly wrenched from the Thjorsa's grip and surfed to shore by its rescuer, the crane, pausing a moment to be photographed, before it proceeded to lower the plane onto its drum platform at river's edge. Mission impossible had been accomplished!

Figure 49 shows the crane in position at the river's edge, ready to lift the airframe at sunrise on Saturday, August 11, 1979; and also shows the plane as it surfaced, with Jan Bulukin observing from the offshore barge. Figure 50 shows the airframe immediately after being raised, as it is being swung around by the crane to be lowered onto its temporary platform of metal drums. In this picture, note in particular the cables hanging beneath the wing. This figure also shows the airframe after being placed on the drums. Note that the number "20" – this particular N-3PB's official serial number – is still visible on the side of the fuselage, just forward of the RAF insignia.

The question remains: Why did it take so long, to do what Cornish had said could be done quickly? All thought was on the apparent weight of the plane from infilled riverbed material; it was common sense to imagine the plane, hidden from sight in the muddied water, burdened down by this material.

The author, however, in questioning Jan Bulukin, who spent hours underwater contending with the persistent infill of the riverbed, was directed by Jan to another possibility, one based on a natural phenomenon known as capillary action. This is a condition that develops when a flat object is resting on a flat surface in liquid. Just about everyone has experienced the consequences in trying to pick up a relatively flat object, for example a flower pot or plate, setting on wet ground. It seems like the thing is glued to the ground. One has to tip the pot or plate to one side to break what seems like suction between the two surfaces. That "suction" is the result of capillary action: the natural characteristic of water to ascend against an object, especially metal, it is in contact with. The attractive force generated can become tons, in the case of large objects.

Baldur Sveinsson

Baldur Sveinsson

Figure 49. "Mission impossible" becomes highly probable! Bottom, the crane in position to lift the plane from the riverbed; Top, Jan Bulukin looks at his air-bagged opponent finally surfaced; freed from the bottom, it floated!

Baldur Sveinsson

Baldur Sveinsson

Figure 50. Landed at last! Top, getting ready for the turn to platform; Bottom, beached on the platform. Note the number "20" and all the dangling ropes and cables.

Referring again to Figure 50 and the cables stringing below the wing, it appears that what had held the airframe tightly to the riverbed was a combination of capillary forces other than the infill of silt and sand first thought to be the reason the plane couldn't be raised by either of the airbag approaches. Jan Bulukin was in full agreement with this assessment, and expressed the opinion that had a hydrodynamics engineer been at the site, he would have immediately suggested a different approach to free the airplane.

The bottom of the wing, except where the two pontoon pedestals had been ripped away, was a smooth aerodynamic surface, to which the riverbed, over a short time (not counting the years the plane had been buried) would have conformed, molding itself to the curvature of the wing. The wing, pressed between this conformal bed of mud and the water above, would be effectively stuck to the bottom, almost as though glued. Even without the pressure of the overhead water, the plane would have resisted being separated from its "bed" in the riverbed due to the capillary attraction between the wing and the wet mud of the riverbed. Such capillary attraction is a natural phenomenon and is commonly encountered by most people at one time or another in trying to lift something flat, like a stepping stone or flower pot dish, that has sat for some time on wet ground. Considerable effort (and potential backache) is required to separate the stone or dish from the wet soil. What has happened is that water molecules in the wet soil cohere to the object and to each other, forming a water column beneath the object. The interactive cohesion of water molecules in this column keeps the water in the column from draining away as it normally would; the weight of this column effectively holds the object in place, hence the difficulty in lifting it; the object becomes drawn down (effectively weighted down) by a column of water held in position by capillary attraction. The force asserted in such cases is given by the cross-sectional area of the surface in contact (in this case the bottom surface of the wing) multiplied by the height of the column of water attracted and the density of water. Just to approximate this force, so as to appreciate the situation the airframe and divers were caught in, if the wing area was just 150 square feet (versus 376.8 square feet overall for an entire N-3PB wing) and the water column is taken as one foot, the weight imposed by the capillary attraction would be 9,360 pounds or 4.7 tons.[92] Assuming that an equivalent area of fuselage was subject to capillary attraction, this tonnage would be doubled to 9.4 tons. Added to this would be the remnant weight of the airframe, estimated to be half its normal mission weight, or 2.5 tons, bringing the total to almost 12 tons, not including the weight of silt and sand within the airframe.

There was yet an additional weight acting on the airframe due to capillary attraction. Looking at Figure 50, one can see numerous wires, ropes, and cables dangling beneath the airframe. Many of these are remnants of the 60 or so cables used on the N-3PB to control ailerons, elevator, rudder, associated trim tabs, pontoon rudders, guns, and bombs. As the ailerons, tail section, and pontoons were torn loose over the years, the associated cables were left to dangle and eventually to become buried deep in the compacted layer of the riverbed. An example of the anchoring force these cables applied to the airframe is

---

[92] Calculated as cubic feet of water column multiplied by the density of water, or 150 ft.^{3} x 62.4 lb./ft.^{3}. See Appendix K for an application of the general capillary attraction math model to an analysis of the overall complement of capillary forces weighing down the airframe.

seen in the fact that the tail section, even after being adequately excavated, would not lift from the riverbed until the flight control cables running to it were discovered and cut. When the right wing panel and the pontoon pedestals broke loose, the associated cables were left dangling under the airframe and became buried in the same way. The anchoring force of these cables was substantial, as shown in the case of the tail section, and the greater the number of cables, the more force held the airframe down. Each cable in effect constituted a pathway for capillary attraction; that is, over the years as the riverbed drained itself due to gravity, these cables would become flowpaths for water, again due to capillary attraction. If a dangling cable were, on average, 10 feet in length and ¼ inch in diameter, the water column represented would be 2 cubic feet. Multiplied by the density of water (62.4 lb./ft.^{3}), this water column would impose a weight of 125 pounds on the airframe. If there were 50 of these broken cables serving as pathways for water drainage beneath the airframe, their combined weight would be 6,250 pounds or over 3 tons, increasing the total weight due to capillary attraction to 12.5 tons. With the airframe weight added, the total weight the divers were trying to lift would have been 15 tons. Note that this figure does not include the infilled silt and sand that, relatively, was not any where near the problem that capillary attraction posed.

No wonder the flotation bags merely eddied about in the current, creating the impression for those seeking positive signs that the airplane was rocking on the bottom, struggling to rise; and no wonder the 12-ton lifting bag popped out of the hole each time, seeking the path of least resistance. The key to lifting the airframe was to break it loose from this capillary attraction effect, because, then, only the 2.5-ton weight of the airframe would have to be lifted. Breaking this attraction would not have been easy, because the entire bottom of the wing and fuselage would have had to be cleared from its interface with the riverbed and all dangling cables and wires cut. The crane was the optimum solution, because it could be manipulated by the operator to pulse the airframe with a moment of inertia greater than 15 tons, even though the capacity of the crane was 7.5 tons. The operator was able to generate this moment of inertia by alternately loading and unloading the boom and lifting cable, with the latter attached to the airframe. Since the limit load of such machinery typically is specified at two times the design load, the crane could have pulsed the airframe with a lift force of up to 15 tons. That this limit was actually exceeded is shown by the fact that so many strands of the metal lifting cable were broken during the pulsing that the cable finally broke completely as the crane swung the airframe onto its temporary platform on the beach.

It is evident, given these conservative calculations, that neither of the airbag approaches would have worked. The better of the two used its 12.5-ton capacity to blow itself out of the hole beneath the airframe each time it was securely restrained to stay in the hole. Being unable to apply near the pressure required to lift the airframe, its force went in the direction of least resistance and blew out the entrance to the hole, permitting the airbag to exit in the process.

Resorting to the use of a crane and being able to get one was the final and only solution in the time remaining. The expedition certainly benefited by having Northrop's Leo Gay at the recovery site to not only suggest that all effort be focused on getting and activating a crane to lift the airframe. It was just the right crane for the job and Leo was just the right man to insist on getting it. He had succeeded against similar odds at Northrop to get the N-3PB restoration project approved and to keep it scheduled for implementation during the two years of uncertainty preceding the final decision to proceed.

By now, the crew had been at work 30 straight hours. A few had been coordinating or at their support stations even longer. Ragnar had been up for 47 hours. With the airframe securely on shore and the day just beginning, everyone tried to rest, forcing themselves to lie horizontal and if necessary, feign sleep just to fool the body.

After a few hours, the beach crew began cleaning the wreckage with high-pressure hoses, while some of the divers went back in the river to uncover the left pontoon and its pedestal. At 9:05 p.m. this last major assembly of the airplane was winched to shore, weighing in, even in the water, an estimated 4-5 tons, so filled with silt and sand it was. It took three of the 4-wheel-drive trucks working simultaneously to drag it to the shore. Holes were punched in the side in order to work out as much silt as possible, but it was still extremely heavy to handle. Coming ashore, it looked like a small submarine approaching as two trucks (a Ford Bronco and a Volvo Laplander) winched it in, as Ragnar said, "By brute force." Apparently what had happened is that the local farmers, in trying to pull the plane to shore, first from the nose and then the tail, had wrenched the airframe off the pontoon pedestal, such that the pontoon turned over on its pedestal (which then became a virtual keel) and sank in the river bed beneath the airplane.

With all the pieces finally ashore, Crewmembers immediately began examining the hulk. The wing guns were found to have ammunition in the ammo boxes, and there were live rounds in the guns. The guns were in surprisingly good condition with the mechanism operable enough that with some prying, the breeches could be opened and the rounds removed.

Some of the team members began removing the wing attach bolts. This was a tedious job because there are fifty in each wing and after all that time in the water they had to be wrenched every thread of the way. It had to be done though, to get the aircraft broken down into manageable pieces. Northrop's Leo Gay watched the tedious process, thinking of how much easier it must have been to put the airplane together piece by piece on the assembly line; and that even Jack Northrop had never anticipated a design requirement that would someday accommodate wing removal on a glacial river beach.

What had been recovered from the river of the total airplane were the following:

a. The fuselage and wing center section with one outer wing panel attached.

b. The tail section, which had already broken loose from the fuselage by the attempts to wrench the plane from the river by the tail.

c. One pontoon with pedestal.

d. Miscellaneous parts of the wing and tail section.

Everyone stood about, pleased and proud of the effort put forth with such final success. Although all were elated that the expedition had come to a successful completion, with the mission impossible having been turned around, the condition of the airplane, now in remnants of an airframe, was disappointing. The savaged condition of the plane prompted speculation as to what had caused all this damage. Some felt that the plane must have incurred more damage during the crash-landing than originally thought. The missing starboard wing left a fracture that indicated it might have been torn loose by the wing hitting the water after the right pontoon broke off when Sevi abruptly banked to the right to avoid flying into the cliff that suddenly loomed out of the snowstorm. Three cuts in the forward area of the left pontoon were thought to have been possibly caused by the float collapsing into the path of the propeller when the plane spun right abruptly as the right pontoon snagged in the water and was thrown over to the left pontoon. But all faces reflected the same impression, that, as Ragnar wrote later, said:

> "This heap of junk is never going to become an airplane again." I had to confess I didn't think there was much chance of that either. But my mission impossible was over. Before long Northrop's restoration team would be embarking on a mission even more challenging and I was trusting that the mystic force watching over the project would not restrict its influence to the Iceland operation alone.[93]

To a substantial degree, the Thjorsa, that powerful glacial river descending to the sea from mid-Island, had lived up to its legend; it had not returned everything and what it relinquished was ravaged and had to be taken from it by force. The Thjorsa had more subtlety than its simple but harsh appearance evinced; it had all the natural laws of hydrodynamics at its disposal and in the final moments of the expedition's allotted time on the river, it almost won: it almost kept what it had taken. In subduing the Thjorsa, man increased his own freedom.

Gradually, responsibility for the airplane would shift to Northrop's Leo Gay. For Leo, a natural-born coordinator, the recovery phase of the overall restoration had provided a welcome opportunity to utilize some of his marketing expertise. He was that rare combination of engineer and marketeer, a talent of great value in the emerging aerospace industry of the U.S. Like most such talents, he tended to be unobtrusive, but always was observing and offering very keen assessments and suggestions on projects in which he was involved. From the Northrop side of the international team aiming to restore the N-3PB, he was the right man, in the right place, at the right time.

The truck, bulldozer, and crane crews who had implemented the final solution to subduing the Thjorsa departed with their equipment after a much deserved expression of

---

[93] Ragnar J. Ragnarsson, Loc. Cit. In regard to the damage to the left pontoon, the author personally examined it when the airframe was returned to Northrop for restoration. The damage was more of a crushed than cut nature and was on the inner side at both the front and rear of the pontoon. The conclusion reached by the author was that the first attempt to remove the plane from the water had been made by tying ropes around the pontoon at the fore and aft locations and trying to winch the plane ashore sideways. Given the weight of the aircraft and the sideways loading, which the airplane was not designed to take, the pedestal would have broken at its wing attach point and turned over on its right (inboard) side, thereby accounting for the fact that the pontoon and pedestal were found upsidedown under the wing yet still parallel to the fuselage.

thanks and appreciation, along with a hearty lunch at the operations center tent mess hall. Ragnar would see that recovered pieces got moved to the airport at Reykjavik and returned safely to Northrop for restoration. The task was now a relatively simple matter of aerospace logistics, though the mission impossible, in many minds, was beginning to border on the improbable.

Before trying to load the riverbed-laden parts on transport trucks, all accessible sand and silt were removed to lighten them and prevent further damage from excess weight. Figure 51 shows a typical cleaning operation on the beach at Camp Northrop. Easier to handle after this cleaning, the parts were then loaded by integral truck-mounted cranes onto two trucks and transported to a hangar at Reykjavik Airport.

There, over the next two months, the center wing section was separated from the fuselage to enable shipment in a C-130 cargo bay and parts were cleaned again. The parts were then crated and loaded on a Norwegian C-130 that came through Iceland in November on its way to a major scheduled maintenance inspection at a U.S. Air Force overhaul depot in St. Louis.

Baldur Sveinsson

Figure 51. The left pontoon was the last major assembly to be recovered. It was indeed weighted down by infill of riverbed material. Here at the operations beach the cleaning operation began.

As Burns had forecast, the plan had "gang aft agley." But it had brought a sense of organization and purpose that the team could not have done without. What endured of the plan and what had worked as planned was the team structure. In the end, the team became the plan, as they finally discovered exactly what had to be done. And they did it!

On September 30, 1982, for Ragnar's exemplary leadership role in the recovery of the N-3PB and his research of Squadron 330(N), King Olav V of Norway awarded him the Order of St. Olav of the 1st degree (Knight 1st Class).

Perhaps the quality of Ragnar's leadership was expressed most appreciatively by Trygve Skaug, who told Sevi Bulukin that the "Northrop Project" was the most professional recovery operation he had taken part in, both in organization and planning.[94] Trygve knew what he was talking about, for he averaged two major archeological diving projects each year for the Norwegian Maritime Museum, a private, civilian museum devoted to the maritime history of Norway and located in Oslo. Because he was a noted expert in archeological type maritime expeditions involving recovery of long-buried historical objects underwater, Trygve Skaug had been selected by Sevi Bulukin to be the leader of the Norwegian diving team, which had grown in number to supply divers in place of the British Sub-Aqua Club. It was a great loss to maritime archeology when Trygve perished on June 29, 1987 in an expedition near Kristiansand, a historical seaport in southwestern Norway, on the Skagerrak Sea. Ironically, an airlifter of the large-capacity type used to excavate the N-3PB, but operating at a much greater depth where the intake pressure could prevent a man from freeing himself, trapped Trygve underwater.

Burns's epigrammatic "the best laid plans of mice and men gang aft agley" was no more aptly demonstrated than in the recovery of the N-3PB Serial No. 320 from the Thjorsa River. Where the mice want the cheese and get defeated by their objective, so the expedition wanted the airplane and faced imminent defeat twice, each time changing its plan to fight the Thjorsa on its own terms, meeting force with force. As the river flowed on, restoring its riverbed, so the airplane was flown to its origin for restoration.

It would take more than cosmetic surgery to renew Sevi's "Grand old Lady." But, after all, not only had the Thjorsa taken her, but she had given more of herself to her mission than any of the other Northrop's. As her flight log shows (cf., Appendix B), she had flown twice the number of mission hours as any of the other N-3PB's. But then she was in C-Flight, the one on the eastern end of the Island, which flew toward Norway.

---

[94] Ragnar J. Ragnarsson, Loc. Cit., citing Sevi Bulukin's August 25, 1979 report on the N-3PB recovery project to the Inspector General of the Royal Norwegian Air Force.

Part III – The Restoration

CHAPTER 10 - RETURN TO PRODUCTION BASE: ZEN & THE ART OF RESTORATION

Patrol Bomber Model N-3PB, Serial No. 320, rolled off the production line at Northrop in December 1940 in the form shown in Figure 52a and returned 39 years later in the form shown in Figure 52b. As Heraclitus said: You don't step into the same river twice. Time effects change and change is major in a river if it's the Thjorsa.

(a) N-3PB No.1 on its first taxi run after delivery to Lake Elsinore, California, in December 1940, nine months after contract award by Norway.

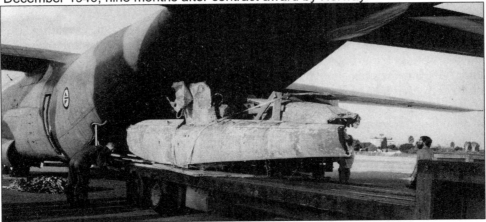

(b) SN 320 on return 39 years later for restoration, November 9, 1979.

Figure 52. As the farmer said, "What the Thjorsa takes, it doesn't give back." (Photo a. by Roy L. Wolford and b. by John Amrhein)

Time and the river couldn't undo the work of the original production team, for the spirit of that team was still at Northrop. The objective now was to reverse nature's entropic deconstruction effects through the Zen and Art of Restoration that only a dedicated team with the Jack Northrop "golden age" spirit could perform. If Zen is the meditative way of reducing the world to nothing, so as to arrive at the truth, the Northrop team was starting with nothing and was then required to restore something. It would take Zen <u>and</u> art to do it.

The Thjorsa River has been a major participant in this story of restoration. It was, in effect, *the* major factor in the recovery and in the restoration. Even in Iceland, this river is legendary and is attributed with special characteristics. One such attribute is that it never gives back what it takes. Another is that its name, "Thjor," in the ancient Norse language, means choppy ice or rapids; thus it is a river that tears up things that get caught in it. The Thjorsa had tried to take this Northrop seaplane first by grinding it with ice and then by burying it in the lava, silt, pumice, and clay of its bed. And it held in reserve yet another means to retain its victim should anyone be able to excavate the riverbed and unbury what it held captive. This backup measure was to set up a powerful capillary attraction between the object and its bed that literally sucked the plane to the bed as though in an eternal kiss. The Thjorsa was determined, it seemed, to take what it wanted using every stratagem given it by nature.[95] It had misled Sevi Bulukin into a crash landing that began the dismemberment of the plane; it had taken Leif Rustad's new flight boots; it had refused to give up its prey to the local farmers; it had tantalizingly withdrawn the plane from human view; it had mauled and reduced it to a "friable" condition; it had buried it in its bed; and, finally when the plane's rescuers came and took its cover away, it had applied its final bonding between itself and the plane where the rescuers couldn't see. It had taken a 7-ton crane to rip the plane from the river's hold.

As Leo Gay said in his reports to Northrop management:

> By three o'clock in the morning the crane crew began preparing the improvised wooden pads (cut from 3-foot diameter cable spools) for insertion beneath the four outrigger leveling jacks of the crane. The wooden pads were improvised as the only immediately available way to keep the jacks from sinking in the jetty that had been extended to the edge of the water. But they show how innovative these guys were, and how determined to let nothing stop them now that we had the crane. During the three hours this took, the divers continued their all-night tours taking turns underwater keeping the airplane ready for lifting by suctioning the infilling riverbed from around the wings and fuselage. At six o'clock in the morning of the 9th day, we were all ready to start trying to get the airplane out by lifting it. The crane operator really knew how to operate this equipment. The cables weren't even strong enough, so he had to double up the cables with a four-cable sling, a bridle of two cables to each of the two support beams beneath the wing center section. It was amazing to watch these guys

---

[95] The Norse meaning of the name "Thjorsa" was provided by Fridthor Eydal in an e-mail dated November 27, 2001.

operate the crane to get this thing out. The first thing to surface were the airbags that had been attached a week ago. Then the next thing to do was to get it over to the beach side. My first impression was that the skin on the upper wing surface was very thin – I knew it was too thin for a wing skin. Suddenly it hit me that for over 30 years the silt in the river had just worn it down, almost like something continually sanding it. It had gone down from 0.030 to 0.015 inch or something like that. There wasn't anywhere that wasn't hit by the silt. Only the stainless steel firewall was still perfect. On the left-hand side of the fuselage, some damage was unfortunately done by the hoist cables, when we had to pull it out (of the riverbed). So there are some wrinkles in the fuselage where something like the hoist might have hit it. So, as far as I can see, the restoration is a little more work than we had planned for originally....[96]

Given that Gay didn't wear glasses, his view of the pending restoration was either a wild understatement, ignoring the reality of what the crane (as stork) had actually delivered from the riverbed, or a calculated ploy to get the plane home again and deal with the consequences later. What was brought to Northrop for restoration were what Cornish had perceptively called the "friable" remnants of an airplane unrecognizable as to origin or model except for the faintly discernible serial number that, in itself, would have been meaningful only to a learned aviation historian or to someone formerly associated with this particular model aircraft. What the Thjorsa had given back was not what it had taken; it had lived up to its reputation.

Over the 1977-79 period Ragnar and the IHAS had struggled with their mission impossible, while the key personnel at Northrop had settled into an attitude of, 'If and when the plane is delivered, we'll restore it.' In January 1977, when Ragnar's letter of introduction to the project arrived at Northrop's Aircraft Division in Hawthorne, California, the reaction among those who would be responsible for the actual restoration was exuberant, even euphoric. Among those who had worked on the plane in 1940 or who remembered its historic position as the first aircraft produced by the new Northrop corporation formed in 1939, its arrival was particularly anticipated. Even before Leo Gay proceeded to Iceland and Norway to coordinate the details of the project, Darrell McNeal, who had worked on the original N-3PB production line as one of Northrop's first aircraft mechanics and who was now manager of Advanced Production, was called into a meeting by Don Page, manager of Aircraft Division public relations, along with the author, then manager of the Division's program planning organization.

This meeting in late-January was an informal one to coordinate the arrival of Ragnar's letter (via Corfield in Northrop's London office) inviting Northrop to participate in the project of recovering and restoring an N-3PB airplane. Page was immediately

---

[96] This text is a condensation and author's edit of two briefings given by Leo Gay to Northrop management personnel, the first on July 11, 1979 and the second in September 1979 following his return from the Phase V recovery operation in Iceland. The briefings were tape-recorded from his extemporaneous talks and the stenographic drafts remained in rough form until edited by the author.

interested in the project because the company's 40th anniversary was coming up in two years. It would be a great public relations ploy to have the first aircraft produced by the company on display. It had been he who had arranged for a $3,000 budget to fly Leo Gay, the company's Advanced Project Engineer, to Iceland and Norway to check out the situation of the airplane and the support for the project in Norway. But, before entering into an agreement with Iceland and Norway, Page wanted to know whether McNeal thought it was feasible to restore an old, wrecked N-3PB and do it in a way that would be a tribute to the company. He knew it was a difficult question with so little information available, but McNeal had helped build the plane, knew it inside and out, from propeller hub to rudder, and was the only management person whose opinion would be respected. Page had to have McNeal's view as to the feasibility of the project before he put his own executive weight and reputation behind it. He didn't want to put over a year's publicity buildup into it and end up holding a bucket of bolts.

To appreciate McNeal's response, the word "feasibility" has to be understood within the context of its use in the aerospace industry; it's a much-used word in the industry. In its aerospace sense, it means two things: (1) can this be done and (2) should it be done? The first question is the purely technical consideration as to whether a project is doable. Here the concern is whether there are technological unknowns that might trip things up downstream; whether the existing state of technology can achieve the required form, fit, and function; and whether personnel with the necessary expertise and facilities with the necessary equipment are available. The second question is that of time and cost: can the required effort be accomplished on schedule and within a reasonable budget? When these two questions are answered in quantitative terms, the project can be evaluated through the use of a cost-effectiveness ratio. Such indices are used in the aerospace industry to optimize a project in terms of its technical content and the amount of time and money required to complete it; and also to compare one project approach with alternatives to select the most optimum in terms of time, cost, and performance. Thus in the aerospace industry the word "feasibility" denotes and covers an array of tradeoffs.

McNeal answered, "Who's going to pay for it?"

It was the perfect response. Of course, Page was using the term "feasibility" loosely, conversationally; and everyone at the table knew it, but McNeal's response answered the question of feasibility by jumping to the next question, "Who's going to pay for it?"

This response told everyone that there was no question of feasibility, but simply one of funding the necessary budget. First of all, there was no question of feasibility, because McNeal, as Northrop's first and only manager of Advanced Production to that time and an expert manufacturing executive, would have instantly identified any question of feasibility pertinent to the project itself. By jumping to the question of funding, he was not evading the question, but in effect saying there's no problem with the feasibility of rebuilding this airplane, just bring me the propeller hub; or, even, just give me the serial number. Clearly, at Northrop, there was the same kind of wartime "mission impossible" spirit present – as in Iceland with the ilk of Ragnar J. Ragnarsson – and Darrell McNeal personified it.

When the Norwegian C-130 carrying the remains of the N-3PB landed at Hawthorne Airport and taxied back midfield to the Northrop airport office, there was a small crowd of Northrop executive personnel, managers, volunteers, and visitors waiting in the noon sun to get a first look at what had returned after leaving 39 years earlier brand new. When the tail cargo ramp was lowered and the ragged remnants came in view, there was a noticeable pause in breathing and talk as everyone stared in disbelief or smiled awkwardly in having expected more. Here was a crowd that had grown up with and whose livelihood involved airplanes, and what they were seeing was scarcely an airplane. For those who had never seen an N-3PB, there was no way to visualize what these pieces of metal might have looked like when assembled as the original airplane. For those who knew the airplane either from having worked on it or seen pictures of it, a substantial stretch of imagination was necessary to visualize it as the plane they knew.

Typical comments were as follows:

Elizabeth McNeal to her husband Darrell: "This is nothing but crap. You'll never get an airplane out of this."

McNeal, in response to his wife, thinking of the team he had assembled: "We'll do it, honey."

Leo Gay, to no one in particular: "It looks better when you see all the pieces laid out."

Don Page, shaking his head as though awakening from a bad dream: "Is this an airplane?"

The author, moving forward to look into the cargo compartment: "Is this everything we're going to get?"

Bub Larsen, Advanced Production manufacturing manager, to McNeal: "This is a mess. First thing is we've got to clean it up."

Bob Lovell, vice president of Manufacturing, as he, McNeal, and Larsen left the unloading pad: "You SOB's have bit off more than you can chew, this time."

Lovell, of course, was of the temperament usually required and found in a top level manufacturing executive –with a common sense, no nonsense, and straight-from-the-shoulder kind of mentality. His off-color comment was in a sense a form of compliment – a challenge to prove him wrong, knowing that if they went ahead with the project in spite of his putdown, he probably would be – and no doubt inwardly he was smiling, knowing that these "SOB's," whom he admired and respected, would no doubt prove him wrong.

But Lovell, being pragmatically engrossed in his executive job function, himself underestimated and misconstrued what was in process here. In the end it was not this "mess," as Larsen described it, that would be restored, but the pure wartime spirit of human teaming that had made the mission-capable aircraft feasible. It was not a glacially deconstructed airframe that was to be rebuilt, but the infinite spirit that vectors beyond space and time into the eternal unity of the team. While in the pragmatic world it is always necessary to divide to conquer (no matter what Benjamin Franklin said[97]), eternity requires unity (a.k.a. order) to conquer. McNeal knew that there was plenty of unified human spirit ready to take on that "mess" of remnants left over from the Thjorsa River's attempt to ravage and entomb the N-3PB. He had no doubts that the team he was forming would soon sort and parse the pieces and patiently restore what time and the river had been unable to destroy. The international team of Iceland, Norway, and Northrop had acted just in time and now Northrop would carry the project forward to completion.

Darrell McNeal had been captivated by aviation since childhood. Born in 1919 in Sandstone, Minnesota, just 15 miles from Lindbergh's hometown, he was introduced to aviation as it emerged from its first colorfully heroic days in the First World War. It was a time when youth entering into their manhood dreamed of the dogfights they read about between begoggled, scarf-streaming aces flying Spads and Fokkers over no-man's land in France and Germany; and, of course, saluting one another as gentlemen knights aloft as they flew away, neither able to defeat the other, so at one with their planes. It was a time when a young, spirited male could live his dream barnstorming in a surplus Army Air Corps plane, the very way Lindbergh was earning his living in the early 1920's. Born on a Minnesota farm, McNeal, at 18 years of age, bought a set of drawings for the Pietenpol homebuilt, by mail order as advertised in Popular Mechanics magazine.[98] He built this high-wing monoplane in a corner of the barn, working on it every spare hour of the day. Since he had already learned how to fly, he took off in it as soon as it was finished, for he had already lined up a job with Vogue Theater in town, delivering leaflets around the countryside to farms and towns announcing upcoming events, such as theatrical productions, circuses, evangelical meetings, and barnstorming tours that people otherwise would not know about. For the rest of his life, aviation would be his main source of income.

McNeal's wife Elizabeth recalls that when in her teens she had worked at the Sandstone Hotel, he would fly over and wigwag the wings of the Pietenpol, waving to her from aloft. She always knew when he was approaching, because the Model-A engine powering the plane could be heard huffing and puffing miles away. She would run to the roof to wave at this mustachioed hero of the air; and that's how they first saw one another: she on the roof waving and he, flying back and circling to show off his prowess,

---

[97] Franklin, of course, said, "United we stand, divided, we fall."

[98] This was a Bernard Pietenpol-designed 1929 Air Camper with a Ford Model A engine. Known popularly as "The Pietenpol," the Air Camper, made mostly of lightweight spruce, was one of the first widely constructed and flown "homebuilt" aircraft, and is still a favorite today. The author bought one and flew it after joining Northrop Aircraft, Inc., following service in the Army Air Corps during WWII. McNeal's discovery that the author had a Pietenpol was a permanent bond between the two. Bernard Pietenpol (1901-1984), the "Father of Homebuilt Aircraft," was inducted in the Minnesota Aviation Hall of Fame in 1990. Over the years, the basic Air Camper design has remained the same, except for minor changes to accommodate more modern engines such as the Chevy Corvair and Continental 65, plus a radio and battery. With Pietenpol's drawings one can go to a lumber yard and hardware store and buy all the basic materials for the airframe.

attracted to this lone waif. Four years later they married and moved the same day to Hawthorne, California; McNeal had followed Jack Northrop's aircraft design breakthroughs since the mid-1930s and, having recently learned about the formation of Northrop Aviation, Inc., he was determined to work for Jack Northrop, because that was where the center of aviation would be, in his view.

Arriving in California in mid-October 1940, McNeal used their remaining funds to sign up for a training course in aircraft riveting, metal fabrication, and assembly offered by an aeronautics trade school in downtown Los Angeles. Completing the course in two months, he interviewed at Northrop on 16 December 1940 and was hired as an assembler on the spot. Elizabeth McNeal remembers the date well, because Christmas was approaching and they had no money and no paycheck would be forthcoming for two weeks. But, as always, Santa Claus saved the day, because her last paycheck from the Sandstone Hotel suddenly arrived; so there was double cause for celebration: Darrell had the job he wanted and they had money to enjoy the holidays. In January 1941, McNeal was put on the night shift where he would earn 7 cents more an hour, raising his hourly rate to 50 cents. The first airplane he worked on was the N-3PB. His assignment was to install the engine cowling. Having previously built an entire airplane himself, he quickly saw ways to improve assembly operations at the new company. Not only did he make major innovations enabling the company to beat schedule on Norway's urgently needed WWII seaplane, but he worked on all the succeeding aircraft designed by the company, except the B-2 stealth bomber, which was built by a separate, specializing division operating under "black hole" security controls, but staffed by many McNeal "graduates."

When N-3PB Serial No. 320 arrived at Northrop on 9 November 1979, McNeal had been manager of the Advanced Production organization for 23 years and a Northrop employee for 38 years. He was 59 years old, in the prime of his career. The first N-3PB had come off the production line just three days before he was hired and now the 20th, on which he personally had installed the engine cowling, was returning to production base 39 years later. It was bound to be a milestone in his career: the first Northrop-designed and-produced airplane and his first professional job. Over the years he had participated in virtually every facet of technological growth in the manufacture of aircraft and here, though bedraggled, was the first airplane he had worked on.

In fact, a technological transition was in process at Northrop, for in one more year the company would be the leading competitor on the B-2 stealth bomber program and Northrop's Tom Jones, chairman and chief executive officer, would take the highly innovative, yet risky step of trying to produce the first commercially-developed tactical fighter, the F-20. Having been through the F-89, P-61, F-15, XP-56, N-156, and F-17 prototype developments, McNeal would retire in 1986 with his career culminating in what many considered Tom Jones's Folly, the F-20.[99] Having this opportunity to restore the N-3PB was, in the long run, something he would look back on fondly as a restoration

---

[99] McNeal and his Advanced Production organization built three prototypes of this outstanding, advanced lightweight fighter over the next five years before the company, because of political considerations, suddenly dropped the program.

of his faith in the industry that Jack Northrop had pioneered. The N-3PB represented all the fundamentals of airframe technology as formulated by Jack Northrop. And for McNeal himself, the restoration would provide proof of origin of his career. Being a man of quiet certitude and one who decentralized power of authority through delegation of responsibility, he similarly delegated the meaning and power of the restoration.

McNeal had reached this point of self-realization relative to the N-3PB in several stages since that first meeting with Don Page, Leo Gay, and the author in January 1977. With his question to Page, "Who going to pay for it (the restoration)?" he had cut through a lot of technical boilerplate as to feasibility. He had learned through the years that by the time a project got to the conference stage, the question of feasibility really came down to the basic issue of not just whether it was affordable, but was there a budget for it. He knew nothing was done in business unless there was an accounting number to charge to. He didn't want to turn on his key people who, in turn, would assign their workers, without knowing that there was money to complete the project.

It was the best question he could have asked, because Page quickly made it known that he had managed to scrape together just $3,000 to cover Gay's trip to evaluate the project. Subsequently, when it took two years to prove the plane was indeed in the river, Page's appeals for budgetary support at Northrop were responded to by the Aircraft Division's General Manager in quid pro quo terms: "We'll authorize you to proceed and provide a work area for the restoration if you can get volunteers to do the work."

The General Manager was simply being realistic, for it was a time at Northrop when the company was "in between" major programs and there was no management reserve or surplus budget to engage in what was basically viewed as a part of Northrop's history based on the Jack Northrop years. The company was moving into a new technological era: stealth aircraft were the main topic of discussion in aerospace boardrooms and highly secret design developments were in process under Department of Defense contracts by Northrop and its aerospace competitors. The Stealth Fighter and the Stealth Bomber would be the next generation aircraft. Since flying wing type designs were the most compatible for the stealth mission, Northrop at least had a credible image going into this competition. It had to back that image with the necessary stealth technology to optimize the all-wing configuration. To reach and sustain a competitive edge, the company itself had to invest in its own proprietary research and development and also conduct a comprehensive marketing program. The most enlightened strategy, rigorously conducted, had to be planned and implemented.

Not only was this investment in the prime aircraft candidates for next-generation military missions absorbing company dollars, but also Tom Jones, now at the peak of his aerospace executive management career as Chairman and CEO of Northrop Corporation, had long advocated a commercialized defense industry. Jones's view was that Adam Smith's "magic hand" of the marketplace was the most cost-effective way to produce the aircraft needed by the Department of Defense for its own use or for export.[100] Jones was not alone among aerospace executives who thought the same way, but he was the most

---

[100] Adam Smith, *The Wealth of Nations,* published by Great Books of the Western World, Vol. 39.

articulate and consistently assertive. The idea he put forth was that the defense industry should be run the same way as other industries, strictly on a competitive basis that would include defining the original specifications that weapon systems should meet. Eventually most of Jones's ideas were in some degree incorporated by the DOD, as, for example, the use of "design to cost" principles and industry's response to basic mission needs statement with alternative weapon system specifications. But Jones was still more competitively minded, still more of a competition purist. He thought industry should not only specify the weapon system but also build it and demonstrate it using company funds. This extreme was that of pure commercialism, pure competition in the maul of the marketplace. Furthermore, Jones had the courage of his convictions to do that very thing. With the Northrop F-20 Tiger Shark he was to spend $4 billion of Northrop's retained earnings in an unsuccessful attempt to prove his point.[101]

But driving Jones's highly publicized objective of building better airplanes to meet national and global security needs by commercializing the industry was the accompanying but unannounced objective of making more money; profit maximization was the real goal. Profit could be maximized if the company was freed from the increasing number of DOD directives and program management systems that gave the government access to the actual cost of an aircraft; for with the cost known, the government could take the next logical step of stipulating the profit margin. Jones saw that he could defeat the government's increasing visibility and control of the financial strategies of defense companies like Northrop by commercializing the entire aircraft development cycle. Northrop would be a pure manufacturer and the DOD would be a pure customer. Northrop would develop, demonstrate and produce; DOD would shop and buy: defense transactions would be conducted in a form of aerospace mall.

Included in this clinically clear management separation of producer and buyer was a similarly clinical view of employees. As time has shown, at many large and small companies employees have become treated as "temps" and "independent contractors" to complete the separation of the company from any responsibility other than for the product to be sold or the "bottom line." What had been the freedom and spirit and love of aviation – the dream of flight and the flying machines envisioned by the Wright Brothers and the other pioneers of aviation was now a financial process for maximizing profit; effectiveness was now measured by the stock price and the amount of profit the company made on its product; employees were now just "labor" as a secondary factor of production, capital being primary. All over the industry it seemed that Jack Northrop's management concepts were rapidly fading away.

What was happening is that as the 1980's approached and the N-3PB was recovered for restoration, "aviation" was transitioning into "aerospace" and aircraft such as the N-3PB were taking on new historical importance as roots of the vital origin from which it had all begun. These were roots that had to be nurtured if workers of the future were to

---

[101] A photo of the F-20 is shown in Chapter 14, where the significance of this airplane as the beginning of a turning point in the business strategy and attendant work environment of Northrop is further noted.

avoid being totally mechanized and robotized by the new corporations. As McNeal, the hands-on aircraft builder from Lindbergh's Minnesota well knew, the Jack Northrop days, when the company executive was also the designer who worked in direct coordination with the employees as part of a team to make the product succeed, were about gone. Now most of the decisions were made by boardroom engineers who, if they were wrong, used the error in judgment for tax write-off purposes to engineer and optimize the balance sheet to maximize profit.

The competitive forces of the marketplace had indeed forced Jack Northrop into retirement in 1952 at age 57, well before the realization of his visionary flying wing approach became operational practice 28 years later in the B-2 bomber. Looking back in later years, Jack Northrop reflected that he had lived in the golden years of aviation, when it "was a fun job":

> I would get up in the morning, eager to see what we could do with the planes. And at night, I would say, 'Tomorrow we'll see what we can do to make them fly better. It was a big thrill every day.... It was before the computer age. It was before the growth of giant corporations where a committee makes every decision. We were never told "you can't do this or don't experiment with that." Everything we did was aimed at making a better aircraft and we had a lot of successes. Aircraft designing will never be the same again.[102]

McNeal knew that restoration of the N-3PB, though of minor impact financially for a company the size of Northrop, would be a major fulfillment for those who were still "Norcrafters" of the Jack Northrop variety: those who loved what they were doing and who worked extra hard for excellence in their respective functions with small regard for recognition because Northrop had built a company that was "a good place to work." He had done this by encouraging individual initiative as an indispensable element of the teamwork necessary to excel; and this individual initiative in the context of teamwork is what needed to be restored.

In his usual quiet, self-assured way, McNeal accepted the fact that the company would only authorize restoration of the airplane on-site if it were done by volunteers: "Fine, that's the way we'll do it," he thought. It would prove a point about the people that Jack Northrop had cultivated to build his company. So when Leo Gay returned from Iceland in February 1979 with the news that the N-3PB was recoverable for restoration, within a week McNeal, Larsen, and the author had 85 volunteers signed up. By the time the airplane arrived 10 months later, 213 volunteers were ready to proceed, including, with McNeal himself, 10 who had worked on the original production contract in 1940. Even Clete Roberts, L.A.'s prime time TV commentator and aviation history buff (seen in Chapter 3, Figure 17) joined as a volunteer. At the project's peak, over 300 men and women volunteers (some, husbands and wives of employees) were onboard. Restoration fever was so rampant that W. J. Minner, Quality Assurance department manager, worked under a technician's direction cleaning parts. The team consisted of such a mixed group

---

[102] Margaret A. Kilgore, "Northrop, Early Aviation Idea Man, Remembers," *Los Angeles Times*, September 3, 1979, Part VII, p. 3.

of employees and outsiders, working various days and hours of the week that the company issued a special badge so that security guards would know whom to let in at the entry gates to the plant.

What soon became clear to McNeal was that when the General Manager had said the restoration would have to be a volunteer effort, he meant that even materials and parts would have to be voluntarily supplied by vendors.[103] The volunteers would manage that, too.

The Norwegian C-130 delivered the following assemblies, subassemblies, and parts of Northrop N-3PB, Serial No. 320, as one "mess" of an airplane:

- The fuselage, broken at the separated tail section, lacking a forward firewall and engine section, and with the integral center wing section removed.
- The wing center section with the cockpit floor and control stick exposed.
- The left outer wing panel with wing tip missing.
- The right outer wing panel as far as the second rib from the wing root at Station 112.
- The remains of the fuselage tail section beginning at Station 204.5, missing the vertical stabilizer except for the tip and lower fuselage fairing, the right elevator and horizontal stabilizer, and the left elevator trailing edge and ribs outboard of the left trim tab.
- The left float with pedestal and small sections of the right pedestal.
- Accessory equipment such as the radios, seats, battery, and installed equipment such as the pilot's electrical control panel.

The first official step was to transfer possession of the airplane. This was a technicality that had to be taken care of, because the airplane, though produced by Northrop, was owned by Norway and was not being imported to the U.S. Even though the airplane was being returned for restoration as a nonfunctioning military aircraft replica, someone had to take possession of it. Because of the cost of insurance, Northrop had made arrangements for the San Diego Air Museum, a nonprofit organization, to be the legal recipient, while Northrop would provide storage room. Thus all personnel who worked on the plane would have to be volunteers acting independently of their employment by the company. Figure 53 shows the C-130's arrival, reception, key personnel, and the turnover meeting.

Once the C-130 parked, the N-3PB assemblies and parts for Serial No. 320 were immediately removed from the cargo bay by the Northrop transportation department and

---

[103] It was only near the end of the restoration, when key executives could see that the restored aircraft was going to be a major coup for Northrop internationally, that this all-voluntary policy was relaxed, as described later. By the time the airplane was set up by the Bub Larsen team at its final exhibit site in Norway, Northrop would have subsidized the project with over $1,000,000. As McNeal noted later, it would be difficult to calculate the cost of time, equipment, and parts contributed by volunteer workers and suppliers. Sometimes a price cannot be put on value.

Figure 53. Top, Norway's C-130 arrives at Northrop Field; middle, Jack Mannion and Leo Gay greet Baldur Svendsen, of IAHS, and Col. Nils Magne Joergensen, Royal Norwegian Air Force; bottom, Leo Gay coordinates transfer of N-3PB SN320 for Northrop voluntary restoration. (Photos by John Amrhein.)

trailered to a hangar at the east end of the Northrop 72-acre complex, which ran parallel to the Hawthorne Airport, known historically as "Northrop Field." Murray Lahue, the transportation manager remembers the event well, because the only item that seemed to have survived intact was the battery. He recalls that Manny Rubio, his service manager was so impressed with the apparently undamaged condition of the airplane's battery that he took it by the battery shop and found that it still held a charge. This discovery was later to gain some publicity for the project and for the battery manufacturer, Exide.

For the next year, the hangar just north of the Boeing 747 manufacturing facility at Northrop was to take on the character of a "Skunk Works" where secret government programs are conducted. That facility would be dedicated to the restoration project and become the offtime workplace of a highly dedicated group of aerospace workers of various job classifications and positions, ranging from assemblers to executives.

Key personnel of the McNeal volunteer team accompanied the parts and positioned them on the concrete floor of the high-bay, hangar type building assigned for the restoration. Their reaction on getting a closer look at what had been sent from Iceland for restoration was surprise, mixed with concern over the task ahead. Some wondered why the parts had even been returned. What they had to work with was the ravaged remnants of a purported airplane scarcely recognizable as such. Why not start from scratch?

The general feeling of the initial inspection team was expressed aptly by R. B. Mackay, a volunteer from Leo Gay's Advanced Project Group: "The initial inspection made after unloading the Norwegian C-130 at Hawthorne Airport showed that early reports of the condition were very much in error." [104]

In general, everyone at Northrop had been led to believe, based on the February report from Leo Gay, that the airplane was in reasonably good condition. These reports were so positive that when attempts were made in June to round up engineering and tooling drawings and produced no results, no one was disturbed; it was concluded that even without drawings the airplane itself, assuming it were complete, would serve as the model by which to configure the few parts that would have to be made. The team was surprised at the disparity between what they had been led to believe and what had been unloaded on them, but not discouraged; they simply had to recalibrate their concept of the effort that would be required to restore the airplane.

Mackay spent most of November examining the condition of the airplane so as to establish a baseline assessment of what would have to be done to restore it. He documented his findings graphically by means of the sketches shown in Figure 54. As indicated, only about 50 percent of the airplane had survived the ravages of time in the river and the mauling of man. Not only was a great portion of the airframe missing, but at least 40 percent of the assemblies delivered were severely damaged to the extent they couldn't even be used as patterns to make new parts.

Mackay's report on his assessment of the airplane's condition succinctly conveys what the volunteer team had to cope with:

---

[104] Northrop Memorandum 2246-80-VE-77, "Design Note 80-1 N-3PB Damage to Airframe," dated December 4, 1980, R. B. Mackay to Those Noted.

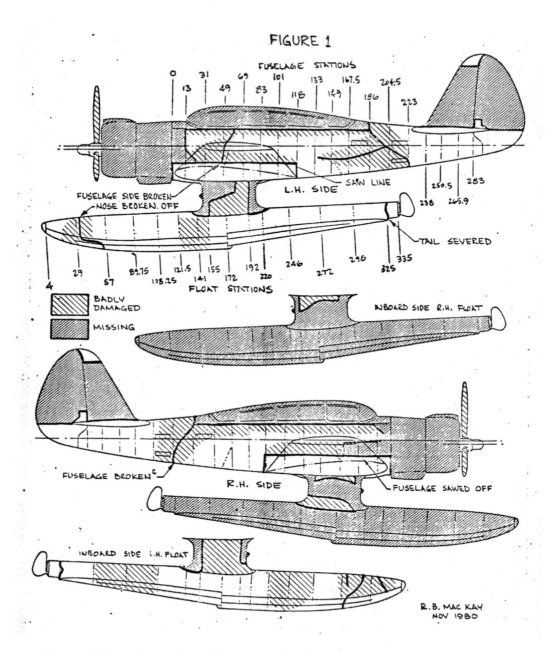

Figure 54a. Generic left- and right-hand side views of the N-3PB identifying badly damaged and missing assemblies on Serial No 320 as returned for restoration.

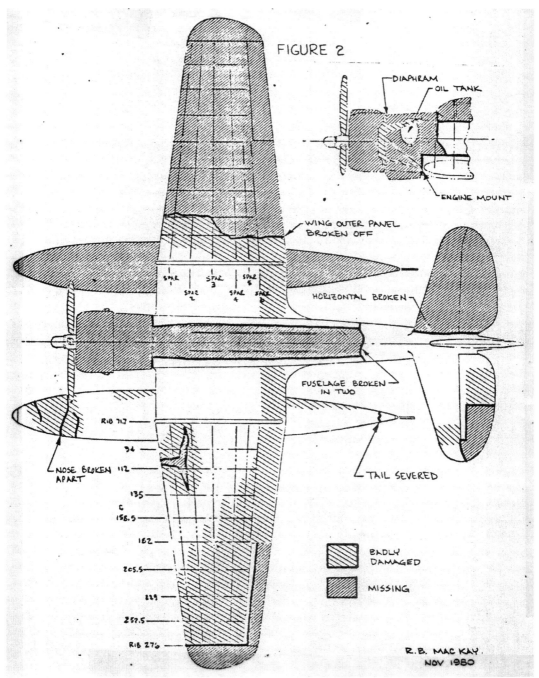

Figure 54b. Generic top view of N-3PB identifying badly damaged and missing assemblies on Serial No. 320 as returned for restoration.

The recovered airframe was in very poor condition. The outer skins were pitted and showed extensive evidence of corrosion (more likely 'erosion'), which had been expected. However, the entire vertical surfaces with the exception of the tip of the fin and the bottom 18 inches of the rudder were missing. The right elevator and horizontal tail from the fuselage attach point outboard were missing. The left-hand elevator trailing edge and ribs were gone from the trim tab outboard with much of the remaining structure deformed.

The wing center section was probably the least damaged component of the entire airframe. The center section did, however, have major damage or missing structure along the trailing edge above the flap area. The left outer wing panel was crushed between each spar, with the trailing edge of the tip rotated about 30 degrees above its proper location, kinking the spars in a diagonal pattern across the wing. Extensive damage (had) occurred in the area of the gun bays in an apparent attempt to recover the guns. The left aileron nose section was still attached to the wing, but all the structure aft of the aileron spar was gone. The left wing tip was not recovered. The right outer wing panel was not recovered outboard of Rib Station 112 (second rib from the root) and major damage was done to the root area.

The right float was not recovered (the one ripped off during the crash-landing). The complete left float was recovered with the nose and tail severed and crushed inward in three areas (see Figure 30a). The nose of the float was broken off three feet aft and the tail (was broken off) complete with (the) water rudder at Float Station 325. The left side was crushed just forward of the step with the right side crushed between Float Station 89 and 121 (and) also between 246 and 298. The left pedestal was still attached to the float with the forward outboard and upper area either badly damaged or missing. Small sections of the right pedestal (near the wing attach point) were recovered with severe damage.

The fuselage has suffered considerable damage during its years in the water; (and) in addition the recovery team sawed through the fuselage frames approximately 6 to 12 inches above the wing surface to allow (separating the wing section) for shipping in the C-130 aircraft. The fuselage was broken in two at Fuselage Station 204.5, with severe damage to the frames at Stations 167.5, 186, and 204.5. The frames were broken into 6 to 12 inch segments, some of which were not recovered. The frames forward of the break, to the pilot's bulkhead, were crushed and deformed. The left side of the fuselage was separated at the bulkhead. The right side was torn apart between Station 13 and 31. The Station 0 (Firewall) lower section, missing the lower right-hand engine mount area, was still attached to the center wing. The structure forward of the firewall, except for the badly bent and broken engine mount and engine diaphragm, was not recovered. This (not recovered) included the engine, engine cowl, accessory cowls with the oil scoop, but the oil tank was recovered.

The interior parts were in general recovered in fair condition including radios, seats, battery and most installed equipment. The major exception in interior equipment (not recovered) was the control system, since most of the brackets were magnesium castings which dissolved (electrolytically) after 35 years underwater.[105]

Clearly this was a rather grim picture. Lovell might have exaggerated the size of the bite, but certainly they had taken a big one. Figure 56 shows the actual condition of major parts as received on the C-130 from their recovery in Iceland. No wonder that at the dinner reception on the evening of the arrival of the Norwegian C-130 with these remnants of an airplane to be turned over to Northrop for restoration, Col. Nils Magne Joergensen, representing the Royal Norwegian Defence Museum, got the biggest laugh of the evening when, in his after dinner talk, he said, "The first thing I noted were the tears in the eyes of the Northrop people when they saw their old airplane again after 40 years."

Even the few electrical system parts returned were in virtually unrecognizable condition, except for the indestructible Exide battery, which apparently thrived in the Thjorsa's frozen or near-freezing environment. Figure 55 shows how the pilot's master electrical control panel looked, as returned, compared with the original installation.

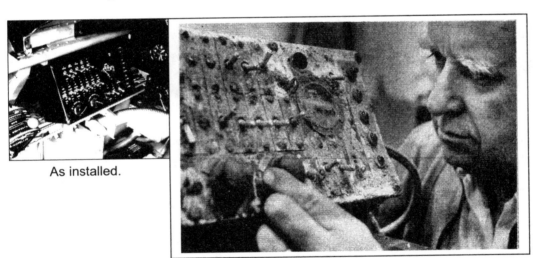

As installed.

As returned for restoration.

Figure 55. The author checks whether the Bomb Indicator Light rheostat of the Pilot's Electric Switch Panel (left front cockpit) still works.

---

[105] Loc. Cit., pp. 1 and 2, excerpted with changes in punctuation and additions noted in parens.

Forward Fuselage and Tail Section (left)

Forward Fuselage and Left Pontoon

Left Wing

Right Wing with Center Wing (rear)

Rudder Base and Left Horizontal (rear)

Pilot's Floor on Center Wing Section

Figure 56. The parts recovered from the Thjorsa River could be likened to artifacts from a pre-Columbian archeological dig. (Photos by John Amrhein.)

New, the N-3PB had taken nine months to manufacture. The question now was how long would it take to restore what once had been new. These remnants of the airplane would not only have to be rebuilt, but the pieces taken apart, cleaned, scraped, sanded, parts cut from new metal and shaped, formed, drilled, and riveted together. Since many of the parts were so damaged they couldn't be restored or even used as patterns and since hundreds more were missing, much of the effort would have to start from the beginning, with drawings.

But were there drawings? Given the condition of what had been recovered, it would have been easier to build the entire plane anew than to restore it. But there was no money for that; this was an all-volunteer effort by a team motivated by more than money.

Time was clearly the major constraint. Mackay's memo had documented the structural condition of the airplane within three weeks of its arrival. In parallel, McNeal, the author, and Larsen defined a work plan based on the time constraint of having the restored aircraft ready for rollout on Jack Northrop's 85th birthday on 10 November 1980, one year and one day from receipt of the plane at Northrop Field.

Ambitious? Had they bitten off more than they could chew? There were a lot of unknowns, but the team was confident that its skills in combination with its determined spirit and the value of what was being done would enable it to achieve the goal.

After the remains of the N-3PB were reviewed, it was obvious that a new approach to the restoration would be required. The piecemeal nature of the remains would affect how the volunteers were organized as well as the tooling sequence (discussed later, separately). The task prior to receipt of the remains had been perceived as a one-of-a-kind prototype project, in which McNeal and his top, handpicked managers had become expert. In fact, because of the constant stream of Jack Northrop's experimental concepts for new aircraft and his hands-on involvement in their construction, McNeal in the early 1940's had begun to conceptualize a compatible advanced production approach to prototyping aircraft. This approach featured an expert team of managers and craftsmen who worked on the aircraft as a whole structure and not piecemeal. These were people who knew every piece of an airplane by first-hand fabrication and assembly experience.

The concept of McNeal's Advanced Production Department matched Jack Northrop's innovative, experimental nature, and the department was an advance form of the "Skunk Works" team approach that also became standard practice at Lockheed Aircraft Company in Burbank, California. The "Skunk Works" approach got its name formally coined in the 1960s when around-the-clock prototyping of secret or "black hole" aircraft was being done at Lockheed and at each 8-hour shift breakpoint in the 24-hour workday a stream of workers could be seen scurrying from the parking lot to the prototyping plant like skunks moving back and forth to build their den. [106]

---

[106] The true "Skunk Works" requires inspirational leaders like Jack Northrop and Darrell McNeal. At Lockheed, that person was Kelly Johnson (1917-1984). Ed Heinemann (1908-1991), whom Jack Northrop knew at Douglas, was a similar force at Douglas Aircraft Company. Interestingly, these men were not so much noted for their educational credentials as for their ability to get a complex manufacturing job done fast with quality results, even though the configuration of the

The Advanced Production Department at Northrop was, in fact, an aircraft factory capable of performing all the operations required to build an airplane short of mounting a sustained production rate. Under this concept, all the key people in the department had to be multi-skilled but able and ready to perform specific responsibilities. McNeal had staffed his key managerial posts with just such people. All were long-term, career-oriented Northrop employees schooled under managers who had worked directly with Jack Northrop and understood perfectly his management policies. Each was an innovator who knew how to get a job done with no excuses and who would never let bureaucratic obstacles stop them. They knew that "Northrop is a good place to work" was more than a slogan and they inspired, by example, the kind of company loyalty in their people that made that motto a reality. They led the signup of volunteers and by being volunteers themselves they made sure all were onboard who would be needed to restore the N-3PB.

The restoration plan as perceived prior to the receipt of the airplane's remains was reworked within a matter of days from one that had envisioned the restoration of a generally intact airframe, to one that was actually a build-from-scratch project. McNeal made the following assignments from his key personnel to ensure that all hardware requirements had an immediate person responsible for coordinating requirements:

- Overall Project Management – Darrell McNeal
- New Parts Fabrication – Bill Martin
- Engineering – Dick Mackay
- Wing – Harris Stone
- Fuselage – Les Epperly
- Engine – Dale Brownlow
- Aft Fuselage Section, Flight Control Surfaces, Floats – Oliver Larsen
- Engineering Coordination, Tooling, Flight Instruments, Guns – Ed Weaver
- Purchasing - Ron McAlpine

At the same time, these personnel were not boxed in. There was an implicit working condition allowing and encouraging across-the-board help in getting things done and in problem solving. For example, it took a lot of coordination to decide on the best way to make the restored airplane easily shippable by air or sea. As work on some sections proceeded faster, there was subsequent downstream mixing of crews and responsibilities to concentrate effort where needed most to keep the project moving ahead on schedule. If one section were held up for material or parts still in fabrication, the crews would work on something available, as members of Larsen's crew did on the ailerons, flaps, and floats. There was no hesitation to work flexibly wherever help was needed; it was not "work" in the usual sense of gainful employment: it was a restoration of something beyond work for material gain.

---

product is constantly changing during manufacture. What separates them from the general workforce is their ability to master and absorb changing complexity while sustaining the continuum of the manufacturing sequence in a seemingly uninterrupted flow under tight schedule.

The plan agreed to among the key personnel time-phased the major end-item subassemblies for integration into the final aircraft assembly, including painting and decaling, by the specified completion date, as shown in Figure 57. This was the kind of plan that the key personnel could work to most adeptly. Being so expert in their fields they were the kind of people who didn't have to be told how to do their work; all they needed to know was what needed to be done and by when. Hence the plans shown are "what" and "when" plans. No work statement or work orders were needed. Once the key personnel knew what was expected of them, from then on the restoration took on its own rhythm, like a ship sailing across uncharted seas with expert sailors aboard. It was the *SS McNeal* with all its hardy and ready crew, who could bite off anything and chew it.

The team had an excellent building to work in, conveniently located near a main guard gate for 24-hour access all week. With over 10,000 square feet of overhead lighted floor area covered by an arched high-bay roof with skylights and opening through full-width sliding hangar doors onto an aircraft parking pad, the building could accommodate the entire airplane as it was re-integrated, while providing ample adjacent areas for positioning assembly fixtures and tools for building up the major subassemblies. Having a dedicated building like this added to the cohesiveness of the team and sparked further enthusiasm to restore this airplane on time and with quality results. It was a one-of-a-kind airplane being brought back to earth by a one-of-a-kind team. It was a nonrecurring effort that would go onward in the spirit of the restoration, like the Thjorsa flows ever onward into the vastness of the sea, returning what the sea has bestowed.

Additional facilities were made available to support the main restoration area, including standard functional areas and equipment for parts cleanup and for the forming and machining of new replacement parts. Such access was provided on a noninterference basis with ongoing contractual work of the company and the labor expended was voluntary.

At the meeting where the author presented the program plan for sequencing the restoration effort in a logical flow of subassemblies for final integration into the airplane as an assembly, it was agreed by all the key personnel that the airplane would be completed and rolled out on Jack Northrop's 85th birthday. What better way to show him that his company was still alive than to roll the N-3PB out of its restoration area, replicating the first production delivery of an airplane made by Northrop Corporation?

It was so perfect a gift for the aging aircraft design genius and business entrepreneur that everyone participating in the restoration felt a sense of excitement in doing something so especially meaningful for the man who had made such a vital input in making their own lives meaningful. In working on this gift it was a form of gratitude for his part of their lives and also a display of their own ingenuity and expertise. For the volunteer team, that was the real goal of this restoration: to show that they could do it for the man who had made it possible for them to do it. It was a project of mutual esteem and gratitude.

With this goal as the focus of the program planning kickoff meeting, group leaders were assigned, operating ground rules were established, a numbering system was established for identifying and accounting for parts, special badges were issued to be

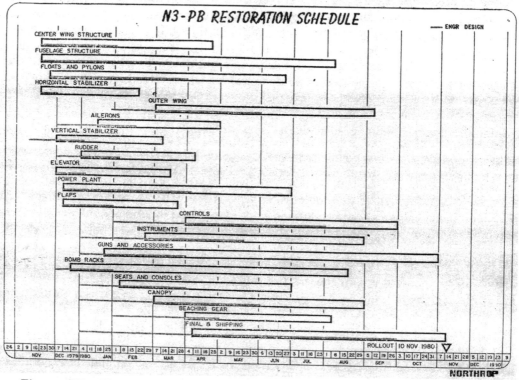

Figure 57. The project plan for restoring the N-3PB told the volunteers what needed to be done and how long they had to do it; and the team was organized accordingly: rollout was November 10, 1980, Jack Northrop's 85th birthday and the N-3PB's 40th!

worn by all team members, and logbooks for recording volunteer time worked were provided to each lead person of the key personnel organization.

With the project plan now formally agreed to, key project lead personnel were officially assigned to each major aircraft subassembly as shown in Figure 58. No titles were necessary, as management and control was distributed to each volunteer at the piece level of assembly worked on. Lead personnel, while working shoulder-to-shoulder at the piece level like everyone else, had the additional task of coordinating questions and requirements among the other key personnel and obtaining or arranging for equipment and materials needed at the piece level. Thus the lead personnel were distinguished by being "runners" and "go-fors" for the hands-on workers, while also doing their share of hands-on work. It was the ideal organization from the workers viewpoint, because being a key person meant you had more work to do. Using music as an analogy, the key personnel had to play an instrument while also orchestrating the band. The key to meeting schedule was coordination; hence the key personnel were called "coordinators." Historically, in the early aircraft industry, having the job title "Coordinator" was a coveted position denoting a person who knew the entire manufacturing and production process from design to shipping and followup spares provisioning. To be classified as a "Coordinator" was prestigious; you were a person who knew it all.

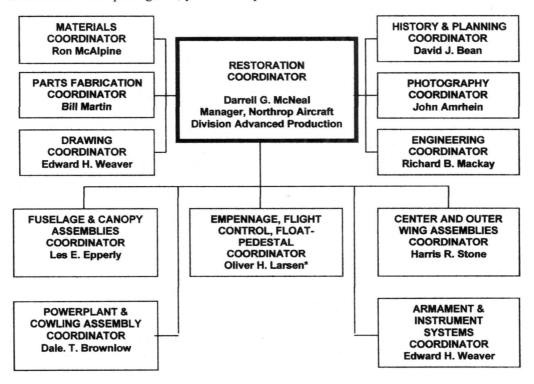

*Larsen led his overall crew participation in assembly of empennage (consisting of vertical stabilizer, rudder plus horizontal stabilizer and elevators, and aft fuselage section), assembly of wing ailerons and flaps, installation of flight control mechanisms, and assembly of floats and pedestals with beaching gear.

Figure 58. A key person was assigned to coordinate completion of each subassembly and subsystem of the airplane in accordance with the restoration schedule. These were the most knowledgeable and capable of the volunteers who agreed to coordinate requirements within and between subassemblies, while also working on their own end-items.

The assignments shown in Figure 58 are primary and do not begin to reflect the overall range of activity of these personnel or of many of the other volunteers. The assembly functions performed by volunteers ranged from scrubbing parts to remove lava silt, sanding to remove corrosion and surface scratches, cutting metal, shaping to size by filing, drilling attach holes, deburring, bending to shape, caulking, painting, clamping in position, riveting, mating with other subassemblies, and integrating the entire plane. In addition, tooling had to be designed and fabricated, including holding fixtures and assembly jigs. These had to be optically aligned to ensure boresight trueness of the fuselage, tail, wings, and floats.

The entire operation was like a regular production line compressed into one station. Parts were made and brought directly to the fuselage jig, the empennage jig, the float and pedestal jig, or the wing jig. The latter was the center of operations in the restoration building, and the subassemblies from the other jigs were brought to it for final integration. The flow diagram of Figure 59 shows the overall steps of the restoration process from detail part to final assembly.

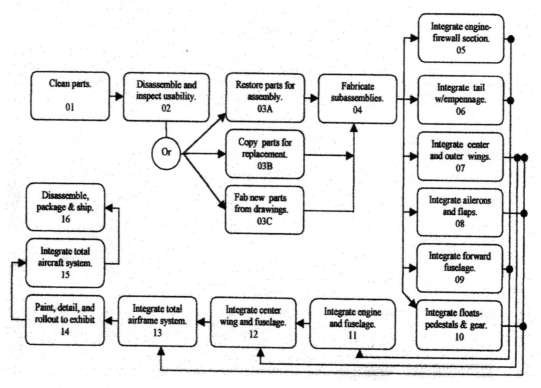

Figure 59. A mini-production line was set up to organize work areas for the restoration team, leading to scheduled rollout of the detailed aircraft.

Of course the actual process did not flow with such methodical precision. Step 01 was absolutely necessary, so as to assess the detail condition of each part. For an airplane that had a maximum gross takeoff weight of 10,600 pounds, the one returned for restoration was incredibly overweight. With all the Thjorsa River silt and lava sand that filled every compartment and covered every surface of the recovered airplane, it was estimated that the C-130 that arrived at Northrop Field on November 9, 1979 carried an N-3PB cargo that weighed almost 6 tons, even though incomplete! It was estimated that 1,200 pounds of Thjorsa riverbed was removed from the returned airframe during the cleaning process.[107] Two 55-gallon drums were filled up with lava silt and pumice washed out of every crevice of the returned parts. No wonder that the main gear of the C-130 transport aircraft sank to their axles as the cargo plane waited on the tarmac to be unloaded.

So the first act of restoration was to clean the parts of the mud and silt from the Thjorsa River that, as Farmer Johansson had said, never gave back what it had taken; only then would the airplane be truly free of the Thjorsa River curse. For the river hung on to its prey even after the victim was pulled free of its intended grave. This first step, while entailing hours of tedious scrubbing, scraping, and rinsing, was not without its rewards, for it soon became a treasure hunt by all the volunteer team to get a rock or even a vial of volcanic sand or silt from Iceland. The first volunteers had the best choice of these sedimentations, but word soon spread throughout the Northrop facility that a rare form of "gold" was being mined at a location known as the "Restoration Building" on the Northrop complex. To get some, of course, one had to volunteer, and so the ranks of volunteers grew. While the airplane would eventually leave, the treasure it had bought in would remain. Today, the volunteers still talk about the size of the rock or the quantity and variety of silt and sand they got from the cleaning of the parts, when they meet another volunteer and reminisce about the restoration.

The cleaning task was necessary so the parts could be inspected in Step 02 to determine whether they were acceptable for use in restoring the airplane. While the condition of the airplane precluded its being restored to flight worthiness status, the rule followed in the restoration was that any part had to be capable of carrying its original static load.[108] Such loading, of course, depended on where the part was located in the airplane. If the part was installed along a primary load path, it would have to carry the full static load experienced on that path. It is estimated that while 40 percent of the airplane was recovered, only about 30 percent was reusable in the restoration; thus 70 percent had to be remade.

As Figure 59 indicates, this refurbishment was done either by copying recovered parts, by fabbing parts from original drawings or, as volunteer Robert L. Gunter said, by using sketches drawn by the "guess and be damned" method (Gunter's excellent reminiscence on the restoration effort is presented in the next chapter; as Elizabeth McNeal recalls, he was an engineer who wrote poetry, hopefully not more rhyme than reason). So the second step became a major decision point. Basically, a part had to meet two criteria to be acceptable for use: it had to be cosmetically free of obvious defects not treatable by filling and painting; and it had to meet a minimal 1-g static load condition.

---

[107] Harris Stone found a California lizard preserved in a center wing compartment. California? Well it wasn't from Iceland.

[108] A flight worthy airplane has to be capable of withstanding static and dynamic loads. Static loads are those imposed by the g-loading of the airplane as it sits on the ground, whereas dynamic loads are those experienced in flight under the anticipated worse conditions of weather and mission profile maneuvers. Dynamic loads typically reach multiple gs. With 1-g equaling the plane's maximum static weight, a dynamic load of 5-g's would equal 53,000 pounds (5 x 10,600) in the N-3PB's case, an overall increase from 5 to 25 tons in weight experienced.

What this meant in practice is that the part had to look defect-free after painting and had to be able to carry its share of the airframe weight after installation.

Parts meeting this mostly visual check entered into the flow of the restoration process in Step 03A. All parts used in the restoration, old and new, were primed with an epoxy primer made and supplied free by the Deft Company, who guarantees absolute protection of the metal for decades under even extreme environmental conditions such as might be found in regular operational usage (though not in the Thjorsa River). The final coat was an epoxy lacquer, also supplied by Deft, matching the original camouflage in colors.

But 70 percent of the airplane had to be rebuilt. The effort facing the restoration team was virtually one of manufacturing a complete airplane, but without drawings! Even a model airplane built out of balsa wood requires drawings. The project, now organized, staffed, and with a scheduled plan of how to proceed was stymied for lack of drawings. The mystic of recovery had come to the rescue of Ragnar J. Ragnarsson's recovery expedition. Would it also rescue the restoration? The team was getting discouraged, realizing the schedule that had to be met was a fixed timeline and that if drawings were not forthcoming, something had to give. The question wasn't so much whether the plane could be restored, but when. And the answer depended on how they were going to have to proceed – with or without drawings.

The C-130 transport that flew the recovered remnants of N-3PB SN320 back to production base brought with it a full flight crew, representatives from the Royal Norwegian Air Force and its Air Museum, and a representative from the Icelandic Aviation Historical Society. This particular C-130 was not primarily assigned to bring the N-3PB back for restoration, but was in the U.S. for a major maintenance modification by Lockheed in Dallas, Texas, and then was headed for various air bases in the eastern U.S. to pick up spare parts for the return trip to Norway, via Iceland. Having arrived at Northrop Field on Friday, these personnel would spend the weekend in Southern California as Northrop guests.

On Saturday evening of the second day, after an all-day shopping tour, the personnel were hosted by Northrop for dinner at Castagnola's restaurant on Redondo Beach Pier, which juts on piers from the beach out over the Pacific ocean; and then on Sunday it was to Disneyland during the day, followed by another dinner hosted by Northrop. Figure 60 shows the flight crew and dignitaries on arrival and then at the dinner party where Leo Gay served as master of ceremonies.

It was in his after-dinner commentary, that Col. Nils Magne Joergensen finally broke the ice on the formality of the occasion by remarking that, instead of happiness, he had witnessed nothing but teary eyes when the Northrop people saw what was being returned to them for restoration. Of course he was jesting and everyone knew it, but what his words portended, as all also knew, was that what the Thjorsa had taken and not returned was now to be restored by the Northrop team of volunteers, fortunately a highly capable team. Somewhere in its silty riverbed the Thjorsa still retained half an airplane. What had been ripped from the riverbed was that portion Jack Northrop was noted for designing as integrally lightweight, strong structure with cellular composition. It was that organic, humanlike portion the river – which was like time – couldn't keep.

RNoAF and IAHS rep's on arrival 11/9/79, from right, Baldur Sveinsson, Col. Nils Magne Joergensen, Lt. Col. Scheie, Capt. Lerstein, Capt. Lyssan and crew (K. Berg, O. Oevrum, F. Svenkerud, J. Brannvoll, E. Kjoeren, absent H. Dalen, K. Skotvedt, K. Finnebratten.)

Northrop Host Leo Gay and wife (center) and Paul Spikula (left) and wife lining up for Norwegian and Iceland guest photo at the Squadron 94 restaurant, Torrance, 11/11/79.

Figure 60. The official end of the recovery and beginning of restoration (Photos by John Amrhein.)

CHAPTER 11 – A NEW PHASE OF RECOVERY: THE SEARCH FOR A BURIED DESIGN BASELINE

By mid-December, with one month of the restoration project already gone and nothing done but partial cleanup of the remnants, the scope and magnitude of what had to be accomplished suddenly became clear. The goal was to rollout the restored aircraft by November 11, 1980, one year after receipt. With one month having passed with mainly paperwork accomplished but no real metal bending or cutting, the key personnel of the project began to realize that what they had "bitten off" was virtually to repeat history; that is, to do in one year what had been done in the original production program in 1940: what they had committed to do, given the virtually useless remains of structure recovered from the Thjorsa River, was to produce a new airplane.

Labor was no problem; volunteers in all the necessary specialty capabilities were continuing to sign up. Material was no problem, either, because there were supplies on hand and donated materials from suppliers who were ready to participate at no cost; and only one airplane had to be built. Plant was not a problem, because Northrop Corporation had set aside a dedicated prototyping facility area just for the restoration.

So all the basic production factors appeared to be under control. But there was still a major element missing, perhaps the most crucial factor for such a manufacturing effort: there were no production drawings! It seemed that the Thjorsa still had the plane (and now the project) within its silty, clay-sticky grip; and time was now the current flowing fast toward November.

Despite the desire and expectation to maximize use of existing parts, the fact that 80 percent of the airplane had to be refabricated sent an immediate alarm through the key personnel, who were the coordinators everyone came to for direction on how to proceed. How were they going to make all these replacement parts without drawings?!

The entire project was suddenly in crisis; none of the original drawings could be found! A plantwide search was immediately mounted to locate any kind of data that could be used to make replacement parts. Parts that could not be used suddenly became valuable molds or patterns for their replacements. Photographs of the airplane, artist's renderings, and planform views – all became potentially valuable manufacturing media. It was in effect an archeological dig. Everyone and anyone who had worked on the original production program were contacted to determine what they knew about the existence and location of any kind of data or documentation, in any media, that could be retrieved.

If the key to repeatable production of aircraft is what is known as configuration management, this situation was configuration management at its most fundamental level. Bub Larsen immediately began compiling a configuration baseline for his sections of the airframe using his own part-numbering system. The list added up to over 400 parts, counting right- and left-hand copies. For those parts that had to be re-made, absent any known drawing database at the beginning of the project, Larsen made his own drawings. But, overall, from the viewpoint of the entire airframe, there were still major chunks of information missing. The complete design baseline consisted of several thousand drawings of every type specified by U.S. Military Specification MIL-D-1000. Could the gaps be filled? And in time to meet the rollout date? Those were questions that began to loom for and haunt the key people who did not have parts to copy. Larsen's tail section was relatively simple compared to the main forward fuselage, wings, and pontoons.

The obvious place to check for drawings was the blueprint control organization, but the equally obvious answer received there was, why would we be controlling the drawings for an airplane produced 40 years ago that had been struck from operational usage ("struck off charge" or SOC'd) for 37 years? The technical library had only a few company brochures that showed pictures and brief stories of the airplane. Ironically, more information could be obtained from the 40-year-old back issues of local newspapers; but still no real technical data showing useful structural configuration was uncovered anywhere. Word and contacts spread beyond the ranks of volunteers, beyond Darrell McNeal's Advanced Production organization, to those whose career paths, unforeseen, had been built on the N-3PB.

Darrell McNeal was quietly consternated but not surprised that the drawings for the airplane were no longer available. But it was his job to build airplanes, not record them. There had been a major break and shift in the company's management structure and philosophy with the early and sudden retirement of Jack Northrop in 1952; and in the next 18 years the fact that he had been the founder of the company and the premier originator of modern aircraft design became almost as buried in the company's history as the N-3PB had been in the Thjorsa River.

Fortunately, McNeal was an instinctive historian. Since this airplane was the first he had worked on – was in effect his rite of passage into modern aircraft manufacture – he had kept two of the aircraft manuals in his personal history file: the *Handbook of Service Instructions* and the *Overhaul Manual*. He knew immediately that these would provide basic undimensioned configuration data. The next step was to get this information into the hands of the engineering personnel who would know how to establish basic dimensioning using key parts recovered from the river.[109]

The fuselage was the main concern because the entire engine and its mounting structure was missing forward of where the firewall (also missing) should have been. The rest of the fuselage, originally manufactured as one assembly from engine firewall to tailcone, was broken in two, with the tail separated just behind the rear cockpit compartment. The forward portion (where the crew had sat) was missing the entire

---

[109] Since Leo Gay had reported on his return from the recovery site in August that major structural items such as the vertical stabilizer and firewall were missing, arrangements to prepare drawings to re-make those parts had been started before the remnants of the airplane arrived for the full-scale restoration. By the time the airplane arrived, the situation regarding the lack of original production drawings had become well defined. The impact of the lack of these drawings struck in all its adversity when the deteriorated, ravaged, and decimated condition of the plane was seen.

canopy assembly and, having been sawn away from the wing center section in Iceland to expedite shipment, lacked flooring and substructure. The aft portion was without the vertical stabilizer, which was missing, and also without the horizontal stabilizers, of which only the left was recovered. The question – and its accompanying quandary – was how to reconstruct these two portions so they could be reintegrated in conformity with the original aerodynamic moldline?

McNeal met with Dick Mackay and E. A. "Gene" Smith to establish an approach by which to answer this question. With no drawings available, the usual approach would have been to "reverse engineer" the fuselage from the parts available. But with so many of the key, controlling parts missing, there was an inadequate basis for that fallback. Mackay, a key aircraft engineering volunteer from the Northrop Advanced Projects organization, had led the initial inspection of the airplane, as reported above. He knew that the engineering effort that would be required to restore the airplane was to be much greater than had been expected. Smith, too, was an engineering volunteer, from Conceptual Design, working under Mackay.

Both were expert generalists in aircraft design and knew how to generate aerodynamic moldlines from the controlling fuselage station geometries. They knew that the master station for a propeller driven airplane was the firewall bulkhead where the engine mounted. On the N-3PB the firewall was Fuselage Station 0 (Zero), meaning that the firewall set the x, y, and z coordinates for all other stations of the entire airframe, including wing and empennage stations. Given the shape of the firewall and the longeron placements about that shape, plus the shape of the recovered bulkheads, they could reconstruct the structural layout of the entire fuselage "to its tailcone" and integrate the wing and empennage structures just as in the original production aircraft.

Smith found just what he needed in McNeal's *N-3PB Handbook of Service Instructions*, which showed a head-on photo of the firewall bulkhead. Reproduced in Figure 61, this photo showed just what they needed to prepare a drawing by which to fabricate a new bulkhead for Fuselage Station 0: the firewall contour showed the aerodynamic moldline and the locations of the major longerons carrying engine loads throughout the fuselage; and it also showed the geometry of the engine mount attach fittings to which the oil tank (recovered intact), the engine and accessory section cowling, and the engine and anti-drag ring attached.

With this bulkhead as benchmark for xyz coordinates, the entire primary fuselage structure could be generated in drawing form. It was a crude, but effective beginning.

There were problems, however. The photo shown in the handbook had not been taken directly head-on; the camera angle had been slightly off center and the distortional effects of this misalignment were significant: the hole pattern for the engine mount bolts was distorted, there was no clear horizontal reference point from which to scale, and the contour in the vicinity of the maximum diameter were obscured. These problems, unless resolved, would have a ripple effect throughout the length of the fuselage.

So the project was stymied again. The possibility of this situation developing had not been considered, because of the excitement surrounding the idea of restoring one of the

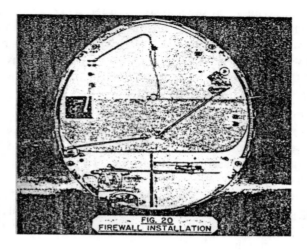

Figure 61. With no drawings available, a copy of a photo of the engine firewall at FS 0, reproduced from the "N-3PB Handbook of Service Instructions," was the starting point for generating the overall airframe configuration. (Photo by Roy L. Wolford.)

N-3PB's for Jack Northrop's birthday and the glowing reports coming from Leo Gay as to the "only slightly damaged" condition of the airplane. Ed Weaver's report on the restoration captured the situation quite well:

In about June of 1979 it appeared that we were seriously in the restoration business. Teams were established and volunteers were solicited and assigned to teams. The team responsible for engineering, tooling, and external stores began searching for any scraps of information that might become useful in the restoration. An original handbook of service instructions dated January 1941 and a handbook of overhaul instructions of the same date were found in the Nortrhop Library and six copies were reproduced by Kathy Seay in our Service Center. Microfilm of some test reports were also found and reproduced. Because of the reportedly good condition of the aircraft, the news that a thorough search of our engineering files had not turned up any N-3PB drawings wasn't particularly disturbing. Gene Smith made contact with Gerald Balzer (an ex-Northrop employee and historical aircraft bug) and found that he had a few original drawings, pictures and negatives. Gene borrowed the only known assembly drawing, took it home over Christmas holiday and traced it on vellum so we could make blueprints. John Amrhein contacted Balzer and arranged to borrow the N-3PB negatives he had. These negatives turned out to be a treasury of views including those used in the handbooks mentioned previously. (I believe these pictures were all originally taken by Roy Wolford.) John made two copies of each of these pictures; one was given to the group leader it would most benefit and the other kept in a master book from which extra copies could be ordered.

That was our engineering! We were relatively comfortable with it until 9 November 1979 when we met the C-130 and first saw what we were going to make an N-3PB from.[110]

It wasn't that Leo Gay was flagrantly unreliable or a maverick. Rather, he was too reliable and definitely a team player. Along with Don Page he had been one of the most enthusiastic supporters of engaging Northrop support for the restoration and, as he had said, "I want to bring this baby home." He felt that way because he agreed with everyone else that it would be the best possible gift for Jack Northrop on his birthday and also because he himself was a historical aircraft restoration hobbyist. Since the company had assigned him to coordinate the project internationally, he considered it his responsibility to make sure the plane returned for restoration no matter what shape it was in. It had been his decision in Iceland at the recovery site to not retrieve the engine remains from the nearby Farm Skridufell, as a similar engine and cowling could be obtained in the U.S. and save the time and effort for more nonstandard restoration requirements. Leo knew that the key requirement was to bring the airplane back regardless of its appearance and that after the complaints and criticisms were expressed, a team of Northrop aviation loyalists would take over and get the job done. The complainers and the critics, he knew, though the loudest, were in the minority; they were the problem-oriented people, the ones who used most of their time looking for problems. Most people he knew at Northrop were solution-oriented, like himself. They would not only find a solution to the restoration, but have fun doing it and relish the results all their lives.

Fortunately, the author, too, having taken on the responsibility to document and plan the project, was contacting the people he thought might know where the original drawings were stored. Dr. Ira Chart, with a doctorate in Languages from Harvard, had joined Northrop Aircraft Division in 1964 to work on new business proposals from a semantics viewpoint. Initially, he had worked for the author, who, at that time, had been manager of major R&D proposals. Over the next 15 years, Dr. Chart became known as Northrop's historian. He had assembled a virtual library on the aircraft the company had designed and built. He instantly identified who should be contacted regarding the N-3PB engineering data that no one could find: Roy Wolford, Northrop's chief photographer! He had taken the photo of the N-3PB engine firewall and a thousand others.

Like most photographers, Wolford was not one who wanted to be in front of the camera. He was the photographer, not the object being shot. However, though relatively obscure among Northrop managers, Wolford had a most notable career, which he had made out of what had begun as an avocation. His background in aviation began in 1934 when Jack Northrop's second corporation, formed with Donald Douglas, Sr., in 1931, employed him. Initially he worked in sheet metal fabrication and then in heat-treating. During the six years at what became Douglas's El Segundo Division, he worked on the Northrop Gamma, A-17, and 8-A series of aircraft.

---

[110] Edward H. Weaver, "The N-3PB Story," dated November 21, 1980. Ed was team leader for N-3PB restoration engineering, tooling, ordinance, and instruments (cf., Figure 58).

Wolford's career became specialized in photography after he met Harold Jackson, who also worked in manufacturing at the Northrop El Segundo facility where Jack Northrop worked, essentially, for Donald Douglas. Jackson was an aerial photographer in the Air National Guard, and soon Wolford was spending every leisure hour learning about cameras, photography techniques, and the relevant technology in general. The two convinced Jack Northrop in 1935 that the manuals published for each aircraft would benefit from having more photographs. To demonstrate what could be done, they took photos during the day and developed them at Jackson's home in the evening, driving the 80-mile roundtrip to Eagle Rock each day. Nine months later, Jack Northrop authorized them to build a photo lab at the El Segundo facility. By the time Northrop parted with Douglas in 1938, the two were recording flight tests of Douglas's DC-3 series of aircraft.

But Wolford was more interested in working for Jack Northrop. As the latter began building his new 72-acre aircraft production plant in Hawthorne, California, in 1939, Wolford volunteered his own time to photograph the construction of the new plant. Then in April 1940, just as Northrop signed the contract with Norway for the N-3PB airplane and just as Wolford was considering enlisting in the Army Air Corps as an aerial photographer, Jack Northrop offered him the opportunity of setting up the new company's first photo group. Wolford seized the offer, for he knew just what Jack Northrop wanted this new organization to do: record static tests of new aircraft; record ground and flight tests; record aircraft structures, equipment, and systems for operations and maintenance manuals; and, increasingly important for configuration management of rapidly changing technology and aircraft upgrades, recording all engineering design data and drawings on microfilm.[111]

The N-3PB was the first airplane Wolford documented photographically in all these categories. He personally recorded the first taxi tests of the N-3PB at Lake Elsinore, California, and photographed flight tests as onboard crewmember. On the trips to Lake Elsinore, California, where the flight tests of the seaplane were conducted, he took his wife with him. She was a loyal booster of his talent, which was that rare synthesis of vocation and avocation, throughout their 54 years of marriage.[112] On one acceptance flight, the pilot was Commander Kristien Ostby, the Norwegian Royal Air Force officer who had coordinated the contract with Northrop and remained at Northrop until all the aircraft had been accepted by his government through him. But most importantly, Wolford microfilmed the N-3PB engineering database, including the model specification,

---

[111] The story, according to Wolford himself, is that he went to Jack Northrop in April 1940 and said he was going to join the Army Signal Corps as an aerial photographer – a whole new field of warfare reconnaissance and the forerunner of modern airborne surveillance systems. Northrop, having just signed the contract with Norway to deliver 24 N-3PB seaplanes, with first delivery in one year, said, "Oh no you're not. As of this moment, you're hired as my manager of photography. I want every drawing on microfilm and I want every flight test documented in film and photos." What Northrop didn't mention, but knew, is that fatigue tests of airframes would also be recorded photographically by Wolford, who would apply photo technology in every way that would improve engineering and production efficiency along with customer support.

[112] Mrs. Wolford died July 25, 2001.

stress reports, performance analyses, vibration test reports, weight and balance reports, flight test reports, and drawings. When no information could be located initially by the volunteer team, Wolford went to an obscure data vault in Plant II where rows and stacks of storage boxes containing canisters of 35mm microfilm reels were found along with rows and stacks of boxes containing company financial records. Bob Korn, the manager of the photo lab within what was now the greatly expanded Graphic Arts Department, had accompanied him. Korn agreed to notify Dick Strawn in the Micrographics organization that what was thought to be a complete microfilm record of past Northrop aircraft engineering drawings had been found and that arrangements should be made to convert any drawings of interest to vellum form for subsequent reproduction of blueprints for distribution to the volunteer restoration team.

Hundreds of reels of microfilmed drawings had been found, but which contained the N-3PB drawings? It would take weeks, if not months, to manually search thousands of frames of drawings to locate those needed. Also, it would have to be a volunteer effort, because this was an unfunded project. Valuable time had already slipped by. April of 1980 was approaching, and the airplane had been in the restoration process over five months already. Progress was being made, but at the piece-part level, not at the major assemblies needed to integrate the total airframe for rollout by 10 November.

When microfilm of the key N-3PB technical reports had been discovered in the main Technical Center Library, it had been quickly coordinated by John Reynolds and Bill Jones of the Library for reproduction by Tom Strawn of Micrographics, to get copies to the key restoration coordinators. Even Ed Weaver, who had volunteered out of McNeal's Advanced Production organization to handle tooling, armament, and instruments, took time away from his main tasks to help with the microfilm reader machine; and Dick Mackay, while originally looking for drawings of the vertical stabilizer as his main objective at the time, helped with the reproduction and distribution of the second-generation paper copies. These reports were eagerly worked over to find airframe geometry data showing reference lines for the primary longitudinal, vertical, and transverse coordinates of the wing and fuselage; dimensions for degrees of movement for flight controls; cross sections of bulkheads; control surface airfoil shapes; and equipment lists.

Fortunately, the search for possible sources of drawing information had by now reached beyond Northrop. A stroke of good luck was needed, and as most successful people know, having good luck is often a matter of having good instincts. All of the key coordinators were engineering or manufacturing generalists who operated a lot on instinct when detailed information was not available or was sketchy or preliminary. Gene Smith, having for the moment resolved the issue of the engine firewall configuration in coordination with Mackay, was now working equally hard to find drawings of the pontoons. Meanwhile, to reconstruct the configuration of the badly damaged front end (3 feet in length) of the recovered float, Smith and Ed Ayers of the Division's Master Dimensions organization were redefining the pontoon contour lines, using lines from the recovered left pontoon and drawings provided by Edo Corporation, the original designer and producer of the floats.

The floats were particularly challenging because of their 30-foot length, which was only 6 feet less than the overall airframe length. Their restoration typifies how a combination of drawing data and direct replication of existing parts was used in restoring most of the airframe. Since the two pontoons were symmetrical, usable parts from the left pontoon could be copied to provide drawings for fabrication of new parts required for both pontoons. In late February 1980, Smith was assigned to prepare drawings showing contours of the keel, keelson, chines, and cross-section contours for the bulkheads and frames, for use in making these parts. To replace the parts in the severely damaged bow, it was necessary to redefine the pontoon contour lines. In this redefinition, Ayers discovered that the drawings provided by Edo were for a Vought Aircraft XSB2U-3 configuration that had slightly different offsets along the center reference line for the bulkheads and frames, though the outside moldline configuration was the same. This discovery added to Smith's incentive to find the actual N-3PB drawings.[113]

Since the first of 1980, as part of his network for getting more specific design data, Smith had made frequent contacts with Gerry Balzer, a former Northrop engineer who had become such an avid aviation historian that he had made a major mid-career change to specialize in writing histories of aviation companies. Balzer had been tracking the progress of the N-3PB recovery and restoration project and responded to the volunteer team's urgent search for configuration data after the plane arrived, by providing photos of the fuselage and wing loft boards; over 100 photos of the plane's evolution through design, production, and test; and copies of two original N-3PB drawings, Drawing No. 500301, General Arrangement, and 504282, Insignia and Marking Plan.

Three months later, in April, Balzer called Smith to say that he had found a note in his records identifying Microfilm Reel 312.42 as the one containing N-3PB Drawing 500456, Cockpit Enclosure Layout. This drawing was not only crucially needed, but the fact that it existed on a microfilm reel cracked the code on the rolls of historical microfilm discovered four months earlier, through Roy Wolford. It was like the Rosetta Stone had been deciphered anew. With this one lead, it was possible all the drawings needed would be found on the same reel. Smith notified Micrographics' Dick Strawn who assigned Brian Seltzer to (a) locate the reel and (b) locate the drawing on it. Again, though a breakthrough had been made, another obstacle loomed; the reel could not be located on the list. But persisting in his assignment, since a previously known reel had been identified, Seltzer learned that the filing records for the reels had been recatalogued in the mid-1960s. He now knew that there were only two possibilities of finding the data: either one of the reels had original filing information on the storage can or inside it; or

---

[113] The pontoon drawings found two months later showed only the installation of the floats and the controls for the water rudder; however, by mid-July the pontoon lines developed by Ayers had enabled accurate re-definition of the damaged upper portion of the 15 bulkheads and 56 frames in each pontoon. With the bottom portions having been defined in parallel by using the Edo "method of templates" as shown on the Edo lines drawing, these were combined with the uppers to complete the definition of external lines for the pontoons. Full-size prints were provided to Bill Martin's restoration machining crew to use as patterns for the new bulkheads and frames. (Based on Footnote 114 reference.)

each reel would have to be screened to find the right one. None of the reel cans gave any clue as to containing what he wanted. But he could guess the approximate chronology of the reels by their design and aged appearance. So he began by screening what appeared to be the older cans. In the third can, his logic proved correct; when he mounted the reel in the viewer and turned it to the title frame, he saw the words, "N-3PB Roll D." Smith rushed over. There on the microfilm viewer he saw unfold before his eyes an incredibly awesome display of over 400 of the "lost" N-3PB drawings.

As Smith wrote months later, recalling this event:

> The discovery of this roll of N-3PB drawings, due primarily to Gerry (Balzer's) call linking an N-3PB drawing to a specific roll of microfilm and to Brian (Seltzer's) interest in searching for a roll with a lost identity, is probably the single most important incident contributing to a successful and accurate restoration of GS-U (Serial No. 320). There is no way that items such as the canopy, cowling, fuselage, and many others, could have been defined with even reasonable accuracy, even for a replica, from the photos and wreckage by the engineering cadre of the N-3PB team and especially in time for the November rollout. And I seriously doubt that it could have been accomplished by a larger and more experienced team. Further, the myriad details associated with items such as markings, mechanisms, substructure hidden to the cameras, etc., would in all probability have been lost to the restoration.[114]

Continuing with Seltzer's logical reasoning process, Smith felt it was common sense to conclude that if the reel he had found was "Roll D" there must be, at least, a roll "A", "B", and "C". Since there were known errors in the "reverse engineering" method used on the engine firewall bulkhead, plus the fact that the float drawings provided by Edo were for a float design used for the Vought XSB2U-3 seaplane and did not directly match the N-3PB float, Smith and Mackay decided to exercise common sense logic and devote precious time to locating Rolls A, B, and C. If 400 drawings were on Roll D, there were at least 1,200 more awaiting discovery. The probability of finding more was judged high enough to warrant risking time that was also needed on other restoration problems. If all needed data were found, the shortest path to completing the restoration would also be found.

With McNeal's help, Smith and Mackay made arrangements through Dick Strawn and Brian Seltzer of Micrographics to provide access to the vault-stored microfilm rolls. Also, the Micrographics organization provided access at all hours to the only viewer in the company that could still accommodate 35mm film on 8-inch-diameter reels; and, in addition, dedicated priority access to vellum and blueprint reproduction machines. In early May, Smith and Mackay began their concentrated survey of all the early company microfilm recorded by Roy Wolford. Mackay and Smith took turns, one carrying the film canisters and the other viewing film and recording frame and drawing numbers, subjects and titles, plus pertinent drawing comments. For the next two months the two

---

[114] Eugene A. Smith, Conceptual Design Engineer, Organization 2151/83, *Design Note 80-6: N-3PB Drawings and Reports*, dated November 5, 1980.

worked almost every lunch hour reviewing the reels of data. By the first of July, they had scanned over 50 rolls of microfilmed drawings, equivalent to over 20,000 drawings.

As their logic had convinced them, they found over 1,800 N-3PB drawings that were pertinent to the success of the restoration, and all were reproduced on vellum so copies could be made for anyone needing them. Jack Northrop had not only adequately documented the design of the N-3PB, but he had anticipated that Roy Wolford would adequately record them for posterity.

This type of "global" perception of what was necessary, useful, and efficient was typical of Jack Northrop's hands-on management approach. His mind was as much at work on the problems likely to be encountered on the production line as on the flight-efficiency problems he was solving on the drafting board. How to communicate the flight solution to the production line and thence to the field maintenance and flight operations crews by means of the most meaningful, readable drawings and manuals was as important to him as flight safety itself. If his airplanes were operated the way he designed them and specified them to be built, maintained, and flown, they were safe, dependable machines, as all of his early test pilots (Edward Bellande, Vance Breese, Max Stanley, et al) discovered, though initially awed by and maybe even skeptical of his advanced flying wing designs.[115]

By the time Smith and Mackay had completed their compilation of drawings, only five months remained before the rollout date. The question now was whether the airplane originally built in nine months could be rebuilt in five. Fortunately, the volunteers had not waited for drawings. Major progress was being made, especially in two areas: the Bub Larsen team (cf., Figure 57) had the empennage and flight controls well underway and the McAlpine and Koller team had taken the list of off-the-shelf equipment uncovered in the initial search for data and made contacts with the original suppliers to solicit their help in locating flight instruments, switches, seats, crew harnesses, canopies, lights, hydraulic cylinders, flight control cabling, aluminum and cloth materials,

---

[115] A relevant anecdote is the case of Vance Breese, who was test pilot for the P-61 night fighter (the famous Black Widow) designed and produced by Northrop during WWII. On the first flight of this highly distinct and innovative radar targeting, attack aircraft, which looked somewhat like the Lockheed P-38 with its twin-engine-nacelle tail booms juxtaposed on each side of the center cockpit nacelle, Breese taxied the airplane up and down the runway of Northrop Field (a.k.a. Hawthorne Airport) so many times that he wore out the brakes and the flight test had to be cancelled for repairs before it had even flown. Max Stanley, the competing Northrop test pilot, according to well-placed sources, used this apparent trepidation on the part of Breese to get him fired. Like "Suitcase" Simpson (a well-known test pilot and author), Breese was probably so exhausted from a night of partying that even the full-flow of the oxygen mask couldn't sober him up to the point of giving him the confidence to take off in an airplane that had never flown before, yet alone with him as pilot – and one with two high-powered engines. He no doubt wore out the brakes just trying to keep the airplane on a straight line while taxiing. Stanley denied the accusation but Breese believed it and always blamed Stanley for his firing. Stanley was to be test pilot of the Northrop B-35 and B-49 series of Flying Wing bombers (for photo of Stanley see Chapter 14). Test pilots who survive are those who find some way to control their natural tendency toward hubris; like "Suitcase," who found Socrates protecting him as wingman.

fasteners, bearings, navigation equipment, radios – in sum, all the equipment needed to make the airframe structure function as an operating aircraft system, in this case a seaplane with floats and wheeled beaching gear. As shown in Appendix F, over 70 supply sources responded. In almost all cases original or upgraded replacement equipment was obtained, often at no cost.

Ron McAlpine, who was manager of the Materials Procurement Department at Northrop, did an outstanding job in coordinating with suppliers to get, in many cases, their total participation in not only supplying parts and materials but actually working on their installation in the restoration. Notable contributions were made by Kai Kuhl, who bought special materials and supplied them free. The owners of Deft, Inc., Tony Desmond and Bud Levine, furnished paint and also bought lacquer and supplied it free. Alcoa's Richard Mardock arranged for a subtier supplier to his company to furnish aluminum sheets in the quantity required. The president of Pioneer Extrusions, John Castle, furnished extrusions and aluminum sheet, even shipping extrusions from his Georgia warehouse at his own expense to enable the project schedule to be met and buying some extrusions from a competitor of his. Rubbercraft's Stella Dancoes, Glen Werts, and F. N. Merrals, set up and made a special run of rubber extrusions in one week for the canopy seal, overriding their own production priorities at no cost to the project. Liberty engineering's Val Phiffer and Jeff Summers worked on their own time to pull fasteners from stock for next morning delivery. Teledyne's Bill Topliker and R. B. Entzminger researched their archives to supply an obsolete turnbuckle for the wing flaps. Other notable contributions included TriStar's Gene Labelle special air delivery of hose clamps; Aircraft Engine Maintenance Corporation giving the exhaust collector ring for the engine; Swedlow's Dave Swedlow and Irv Miller making the windshield glass twice when the reference lines first specified were wrong. In other cases, many new suppliers pitched in with time and materials when contacted by McAlpine, who got such spirited response overall that he organized a volunteer group of buyers and managers to work on the project. These people (identified in Table 6) had never done aircraft assembly work and eagerly joined the restoration effort, using the opportunity to expand their backgrounds by learning to rivet and form metal for the first time.

Some of the larger and seemingly most difficult supply requirements were surprisingly met early in the project; for example, a new, replacement engine was obtained by Dale Brownlow from Northrop University (another Jack Northrop "first" as described in Chapter 3, especially Figure 17). Brownlow had graduated from Northrop University, certificated to repair and maintain airframes and powerplants, and so he knew the university had a Wright R-1820-40 engine. He was typical of the generalist type of production engineer Northrop sought and nurtured. A hydraulic specialist in the U. S. Air Force, he had worked at the family business, W. W. Brownlow Company, a Northrop supplier of secondary aircraft structural assemblies, while attending Northrop University. At Northrop he quickly rose in production management successively as supervisor of mechanical subassembly, electrical subassembly, and then as head of field modifications and repairs on the T-38 jet trainer and F-5 fighter aircraft. At the time of the restoration project he was McNeal's Advanced Production manager for electrical subassembly and later became manager of F-5/F-18 ground support equipment, special test equipment, major spares, and field service modifications. On the restoration project, he adapted the Wright R-1850-40 engine to the N-3PB, removing most of the internal moving parts to lighten overall weight and converting four sections of a three-section DC-3 cowling to cover the engine. He also fabricated a new engine mount patterned on the old one.

So, as Smith and Mackay obtained the necessary drawings for the missing fuselage and wing structure and for final painting and detailing of the integrated airplane, great progress was being made on the front and tail ends of the airplane. Oliver "Bub" Larsen was the perfect choice to work on this airplane. Being Scandinavian, he could continue with the project as it moved into the exhibit stage and, having the Scandinavian bent for the "mission impossible," he would see that the airplane got restored with or without drawings, on schedule. Bub's talent is his ability to size up a job in a few minutes and develop his plan as he does the work; it's the ultimate form of "rolling wave" planning and implementation, where Bub is the rolling wave – quality and quantity combined in one package. He actually started working at Northrop on the P-61 night fighter while still in high school, in 1944, as a student trainee. This student trainee program was another Jack Northrop innovation, working jointly with local high schools to develop career paths for student employment in local industries – a strategy particularly useful during WWII when manpower was scarce. On graduating, however, Larsen decided to enlist in the Army Corps of Engineers and get some down-to-earth action and experience. When the war ended a year later, he was released from service after an 18-month tour of duty and returned to Northrop, where his employment was counted from the beginning of 1944. So in 1946, just starting again at Northrop, he already had one year of seniority.

With Northrop's postwar goal being to develop the flying wing aircraft for both commercial and military use, Larsen's first job was helping to build the YB-49 flying wing bomber. In 1949, Larsen's and Northrop's world of flying wings changed abruptly when Jack Northrop refused to merge with Convair, as directed by the Secretary of the Air Force. Northrop consequently was ordered to demolish all the flying wing fleet and the contract for the next-generation long-range bomber was awarded to Convair for the B-36, a conventional fixed-wing aircraft.

Afterwards, Larsen's career tracked the subsequent series of prototype aircraft developed by Northrop: the F-89 fighter; the A-9 competitive prototype for the A-10 low-altitude attack aircraft; the F-5 series of international lightweight fighters; and the YF-17 prototype for the lightweight fighter competition. On the YF-17 competitive flyoff program, Larsen was made head of manufacturing and material, because of his ability to meet tight schedules with quality results. When the YF-17 design was selected by the Navy as its next-generation F-18 fighter for aircraft carrier operations, Larsen became operations manager.

On completion of the YF-17 transition to the F-18 production program, Larsen was assigned by McNeal as Support Operations Manager for the Tacit Blue stealth surveillance aircraft (stealth technology development forerunner for the B-2 bomber) and the Northrop-funded F-20 advanced lightweight fighter, which was intended for international customers. Following the restoration of the N-3PB, he became operations manager of the Manufacturing Development Center (MDC) for the B-2 long-range, flying-wing stealth bomber. The Center produced and managed the Engineering Development Fixture, which replicated the flight crew station in detail within the context of the overall wing and was a major aid in showing key government visitors the design and performance features of this highly secret aircraft. Larsen remained with the B-2 program through his retirement in January 1990 and, in addition to managing operations of the MDC was responsible for the Advanced Production Department of the B-2 program management organization.

In 1980-81, having been perhaps the major leader in the assembly functions for the N-3PB restoration and its subsequent display in the U.S. and Iceland and turnover to Norway, Larsen was instrumental in the formation of the Western Museum of Flight, as described later.

As manager of Master Program Planning for the Aircraft Division, the author coordinated Larsen's programs over the years beginning with the YF-17. The two worked closely together to make sure that the rollout date for the restored N-3PB would be met. Their Northrop careers paralleled, with the author's having begun in 1946 also. Having joined the U.S. Army Air Corps as an air cadet in 1943, the author served through October 1945 as flight instructor of B-25 pilots. After discharge, the author returned home to Connecticut where, after a brief respite and reflection on a future course of action, he read a Northrop ad for engineers to work on developing advanced aircraft designs.

By September of 1946, he was sweeping WWII camouflage debris off the rooftop of the main Northrop production facility. This function was quite acceptable at the time, because beneath his feet flying wings were being manufactured and he was attending Northrop Institute of Technology, the forerunner of Northrop University, to become an aeronautical engineer. He was literally on top of his world. This world collapsed suddenly for him and other Norcrafters when in 1949 the flying wing program was cancelled and he had to go to work at nearby Douglas Aircraft for seven months. Returning to Northrop at the first opening, he worked in liaison engineering, a function that brought him in direct contact with Jack Northrop, who regularly came by to check on the status of engineering change incorporation in the manufacturing line and whether drawings were up-to-date and serving their function in turning out a quality product.

During the 1950-57 period, he was liaison engineer on the Northrop F-89 night fighter, spending four years at the flight test facility in Palmdale, California, near Edwards Air Force Base. From 1954-57, he flew F-86 fighter aircraft with the California Air National Guard. Following the F-89 assignment, he went on the Hawk ground-to-air missile program as liaison engineer and then assistant program manager (under Bob Shaftel, the role model for program managers). From 1960-70 he was manager of R&D proposals and then went into management of master program planning for the entire Northrop Aircraft Division.

It was from this position that the author's participation in the restoration proceeded, at least technically. His intense interest in and subsequent all-out commitment to the restoration were due to more than just his functional usefulness to the project: there was a bond between him and Northrop, for it was the company that had provided him a choice career path, a company where he personally knew the man, Jack Northrop, who had started it and made that career path possible – who in fact had served as the critical path of management and technology from which the entire industry had emerged. It was this bond with Northrop as a company and the man behind it that continued to motivate the author beyond the restoration of the N-3PB to the writing of this book, in an attempt to restore it all, if only for the brief moment of recollection.

Operating in its dedicated building, the restoration was effectively in a world of its own. It was a unique operation, because the people were motivated by the common goal of restoring the airplane for the man who had built the company as well as designed the airplane. It was a commemorative effort that documented their own life and work and that of Jack Northrop who had conceived the plane that had set their life and work in motion. It was a coordinated effort of small groups working on designated sections of the airplane under designated section coordinators. Unlike normal management structures, there was no hierarchy of management and control; each group constituted a dedicated functional unit working to complete its section of the plane in direct coordination with the others. There was no star; all were equal in their dedicated endeavor to meet the rollout date for Jack Northrop's birthday. What was being restored was more than an airplane. The restoration was individual and collective and was of the spirit.

McNeal continued throughout as the responsible restoration manager within the Aircraft Division. Don Page and Leo Gay were available to help him coordinate requirements beyond his own organizational lines of reporting, but were mainly waiting for the finished aircraft to be rolled out for display. As his wife, Elizabeth noted, every Saturday he took her with him when he went to assess the progress being made and any critical requirements that couldn't be met by the volunteers. From the beginning he, too, had been impressed by the amount of work ahead of them to restore this airplane. After Dick Mackay's survey of the returned aircraft's condition, McNeal expressed privately that he felt they had an 80 percent probability of meeting schedule. The original production of an airplane is straightforward, sequential: fulltime workers begin by fabricating and joining together new parts and building up subassemblies and systems to be integrated into the overall aircraft assembly; but here the volunteers had to begin by first disassembling the airplane and then cleaning, inspecting, repairing, fabbing anew, and figuring out how to bridge areas where there were no parts and, for months, no drawings, before they could even begin putting the airplane back together.

Even one of his most intrepid managers, Dale Brownlow, had said on first seeing the airplane: "We can't do anything with that!" Later, Brownlow admitted that when he first saw the ravaged condition of the plane, his stomach sank. He was glad that he had chosen the powerplant to work on, for even before the plane arrived he already knew that he could get a replacement engine at his old alma mater, Northrop University; his job would be relatively straightforward, because he could make the engine mount fit the new engine and he had the oil cooler and accessory gear box, which, having been removed by Farmer Johansson before the airplane sank, were in good shape and could be restored. But most fortunately, the engine was still used in the twin-engine Douglas DC-3 aircraft and parts were available. The recovered spinner polished up like new, Farmer Johansson having used it as a feed bowl for his animals.

The engine section was not only the lead item in presenting the aircraft, but was typical of the team effort put forth by volunteers and suppliers. Fourteen volunteers and seven suppliers contributed to this part of the restoration effort. Well ahead of the other assemblies, Brownlow and his team had the engine section completed and attached to a holding fixture ready to be mounted on the firewall bulkhead. Since the Wright R-1820-40 engine had been used on the Douglas DC-3 airplane, the DC-3 cowling could be adapted to the N--3PB installation, using cowling sections provided by Pacific Air Industries of Santa Monica, California. The propeller nose dome and blade insert collars, which had been recovered from Farmer Johansson's place, would be used along with three new prop blades. The accessory gear box also had been retrieved from Farmer Johansson and new engine accessories such as the vacuum pump, generator, starter, ignition harness and carburetor were donated by Aircraft Associates of Long Beach, California, while new magnetos were donated by Bendix Corporation and shockmounts by G&H Air Parts of Santa Monica. The Aircraft Cylinder & Turbine Co., of Sunland, California, donated a modifiable engine mount. Brownlow's father's company, W. W. Brownlow Co., donated machine time and material to make the mounting legs for this modification. In search of the exhaust collector ring, Brownlow drove and, with Ed Weaver as pilot, flew privately 1,500 miles total, first to Fresno, California, then to Tucson, and finally to San Diego before pieces from which to make one were located at Aircraft Engine Overhaul, Inc.

Seeing the powerplant sitting there ready to be mated with the airplane reassured McNeal and gave a sense of empowerment to the other volunteers. The front end of the plane now awaited the other sections and urged them on to completion. The engine, sitting there, represented a readiness, the energy and will, to fly, and seemed to signify that the rest of the airplane was bound to fall into place so as to fulfill the engine's purpose. The availability of powerplants has always been a motivating factor in new aircraft design, beginning with the Wright brothers. Brownlow worked his way on down the airframe, helping get it ready to be mated with the engine. His generalist knowledge of what to do on any part of the plane and his desire to get the job done typified the attitude and capability of all the team of volunteers.

Edward H. Weaver, another of McNeal's Advanced Production managers, became a key coordinator in the restoration for the engineering and tooling requirements. John H. Williams assisted Weaver by designing the assembly tooling for the outer wing panels. Known as "Big John," due to his ability and willingness to take on any assignment, Williams had begun his career at Northrop in 1948 as a tool inspector on the the first YB-49 flying wing bomber. In this job he inspected the author's work on the loft lines governing the configuration of that history-making aircraft. "Big John" retired from Northrop twice, once after working on the U.S. Navy's F-18 Air Combat Fighter tooling and again after returning, by invitation, to work as tool engineer on the B-2 Stealth Bomber flying wing. So he began and ended his aviation career working on Northrop flying wings. Even though "Big John" was transferred in early 1980 to Seattle,

Washington, under the Northrop contract for the "stretched upper deck" version of the Boeing 747 jet liner, he periodically returned to Hawthorne on weekends to assist with the tooling for the restoration.

Gene Smith provided Ed with two copies of each of the drawings as they were found and reproduced and Ed distributed one copy to the applicable airframe section leaders and the other to Bill Martin for use in fabricating new parts where existing parts could not be copied.

Ed also coordinated the construction of tooling. As he later reported, two major factors influenced the design of the major assembly tools. One was that transporting the restored aircraft aboard a C-130 or surface ship to its destination in Norway required that the wing be packaged separately from the fuselage. Whereas in the original production design the center wing section had been an integral part of the fuselage and the complete airplane had been shipped by sea, for airborne or surface shipment the wing would have to be separated from the fuselage.

This tooling concept was extended to the other airframe sections when the condition of the airplane remnants was seen. It was then evident that the original concept of having one assembly jig for the fuselage and one for the wing would have to be changed to one of having a number of individual holding fixtures to accommodate the airframe in major sections. These sections would have to be restored individually before being brought together for final assembly.

This sectionalized tooling approach matched the condition of the recovered airplane and also enabled the restoration teams to be organized by section. Accordingly, separate assembly fixtures were built to support and locate detail parts for the outer wing, center wing, pedestal, float, engine and firewall forward section, forward fuselage, and aft fuselage, plus special fixtures for the flight control surfaces.

Typical tooling setups are shown in Figure 62. For speed and economy, these tools were constructed from wood, except for the engine and firewall forward section and the wings interface tools, where the weight and accuracy requirements necessitated steel frames, which were made from scrap material. The most complex tool was that for the forward fuselage and was assembled on a wood platform 28 feet long, 4 feet wide, and 5 inches high. All the fuselage dimensions were referenced from this platform, which was dimensioned so it was 59 inches below the aircraft's horizontal centerline. A matching aft jig was built to hold the rear end of the forward fuselage 59 inches from the floor. The platform was leveled with optics to ±0.015-inch accuracy longitudinally and transversely. On the forward end at Station 0, a wooden firewall with engine mount locations was installed to simulate the engine section interface. From this station rearward, the platform was marked for fuselage centerline and for each bulkhead and frame station. To simulate where the wing center section normally would have been a wooden center wing contour box was mounted on the platform and rigged for matching centerline and stations.

New firewall with engine mount attached.

Firewall mount with engine installed.

New right-hand wing in overhead jig fixture.

New right-hand pontoon assembly fixture.

New tail section holding fixture.

Basic hand forming a new fuselage skin.

Figure 62. By March 1980, tooling setups had been made for all subassemblies and, though still without detail drawings, fabrication and assembly was in process using mostly original or copied parts. (Photos by John Amrhein.)

When drawings were found, wooden locating rails for the canopy assembly were added. All fuselage outer moldline contours were marked off from a full-size loft board, which was made from a full-size photo of the original loftboard found on an 8-by-10-inch negative by John Amrhein. Dick Mackay converted Amrhein's photo into computer-generated drawings for the moldline at each fuselage station; and then copying the few usable frames from the recovered fuselage and microfilm drawings found by Gene Smith, produced full-size bulkhead and frame drawings for fabrication of new parts by Bill Martin's volunteer machine shop. Assembly drawings were also produced for Les Epperly's fuselage team to use in putting the parts together and riveting on new aluminum skins.[116]

The wing jig also benefited from the discovery of the original drawings. Dick Mackay had used computer-aided design (CADAM) and inputs of airfoil section data found in N-3PB test and fatigue analysis reports to generate his wing drawings. With information on wing twist (i.e., washout) not included in these reports it was assumed, from wings like the N-3PB's of the same period that 2.5 degrees of twist would be the case, and the jig was designed accordingly. When the wing drawings became available, it was found that the wing had zero twist. The CADAM design was modified to match the drawings and the jig corrected to produce a straight wing.

A similar situation was encountered with the wooden assembly fixture made for the pontoons. While the Edo drawings showed the correct outer moldline, the stations for bulkheads and frames did not match those of the recovered left-side pontoon. So the stations were CADAM-located by Gene Smith and Ed Ayers in accordance with the actual pontoon locations and drawings then generated matching the moldline for each station. These drawings were used by Bill Martin's shop to make the necessary parts and the pontoon fixture was reconfigured by Ed Weaver to hold these parts at their respective stations. Last to be completed, the pontoons benefitted from having a number of volunteers ready to work on them, including Stu Schneider, Jeff Stone, Bub Larsen, and the author.

While the volunteers worked on their respective sections according to their personal schedules and agreements, the section coordinators met every Saturday morning with McNeal to report their status and to coordinate with each other on interface and support requirements. Each Saturday began a new week for the team. The normal volunteer schedule was to spend evenings during the workweek and all day Saturday and sometimes Sunday cleaning, repairing, fabricating, painting, and riveting or bolting parts together into subassemblies and assemblies. Some people even took parts home to work on them in their garages.

---

[116] In general, nonheat-treated aluminum sheet metal was used for new skins wherever required throughout the airframe, because the airframe had to carry only static loads and heat-treated material would have been time-consuming and costly to work with. In almost every case, skins were shaped by hand using holding clamps or riveted in place, as shown in subsequent photographs.

Tom and Linda Dozier were examples of this practice, because they worked at other companies. Linda, an executive at then-Western Airlines, had gotten the restoration spirit earlier when she had been project manager of the restoration of one of Western's first airmail delivery planes, the Douglas M-2. As another example of the zeal with which volunteers participated, in some cases executive level people who had never done manual fabrication or assembly tasks worked under the direction of factory hands.

When McNeal met with the key coordinators each Saturday morning, it was evident that many problems were stacking up. As usual, he met the situation calmly, making mental notes and projecting in his mind his own critical path of requirements leading to the completion. He listened intently, sometimes questioning, and when you saw him nod you knew he had thrown a switch on a solution or a way to find one. It was his key coordination between the engineering, manufacturing, and materiel departments of the company that enabled support services and eventually funding to be obtained whenever an impasse seemed to be about to block progress. He wanted the schedule to be met, but most importantly, with quality; he didn't want the airplane to look like a relic: it had to meet the most observant scrutiny as a real N-3PB and do so at the initial glance as well as on followup inspection.

He knew that the first impression people would have of the restored plane was the key. The interior of the airplane could be lacking or awaiting completion if the exterior was impeccably done in detail. To achieve this level of fidelity he knew the pertinent drawings were essential. For that, he was counting on Mackay's and Smith's review of Wolford's microfilm cache. After the cache was discovered, he remembered that Wolford had microfilmed all of the drawings of the early aircraft designed and produced under Jack Northrop's engineering leadership. He had been certain that drawings would be found. The question was one of timing. He made sure that the Graphics Department set aside the necessary budget for one person to focus on reviewing the film in support of Mackay's and Smith's volunteer effort. This was typical of the behind-the-scenes coordination McNeal conducted to remove the obstacles to meaningful progress in achieving a quality restoration.

Since Ed Weaver was the youngest and newest manager in his Advanced Production organization and was eager to demonstrate his prowess, McNeal used him to coordinate both basic and miscellaneous requirements to keep activities moving forward and, as much as possible, on schedule. After finishing the tools for assembling the major sections into which the airplane had been divided, Weaver focused on coordinating the fabrication of new detail parts for those sections and finding replacements for the flight instruments, navigation lights, and guns. The similarity of the N-3PB to Jack Northrop's earlier A-17 aircraft series designed for Douglas Aircraft (cf., Figure 9) helped find suitable replacements in many cases. The N-3PB drawings again helped identify these replaceable items.

McNeal was putting in doubletime working on two tightly scheduled projects. During the normal workweek, he had Aircraft Division responsibility for managing the new Production Development Center, where the Tom Jones foray into company-funded "commercialization" of the U. S. defense industry was being materialized in the form of the F-20 Tigershark aircraft. Jones's idea was to cut corners on cost and performance by taking the Welko Gasich-designed F-5 series of lightweight fighters – already a demonstrated production and operational success deployed among 28 "Free World" nations – and "restoring" the design as a super-lightweight, super-nimble, near-hypersonic air superiority fighter. This was to be done in a clever marketing ploy by using one of the same high-thrust engines used on the U.S. Navy's F-18 fighter, thereby gaining for the F-20 the economic-ordering price advantage of a higher quantity buy of engines (the highest unit-cost item of an aircraft).

Thus the F-5 was being converted from a relatively low-powered twin-engine airplane to a more modern single-engine fighter, by inserting into its lightweight airframe the latest advanced engine with a massive increase in thrust over the original engines. In addition, to increase the F-5's aeroagility so the F-20 would be competitive in the lightweight fighter combat mission, wing leading-edge extensions were added along the sides of the forward fuselage, along with a redesigned nose. These LEX's were to provide the aerodynamic "bite" to bring the turn radius down to match if not beat that of competing aircraft already operationally deployed. The redesigned nose would accommodate the latest radar for target detection and air-to-air weapon delivery. Quite a package and quite a restoration, and McNeal had direct management responsibility to meet the rollout schedule within the company's "affordable" budget. And for this project, "affordability" meant whatever it takes to be successful.

Manufacturing the first F-20 (which turned out to be a superb airplane[117]) was a relatively straightforward management task for McNeal compared to restoring the N-3PB, which, without drawings, would turn out to be as much artisanship as craftsmanship. The F-20 was a straightforward, build-to-print task and all his key people were well advanced along its experience learning curve, due to their background on the F-5, the baseline design for the F-20. The N-3PB was far more challenging due to the lack of a design baseline, in the form of drawings, and also because the return of this airplane at this particular time of the company's life had made it a center of both corporate and public interest. The year 1979 marked the 40th birthday of the company and 1980 the 85th birthday of its founder, the designer of the airplane, Jack Northrop. McNeal was getting a lot of attention from the corporate level and from the public, as to progress on the restoration. Local newspapers wanted background stories, pictures, and reports on progress – will it be ready on time and are you having any problems?, they all wanted to know.

McNeal had to schedule visits from corporate executives, the public and reporters; and he had to do so on a noninterference basis with the restoration itself. The project became virtually a company within a company. Of course all the publicity did help

---

[117] In the case of the F-20, history seemed to repeat itself, for even as the government had rejected Jack Northrop's early flying wing aircraft for political reasons, similar obstacles seemed to block Tom Jones's innovative attempt to commercialize production of military aircraft. In the case of Jack Northrop's innovative flying wing, political subjectivity eventually succumbed to time and mission need in the B-2. The F-20 is shown in Chapter 14, Figure 95, with its companion in time, the restored N-3PB.

attract volunteers and build a sense of team responsibility to perform. It was like the period during WWII when everyone counted and no task was trivial.

Figure 63 shows a typical VIP visitor. As the engine was the first evidence of a completed assembly, it provided McNeal with his first scheduled event to demonstrate progress and satisfy the inquisitive that the project was under management control and headed for the designated event of Jack Northrop's birthday celebration.

Before the N-3PB's original microfilm cache was discovered – while Mackay and Smith were trying to reverse-engineer the engine firewall bulkhead from the handbook photo shown in Figure 61 – Les Epperly was trying to restore the main fuselage section from which the tail had been ripped. Now the fuselage was being treated as consisting of two sections, the main forward section to which the engine would attach and the aft section which would attach to the forward one. The forward section constituted the three-man crew stations for the pilot, radioman-navigator, and gunner. While this section was in a demolished state, having been cut with a saw from the wing center section and missing the 14.5-foot canopy that ran almost its entire length, the aft portion was by

John Amrhein

Figure 63. McNeal shows T. V. Jones, Northrop Chairman & CEO, the first product of restoration, the Wright-Cyclone engine. The auxiliary gearbox driven by the engine to power electromechanical accessories sits on the table (foreground) along with the propeller hub. Behind is "Big John's" wing jig. McNeal was concurrently managing the Production Development Center and manufacture of the first F-20 Tigershark, Jones's brilliant but ill-fated attempt to revolutionize the U.S. defense industry's weapon system procurement process.

comparison intact. It was decided to interface the two sections with matching bulkheads where the canopy structure ended.

That decision resolved the terminal point of the interface between the two sections quite well, because the forward section was more intact toward the end of the crew compartment. Remaining unresolved were the three other major interfaces: first was the now well-known engine firewall bulkhead that constituted the front terminal point of the forward section; second was the lack of any drawings for the canopy and the windshield; and third was how to interface the fuselage with the wing. The third interface was an immediate issue, because as originally designed, the center wing box was an integral part of the fuselage. Shipping what was now to be an exhibit model of the N-3PB necessitated that the wing be easily removed and shipped separately and then easily reassembled at the exhibit point. To resolve this issue, it was decided that Epperly's fuselage section would be redesigned at the wing interface so the two could be bolted together as separate assemblies.

The decisions on the tail and wing interfaces gave Epperly enough to start with. He and Ed Weaver, the tooling specialist, decided that a wooden replica of the wing center section would be used as the basic holding fixture for the forward fuselage. Since the wing root extended two-thirds of the length of the forward fuselage, this fixture would provide the main ventral surface from which to build up the new main bulkheads. To pick up the engine firewall bulkhead just forward of the wing and the rest of the fuselage aft of the wing, a wooden keel was incorporated in the wing root fixture. Using the reverse-engineered firewall drawing provided by Smith, Epperly and Weaver added a wooden replica of the forward bulkhead as an interim template for restoring the fuselage. From the recovered fuselage, Epperly's crew removed usable parts for inclusion in the buildup of what was to become a virtually new forward fuselage section.

Like Weaver, Les Epperly also was one of the key managers in McNeal's Advanced Production Department. Like his boss he was working concurrently on the tightly scheduled F-20 program at the Production Development Center, where only the best worked. During the day, he directed F-20 assembly operations for the hydraulic system. At night and on weekends, he had volunteered to coordinate the toughest part of the restoration, the one with the most interfaces and in the worst condition.

Because of the uncertainties concerning the front end of the fuselage where the engine attached, he started his volunteers on the aft end, where the bottom gun door was the main feature and the recovered frames and some skins were restorable. Forward of the gunner's door the structure was either missing or grossly deformed. After all the available and usable structure was tacked in place on the holding fixture, the only alternative was to reverse engineer the structure from photos and by extrapolating from the available structure.

Then, word spread that the drawings had been discovered. Mackay and Smith gave Epperly first priority by locating and reproducing the drawings for the forward fuselage, wing interface, canopy, and the cornerstone firewall.[118] Using the original drawings, new frames and stringers were fabricated by Bill Martin, McNeal's manager of Fabrication Operations. Following the policy set for new parts, only those parts that were missing or clearly unrestorable were fabricated anew. Swedlow, Inc., the leading canopy and windshield manufacturer, made the entire plexiglass canopy free, in return for getting back all the pieces of plexiglass recovered from the Thjorsa River. These pieces were sought for testing, because after over 30 years of submergence in a cold, silt-laden, fast flowing glacial river at the Arctic Circle, they were still transparent. Swedlow made the windshield twice, because more accurate geometric contouring and sizing was possible after the drawings were found.

With the decision to make the wing an entirely separate assembly from the fuselage, Harris R. Stone and his crew mounted the recovered center wing section (which, to facilitate shipment back to Northrop, had been sawn from the recovered fuselage) in a vertical holding fixture where it could be worked on conveniently at standing height (an Ed Weaver human engineering concept). Figure 64 shows the restoration setup and activity on the wing center section and right-hand wing.

The wing, due to the large number of new parts that had to be made, provides a good example of the systematic way in which the restoration of the plane in general was approached; and particularly so, because Harris Stone recorded the wing restoration process in diary form, as shown in Figure 65.

When the fuel cells were removed from their wing cavities, the internal wing structure was found to be in good condition, even though the external skin surfaces were abraded and pitted. Obviously, Jack Northrop's high-strength, low-fatigue web-box panel design had provided an adequate seal against water damage. Most of the internal structure was reused but new aluminum skins were cut and riveted in place to form new upper and lower surfaces. To interface the section with the fuselage as a removable structure, the upper wing skin was provided with access panels through which four frame extensions from the fuselage could be bolted to the front and rear wing spars, two extensions, one right and one left, for each spar.

To mate the fuselage with the wing airfoil curvature, two matching airfoil doublers were installed ventrally in the fuselage; thus when the wing was attached to the fuselage, it rested against these fuselage doublers for stability. Once the fuselage was ready to mate with the wing, the vertical fixture holding the wing would be rotated so that the

---

[118] Emphasis has been placed on the engine firewall bulkhead as the key to the fuselage restoration, because in the overall configuration of the fuselage, the firewall was Fuselage Station 0, the frontmost reference plane from which all the other stations of the fuselage were measured. All reference planes of the airframe, including the wing, originate with FS 0. Thus to have a true geometric translation of the airplane in the x, y, and z axes, such that all flight surfaces were in alignment vertically, horizontally, and transversely and such that the sagittal and transverse planes were precisely located at right angles along the airframe centerline, the FS 0 reference lines had to be precisely known and transferred to the structure as fabricated.

In Weaver's human-engineered holding fixture.

Skin stripping in process.

Harris Stone drilling rivet holes for new skins.

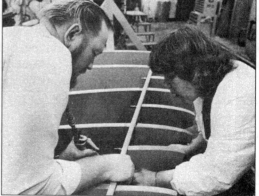

The center wing section restored.

Precision-fit attachment of fuselage, McNeal observing.

R. Antoine and Nancy Larsen at wing fixture designed by "Big John" Williams.

Figure 64. Restoration of the wing followed standard practice procedure. (Photos by John Amrhein.)

THE N3-PB Story

Harris Stone
24 November 1980

N3-PB Wings

November 14-20. H. Stone, D. Kurzenski, A. Zepada, D. Arellano and H. Buckingham positioned and turned over the center wing section and began removal of the bomb rack fairings, bomb racks, fuel tanks and several hundred pounds of river silt and rock. This work continued through December 21 with help of J. Villalobos, J. Spangler, V. Bladel and F. Armstrong.

January 2-21. Continued to remove dirt from c/w section; also removed fuel lines, fuel valves, and the remains of F/S 13 bulkhead.

January 15-31. Began to remove outer wing attach angles and doublers common to center wing section, and the lower outer moldline skins.

February 2-23. Continued removing wing skins, the remains of the trailing edge section on the center wing, also the refurbishing of the l/h and r/h wing shear plates.

February 26-March 29. Started to refurbish the skin stringers in c/w and make new parts for the lower c/w surface; installed the c/w section into a routing fixture to increase accessibility; moved the l/h o/w into a new work area and began to disassemble. Mr. Buckingham's wife Mary joined the work crew; also D. Abler, E. Green, R. Bunch, D. Banach. All the parts removed that were of a reasonably good configuration were used as patterns to make new parts for both l/h and r/h outer wing sections.

April 1-30. Lower side of c/w section refurbished and painted and ready for installation of new parts; installed bomb rack fairing support structure and new outer moldline skins; assembled the substructure of the c/w trailing edge section, fitting the bomb rack fairings to substructure. Disassembly of the l/h o/w continued as planned with new parts being fabricated.

Figure 65. Harris Stone's Record of the N-3PB Wing Restoration (page 1 of 3), showing the typical care given to managing the restoration.

The N-3 PB Story - N3-PB Wings

May 1-31. Removed the upper moldline skins from c/w section; refurbished the substructure such as stringers, spar caps and brackets, making new skins for upper surface by using old skins as patterns. All substructures refurbished and painted; began installation of skins. Left-hand o/w completely disassembled; new parts fabricated using old parts as patterns. The work was reinforced: D. McCormick, J. Larson, F. Lincoln, L. Mortz and T. Robinson worked on both sections of the wings.

June 1-31. Right-hand and left-hand o/w main spars were assembled; the assembly tool was ready for installation of subassemblies. The c/w trailing edge section was completed and wing attach angles and doublers common to c/w installed. The fuel scoopers, doors and drain valves were being installed, and fuel lines in mockup. Fairing skins were complete and ready for installation.

July 1-31. Center wing section was completed except for some small detailing. Outer wing spar assemblies and skins panel assemblies were being worked. Parts that were in a restorable condition were refurbished and readied for installation when major assembly starts on o/w.

August 2-30. Continued with spar and skin panel assemblies for outer wings. Worked some wing ribs, located stringer cutouts and joggles, and made r/h wing stringers. Began loading l/h wing assembly into assembly jig.

September 2-30. Left-hand, outer wing assembly progressed very well; still worked small assemblies and parts for r/h o/w on the bench. September 25, removed l/h o/w from assembly a/j tooling converting a/j to r/h. September 29, began loading r/h o/w into assembly aj, working gun doors, trailing and wing tip structure on l/h o/w.

Figure 65. (Continued, page 2 of 3.)

Harris Stone
24 November 1980
Page 3 of 3

The N-3 PB Story - N3-PB Wings

October 1-30.   Right-hand outer wing progressed very well in assembly a/j. October 10 mated l/h o/w to center wing section and continued working gun mounting structure and wing tip installation.   October 17, removed r/h o/w from assembly a/j and began cleanup of work required in preparation for mating. October 23, installed r/h o/w to center wing section. Continued work on r/h trailing edge, tip installation lights, etc. Both l/h and r/h wing attach fairings were progressing well--completion expected by November 4, the scheduled day to start painting the aircraft.

Center wing _ _ _ _ _ _ _ _ _ _ _ _ _ _ approx.	480	old parts
Center wing _ _ _ _ _ _ _ _ _ _ _ _ "	172	new parts
Left-hand outer wing _ _ _ _ _ _ _ "	68	old parts
Left-hand outer wing _ _ _ _ _ _ _ "	474	new parts
Right-hand outer wing _ _ _ _ _ _ _ "	17	old parts
Right-hand outer wing _ _ _ _ _ _ _ "	525	new parts

- - -

H. R. Stone
Wing Group Leader

Figure 65. (Continued, page 3 of 3)

wing was horizontal. The fuselage would then be lifted by crane from its own wing-conformal assembly jig and lowered onto the center wing section. This procedure would be reversed when the airplane was prepared for shipment.

While some of his volunteers riveted new skins to the center wing section's web-box of ribs and spars, Stone had others disassemble the left outer wing panel, which was intact to the extent that it still resembled a wing. Since the two outer wing panels were mirror images, Weaver built an assembly jig that could be used to hold the left panel for restoration and then modified to build the new right-hand panel. Initially, the plan was to duplicate the parts of the left panel for the right panel, but when the wing drawings were located and reproduced from the microfilm cache, Bill Martin had new parts fabricated from the original production drawings.

The many shear webs and caps that fastened to the wing ribs, plus the manufacture of spars, consumed substantial lead-time for the ordering of fabrication materials, so the wing panels became a critical time path item and were not completed for attachment to the wing center section until mid-October. For this reason the wing work area became the center for final mating of wing and fuselage. First the fuselage forward section (with engine section installed) was mated to the wing center section and then the outer wing panels were attached. In parallel, the tail section was attached to the forward fuselage. All mating points were equipped with large precision-machined bolts that could be quickly removed to disassemble the airplane for shipment.

That the three wing panels became the main activity-event item on the critical time path of the restoration is a result of the ravaging they took all the years they were either submerged in the fast-moving, ice-chunked current of the Thjorsa River or buried in the shifting lava silt and sand of the riverbed. The center wing section got some protection from the fuselage above it. Since the airplane was facing upstream, the right wing panel took the brunt of the river's attack, but in the process put heavy, surging loads on the shoreward left wing.

Table 3 shows the immensity and pattern of the demolition effects the river had on the panels. Overall, more than two-thirds of the wing panels had to be fabricated new, a figure representative of the entire airplane.

TABLE 3. SALVAGEABLE VERSUS NEW PARTS REQUIRED FOR THE WING RESTORATION

WING SECTION	SALVAGED PARTS	NEW PARTS	TOTAL PARTS (Qty.)	% NEW
Center Wing	480	172	652	26
Left Wing	68	474	542	87
Right Wing	17	525	542	97
TOTAL PARTS	565	1,171	1,736	67

It was the ravaged appearance of the wing and forward fuselage that had elicited the generally negative comments from those who had attended the reception of the Norwegian C-130 on its arrival at Northrop with the remains of the airplane. While the forward fuselage section had similar ravagement to that of the wing, it was largely the early attempts by the Icelandic farmers to pull the airplane from the river by brute force that enabled the river's subsequent relentless attack. With the engine section ripped off and the canopy gone for years, the interior of the crew compartment had been fully exposed to the river's onslaught. Nevertheless, fewer structural parts had to be made new, because this section contained most of the avionics, flight and engine controls, and crew stations that constitute system type installations. Almost the entire upper portion of this section consisted of the canopy assembly that covered the three-man crew and that had to be made new along with its support railings, cockpit sides, and slide tracks. Surprisingly, many of the original interior details of the crew stations, once cleaned up, were found to be restorable. The radios and most of the electrical boxes, once cleaned, were restorable to look new even if they were no longer hooked up or required to work. Filling of corrosion pits and repainting was all most of the so-called "black boxes" required. The fire extinguisher and emergency flare tubes were restorable along with the reel mechanism for the trailing radio antenna. Everything magnesium, however, had dissolved in the river water, so the bell cranks and fittings for the flight control system, the trim tab wheels, and other castings made of Jack Northrop's favorite lightweight, but strong metal, magnesium, all had to replaced.

The tail section similarly had major subassemblies that had to be replaced with newly fabricated ones. Where the right wing had taken the brunt of the river's attack, the aft fuselage section, as configured for restoration purposes to mate with the forward fuselage section, was missing the entire right horizontal stabilizer and elevator along with the entire vertical stabilizer and rudder except for a stub at the base and the top leading edge of the vertical. Only the fuselage substructure and the left horizontal and elevator less tips remained. Overall, about two-thirds of what was now called the aft section was missing. The front end of the section had to be mastered according to the original moldline so as to interface compatibly with the forward fuselage and, in addition, about 80 percent of the tail flight control surfaces had to be fabricated anew. This task was a scaled down version of the wing and forward fuselage combined.

Figure 66 shows restoration of the major subassemblies of the tail section taking place.

Fortunately, the most energetic and talented "generalist" in McNeal's Advanced Production Department took on this assignment. "Bub" Larsen, too, was concurrently responsible to McNeal as prototype manager of the F-20 across the street from the restoration building at the Production Development Center. Larsen was not only enthused about restoring the N-3PB, but determined, because he was, ethnically, Danish and could identify with the Norwegian's spirited struggle for freedom during WWII. For him it was a personal matter as well as company pride to make a gift of this airplane to Norway as a show of appreciation for the contract that put Jack Northrop and the company truly in the aircraft business in 1940.

Vertical stabilizer in place for skins.

Horizontal stabilizer in holding fixture.

Larsen skinning horizontal, author assisting.

Author skinning the horizontal with Antoine.

Full empennage ready for fabric.

Fully restored empennage.

Figure 66. Restoration of the tail section in major stages.

Larsen's team began the aft section restoration in two parallel steps. Part of the team cleaned up the recovered aft section and began restoring the front end to mate with the forward fuselage at the rear gun bay bulkhead; and another group focused on building a new horizontal stabilizer and elevators out of the remnant of the left-hand unit recovered from the river. Larsen concentrated on the vertical stabilizer and rudder, of which almost nothing had been returned to reverse engineer other than a 1.5-foot piece of the vertical stabilizer root and the rudder pivot block at the top end. Everything else was gone. These two opposite ends of the vertical stabilizer, however, proved valuable in establishing the airfoil cross-section of the leading edge of the stabilizer. While the horizontal remnant was disassembled and copied to build new ribs and spars for the right-hand unit, Larsen made his own drawings for the vertical stabilizer and rudder portion of the empennage, including detail drawings for ribs and spars.

When Martin's volunteer fabrication group had the parts ready, Larsen built up the vertical stabilizer in a separate wooden holding fixture. The rudder was drilled and assembled in a separate wooden fixture and mated to the vertical stabilizer after the latter's installation on the aft section. Similarly, wooden holding fixtures were used to drill and attach new skins to the ribs and spars of the horizontal stabilizer. Students at Northrop University covered the elevators and the rudder with aircraft fabric after their basic frames were assembled. The horizontal stabilizer was first installed in its slot in the aft section and then the vertical stabilizer was installed. Then the movable flight control surfaces, elevators and rudder, were installed on their respective stabilizers.

Both the front end and the aft end of the airplane were finished first, with the engine leading, logically, of course. Completed in early April 1980, the aft section was displayed in the company cafeteria for several days, as a showpiece that stimulated new interest in the project and anticipation of the approaching rollout.

Having claimed the distinction of restoring the first airframe section, Larsen's volunteers joined the wing group to assist in its more complex restoration task, which was now the critical time path to meeting the scheduled rollout date. Fortunately, concurrent with completion of the aft section, Mackay and Smith found the missing N-3PB drawings, which included drawings for the outer wing panels. As Larsen applied his volunteers to making new ailerons and flaps, Harris Stone, the wing group coordinator, divided his volunteers among the center section and the two outboard panels. With detail wing rib and spar drawings now in hand, Martin's fabrication department could proceed confidently, without the time-consuming coordination inherent in extrapolating and reverse engineering detail designs between manufacturing and engineering personnel. To a fabrication man, having a drawing in hand is like holding the part. A new time-to-complete projection by the author showed that the wings could be completed by mid-October, if all the assigned volunteers worked consistent hours.

As usual with an airplane, the landing gear is the last thing installed. The N-3PB was no different; the floats and pedestals, which constituted landing gear, had not yet been seriously worked on. McNeal had assigned his son Gary, who worked in Advanced Production under Don Small and Dale Brownlow, to clean up the one recovered float and pedestal and begin restoring it. Gary was an enthused volunteer not only because the N-

3PB was the first airplane on which his father had worked, but he had met Jack Northrop briefly at an airshow at Edwards in 1976. He was relatively new in the Advanced Production Department, but had worked with Northrop since 1974 at the flight-test facility at Edwards Air Force Base. In examining the recovered parts he found that the center wing section still had the missing upper part of the left pedestal attached to it, so between the two a complete pedestal could be restored and used as a model for the missing right pedestal. Discussing the badly damaged right float with Larsen, the latter suggested that he stabilize the float in a wooden floor fixture with endboards at the forward and aft ends. Strings could then be tied between the endboards to establish longitudinal and transverse reference lines along which the actual float stations could be marked. Gary had the holding fixture constructed and skins removed for access to pontoon bulkheads, frames, and longerons by the time the production drawings were found. Instead of having to copy from the extant parts, new parts were made.

In addition to his initial volunteering to plan and document the restoration, the author assigned himself as volunteer assistant to Larsen, who was getting spread thin between the aft section, the wing, and the floats, given his fulltime responsibility on the urgent, hush-hush F-20 program. When Edo Corporation couldn't provide the original drawings for the floats, in desperation, an ad was run in a widely read aviation newspaper to see if any of the original floats from N-3PB's that crashed during training operations in Canada might have ended up in private or commercial hands. When no response was received, the decision was made to reconstruct the damaged left-hand float and copy it to build a new right-hand float. Similarly, the left pedestal would be restored and copied for the right.

The author became Larsen's lead assembler on the control surfaces and mechanisms of the empennage and wings.

Gary McNeal was now concentrating on disassembling the left-hand pontoon so the parts could be replaced or restored. Fabricating and assembling new parts was a time-consuming, repetitive task, because there was a continuous taper along the length of the float and each bulkhead was of a slightly different configuration in its planform and with tailored webs and t-shaped caps that interfaced with the longerons and skin. Because of the high g-forces the pontoons had to withstand during takeoff and landing on usually choppy water, each float station had its tailored bulkhead. In general, the floats were monocoque structures similar to the fuselage. In fact, Gary had worked some on the fuselage and quipped that working on the floats was like building two more fuselages. Because the floats were identical, once the drawings were computer-generated, Ed Weaver's single wooden assembly fixture enabled the pontoons to be built in succession.

Figure 67 shows the pontoons in their side-by-side assembly position just like they would be located on the airplane. Each pontoon could be equipped with a set of wheeled beaching gear that enabled the plane to be rolled from the water onto a beach or about on land for servicing and maintenance. Each set consisted of a forward two-wheel strut system and a single tail wheel for steerability. The forward wheels were larger than the tail wheel and were self-clamping to the float once inserted in special recesses and strapped in place, one wheel on each side. The smaller tail wheels also clamped in place along the outboard end of each float on single vertically housed axles that permitted them to rotate directionally.

Indicative of the outreach the project was generating, two sets of the forward gear were located in Norway in early May 1980 by McAlpine, who maintained constant search for required items among his qualified vendor sources of supply and other nonstandard, special sources, such as, in this case, Sevi Bulukin of the Norwegian Royal Air Force.[119] These sets had been used on N-3PB Serial No. 322, one of two of the fleet to survive operations in Iceland only to be eventually scrapped (No. 322 was scrapped on 26 May 1958 in Kjervik, Norway). The sets were refurbished by the Norwegian Air Force and returned to Northrop. The aft wheels were reverse-engineered by Gene Smith and manufactured new from a photograph.

The pontoon pedestals were assembled in a wooden holding fixture one at a time, using, in the case of the left pedestal, most of the original heavy attach fittings (perhaps made in Iceland by Sevi Bulukin's alchemist blacksmith, as described in Chapter 5). The wing attach holes of the replacement pedestals were located directly from the existing holes on the center wing section. Each float was equipped with its beaching gear before being lifted from the assembly jig, so that, once out of the jig, each float-pedestal unit could be easily rolled into position for mating.

Figure 67. The pontoons were restored last; if the plane wasn't finished they wouldn't be needed. Inset: Beaching gear. (Photo by John Amrhein.)

---

[119] Sevi Bulukin, the pilot of the crashed airplane being restored and a Colonel in the Royal Norwegian Air Force, had been in contact with Leo Gay, who had invited him to the rollout. Gay told McAlpine that Sevi had indicated some N-3PB parts were in storage from the aircraft that had returned to Norway at the end of WWII. The parts had been salvaged when the aircraft were scrapped as they became outmoded.

The aerodynamic fairings about the pontoon and pedestal interface were made from fiberglass and installed after the two were mated.

In all the above restoration activity, while each section of the airframe had an assigned lead coordinator and crew, there were key support services provided across the entire operation. Bill Martin, McNeal's manager of Fabrication Operations, was chief coordinator for fabrication of all the new parts made. John Amrhein, who photographed the entire one-year restoration process, was a volunteer from the Graphic Arts Department under Bob Korn, who was manager of the Photo Lab that Roy Wolford had started under Jack Northrop in 1940. Mackay, Smith, and McAlpine also were valuable coordinating volunteers from departments outside McNeal's Advanced Production, the first two from Engineering and the third from Materiel.

Similarly, there was a large pool of volunteers that moved from one airframe section to the next according to the priorities and exigencies of the moment. During September inside the restoration building it was beginning to look like an airplane was being built. Brownlow's engine section, the powerplant portion completed in April, was ready for installation, having been finalized in August with installation of a newly-made diaphragm that directs slipstream air behind the engine cylinders to cool them. Larsen's tail section, complete with new empennage, had been sitting on display since April; and his wing flaps, ailerons, and flight control mechanisms had been completed at the end of June. The forward fuselage, wing, and floats were on schedule to be completed by mid-October. Three weeks would be left to integrate these sections and the control systems and then finish paint and detail the aircraft for rollout.

Earlier in the year, a couple of parties had been thrown to cheer the volunteers. Since July, however, a celebratory mood was evident among the team, especially on weekends. The sense of quiet desperation and the no-nonsense attitude that had fallen over the project with the arrival of the remnants of the airplane had gradually been replaced in stages by more relaxed looks, then smiles, later grins, and now occasional laughter. Every time a major subassembly or assembly was completed, cheers went up from the responsible crews and the others gathered around to congratulate them and examine their work with appreciative critiques. When John Hardman put his last touches on the assembly and covering of the ailerons, he swore to everyone around that they were flightworthy: "I would trust my mother-in-law's life in this airplane with those ailerons," he boasted. Thereafter, it became his standard oath on special occasions.

From April on, volunteer participation was mounting every month in daily numbers and time spent. Indeed, as Gene Smith had noted, the discovery of the N-3PB microfilm drawing cache seemed to be the turning point for the project. Prior to April, everything seemed to go in reverse as more and more parts needed were identified and major airframe sections had to be taken apart down to the last detail for use as patterns to make new ones and photos used in many cases to make drawings for missing parts. Through Christmas and late winter, the restoration area looked more like an aircraft junkyard than a manufacturing facility. The discovery of the drawings gave a sense of organized surety to the project. Now there was a documented design baseline to work to: the drawings turned the project from one of artisanship to craftsmanship; no longer would parts have to be created, they could be manufactured. All at once, the project began to operate like a factory operated by specialists in material supply, tooling, fabrication, and assembly. In microcosm, the project began to function like McNeal's Advanced Production Department.

What this shift means, in essence, is that the right people were there all along. All they needed were all the basic tools. The drawings completed the set of tools needed to make an airplane! What this proves is that there is a fourth factor of production to the three that Adam Smith defined. Granted you must have labor, plant, and capital, as Smith said. The team of restoration volunteers had all three, but at the last minute they had still lacked something: the design of the product to be produced; i.e., the objective of production. With that in hand they were ready to proceed to meet schedule. Thus does restoration teach us something about production.

CHAPTER 12 – HAPPY BIRTHDAY, MR. NORTHROP!

By July 1980 the major subassemblies of the airplane were beginning to take shape within the restoration area and one could begin to picture the plane as it would look when all the pieces came together. Concurrently, the team spirit of the volunteers began to rise as individuals saw how their respective work sections were progressing compared to others and how their contribution to the restoration was going to fit and prove essential.

Figure 68 indicates the increasing coordination that was taking place as personnel came to the main fuselage section to check and verify interfaces for their subassemblies. Figures 69 and 70 show volunteers at work to finish subassemblies.

Against the general background of problems, there were a few interesting, even intriguing surprises that provided some distraction. For example, Gary McNeal, in removing the battery from the forward fuselage section and cleaning it up thought it looked so new that he would see if it still worked. The news quickly spread that this battery, manufactured by Exide, still had a charge when first tested after 35 years underwater in an icy cold glacial river. Moreover, when recharged, the battery performed like new, as shown in Figure 71. The manufacturer used this battery in a special promotional ad campaign. At exhibits of the restored airplane, an airborne beacon light was kept in sustained rotation by the battery, to the amazement and wonder of all viewers.

Don Page was now stepping up coordination with corporate headquarters in Century City to prepare for celebrating Jack Northrop's birthday concurrent with the rollout on 10 November. Leo Gay was beginning to visit the restoration building more frequently and to spend more time looking on and talking with the crews, especially when John Amrhein, the official project photographer, scheduled photoshoots. After all, Gay was a volunteer, too. He had coordinated the project from the first; delivered communications equipment for the divers and shore lookouts; assisted in getting the crane, trucks, and roadbed gravel for the final recovery operation at the site; and helped locate parts for the restoration. However, Gay's volunteering to deliver a complete canopy set caused a crisis when after months of promises and waiting, backed by Gay's reassurances, it was learned in September that the vendor Gay had selected couldn't meet the delivery schedule.

Ted Mothershead of Les Epperly's fuselage team took the canopy drawings and personally built all three canopies in a closely coordinated, intense effort with vendors. The close call resulting from this management oversight is shown by the dubious distinction that the canopies were the last items installed, just two days before the promised rollout on 10 November. Using contour boards made from the moldline drawings, Mothershead made male and female molds to the respective shapes of the canopies (pilot's, radio-navigator's, and gunner's) and had them formed by a local (paid) supplier from plexiglass donated by Swedlow and the Plastic Center, Inc. The frames were handformed over plywood formers and attached to the mold-formed plexiglass.

Coordinating the next step.

Ready for wings.

Measuring the wing fairing.

Installing the engine.

Center wing installed, tail surfaces next.

Epperly, Larsen, and Motherhead checking.

Figure 68. As subassemblies were nearing completion, coordination centered on the main fuselage to verify installation interfaces. (Photos by John Amrhein.)

Recovering the Thjorsa by hand.

Northrop Institute covering the elevator.

Splicing tail section to forward fuselage.

Schneider and Stone on the left pontoon.

Oiling the auxiliary gearbox.

Securing the prop with restored spinner.

Figure 69. As the main fuselage became integrated as an airframe, the remaining subassemblies and subsystems were prepared for integration. (Photos by John Amrhein.)

John Amrhein

Figure 70. Proof that the author did indeed perform as volunteer in the restoration, shown here apparently hitting Bub Larsen's thumb although actually driving rivets from the recovered left-hand horizontal stabilizer.

John Amrhein

Figure 71. Surprising everyone and delighting the original manufacturer, the Exide battery was demonstrated by Bub Larsen to be still working after 37 years of submergence in Iceland's Thjorsa River. Ed Weaver at engine, rear.

Epperly already had built and installed the railings as part of the fuselage restoration. But the canopy seals that installed in the frames were a last-minute rush order filled on a donation basis by Rubbercraft Corporation of America. Rubbercraft's Stella Dancoes, Glen Werts, and F. N. Merralls set up and made a special run of the required type of rubber extrusions in one week to enable the November 8 installation date to be met, overriding other priority production orders at their company, all at no cost to Northrop.

Note that up to this point the restoration project has been recounted as an all-volunteer effort that was to cost Northrop nothing in labor, material, or legal exposure in the event a volunteer got injured. As noted in Chapter 10, Northrop had agreed to provide a facility in which the restoration could be accomplished by volunteers, plus machines and other tools by which the fabrication and assembly of parts could be accomplished by volunteers.

There was to be a change in this policy, due to another crisis impacting, most severely, the main objective driving the spirited effort of the volunteers. In early September, the first report of approaching tragic news was fedback from the corporate level to the project members by Don Page. Jack Northrop's health was failing rapidly.

McNeal learned of it first, and after confirming the rumor with Jack Northrop's son, John Northrop, briefed Bub Larsen and the author in a meeting the same morning. John Northrop had informed McNeal that his father had already been hospitalized with breathing problems due to a stroke and that the prognosis for the long run was bleak. He knew how important the project was to the volunteers because of its link to his father. As winter came on, with colder weather and rain, his father's health situation would require that he remain indoors and not travel about or be in public places where he might be exposed to colds or flu bugs. So John requested, speaking for his father, that he be shown the restored aircraft no later than the first week of October, after which both time and the weather were likely to turn against him healthwise.

The question from McNeal now was, "Can we have enough of an airplane to show Jack Northrop no later than October 7?" The logical response to this requirement for schedule acceleration was the same as McNeal himself had made when Don Page first had introduced the prospect of restoring the N-3PB: Who's going to pay for it?

This time it was the author who brought up the issue; for, clearly, to accelerate the schedule enough to have an integrated aircraft to show Jack Northrop within the next 30 days would require that budget be allocated so that people could work fulltime in addition to volunteering in their offtime. This arrangement would effectively double the manhours being put into the restoration; and would be the only way the schedule could be reduced by one-half as the new schedule would require. Larsen pointed out that even with people working fulltime, the remaining material efforts (I.e., getting material and fabricating parts) on the fuselage, wing, and floats had lead-times that couldn't be improved by applying more labor. From this time forward, the critical pacing requirements timewise were the parts needed to complete assembly. Pumping budget into fabrication labor would certainly shorten the schedule, but not proportionately; i.e., by doubling fabrication labor, the schedule for parts wouldn't be shortened by one-half. In fact, Larsen pointed out, just putting budget into fulltime integration of the already restored sections might enable the fuselage, engine section, tail section, and center wing section to be integrated by the first week of October.

McNeal knew there was no need to call John Northrop back to see if this would be acceptable, because there was no alternative. There was only so much time left, no matter how much money was spent. Accordingly, it was agreed by the three, that fulltime budget would be arranged for only those volunteers employed by Northrop who were working on those sections that could be integrated with the fuselage by 5 October, one month away.

The question now was how to get the money to pay for fulltime labor and get permission for people to leave their regular work for 30 days. McNeal made the decision that he and the author would meet with Jack Mannion, the vice president of the Manufacturing & Materiel Department for the Aircraft Division, and convince him that budget and time should be allocated to have the N-3PB in some integrated airframe shape to show Jack Northrop on October 7, 1980. Concurrently, Larsen was to organize the volunteers to proceed with full-scale integration of assemblies, assuming that Mannion would be swayed to budget the project.

Because of the investments the company was making on the F-20 program and startup preparations just getting underway for a major proposal to win the B-2 flying wing bomber program (which was to be an intensely competed multi-billion-dollar contract award coveted by all the major aerospace contractor teams industry-wide), convincing Mannion to support what, by comparison, could be construed as a sentimental celebration of the past unrelated to the company's sustained growth in the future would be equivalent to a major marketing coup. McNeal and the author were anxious as to how to proceed, both holding major management responsibilities on both the F-20 and upcoming B-2 programs. Would they look foolish making such a request, in the face of what the company was risking on the F-20 and the B-2 proposal. The fact that both were known within the company as generalists who could manage any assignment successfully meant they were also realists; this self-knowledge made what they had decided to do a difficult adjustment, given the relatively minuscule, even obscure, importance the restoration project really represented in relation to the overall business activity of the company.

As in many past situations they had been in, the pressure of making the right decisions quickly and following through to get things done worked in this instance too. As John F. Kennedy once said, "In every danger there is opportunity." Having worked in major contract acquisitions for 10 years, the author knew how to put together winning proposals. The number and quality of the people who had volunteered to restore an old but uniquely historical airplane had impressed him. It was evident that such restorations could be organized to bring in similarly qualified and motivated but younger, beginning aircraft manufacturing personnel, if similar projects were organized by a company like Northrop on a regular curriculum basis. With the F-20 and B-2 programs coming online in the near-term and the F-18 and Boeing 747 programs continuing at high production levels, getting new employees would require that the company organize and staff special, recurring, long-term programs that would be quite expensive.

Discussing how to approach Mannion on the N-3PB budgeting requirement, McNeal and the author quickly reached a consensus that the restoration project itself was the key to solving the major employment buildup the company was presently trying to meet: they would turn the restoration project into a training program. They now were eager to proceed. Volunteerism could be organized as a training program that could provide a new approach to educating candidates in aircraft manufacturing skills and career paths. This approach would be a special application of Jack Northrop's idea of a university for aviation job entry. The company would meet its recruiting needs by offering candidates special, hands-on training in return for their volunteer participation. This approach would offset its costs by getting free labor in return for training.

With McNeal's ready concurrence, the author documented a summary of the strategic concept and its benefits to the company, along with a curriculum outline. Of course the manifest success of the ongoing N-3PB restoration and its volunteer team provided real-time evidence that the strategy would work. The proposal was readily accepted by Mannion as a most welcome, cost-effective solution to a difficult problem facing the company and the industry in general, as the Cold War and defense spending mounted. It was a most enlightened idea that he wanted to implement right away. The N-3PB volunteer restoration would serve as a prototype demonstration to work out all the details for formal implementation. Northrop would change not only the way the industry contracted with government but the way employees were trained. The approach would help win new contracts and show customers that Northrop was not only an advanced technology company but one with the most enlightened management solutions. It was an idea that would result in the formation of the Southern California Historical Aviation Foundation and its operating arm, the Western Museum of Flight, in which McNeal, Page, Gay, Larsen, and the author subsequently would participate operationally. McNeal in particular was to become most active as director of WMF after his retirement from Northrop in 1986 immediately following the F-20 crash in South Korea that killed Northrop's test pilot, Don Cornell.

Even with a 30-day budget approved for daytime employment of volunteer employees, Larsen concluded after surveying the work remaining to complete the integration of a fullup airplane, that a schedule reduction of 30 days just couldn't be met, at least for the entire airplane. The most realistic objective was to apply the budget to completing the forward fuselage section and the center wing section on an accelerated schedule and then integrate those sections with the already completed engine and tail sections to form a completed fuselage, less the canopy, the outer wings, and the floats.

Seeing the completed fuselage and wing integrated as an assembly would impress Jack Northrop most, because it would represent the main body of the airframe in the configuration as he had designed it; with the center wing integral with the fuselage, he would immediately picture the entire airplane as though fully assembled, with the other sections being worked on nearby in their almost completed stages. It would be more dramatic for him to see the restoration almost complete and still in process. After all, it had been the dynamics of the design and manufacturing process that had interested his creative talent more than the end product. In a way it would let him participate in the restoration by still having time to make suggestions and to mentally integrate the remaining sections, than for him to walk in and see the whole job done. Having devoted his life to aviation almost exclusively, he was the ultimate volunteer and should be given the opportunity to make suggestions or to point out improvements or oversights, if he wanted – at least this would show that he hadn't been presumptuously excluded as no longer needed. In this sense the airplane would be more his than if fully completed.

This plan to integrate the main fuselage sections, complete with engine, was adopted; and October 7 became known as "D-Day." Larsen was thankful for the budget coming at the finale of the restoration because, all along, relying solely on volunteer availability, the project had suffered from having 1 or 2 volunteers one day and 15 or 20 the next. Trying to schedule such a workforce had resulted in the project surging forward and then ebbing like waves at the beach. Now with all the remaining work well-defined, having budget to work fulltime on a regular schedule would ensure a quality product at rollout.

To implement this budgeted effort under efficient management control, McNeal issued the revised organization chart shown in Figure 72. Only the key functional personnel were identified. The scheduled objective was now spread among more lead managers so that each of the major subassemblies would have an assigned leader to ensure the new D-Day schedule was met. Sometimes the best mystique is money.

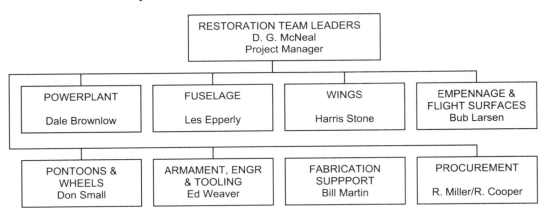

Figure 72. On June 3, 1980, McNeal restructured the restoration project, to ensure meeting the D-Day schedule for delivering Jack Northrop's birthday gift. All necessary resources were now available; he was making sure that the original reason for recovering this plane would be upheld.

A fulltime effort proceeded on the forward fuselage to complete fabrication of the new frames for the ones that had been completely missing over about eight feet of the crew compartment and to fabricate new skins and rivet them in place over the entire section. After the rear portion of the forward fuselage was completed the tail section empennage was mated to it, less the movable rudder and elevators, which would be added at final integration before rollout in November. As the rear fuselage area was being integrated, the front was completed, after which the engine section was installed.

The full-length integration of the fuselage was completed on September 27. When the center wing section was completed three days later, the fuselage was rolled on its wooden assemble fixture over to the wing assembly area, as shown in Figure 73. There lifting straps were placed around the fuselage and it was hoisted onto the waiting center wing section, as shown in Figure 74, and the two were bolted together. This was to become the standard procedure for setting up the airplane for exhibit and, in reverse, preparing it for shipment.

John Amrhein

Figure 73. The fuselage with empennage, less engine and canopy, was rolled on its wooden holding fixture to the wing assembly area for mating with the center wing section, so Jack Northrop would see the fuselage just as he had designed it – with integral wing box!

First, separating from the wooden form box. Next, lowering onto the center wing section.

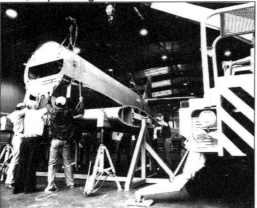

Then, aligning over the connecting frames. Finally, fastening in position.

With the center wing and engine installed, work is in process to install the cockpit canopy framing (sitting on the workbench, foreground) and also the left wing (sitting left, foreground). The right wing is being installed on the opposite side of fuselage and installation of the empennage flight control surfaces is about to begin.

Figure 74. After fuselage and center wing section integration, the other airframe subassemblies were installed, pontoons last. (Photos by John Amrhein.)

"D-Day" would be met! It was now definite that the fuselage would be the centerpiece of Jack Northrop's preview of the airplane he had created and brought into being. What a birthday present, early though it was, to see, once again, in the process of major assembly, an airplane designed and produced in the beginning of one's professional life. What a feast this would be, with Jack Northrop the centerpiece genius surrounded by his centerpiece airplane. The beginning he had created for so many people would now be in restoration before him.

On October 7, as planned, Jack Northrop, accompanied by his son, John, arrived at Northrop as scheduled. The event was deliberately low key, as John had requested, so that his father, now frail and suffering from initial Parkinson's symptoms as well as a congestive heart condition, would not be pressured by having to interact too much socially and become unduly fatigued. Dick Millar, secretary and treasurer, was the only corporate representative, and Jack Mannion represented the Aircraft Division.

It was like any other Saturday. The volunteers were at work as usual and as usual Elizabeth McNeal, whom Jack knew from McNeal's early years at the company, was there with her husband for his weekly project status meeting. John handed over his father's arm to McNeal who led the founder on his restoration tour.

As Elizabeth McNeal, who remained in the background observing, later said, "His appearance noticeably perked up as he saw the main fuselage. He removed his arm from Darrell's grasp and walked spryly up to the wing, smiling, and patted it approvingly. I couldn't hear what was said and there wasn't much said anyway, but you could tell he was very pleased by what he saw."

Figure 75 shows the guest of honor arriving with his son John Northrop and being greeted by Dick Millar, a corporate director, and Jack Mannion, administrative vice president of Northrop Aircraft Division. He immediately linked his arm in McNeal's to be shown around the restoration area. He didn't say much, but smiled at the obvious attention he was getting and donned a special baseball cap labeled with the Northrop insignia. McNeal pointed out the work that Northrop University (formerly the Northrop Institute of Technology) had done on the restoration, in particular the elevator the University had volunteered to cover.

Jack Northrop didn't have to walk around the entire area. Rather he stood where he could look around, with McNeal pointing out what the status of everything was and what had to be done and when to complete the final integration. Northrop nodded in affirmation. It was clear everything was under control and schedule would be met. Norway would get a good product, as they had in the beginning.

It was to be the last time Jack Northrop would be at his homeplant. He wouldn't be at the rollout on November 10 when he would be 85 years of age. He would be in the hospital, which he would soon enter due to advanced Parkinson's. He would see the rollout, however, from his hospital bed on television, in a special news report arranged and broadcast by Clete Roberts, celebrity news commentator and himself an N-3PB restoration volunteer. Roberts, an aviation history enthusiast and pilot, had known Jack Northrop since his retirement in 1952 – a news event Roberts had covered as a reporter.

McNeal, Jack, Dick Millar, and Jack Mannion.

John H. and John K. Northrop

Team leader.

Les Epperly explains restoration process.

Northrop Institute helped restore this part.

Recalling the "Golden Years."

Figure 75. Jack Northrop's special review of the N-3PB restoration was a historical event for dignitaries, volunteers, other employees, and family. (Photos by John Amrhein.)

Jack Northrop sent a "Thank You" note to McNeal and his team of volunteers for such a very special, restorative gift. And he added that like all airplanes produced by Northrop it would go on to its customer's destination, the most fitting destiny for a quality product.

Meanwhile, the restoration proceeded toward the formal rollout date of November 10 when key personnel of the international team and Norwegian dignitaries would be present, along with Northrop's Tom Jones, Dick Millar, and Jack Mannion.

Both outer wing panels were attached to the center wing section by mid-October. The floats were completed in mid-October; and then, less beaching gear, were installed with their pedestals to the center wing section on October 25. The airplane now sat on its own support carriage for the first time in 37 years.

Figure 76 shows a particularly historical view of the N-3PB being restored in a similar photo angle to another taken during the original production in 1940. The lower photo shows the final stage of restoration, before final painting and detailing, just after the floats were installed and as the fairings and the canopy assembly are being fitted. The upper photo shows the first N-3PB at the same stage of assembly during production in November 1940.

The morning of November 8 was the dropdead date for towing the airplane on its beaching gear over to Plant I for final painting and detailing with camouflage, insignia, identification number, and decals. The paint shop needed 24 hours to complete the restoration and allow the airplane to dry as an accurately camouflaged and serial-numbered aircraft of Royal Air Force Squadron 330(N) – Norway.

The 8th of November was one month and one day from the memorable presentation of the airplane to Jack Northrop in the restoration hangar. In 31 days, the restoration was to proceed from the fully assembled fuselage, less wings, flight control surfaces, and floats, to a fully integrated airplane – at least in outward appearance, for there would be some of the system elements that simply could not be completed and installed in time for the rollout on November 10.

At the time of the public ceremony celebrating the rollout, the pilot's seat and control stick, the instrument panels, pilot's floor, radio-navigator and gunner-bombardier's seats, and other interior accommodations and accessories would not have been installed. But for this event, the plane would be sitting high on its floats and beaching gear and no one would know the difference; the airplane as the restored embodiment of the N-3PB was what everyone would be looking at and that would be quite sufficient for this initial viewing, for the airplane was a thing of beauty that filled everyone's field of view and captivated the imagination with its reality of presence and the history it represented and brought back to life.

The history of the Second World War and Northrop's beginning was there before the eyes in three-dimensional space, in color. It was to be a moment of great recall, nostalgia, pride, and hope for the future. Yet, as Heraclitus had said, "You never step in the same river twice." The restoration of this first Northrop-produced airplane marked a time of great change.

Source: *Northrop Update*, November 7, 1980.

Figure 76. Below: November 1980: N-3PB Serial No. 320 in final stage of restoration prior to painting and detailing. Above: November 1940, Serial No. 301, the first of 24 N-3PB's, at the same stage in production. Below, right to left, Chino Forester, Darrell McNeal, Jerry Alpern, Frank Blair, Fred Armstrong, Robert Cooper (propeller), Harold Buckingham (rear cockpit), Roy Wolford (on wing), Art Cerny, George Babajian, and Robert Gunter on opposite wing.

Since this story is really about the people who performed the restoration, Table 4 identifies all the team members alphabetically, all equal for having volunteered. The variability and range of work performed by each member of the volunteer team shows that this was a true team effort. Each person enthusiastically did whatever was necessary to complete the project on schedule and with the quality results everyone at Northrop would be proud of, especially Jack Northrop. Since each hour spent by these people contributed indispensably to the success of the project, the time each spent is a quantitative factor that doesn't compare with the quality of their performance or what they did. So only the names are listed; and in alphabetical order.

McNeal's wife, Elizabeth, especially remembers volunteer Robert L. Gunter, who had worked in tool development at Northrop from 1940 through 1949. He remembers Jack Northrop's interest in expanding the use of new metals and wrote a manual titled "Northrop Manufacturing Methods." The first tooling he developed was for the N-3PB's production in 1940. As part of his hobby class at Northrop in jewelry making, he made N-3PB pins and tietacks for coworkers. Retired from North American Aviation when he heard about the N-3PB restoration, he contacted Larsen who forwarded him to McNeal, whom he had known in 1940. After his outstanding volunteer role in the restoration, McNeal asked him to write a summary of his experiences on the project. His letter to McNeal, shown in Appendix G and excerpted below, describes first-hand the typically widespread contributions made by volunteers and the return benefits they got:

I heard about the N-3PB program thru a friend and that it was for Jack Northrop's birthday. I was approved for work and given a badge. It was so nice to be back in the shop after being retired. . . . I worked on untangling the bent metal, removing the rivets, flattening the parts, straightening and painting. Other (parts) were hopeless. With no drawings, the 'guess and be damned' method was used. In most cases we were right.

I furnished and installed two lights on the vertical tail. There were so many things to be done, errands to be run for parts and tools, shop to be kept workably clean, so as my memory assures me – we were kept busy at one task or another. All the fellows worked as if it was their own ship – and enjoyed it. These fine craftsmen had their own private tools and were willing to share them with the other workmen. The entire shop attitude was the finest that I have ever encountered anywhere.

I met and worked with Clete Roberts, whose father was a blacksmith and a carriage builder. He was good with his tools. I met old friends like Roy Wolford and talked about people and past history. It was great fun and interesting. Roy has my lapel pin (N-3PB).

All in all, it was a great pleasure to see a corroded pile of scrap metal slowly unfurl and develop into a beautiful "Proud Bird" (that would) leave its nest to greet the world. It's the most outstanding development of the year: 1940 to 1980.

It was a great thrill and a wonderful program to honor a great man and the world's greatest aircraft creator – Mr. John (Jack) K. Northrop. His other accomplishments in other fields are not well known but they are numerous. His prosthesis developments are outstanding. He is a master in his own rite.[120]

Gunter identified himself as a project engineer, which is a later version of "lead coordinator" or "responsible engineer" and one of the most demanding "generalist" jobs in the aerospace industry. A project engineer is given a one-time assignment to manage a nonrecurring project. His responsibility is to meet or better all the requirements on time and within budget, on a project that he usually didn't plan, schedule, or budget. He subsequently either finds out that the project was well planned or begs, borrows, and steals to meet the requirements as packaged for him. After finishing the job, he is given a few days off as a gratuity for the many hours of unpaid overtime he worked to meet requirements as planned. He then disappears into the ranks of employees until the next project comes his way. As one aerospace executive once said, "There's no limit to what you can do, as long as you don't want to take credit for it."[121]

In Gunter's case, both McNeal and his wife considered him exemplary of the volunteer role. He was not only a great generalist, but he did things without having to be told. He was solution-oriented. Elizabeth McNeal recalls that in addition to making jewelry, he was a poet; and in the Darrell McNeal archives that she keeps, there are some Gunter poems that someday might be restored and, as she said, "Greet the world."

At 3:00 a.m. on 9 November the airplane was towed out of the paint shop, detailing just completed, to accelerate the overall drying process in the open air. When the sun came up, the plane was parked just east of where the tent for the rollout ceremony was being erected.

John Amrhein took the first picture of the restored aircraft, shown in Figure 77, as the day began. Since the plane would be inside its rollout tent within the hour, it had been decided in October to utilize this same day for a sneak preview by all the volunteers and their families. Thus the team beat the rollout schedule by one day! In true Jack Northrop tradition, the plane was delivered ahead of schedule.

The Zen of restoration is in the contemplation of the object's total history for enlightenment as to its meaning; the Art is in the restoration of the meaning to sense the enlightenment: the Zen and the Art restore the object for contemplation of past and future, returning what had been object as subject.

---

[120] Robert L. Gunter, excerpts from letter to D. G. McNeal dated November 20, 1980, reprinted in full in Appendix G. The word 'rite' may be more correctly intended by Gunter to read 'right'; however, the author has left it as written, because Jack Northrop's life was certainly lived as his own rite.

[121] William H. Ruddy, 1963, when manager of Northrop Aircraft Division's Proposal Group.

Finally, as the sun was rising, the pontoons were installed; first off, last on.

Figure 77. At sunup, on November 9, 1980, freshly painted and detailed, the restored N-3PB Serial No. 320 was rolled out on beaching gear for its first official photo. It was a day ahead of Jack Northrop's birthday and one year after arrival in Thjorsa-ravaged pieces. (Photos by John Amrhein.)

TABLE 4. MEMBERS OF THE VOLUNTEER RESTORATION TEAM

NAME		NAME	
Abler	0. R. Abler	Caruthers	A. E. Caruthers
Albert	R. A. Albert	Castro	A. C. Castro
Alien, Jr	R. C. Alien, Jr.	Causey	J. C. Causey
Anderson	M. A. Anderson	Cerny	A. P. Cerny
Andren	M. G. Andren	Chabrow	P. J. Chabrow
Antoine	R. L. Antoine	Champion	J. F. Champion
Arellano	D. Arellano	Chaplin	G. A. Chaplin
Arellano	D. R. Arellano	Cobbs	J. R. Cobbs
*Armstrong	F. M. Armstrong	Coffman	M. F. Coffman
Arnrhein	C. J. Arnrhein	Color	J. M. Color
Ayers	E. D. Ayers	Cook	B. R. Cook
Babajian	G. A. Babajian	Cook, Jr	B. R. Cook, Jr.
Bach	R. Bach	Coonce	W. E. Coonce
Baez	R. Baez, Jr.	*Cooper	R. M. Cooper
Banach	D. R. Banach	Cooper	L. Cooper
Barajas	J. Barajas	Corbett	L. Corbett
Barboza	E. J. Barboza	Costa	W. A. Costa
Barrett	C. P. Barrett	Crawford	R. Crawford
Bean	D. J. Bean	Cumins	J. Cumins
Beedon	C. L. Beedon	Cwynar	T. J. Cwynar
Benedetti	R. Benedetti	Del Haro	A. L. Del Haro
Billings	D. G. Billings	Delgado	R. A. Delgado
Binding	B. C. Binding	DeRitis	R. G. DeRitis
Bladel	V. H. Bladel	Dozier	L. G. Dozier
*Blair	F. J. Blair	Dozier	T. J. Dozier
Blair	M. Blair	Dukeman	J. K. Dukeman
Blaize	W. B. Blaize	Duncan	E. D. Duncan
Boyer	L. J. Boyer	Dunnegan	E. R. Dunnegan
Brown	E. Brown	Dyer	W. T. Dyer
Brown	R. D. Brown	El-Sayed	K. M. El-Sayed
Brownlos	J. W. Brownlos	Ensign	M. Ensign
Brownlow	D. T. Brownlow	Epperly	B. M. Epperly
Brownlow	W. Brownlow	Epperly	L. E. Epperly
*Buckingham	H. V. Buckingham	Erwin	R.C. Erwin
Buckingham	M. H. Buckingham	Erwin	S. J. Erwin
Bunch	R. T. Bunch	Fariell	L. L. Fariell
Burnett	L. Burnett	Fernandez	D. S. Fernandez
Carruth	W. Carruth	Figueras	W. Figueras

281

TABLE 4. MEMBERS OF THE VOLUNTEER RESTORATION TEAM (Ctd.)

NAME		NAME	
Flippen	W. F. Flippen	Holtsman	F. R. Holtsman
Ford	B. H. Ford	Hopper	E. S. Hopper
*Forster	Y. J. Forster	Hutchinson	V. Hutchinson
Fortier	C. C. Fortier	James	T. James
Frangos	E. Frangos	Jannson	A. Jannson
Freeman	J. L. Freeman	Johnson	A. D. Johnson
Fulmer	R. Fulmer	Johnston	O. Johnston
Gabsa	0. J. Gabsa	Jones	D. E. Jones
Garcia	D. P. Garcia	Karmellch	F. R. Karmellch
Gay	L. 0. Gay	Keehart	H. A. Keehart
Gilbert	J. E. Gilbert	Kelecy	W. G. Kelecy
Gill	G. E. Gill	Khan	M. Khan
Girton	W. T. Girton	Killeen	M. Killeen
Gonez	A. M. Gonez	Kimball	J. A. Kimball
Goodlander	C. R. Goodlander	King	F. King
Gornez	D. M. Gornez	Kitahata	S. M. Kitahata
Graab	R. L. Graab	Koller	B. Koller
Graham	W. L. Graham	Knaus	J. F. Knaus
Greear	G. T. Greear	Knutson	D. A. Knutson
Greek	J. Greek	Kramer	F. Kramer
Green	E. Green	Krause	M. P. Krause
Green	M. R. Green	Kreide	B. L. Kreide
Green	R. W. Green	Krumbine	M. R. Krumbine
Gruba	B. G. Gruba	Krystyan	J. M. Krystyan
Gunter	R. L. Gunter	Kueblar	J. R. Kueblar
Hardman	D. D. Hardman	Kuebler	J. R. Kuebler
Hardman	J. D. Hardman	Kurzenski	D. F. Kurzenski
Hayos	R. Hayos	Lackey	M. H. Lackey
Heard	H. F. Heard	Laliberte	F. Laliberte
Heimbuck	H. Heimbuck	Langston	L. Langston
Helfrich	R. J. Helfrich	Larsen	D. T. Larsen
Hennrick	D. F. Hennrick	Larsen	G. Larsen
Hick	D. Hick	Larson	J. R. Larson
Hiller	C. H. Hiller	Larsen	N. Larsen
Hobson	F. T. Hobson	Larsen	0. H. Larsen
Hock	J. W. Hock	Lee	J. D. Lee
Hohn	C. S. Hohn	Leonard	P. Leonard
Holdsworth	R. F. Holdsworth	Lester	C. W. Lester

TABLE 4. MEMBERS OF THE VOLUNTEER RESTORATION TEAM (Ctd.)

NAME		NAME	
Linardos	J. N. Linardos	Nolan	L. J. Nolan
Lincoln, Jr	F. A. Lincoln, Jr.	Nolan	S. L. Nolan
Locher	A. Locher	Noonan	E. J. Noonan
Low	N. S. Low	Nunez	D. Nunez
Luce	S. E. Luce	Oliver	D. Oliver
Mackay	R. B. Mackay	Ortiz	G. L. Ortiz
Malcolm	R. E. Malcolm	Page	E. Page
Malden	D. S. Malden	Page	W. R. Page
Malo	R. P. Malo	Palombi	E. L. Palombi
Martin	B.K. Martin	Parenteau	G. J. Parenteau
Martin	D. L. Martin	Patterson	R. Patterson
Martin	R. Martin	Pereira	F. A. Pereira
McAlpine	R. L. McAlpine	Perkins	M. C. Perkins
McCormick	D. H. McCormick	Perkins	S. T. Perkins
McEuen	G. F. McEuen	Pettigrew	K. L. Pettigrew
McGlibery	L. B. McGlibery	Pierce	D. L. Pierce
McMahon	B. S. McMahon	Polliard	J. V. Polliard
*McNeal	D. G. McNeal	Potter	F. I. Potter
McNeal	G. E. McNeal	Quinn	J. E. Quinn
Merizan	J. R. Merizan	Rahlf	D. W. Rahlf
Michaelson	M. A. Michaelson	Randall	J. F. Randall
Miller	L. Miller, Jr.	Ranoa, Jr	V. M. Ranoa, Jr.
Miller	R. M. Miller	Redmond	G. A. Redmond
Minner	W. J. Minner	Rich	D. W. Rich
Monsisvais	M. Monsisvais	Rinnert	E. A. Rinnert
Montez	D. Montez	Rinnert, Jr	E. A. Rinnert, Jr.
Morales	R. J. Morales	Roberts	C. Roberts
Moran	M. Moran	Roberts	J. Roberts
Morfis	C. Morfis	Robinson	S. M. Robinson
Morgan	T. Morgan	Robinson	T. W. Robinson
Mothershead	T. Mothershead	Rohrberg	R. R. Rohrberg
Moulton	L. Moulton	Rosentiel	M. R. Rosentiel
Mrotz	L. J. Mrotz	Roshan-Zamir	S. Roshan-Zamir
Murillo	P. Murillo	Ross	J. Ross
Naulls	J. W. Naulls	Rothermel	M. Rothermel
Nelson	B. E. Nelson	Ryder	P. Ryder
Nelson	E. P. Nelson	Saladana	D. G. Saladana
Newman	J. Newman	Sardegna	N. Sardegna

TABLE 4. MEMBERS OF THE VOLUNTEER RESTORATION TEAM (Ctd.)

NAME		NAME	
Satalich	R. Satalich	Underwood	C. E. Underwood
Schneider	S. L. Schneider	Villalobos	J. M. Villalobos
Schubert	L. D. Schubert	Warwick	B. J. Warwick
Scrugs	J. F. Scrugs	Watson	R. Watson, Jr.
Sellinger	T. N. Sellinger	Weaver	E. H. Weaver
Sepeda	A. M. Sepeda	Webber	A. L. Webber
Serna	R. Serna	Welch	N. L. Welch
Shellum	G. L. Shellum	Weston	R. C. Weston
Shirrefs	W. G. Shirrefs	Wilkinson	W. B. Wilkinson
Shreve	H. R. Shreve	Williams	H. G. Williams
Small	D. J. Small	Williams	J. H. Williams
Smith	E. A. Smith	Wilson	D. Wilson
Smith	J. W. Smith	Wilson	J. P. Wilson
Smith	M. J. Smith	Wilson	T. L. Wilson
Smith	S. F. Smith	*Wolford	R. L. Wolford
Smuck	R. B. Smuck	Woody	W. P. Woody
Sordelet	F. A. Sordelet	Wooton	R. W. Wooton
Spangler	J. A. Spangler	Wright	G. S. Wright
Spangler	L. A. Spangler	Wright	J. R. Wright
Spaunhurst	E. M. Spaunhurst	Zollinger	D. Zollinger
Spencer	W. F. Spencer		
Spikula	P. J. Spikula		
Steele	R. Steele		
Stephens	J. L. Stephens		
Stone	H. R. Stone		
Stone	J. A. Stone		
Stover	J. R. Stover		
Strasser	E. Strasser		
Tancre	H. W. Tancre		
Tancre	W. D. Tancre		
Tazza	N. P. Tazza		
Thompson	S. A. Thompson		
Thordason	S. Thordarson		
Toller	T. F. Toller		
Toller	B. Toller	*Denotes those volunteers who also worked on the production N-3PB in 1940-41.	
Trunble	R. B. Trunble		
Tyler	T. Tyler		
Ulyate	M. Ulyate		

CHAPTER 13 - FINAL ROLLOUT AND TAKEOFF

From production to restoration rollout, the life of N-3PB Serial No. 320 spanned 40 years. Much happened to change the airplane and the world inbetween the two rollouts. However, on Sunday, November 9, 1980, when the restored airplane was rolled out ahead of schedule, it would have been almost impossible for the observer, whether an aviation professional or average spectator, to see any differences from the way the plane had looked 40 years earlier brand new. There were no signs of aging or wear and tear. It looked like it was flight ready and any aviator could imagine jumping into the cockpit and taking off, water or not. As Sevi Bulukin recalled after seeing the restored airplane for the first time on November 10 at the formal presentation, "She's never looked so pretty. I would like to get in the cockpit and fly it again."[122]

One thing was sure: this airplane would never suffer the fate of a lot of old, though well-tended airplanes, of becoming an abandoned "hangar queen": this airplane represented something memorable. While it might not be actually flown again, it would be mentally by everyone who viewed it, either as pilot or passenger. This plane would serve mission after mission in the imagination of viewers, never breaking down or succumbing to old age. The Thjorsa had been beaten.

The rollout, however, while marking a restoration of the Jack Northrop spirit as well as of the spirit of those who had fought and won the war, also marked a change in Northrop and the industry, that over the next decade would result in a diminishment of the Northrop spirit. Some of this change would be due to a hardening of what might be called the management mindset of executive management at the corporate level. With the rollout of the N-3PB an era was ending; as Jack Northrop had so well expressed it, "The golden years are gone." When he had begun his career in aviation in 1916 at the Loughead (Lockheed) brother's plant in Santa Barbara, California, a seaplane had been the first type of aircraft he had worked on – a seven-passenger, float-type, twin-engine seaplane. Known as the F-1, it was one of the biggest flying boats of the time. The N-3PB had been the fastest seaplane. A historical cycle was being completed, begun by an individual named Jack Northrop and now ending with him. The rollout marked both the ending of a cycle and the beginning of something new that could not be defined as yet, but could already be seen as less personal, more systematic and programmatic.

The new cycle augured decreasing value for the humans on whom the industry depended, as the mindset of those leading and deciding on change increasingly sought not

---

[122]Quoted from Norwegian Aviation Historical Society Letter dated December 1, 1980, from Cato Guhnfeldt, NAHS Director, to Darrell McNeal, Manager, Northrop Aircraft Division Advanced Production; and "Northrop Update," Vol. 5, No. 36, p. 2, dated November 14, 1980 As noted in Chapter 9, Sevi Bulukin, at the instant the remains of the fuselage were beached on removal from the Thjorsa River, had jumped in the cockpit and waved, ready for takeoff. Whether in ruin or restored, the airplane had an instant restorative effect on him.

individual human quality, but "total quality" based on technology and computer-generated accountability in place of human direction. This trend was not clearly seen at the time of the restoration, but was implicit in the increasing division of management into higher and lower echelons, with a commensurate dichotomy between those with decisionmaking authority and those responsible for implementing decisions and bearing the consequences. The "golden days" when responsibility for the outcome of decisions had been taken by those who made them would be seen in retrospect as gone – gone with Jack Northrop and then later gone with the men and women he had cultivated and grown to follow after him. In retrospect, it can be seen that the restoration was made to honor this "golden age" and, if not to resurrect it, to leave a sign for those of the future that would manifest the fellowship and community of effort, in essence, the value, that age had bestowed on them.

N-3PB Serial No. 320 was towed on its beaching gear out of the Plant I paint shop early on the morning of 9 November 1980 and taken to the Northrop air terminal at Hawthorne airport where a tent had been erected for its formal presentation to representatives of the international team on Monday, 10 November. On Sunday afternoon, a "sneak preview" was held, open only to the volunteers and their families. Figure 78 shows the airplane mounted on its stage, as it was being prepared as the star of the show.

John Amrhein

Figure 78. N-3PB Serial No. 320 being prepared for unveiling to the international team that had made the restoration possible.

The following day, Jack Northrop's 85th birthday, was the official rollout date for the unveiling and exhibit of the airplane. Not all the organizations that had participated in the recovery and restoration operations had separate representatives present, but were nevertheless present in the form of the restored airplane. At the international level of the project, it is appropriate to re-identify them at this juncture, for the rollout and unveiling culminated what, at its most incipient beginning, was an 8-year effort on the team's part:

- The Icelandic Aviation Historical Society
- The Icelandic Lifesaving Association's Rescue Team "Albert"
- The Icelandic Diver's Association
- The Icelandic Coast Guard
- The National Power Company
- The Royal Norwegian Air Force
- The Norwegian Defense Museum
- The Norwegian Maritime Museum
- The U.S. Navy's Electronic Ordnance Detection Group 2
- The San Diego Aerospace Museum
- The British Sub-Aqua Club
- The U. S. Navy's Icelandic Defense Force
- Northrop Corporation

Within each organization, numerous individuals and many other companies gave freely of their time and materials. On the Northrop side alone, it is estimated that the restoration itself had involved some level of direct participation by nearly 500 people, many of whom have been identified in the preceding chapter. Overall, the project must have involved on the order of a 1,000 people in Iceland, Norway, England, Canada, and the U.S. At the unveiling ceremony, there were 62 representatives from Iceland and Norway (cf., Appendix H). Notable among these were Ragnar Ragnarsson, the "mission impossible" Icelandic force behind the project; Gudmundur Vignir Josefsson of Iceland; Sevi Bulukin, the Royal Norwegian Air Force pilot whose deft handling of the airplane during its forced crash-landing on the Thjorsa River made the restoration possible; Cato Guhnfeldt, Director of the Norwegian Aviation Historical Society; Col. N. M. Jorgensen, Royal Norwegian Air Force; and Sverre Thuve, Manager of the Norwegian Einar Bakkevig shipline that was scheduled to transport the plane to Iceland and then to Norway for permanent display.

Notably absent was Jack Northrop himself, who, through the special arrangements made by Clete Roberts, Los Angeles Channel 4 television news commentator, would be watching the entire ceremony from his hospital room. Standing in for him was his son, John. For Jack Northrop and his fellow Norcrafters, the rollout signified the excellence of the golden age of aviation that was passing on into the entirely new and different age of aerospace – different because its values were different: no longer human, but technological and seemingly profit seeking at any cost, human, animal, or environmental.

Tom Jones, Northrop's top executive, represented the company and was the keynote speaker.[123] Though traveling in his favorite Porsche mode of transportation, Jones was late getting to the unveiling. According to Gary McNeal, Jones was late because, having arrived tardily he was further delayed at the Gate 5 main entry because he didn't bring his company badge.[124] By the time he got to the rollout tent, the crowd was seated, waiting for the ceremony to begin, all eyes on the golden curtain that hid the plane from view.

With his customary athletic, on-your-toes alacrity, Jones sped at double-time up the steps of the platform to the speaker's podium without introduction. At his signal the golden curtain fell. A gasp, followed without hesitation by spontaneous applause and shouts of appreciation and approval, came from the audience of select guests. As Dale Brownlow later reported, "Seconds after the aircraft was unveiled I started watching the onlooker dignitaries from Iceland and Norway. Many of them had tears in their eyes."[125] These mainly were those courageous members of Squadron 330(N) who had been able to attend.

Jones used his tardiness and the event to his advantage as an icebreaker for his speech. He, too, was excited, not only because he relished the international ambiance of the audience and the opportunity to market Northrop and its management approach, but because in January of the year now almost past he had signed the one-page corporate directive that authorized manufacture of the F-20 advanced lightweight tactical fighter by Darrell McNeal's Advanced Production Department. At this very moment, rollout of the first F-20 was just two months away. While the N-3PB had marked the beginning of Jack Northrop's modern career in aviation, the F-20, 40 years later, marked the beginning of Tom Jones's breakthrough in technology that wrapped up and advanced everything Jack Northrop had ever done. Jones was excited, because his name would be associated with the first double coup in aviation and in national security; it was a technoeconomic breakthrough no other executive within the industry had the vision and guts to go for. While the day's event was recognizing history past, he was making history by opening the path to a new future.

Shown in Figure 79, Jones began his talk by noting the international cooperation that had characterized the restoration and made it possible. He also praised the efforts of Northrop employees who had volunteered their personal time to the project. In tracing the history of the N-3PB, he put it in the context of the contribution its technology had made to the current aircraft programs of the company. But his main theme was that international cooperation had made the project possible and successful. He noted the

---

[123] Sheer coincidence, of course, but Jones's full name, Thomas Victor Jones, or T. V. Jones, was so apt for the emerging age of technology.

[124]The story goes that Jones told the guard who he was, reasoning that his well-known name alone would gain him entry to the DOD-security-restricted facility without the formality of a badge. When Jones said, "I'm Tom Jones, you know who I am," the guard reputedly said, "I don't care if you're Petula Clark, you can't come in here without a badge. It took several phone calls and 15 minutes to locate and reach the right level of authority to convince the guard that this was the real Tom Jones, not Petula Clark.

[125] Dale Brownlow memo dated November 20, 1980, "The N-3PB Story."

continued success of the F-5 international fighter, the long and strong potential for international sales of the land-version of the F-18, for which Northrop was a prime associate contractor. He noted that technology had enabled the N-3PB to survive and that the future success of aviation rested similarly in organizing technology. Northrop, he finished, was not just a military company, but had major participation as well in commercial aviation, such as the Boeing 747 program on which the company produced the 20-ton, 153-foot fuselage just a few hundred yards from where "we are gathered."

In addition, he quickly summarized the numerous commercial products the company offered internationally, including airport landing systems, automatic aircraft checkout systems, and navigation systems. But implicit in his talk was the theme that Northrop was a leader in how to manage technology to produce the best products at affordable prices. It was not high level "boilerplate" – the sort of unbridled boasting and hyperbole expected from a company leader – but complex political-economy theory of the marketplace reduced to sophomoric simplicity; perhaps too simply reduced.

John Amrhein

Figure 79. Inside the "Golden Age" tent, Tom Jones representing Northrop in the unveiling and turnover of N-3PB Serial No. 320 to Norway as the restoration of past victory and the beginning of a new era.

Inside the rollout tent, which in the sunlight and with its gold color nylon cast an awesome golden hue inside, the N-3PB appeared monumental, sitting high on its platform and higher still on its beaching gear and pontoons. The airplane had an immensity and presence that not only dwarfed Jones, but a quiet eloquence that drowned his words. Somehow, the plane signified a truth that transcended anything that might be said about a future not yet achieved – a future yet to be demonstrated as feasible. Jones was trying to fly far above and beyond where the people and the plane were, a modern technological Icarus whose wings could melt from such altitudes of aspiration. His words did not fall on deaf ears, but on eyes and minds captivated by the magnificent bird behind him.

The N-3PB was positioned not only high above the audience level, but against a silver screen that reflected the stage lighting and gave the plane an ethereal presence. Interior details such as the instrument panels, the pilot's and navigator's seats, the control stick and other cockpit equipment were on display tables, giving the spectators direct view of what they would otherwise would not have been able to see because of the plane's elevated position and pontoon-stilted height. Several display boards placed at ground level about the stage showed photos of the wreckage of the plane as it had been lifted from its burial in the Thjorsa River; and in sequence, the major steps of the restoration of the plane. A large piece of fuselage skin in the original condition recovered from the river was displayed, along with one blade of the original propeller returned by Farmer Johansson and now gold anodized and mounted on a base that contained a plaque listing the U.S. companies that had contributed materials and services to the restoration. This memorial was to accompany the airplane to its permanent exhibit location in Norway.

A narrated film history of the airplane and the restoration process was shown on four monitors around the stage. Refreshments were served, followed at 1:30 p.m. by a documentary of Jack Northrop's career as an aircraft designer and industry leader. This documentary had been created by Roy Wolford for the early preview of the N-3PB the previous month and the testimonial dinner that followed. Figure 80 shows the Norwegian contingent attending the event and Sevi Bulukin and Jack Northrop's son John, with the plane onstage.

That evening the international guests were hosted by Northrop for cocktails, dinner, and dancing at Marina Del Rey, the prestigious yacht harbor and condo village on the coast just north of L. A. International Airport. A highlight of the evening was the showing of a movie made by Roy Wolford showing Darrell McNeal interviewing Jack Northrop. Some, including McNeal, wondered whether the F-20 would survive as the N-3PB had.

Elizabeth McNeal of course was there with her husband. Since dancing was their favorite recreation, she was most impressed by the adroit, energetic dancing of the Icelandic and Norwegian men (warriors all). Sevi Bulukin explained to her that when you live in cold northern regions where the nights are long, dancing is a favorite social activity.

Norwegians who operated the N-3PB: (from left: Sevi Bulukin, Finn Kristoffersen, Kjell Christiansen (mechanic), Per Christian Aas (pilot), Erik Bjoernebye (pilot), Alf Steffen-Olsen (chief navigation officer), Kaare Skabo (navigator), Thorvald Gunnerud (navigator), Hagbart Falk (mechanic), Conrad Skjoldhammer (pilot), Bredo Thurman-Nielsen (pilot with most N-3PB flight hours).

Looks like John Northrop is trying to talk Sevi Bulukin out of jumping in the cockpit and taking off again (though salty, tears do not make an ocean sufficient for a seaplane).

Figure 80. Norway's team representation at the rollout of N-3PB Serial No. 320, where one in good humor asked, as before, at the recovery, 'Shouldn't that be Serial No. 318?' Did the Thjorsa make a mistake? (Photos by John Amrhein.)

As the celebrity pilot of the occasion, Sevi also gave a short talk after dinner on how he had been forced down and crash-landed the airplane. New and even modified details were shared by him. He and his radio operator, Leif Dag Rustad had a single one-man survival raft that they held onto as they were swept to shore, moving fast downstream with the current in the river bend. His main memory was how cold the water was and that Rustad had lost a pair of new boots. After hitting shore on the west side of the river, they had walked to a farmhouse to get aid; and 40 years later when he was a participant in the recovery of the plane from the river, he had retraced their route and found the same farmhouse and the same farmer. "It was a grand reunion." He noted that after the airplane had been recovered from the river, the team had a farewell party where he told everyone, "Boys, the difficult you did once, the impossible took just a little longer." Ragnar Ragnarsson immediately added, "Having since had the opportunity to follow up on the tremendous work done by the skillful and dedicated group of people responsible for the aircraft's restoration, I might add, 'And a miracle took little less than a year.'"

Sevi Bulukin ended with, "We thought it a wonderful aircraft. It was the world's fastest seaplane at that time. We were very proud of it. We flew it on submarine patrol and used it as a fighter when we had to. I never attacked a submarine in an N-3PB myself, but I did engage in fighter attacks with it." He added that the plane had been called "The Northrop" by its pilots and was the first aircraft used by Norway's first-ever wartime squadron. "It helped in the struggle that eventually led to Norway's freedom. For us it is a very historic aircraft and its return to Norway for permanent exhibition will be a memorable occasion. We are truly grateful to all those dedicated people who worked so hard to bring the aircraft back to life."

McNeal noted that when the N-3PB's were built it "was a period of great patriotism and dedication. . . . It is easy to feel that way during a war, but as the restoration work proceeded, I found the same enthusiasm for the N-3PB now that we had then. Forty years have passed since we received the N-3PB contract. . . . Although people have changed, the spirit that motivated us then is still with us today." Figure 81 shows Darrell McNeal, wife Elizabeth, and son Gary at the dinner celebration following the rollout.

The next day, the plane was taken to Plant III where the group photo shown in Figure 82 was taken with the plane surrounded by many of the Northrop volunteers who had performed the restoration (refer to Table 6, previous chapter, for names).

Since it was mid-winter in Iceland, it was decided to wait until summer to ship it there for a brief exhibit and then on to Norway. This schedule provided almost six months for exhibit in the U.S. With the holidays approaching, the plane was displayed for several weeks next to the Northrop cafeteria at the main entry gate. For the year-end meeting of the Northrop Management Club, it was displayed at the Airport Park Hotel in Inglewood, California. The rear machine guns were prominently exposed and this gave the Inglewood police a problem, for machine guns required permits to be shown in public. The police were chagrin when it was explained and shown to them that the rear guns were wood replicas of the actual 30-caliber machine gun and that the 50-caliber wing guns (two per wing) had their barrels plugged and the firing-pin mechanisms disabled.

Figure 81. The McNeal family, Elizabeth, Darrell, and Gary, at the restoration dinner party. Elizabeth delighted in dancing with the Norwegians. From Minnesota, she was Viking, too. (Photo by John Amrhein.)

John Amrhein

Figure 82. N-3PB Serial No. 320, restored, nestles the volunteers who restored it, signifying that who restores gets restored.

The guns had been one of the last items restored and installed before the rollout. Local and federal gun laws made it impractical to try and bring the original guns from Iceland even though they had been under water for 36 years and would have been useless operationally (though the mechanisms could still be forced into operation). Four surplus 50-caliber machine guns were located in the U. S. Air Force stock inventory and after being plugged were donated for the project. Since the 30-caliber units could not be found, drawings were found from which dummy units were made from wood for the rear upper and lower gun bays. The pilot's gun sight was simulated out of metal from original drawings.

After the 1981 New Year, the plane was partially disassembled and trucked to the corporate headquarters building in Century City, near downtown Los Angeles, where it was reassembled and put on display for a month. It was then returned to the Hawthorne plant of the Aircraft Division for display outside the cafeteria for several months. After exhibit on 16 May aboard a flatbed truck in the Torrance, California Armed Forces Day Parade, the airplane was finally readied for shipment in cargo C-vans aboard the Norwegian freighter Starr Dieppe to Iceland out of L. A. Harbor. The Starr Dieppe was carrying other cargo, but space had been volunteered by Einar Bakkevig shipline.

While Gary McNeal had been in charge of all the local exhibits, Oliver "Bub" Larsen, as the Aircraft Division's lead Scandinavian volunteer on the N-3PB restoration, volunteered to manage the international exhibits. For the next two months, Larsen would lead a five-man team to get the airplane to Norway via Iceland. By this time, Larsen had transferred from McNeal's Advanced Production organization to the B-2 flying wing stealth bomber program, which was being staffed with personnel as a separate division of Northrop Corporation. After installing the N-3PB in its final exhibit location in Norway, Larsen would spend the next nine years on the B-2 program as manager of the Manufacturing Development Center and also the B-2 Advanced Production Department.

With the N-3PB's departure for Iceland and Norway, Darrell McNeal's responsibility for its restoration was completed and he felt relieved that he now could focus on the F-20. Tom Jones had built the Production Development Center so that McNeal's Advanced Production organization would have a dedicated plant for manufacturing aircraft prototypes under the company's new commercialization program. Parallel changes were being made by Jones in the management structure of the Aircraft Division to ensure dedicated focus of the division's attention on the F-20. It was Jones's big venture, one that would prove his executive pre-eminence in the modern aerospace industry. The F-18 fighter, which as the F-17 Cobra prototype, had survived being beaten by the Lockheed F-16 in the lightweight fighter competition, had been relocated to the old Douglas plant in El Segundo, that facility having been recently acquired by Northrop especially for the F-18 and in anticipation of fullup production of the F-20. Jones had been forced by the Navy and McDonnell-Douglas to concede the prime contractor position on the F-18 to McDonnell-Douglas; but as a bone, he was given prime contractor rights on any land version of the F-18, something that no one gave much credence to because of the contractual commitments already given the F-16 for that mission. Even those rights would be lost by 1985, after McDonnell won a six-year legal contest between the two companies over who was rightful prime contractor on all versions of the F-18. Jones's position was weakened by evidence that McDonnell F-18 technology had been used without approval on the F-20. Any Northrop bad feeling was salved by McDonnell's having to pay Northrop $50 million to settle the suit.

Similarly, in 1981, the B-2 program was moved out of the way of the F-20 by locating it in Pico Rivera, 30 miles east of Hawthorne. The original plant in Hawthorne, opened by Jack Northrop in July 1939 on 72 acres of raw land that in earlier years had been farmland, was in Jones's strategic plan to become the aircraft prototype development division. To manage these three divisions, the Aircraft Group was formed. Joe Gallagher, who had been in charge of the advanced development of the F-20, was made vice president of Engineering at the aircraft Division and was in line to take over the position of General Manager from vice president Roy P. Jackson as the F-20 program expanded. Jackson would represent Northrop Corporation in Iceland as transfer of the N-3PB was accomplished and then move on up to corporate. Dr. Thomas Paine, Chief Operating Officer of the corporation, would represent the company when the airplane got to Norway.

With the F-20 online, Jones had his technology programs and handpicked executive staff in place to position him as the "Jack Northrop" of the future. The "mindset" separating corporate level strategic planning from operational level management and control was in effect. Henceforth, the vesting of authority at the corporate level of decisionmaking compromised the capability of the human element at the bottom of the management hierarchy to be fully responsible for the outcome. The Jack Northrop continuum between management policy and its implementation in coordination with the people responsible for product integrity was severed. Granted that the financial decisions being made by Tom Jones and his board of directors were risky, but when one thinks of the tremendous technological leap Jack Northrop made with such success in going from conventional aircraft design to the flying wing, one wonders how this high school graduate did it. The answer is that he didn't do it alone. He documented his design solution on drawings that he then coordinated personally with the workers who would produce the plane. Both management and implementers knew what was to be done and how, where, when, by whom, and, as important, why. The management and control loop was continuous from top to bottom. The responsibility was clearly delegated and the authority to do a job of the highest quality was commensurate.

It was late August before the Starr Dieppe reached Iceland. Had McNeal's N-3PB delivery crew known that the ship had so many ports of call enroute to the Island, they would have scheduled the plane's delivery sooner. As it was, the exhibit of the plane in Iceland would have to be shortened so as to get the plane to Norway before winter arrived again. Assembly of the plane in Reykjavik took two days by Larsen and his team (shown in Figure 83). While waiting for Roy P. Jackson and Don Page to arrive onboard the corporate Gulfstream jet, other photos (also shown in Figure 83) were taken of the plane outside the Icelandair maintenance hangar loaned the IAHS for the one-week exhibit of the N-3PB at the Keflavik International Airport.[126]

---

[126] During WWII, Keflavik Field was a U. S. Army Air Base known as Meeks Field. The base was turned over to Iceland in October 1946 and renamed Keflavik Field.

In Iceland, don't fly me near the Thjorsa.   Larsen shipping crew with Baldur Sveinsson.

Roy P. Jackson (center) with Don Page (to his right) and Icelandic aviation enthusiasts.

Figure 83. On assembly at the airport in Iceland, the airplane was displayed for photo opportunities outside the Icelandic Aviation Historical Society's exhibit museum. (Photos by Larsen.)

On the evening of the formal presentation of the airplane to the IAHS, Iceland's 4-term, first-and-only female president, Vigdis Finnbogadottir, was present. Key personnel at the presentation of the plaque commemorating the aircraft's restoration are shown in Figure 84.

(a) Charlotte Jackson, Roy P. Jackson, the President (b) Conrad Skjoldhammer, the President, and Ragnar.

(c) Iceland's President thanks Bub Larsen. (d) Charlotte, Ragnar J. Ragnarsson, Leo Gay, and Bub.

(e) Jackson, Skjoldhammer, Ragnar and wife Stena. (f) Jackson, wife, Sigretta Thordason, Molly Morton-O'Neil.

O. H. Larsen

Figure 84. Presentation of the N-3PB restoration plaque to the Icelandic Aviation Historical Society, with the President of Iceland, Vigdis Finnbogadottir, newly elected to the first of her four terms, in attendance. In (d), Gay views plaque presented by IAHS President Baldur Sveinsson to Northrop in commemoration of the restoration.

A more permanent commemoration of the recovery and restoration of the N-3PB was made to the Icelandic government in the form of the monument shown in Figure 85. This monument was erected at Fossvogur Bay, from where A-Flight of Squadron 330(N) had operated in the Reykjavik area of southwest Iceland. The "Nissen" huts that had constituted "Corbett Camp" and served as housing and maintenance shelters for A-Flight were now gone, but the memory was now commemorated forever. This monument was paid for by the Northrop volunteers who restored the airplane. Following the presentation in Iceland, Larsen's team disassembled the plane one more time and loaded it onboard the Norwegian C-130 transport that would take it to its permanent home in the Royal Norwegian Air Force Museum at Gardermoen Airport in Oslo. Figure 86 shows Larsen and his wife onboard the C-130 on the final leg of the restoration, which would officially conclude in Norway.

O. H. Larsen

Figure 85. (a) Since Norway was to be the place of final exhibit, the Northrop volunteers made sure Iceland's strategic role in the wartime basing and subsequent recovery of the plane was commemorated by a special monument at the main base of operations at Fossvogur Bay, Reykjavik.

(b) Fossvogur Bay in 1979, showing the approach to mud-hole beach, the revetments (left) and the hangars and workshops right.

O. H. Larsen

Figure 86. N-3PB Serial No. 320 on the final leg of restoration aboard a Norwegian C-130 transport with Larsen and crew in attendance. Bub's wife Mary Ellen (left) entertains the crew with the N-3PB assisting on stage.

On completion of the restoration, a collection had been taken by the volunteers so that the special commemorative monument shown in Figure 85 could be erected in Iceland, where the restored airplane would pass through on temporary display, but not be permanently exhibited. The check for the monument had been presented earlier to the respective Norwegian and Icelandic counsels in Los Angeles. The occasion is documented in Figure 87.

In Norway, Larsen's team restored the N-3PB to its fullup configuration for the last time at the plane's permanent exhibit location at the Royal Norwegian Air Force Museum in Oslo. The airplane was then formally turned over to the Norwegian government at the ceremony shown in Figure 88. The king of Norway, Olav V, was duly represented. The letter from Cato Guhnfeldt, director of the Norwegian Aviation Historical Society (cf., Figure 80), to Darrell McNeal, expresses most aptly the meaning of the plane to Norway:

> To find the appropriate words to open this letter was not easy, so I'll just say THANK YOU! For the wonderful way you and your men have restored the N-3PB, for the magnificent way you and your colleagues looked after us all during our visit to Los Angeles. I think I can say on behalf of every

Norwegian that was present: It was a dream come true. It was something we'll never forget.

.... You can all be proud of what you've done, for several reasons: As far as "all we critical guys from the Aviation Society" could observe, the N-3PB looked just the way we all expected it to look, judging from all the war-time pictures we've collected. The paint-scheme looked authentic, and as we all moved around it with our cameras, I think each one of us suddenly realized how much time and effort you've put into it. In a way, I wish you could keep it to stand by the gateway of the factory as a monument to Jack Northrop, and the early days.

But I remember your words during your dinner: "In Norway you can show it, saying, 'This is what we fought with during the war.'" I did not realize it at the time, but it so happens that the N-3PB will be the only aircraft (the original parts) that actually went into combat during the war, that has been preserved. True, we have two Spitfires in Norway, the same type we flew during the war. But none of these aircraft fought, they were delivered to Norway after the war. The aircraft certainly will be a magnificent showpiece. And it will not only serve as a commemoration of the fighting during the war, but also of the remarkable will, dedication and effort of the people of Northrop, that brought the N-3PB back to us. Big words, but they are true.

But there's another reason why you can be proud, and the fellows with you. It was not mentioned during the rollout ceremony, but the fact is that 330 Squadron during the war not only was Norwegian but it was also very much forgotten. The personnel of the squadron fought on the outskirts of the war in Europe, accordingly their efforts were not given the appropriate attention by the heads of the government and military forces in London. Their eyes were focused on 331 and 332 Squadron that almost daily flew their Spitfires across the English Channel, and 333 Squadron that flew Catalina's and Mosquitoes over Norway, dropping parcels at Christmas, sinking ships in the fjords.

"Sometimes London never quite knew what we were doing," Brigadier Bredo Thurmann-Nielsen once told me (he spoke about the operations after the unveiling ceremony). "And we were the ones that sometimes fought the toughest battles, not against Jerry's, but against nature itself, repairing the aircraft outdoors, leaving the Icelandic coast behind you, and not knowing if we would see it again. Thanks to the Northrops, more of us survived than would have been expected."

330 Squadron was the forgotten squadron indeed, but thanks to your people, Darrell, those that fought have been brought out into the light of appreciation, and given the most fitting token of homage that ever could be made, a real N-3PB. So you see, there was really more to it than just the

aircraft. You've lighted up a spark in many a veteran, and for that we say, 'THANK YOU!'[127]

John Amrhein

Figure 87. Bub Larsen presents check to Norwegian L.A. consul from money raised by Northrop restoration volunteers for monument to be permanently located in Iceland in commemoration of Squadron 330(N)'s heroic performance during WWII. Showing her appreciation is Halla Linker, the Icelandic Consul General in Los Angeles.[128]

---

[127] Cato Guhnfeldt, director, Norwegian Aviation Historical Society, letter to Darrell McNeal, manager, Northrop Aircraft Division Advanced Production, dated December 1, 1980. Refer to Appendix J for full reprint.

[128] At the time of this photo in 1981, Halla Linker, a native Icelander, was the wife of Hal Linker, noted documentary filmmaker. Ms. Linker served as Consul General of Iceland from 1980 through 1998. She is now married to Francisco Aguirre, Former Brigadier General in the Air Force of Ecuador and now Emeritus Consul General of Ecuador, having served as Consul General of Ecuador in the 1980s.

Restoration takes place at many levels in many ways, but all commemorating a struggle from which mankind has emerged victor. Restoration of the N-3PB exemplifies this pattern. Though Norway had been the destination for the restoration of the N-3PB, it was in Iceland that a new cycle of restoration took root. During the week prior to its official presentation to Iceland's president, the airplane had been held on display in front of the hangar at Keflavik International Airport where Ragnar's IAHS had its air museum. During that week the Northrop team was feasted and taken on bus tours of the Island.

On one such trip, Ragnar and Don Page were sitting in front of Roy P. Jackson with Bub Larsen in the seat behind. The IAHS, then in its eighth year of operation, had led the international effort to find and restore the N-3PB that was now bringing everyone together, with Ragnar as principal coordinator. Don Page thought that having a similar organization in Southern California would be most appropriate, with the region's rich history of aviation notables, aircraft evolution, and related technological development, plus the general benefit made by aviation to the region's economic growth and the social welfare of its people. Noting Ragnar's example in forming the IAHS, Page suggested to Jackson that a similar organization be formed at home. By incorporating a Southern California Historical Aviation Foundation, the volunteer team concept could be continued in operation on the restoration of other aircraft. Jackson turned to Larsen and asked, "Can this be done, Bub?"

"We've already demonstrated it can be done," Larsen responded. "That's how we got here." He was eager to see the idea become a reality, so the restoration concept would have continuity.

When Page returned to Hawthorne he called a meeting with the author and Darrell McNeal to discuss the possibility of forming a historical aviation society, as Iceland and Norway had done. The objective here would be to memorialize the splendid world-changing history of aviation as it originated in Southern California. Subsequent meetings were held with the key people of the Northrop Recreation Club and the Aircraft Division's Finance Department invited. It was determined that a historical aviation society could be supported financially by establishing a payroll deduction program open to voluntary participation by all Aircraft Division personnel. This approach was then outlined to the Legal Department, which prepared the necessary paperwork to register a nonprofit organization with the State of California, to be known as the Southern California Historical Aviation Foundation. Northrop Corporation agreed to help sponsor the organization by renting a hangar for SCHAF to set up an aviation museum that is today still in operation as the Western Museum of Flight. Appropriately, WMF is located at Hawthorne Airport (historically and officially known as Jack Northrop Field).

But though the spirit of volunteerism and the training of new personnel to work in the aerospace industry was continued past the restoration of the N-3PB by means of SCHAF and the WMF, what Jack Northrop had called "the golden days" were not restorable. People in the aviation industry were no longer united by the goal of producing quality aircraft and new technology developments as a team, but were carrying out decisions made far above them in the corporate hierarchy where authority was separated and often aloof from responsibility for the consequences. Decisions at the corporate level were "strategic" and "long-range." Responsibilities at the working level were "functional" and "short-range." Quality became managed by technology; so technology produced technology.

After Jack Northrop left in 1952, the company went through three growth stages. First there was the Edgar Schmeud-Welko Gasich F-5 Freedom Fighter which the government authorized as the first "lightweight" tactical fighter aircraft that could be supplied to developing nations under military assistance program funding to keep them from buying such equipment from the Soviets. The F-5 production program lasted from 1960 to 1987, after 1967 in decreasing production quantities. As F-5 production peaked, Bob Lloyd, who had started work as an aircraft assembler under Jack Northrop and became vice president of Manufacturing, enabled Northrop to win a major subcontract on the Boeing 747, due to his manufacturing management ability and the respect Boeing had for him. Then on October 17, 1981, as the Boeing program peaked, Jack Northrop was at last redeemed when the company was awarded the contract for the B-2 flying-wing stealth bomber. He knew this before he died on February 18, 1981, because the intent of the U.S. Air Force to award a "stealth" flying wing bomber contract to Northrop Corporation had been leaked publicly during 1980. In a private meeting held just for him at the company, he had been shown a classified model of the plane. He too might have publicly said: "I knew I was right all along!" But in his more modest manner, he remained reflective, saying, "You know, if I had a chance to do it all over again – I would! And I don't think I'd change much of anything."[129] Most appropriately, the B-2 flying wing stealth bomber was named "The Spirit." So Jack Northrop was restored.

What was restored with the N-3PB, at its highest level of meaning, was the team spirit that brought the airplane into being. Originally the center of importance – the focal point of innovation, enterprise, and strategic need – the airplane, having fulfilled its need, became the symbol and metaphor of the meaning that it had for the team.

Figure 89 shows N-3PB Serial No. 320 as it looks to day, still enabling visitors to Oslo to take off on their respective flights of memory or fantasy restored.

---

[129]Ted Thackrey, Jr., "Aircraft Pioneer Jack Northrop Dies at 85," L. A. Times, February 20, 1981, Section I, p. 8.

Norway Air Defense Museum

Figure 88. Finally restoring the airplane to its original Northrop customer, the Royal Norwegian Air Force in Oslo, Norway, in the Air Museum at Gardermoen Flystasjon airport. (From Left: Thomas O. Paine, Northrop Chief Operating Officer; Ragnar J. Ragnarsson, IAHS; and Col. Sevi Bulukin, RNoAF pilot of the airplane.

Norway Air Defense Museum

Figure 89. N-3PB Serial No. 320 as it looks today, still on-stage after rollout, still restoring one of mankind's great victories over earthly tyranny in the name of freedom. The bent propeller blade was recovered from the crash site in Iceland.

CHAPTER 14 - THE FOLLOWON MISSION

To everyone's great pleasure and relief, the restored N-3PB Serial No. 320 appeared good as new, though the Thjorsa River had succeeded in taking half the plane for keeps and, as Leo Gay observed, had sanded down 80 percent of the remainder. But the effort put forth had done more than just restore a historical airplane. The effort had so energized the volunteer team that it wanted to keep going – to repeat the restoration effort on other historical aircraft and in the process to bring back and experience again the zest of its own professional history. In effect, what had been learned is that restoration is about the act, not the object, of restoring.

So during the following year (1981) there was a lot of discussion about forming an aviation historical society that would implement fulltime what Don Page had suggested the year previously while riding with Ragnar J. Ragnarsson, Roy P. Jackson, and Bub Larsen on the bus in Iceland. What the Icelandic Aviation Historical Society had set in motion with the N-3PB was seen as the seed of a recurring program of restoration that would take root and flourish in Southern California, the birthplace of modern aviation. The idea was not only a natural one for the place that had brought forth Jack Northrop, the Lockheed brothers, Donald Douglas, Claude Ryan, Howard Hughes, and Gerard Vultee, and that had created one of the greatest industries on earth, but it was an idea that had to find expression. The history was not only important for the sake of documenting the contributions of these pioneers of aviation and the hundreds of thousands of employees who implemented their ideas, but for the youth who would follow. Forming an aviation historical society was clearly an obligation, one that rested on the productive spirit of man, as the N-3PB volunteers had demonstrated and wanted to continue demonstrating in follow-on restorations.

Due to the nonprofit nature of such a society for preserving history, its formation required volunteers. Fortunately, the timing was right (once again the mystical Zen of evolving truth seemed to be watching over things), for the very people who had topped out as leaders of the restoration were also in the process of retiring or approaching that historical stage of transition to an individually chosen future: McNeal, Page, Gay, the author – all were planning on what to do next and forming and participating in an aviation historical society devoted to the preservation of their Southern California heritage suddenly became top priority in their list of things to do in retirement.

Of course, there were many factors in favor of this choice. For one, it would provide a smooth transition to the future. Also it would bring closure to their years of work in the aviation industry in a way that would open up a new, even more important future of benefit to that industry, if managed properly. The new team of organizers itself provided the essential nucleus for success. McNeal, as manager of Advanced Production at the Northrop Aircraft Division, had the demonstrated management background of working on one-of-a-kind aircraft, in which prototyping was the main task and much like restoring in that one usually worked with minimal design information. Don Page, as manager of

Public Relations, had access to the essential influential contacts at the corporate level of Northrop and within the local community of Hawthorne, California. Leo Gay, as Advanced Aircraft Project Engineer, had the engineering know-how. The author, as manager of Master Program Planning, had the relevant background in new business venture development and, through his own career as a pilot, personal contacts throughout the aviation community with the key test pilots who had flown the aircraft that had made aviation history, besides contacts with many experimental aircraft developers.

But most important was the fact that all had worked closely together in the history-making N-3PB restoration: the historic restoration of a historic airplane and the beginning of the Southern California Historical Aircraft Foundation.

During 1981, most of the restoration fervor was still arising from and focused on the delivery and exhibit of the N-3PB in the Southern California area, Iceland, and the final destination in Norway. These activities consumed a great amount of the time of the key people such as Leo Gay, Bub Larsen, Bill Sheriffs, Les Epperly, Ted Mothershead, and Dick McKay, while in the background Don Page, Darrell McNeal and the author coordinated the groundwork for starting up the historical aviation foundation. During the spring and summer of 1981, Don Page, operating under the auspices of Jack Mannion, vice president of the Northrop Aircraft Division's Administration Department, held a series of meetings concerning the need for and benefits of forming a fulltime foundation for the preservation and exhibit of Southern California aviation history for the general welfare of the region, the nation, and the world at large. Participating in these meetings were representatives of the Engineering, Facilities, Human Resources, Legal, and Public Affairs departments of the Aircraft Division.

The general conclusion reached after coordination with corporate leaders such as Richard W. Millar, corporate director and treasurer, and Frank R. Smith, corporate counsel, was that a nonprofit foundation, as formed by The Boeing Company in Seattle, Washington, would be the way to proceed. Such a foundation would enable financial and equipment donations to be made with attendant tax benefits and also insulate the sponsors from any legal exposure. Accordingly, in the fall of 1981, the author documented this approach in a proposal to Northrop Corporation to underwrite, through the Aircraft Division, the Southern California Historical Aircraft Foundation.

With delivery of the N-3PB seaplane to the Air Museum in Norway constituting the formal completion of the restoration in October 1981, the key personnel turned their attention to implementing the nonprofit foundation proposal. The initial concept for locating the foundation was to lease what was known historically at Northrop as the Radar Building (Building 3-7) near the east end of the Hawthorne complex. This was a 4,500-square-foot building consisting of 2,100 square feet of low-bay office, tooling, machining, and sheet metal work area, plus 2,400 square feet of high-bay area for aircraft restoration activity. The building had direct access to Northrop Field.

As usual in any matter that was not "business as usual," it was taking time to get corporate level go-ahead on the proposed plan. Already, the author had made contact with his associates in the U.S. Air Force and obtained the right to restore the Northrop X-4 aircraft. This airplane was the culminating configuration of a series of Jack Northrop designs exploring the transition from conventional to all-wing aircraft. Since the formation of his new company in 1939, Jack Northrop had been designing and building flying wing prototypes, such as the N-1M (cf., Figure 8), the MX-324/334 rocket wing (1944), the JB-1 flying wing power bomb (1943), and the JB-10 power bomb (1944), and the XP-79B flying ram (1943). Then with the introduction of the jet engine, aircraft designers had to respond to new possibilities for performance, because now supersonic flight was the next advance required of the airframe. Jack Northrop's entry into this field was the X-4 which, except for the vertical stabilizer, was a flying wing, as shown in Figure 90.

Jack Northrop and designer Art Lusk.   X-4 with Charles Tucker piloting.

Figure 90. The X-4 transonic research airplane on flight test 12/15/48.

Adding impetus to getting the foundation activated was the fact that McNeal and his key personnel, along with Page, Gay and the author, wanted to take advantage of the still highly motivated volunteer corps that was ready to begin restoring another airplane given the go-ahead and a facility to work in. To keep the idea moving ahead, Page decided to file the Articles of Incorporation shown in Figure 91. As shown, his team of incorporators consisted of M'Liss Kane, Frank G. Compton (a well-known program manager of new aircraft developments), Darrell McNeal, and Leo Gay. These articles, signed November 15, 1982, officially established the Southern California Historical Aviation Foundation, familiarly known in aviation history and museum circles as SCHAF.

The X-4 transonic jet aircraft from the U.S. Air Force Museum at Wright-Patterson AFB was immediately moved into Building 3-7 and put under the direct restoration project management of the author. Building 3-7 was technically under the control of McNeal for use in SCHAF restoration projects. McNeal, though now fulltime manager of the Northrop Product Development Center where the F-20 Tigershark was being manufactured under his direction in prototypes, was working evenings and weekends to get SCHAF into fulltime operation as well.

```
                    ARTICLES OF INCORPORATION
                              OF
                 SOUTHERN CALIFORNIA HISTORICAL
                      AVIATION FOUNDATION


                              I

        The name of this Corporation is the Southern California Histor-
ical Aviation Foundation.

                              II

        A.  This Corporation is a nonprofit public benefit corporation and is
not organized for the private gain of any person.  It is organized under
the NonProfit Public Benefit Corporation Law for charitable purposes.

        B.  The Corporation is organized and shall be operated for the follow-
ing scientific and educational purposes:

        1.  To foster, encourage and sponsor the research and writing of
the history of aviation activities in Southern California;

        2.  To acquire, restore, preserve and donate for public display
aircraft and other objects, things and documents of present or
historical value relating to the history and development of aviation
and the role of Southern California therein;

        3.  To assist and make possible the preservation and public
display of such aircraft, objects, things and documents of present or
historical value by establishing and operating, or fostering and
assisting the establishment and operation of a public nonprofit
aeronautical department or section of, or display in, any existing
public, nonprofit museum or similar institution;

        4.  To foster, encourage and sponsor the active participation of
the public, schools, associations and clubs in progress involving the
physical restoration of aircraft, missiles, drones, space vehicles and
other objects that have contributed to the advancement of United
States aerospace;

        5.  To foster, encourage and sponsor the active participation of
the public, schools, associations and clubs in programs involving the
preservation, coalition, cataloging and display of historical memor-
abilia which reflect the history of aviation activities in Southern
California; and

        6.  Such purposes related to those above as its trustees may from
time to time deem advisable.
```

Figure 91. The original SCHAF Articles of Incorporation secured the status of the nonprofit organization on November 15, 1982 (page 1 of 2).

We hereby declare that we are the persons who executed the foregoing Articles of Incorporation, which execution is our act and deed.

INCORPORATORS:

M'Liss Kane
M'Liss Kane

Frank S. Compton
Frank Compton

Darrell McNeal
Darrell McNeal

Leo Gay
Leo Gay

Donald G. Page
Donald G. Page

Figure 91. (Continued, page 2 of 2.)

The first meeting of the SCHAF Board of Directors was held December 14, 1982. The initial board of directors consisted of Richard W. Millar (Northrop corporate director and treasurer), Max R. Stanley (test pilot on the Northrop flying wing bombers beginning with the N-9M in 1942), Donald G. Page (manager of Aircraft Division Public Relations, and Raymond C. Nadeau, Jr. The Board of Trustees for this nonprofit foundation included Richard Millar, Max Stanley, Jack Mannion, Frank Compton, Ray Nadeau, Donald Page, Leo Gay, Bud Mahurin, Clete Roberts, Don Foulds, Willie Hawkings, Darrell McNeal, General Switzer, and Clete Roberts.

Even before the N-3PB became a restoration objective, the Vintage Aircraft Boosters Club had been in existence at the Northrop Aircraft Division since the early 1960s. Primarily a social club, this organization had as its main charter the preservation of historical aircraft artifacts, memorabilia, and documentation, including drawings, photos, films and reports. The organization also had an excellent collection of scale models of historical aircraft. The organization's particularly intensive and extensive pursuit of Southern California aviation history is shown by its interest in the late 19th Century Montgomery glider, a replica of which is shown in Figure 92.

Western Museum of Flight

Figure 92. A full-scale replica of John J. Montgomery's Year-1883 manned and flight-controlled glider is on permanent display by SCHAF at its Western Museum of Fight at Northrop Field, Hawthorne, California.

John J. Montgomery, the Vintage Aircraft Booster's Club research revealed, was unquestionably the first human to fly under his own control in an airplane. Granted this was a glider type airplane, the flight was nevertheless performed in 1883, on August 28, and witnessed by Montgomery's brother. Furthermore, the flight was made in Southern California's San Diego County, off of Otay Mesa, just northeast of Tijuana near the U.S.-Mexico border, where his father owned a ranch. Think about it! Over 20 years before the Wright Brother's flew their engine-powered aircraft, human flight took place where aviation in the U.S. would eventually take root. Montgomery described this first controlled flight by man as a feeling of "self-buoyance."

Montgomery subsequently became better known in the Santa Clara area of Northern California for his man-controlled glider flights over the next 25 years. In 1901 he was awarded a Ph.D. in Science from Santa Clara College. Earlier, in 1894, after earning a master's in science from St. Ignatius College in San Francisco, he began teaching mathematics at St. Joseph's College, Rohnerville, California; and concurrently he helped Octave Chanute write a summary of his aerodynamic results for Chanute's book, *Progress in Flying,* which was read by the Wright brothers in preparing to build their first aircraft over the next 10 years.

While working on his Ph.D., he performed research in hydrodynamics on various lifting body configurations to improve his airfoil designs for wings and flight control surfaces. He even built a wind tunnel to experiment in varying curvatures of wing, rudder and stabilizer airfoils. In 1906, he was awarded the first "aeroplane" patent by the U.S. During this time he continued making actual glider flights to demonstrate feasibility of selected configurations. During two weeks in October 1911, at Evergreen, California, outside of San Jose, he made 55 flights. Though now 53 years old, he wanted to test one more design change before winter came and on this last flight the glider stalled and he was killed in the crash. His last words were, "How is the machine?"

As an offshoot of John Montgomery's historic introduction of manned flight, the Associated Glider Clubs of Southern California was formed in 1930. Anne Morrow and Charles Lindbergh learned to fly gliders in San Diego in the spring of that year and Anne Morrow Lindbergh formed the Anne Lindbergh Glider Club of San Diego shortly afterward. The AGCSC continues to operate at Torrey Pines, flying off the cliffs along the Pacific coast. The AGCSC is the oldest soaring organization in the U.S. and is still active in Southern California.

Montgomery's stellar status in aviation history was not always so well known. It was through the persistent efforts of organizations such as the Northrop Vintage Aircraft Booster's Club that his initiating role in manned flight was restored. Today, one of the two remaining replicas of Montgomery's original glider is on display by SCHAF at its Western Museum of Flight. Through such historical research as that performed on John Montgomery's early aircraft design and flight demonstrations, the Vintage Aircraft Booster's Club at the Northrop Aircraft Division became a major contributor to the success of SCHAF and continues so today.

Within two years of its activation, SCHAF had become so successful that it was outgrowing its location at Building 3-7 on Northrop property next to the airport in Hawthorne. Demand for more space in which to operate soon came about when restoration of a Northrop XP-56 (cf., Figure 36) was assigned to SCHAF by the Smithsonian Air Museum in Washington, D.C. Now the X-4 restoration team found itself contending with another volunteer crew for both assembly room and equipment to fabricate parts, as well as storage space.

Fortuitously, the Zen of Restoration was still working on behalf of the Northrop volunteers. A 20,000-square-foot hangar had just become available at Northrop Field proper. Located at the opposite end of the airport, it was at the northwest corner where Prairie Avenue and 120th Street intersect. This location provided excellent visibility to passersby, was all highbay on the inside, and had extensive paved area outside for display of aircraft. Just two years after its startup, SCHAF relocated to this hangar and concurrently formed the Western Museum of Flight, which continues in operation today at this site. All of the sheet metal, fasteners, fittings, tools, and other hardware left over from the N-3PB restoration project were given to the museum. These materials had been donated by Northrop and its suppliers.

Figure 93 shows the X-4 transonic research airplane after restoration, ready for return to the U.S. Air Museum. In honor of Darrell G. McNeal – who can be called the "Father of restoration at Northrop" – the WMF facility at this location has been designated the Darrel G. McNeal Restoration Facility. Today, about half of the facility is used for restoration projects and the rest for display of aviation artifacts and memorabilia.

Figure 93. With Charles Tucker – the original test pilot – at the podium, the SCHAF-restored X-4 transonic research airplane is rolled out at the Western Museum of Flight ready for return to the U.S. Air Force Museum at Wright-Patterson AFB. The Northrop JB-1 flying bomb is shown in the background. (Photo provided by author, who, seen holding camera, foreground, also was master of ceremonies, as X-4 restoration project director.)

The principal Northrop aircraft displayed at the facility are the world renowned F-5A Freedom Fighter (the first truly "lightweight" fighter offering advanced aeroagility in the 1960s and the airframe baseline for the F-20 Tigershark, Northrop's Tom Jones's proposed Freedom Fighter replacement for the 1980s and beyond); the YF-17 Cobra prototype of the U.S. Navy's carrier-compatible, advanced tactical fighter that has performed so successfully in U.S. air combat operations (e.g., Desert Storm and Afghanistan) since 1990; the YF-23A Black Widow II advanced tactical fighter, DOD flyoff competitor against the Lockheed F-22; the WWII JB-1 (MX-543) Power Bomb glider, one of three Jack Northrop 1940s flying wing aircraft still extant; and the Northrop RP-5A, RP-76, and KD2R-5 target drones used by U.S. and allied air and ground forces for live fire and weapon delivery training. Other historical aircraft produced by Grumman, Douglas, Lockheed, deHavilland, and North American Aviation have been restored and are on display.

Additional rare Northrop aircraft are displayed in scale-model form by WMF, including actual wind tunnel models that were used to design and develop the Northrop Alpha aircraft of the early 1930s and the Northrop A-9A close-air support airplane. The A-9A competed against the Fairchild A-10, the latter known as the "Warthog" because it carried so many external weapon stores and had twin jet engines pyloned externally on each side of the aft fuselage.

WMF also has an outstanding archive of rare films of historical aviation events, assembled by and known as the Frank G. Compton Aviation Film Library. Complementing this treasure of historical film is the Dr. Ira Chart Library of Aviation History. Thus at WMF, students, historians, and visitors can see and have research access to a wide spectrum of aviation history in various media.

When the N-3PB restoration was completed, Darrel McNeal wrote a "thank you" letter to each of his managers who had helped him bring the project to a successful conclusion. [130] These managers are shown with McNeal along with the product of their efforts, in Figure 94. With the letter to them, he enclosed a copy of the picture shown in Figure 95, which provides a rare comparison of the N-3PB, just restored, with the F-20 Tigershark, just off the manufacturing line as Prototype No. 1.

The advent of the F-20 did have a major impact on McNeal's time and it was necessary for him to rely heavily on these key men to take on more responsibility for the N-3PB restoration while also performing their regular assignments on the F-20, which had become a major priority for the Aircraft Division.

---

[130] Darrell G. McNeal retired from Northrop on April 25, 1986, and became fulltime operations director of the Western Museum of Flight, while continuing to serve as a director and trustee of SCHAF, until his death October 31, 1994. Donald G. Page retired on October 21, 1986, and continued to serve as a director and trustee of SCHAF until his death November 9, 1996. Lionel ("Leo") O. Gay retired on June 28, 1991, and served as a director of SCHAF until his death January 9, 1995.

John Amrhein

Figure 94. Darrell McNeal (center) flanked by key restoration managers from his Advanced Production organization, from left, Dale Brownlow, Dick MacKay, Bub Larsen, McNeal, Les Epperly, Harris Stone, and Ed Weaver.

Roy P. Jackson had been made Vice President and General Manager of the Northrop Aircraft Division especially to bring top-level executive management attention to this new initiative by Northrop Corporation to change the way weapon systems were procured to a more commercially efficient approach. This new approach was a logical response to the U.S. Department of Defense's new way of defining weapon system requirements based on mission need. This change gave prime weapon system contractors like Northrop the chance to specify the weapon system that would meet the mission need and thereby enable such contractors to be more innovative in offering the most cost-efficient solution, though at the contractor's risk for the upfront money.

The F-20 was one such innovative solution offered by Northrop. Jackson was a highly qualified executive to lead the F-20 program because he was well known and respected within the industry by military and other government agencies that would or could have influence on the outcome. Prior to taking over the Aircraft Division, he was corporate vice president of program management. Having first joined Northrop in 1953,

John Amrhein

Figure 95. Jack Northrop's restored N-3PB seaplane and the F-20 Tigershark, the beginning and end of the "Golden Years."

he had been chief engineer and assistant general manager of Northrop Space Labs. On his return to Northrop from NASA, he was assistant general manager of the Aircraft Division and then YF-17 program manager, as well as program manager of the F/A-18A during the development and acquisition phase and subsequently vice president of the F/A-18L program. Interim to Northrop, he had been with the Martin Company and Ford-Aeronutronics in the 1958-1962 period and then during 1970-73 with NASA as associate Administrator for Aeronautics and Space Technology. For his distinguished contributions to the U.S. aeronautics and space programs at NASA, he received the Distinguished Service Medal, NASA's highest award.

Driving the F-20 program concept was the incentive for Northrop to maximize profit while offering the latest weapon delivery technology, by using the basic F-5 Freedom Fighter airframe that was already developed and in production and had a known record of demonstrated performance excellence both logistically and operationally. Figure 96 shows Jackson receiving his honorary SCHAF Booster Club Pin from the first SCHAF President Holly Holliday.

In delivering the N-3PB seaplane to Norway in nine months from contract signing, Jack Northrop had had a similar advantage as prime contractor. Norway had a mission need and Jack Northrop had a ready airframe solution based on aircraft he had designed and built with such acclaim and trend-setting technological breakthrough over the past decade (cf., Figure 9). With an already demonstrated airframe, he could select the best systems technology to incorporate and integrate as the airframe went down the production line.

John Amrhein

Figure 96. First SCHAF Booster Club President Holli Holliday pinning Northrop VP Roy P. Jackson with members Bub Larsen (left) and the author witnessing.

So the two aircraft shown in Figure 95 are historical classics. But they also mark the end of something, for what was coming to the forefront of the industry at the beginning of the 1980s was a new approach to systems design. The methodology of the 1960s and 70s known as "system engineering" was being superseded by a new technological methodology known as "total systems integration." In this new approach, the airframe and the systems are integrated as a total weapon system platform responding to a specific mission need in which the pilot and other crew members (if any) are largely weapon system managers; the airplanes for the most part fly themselves under the management supervision of the pilot, who also serves as the decisionmaker for the weapon fire command. Except for takeoff and landing, most of the flight and combat functions are computer-programmed and implemented, including target detection, identification, weapon selection, delivery, and target damage assessment. Navigation is pinpoint and flawless by use of the satellite-based Global Positioning System.

The success of Northrop Grumman Corporation today is the result of its new leader, Kent Kresa, employing this methodology in the selection of technology leaders for acquisition and merger as part of the corporation. From its early business as an integrator of "airborne systems" for aircraft platforms, Northrop today – through Kresa's perspicuous genius for integrating building-block national security systems by means of network-centric technology companies – has become a leading integrator of not just "weapon systems" but "weapon system platforms" for air, ground, sea, and space mission domains covering the entire earth. It's as though Kresa's vision is focused beyond mere national security, on world security. And in the not-too-distant future that may be the main aerospace marketplace. In looking abstractly at Jack Northrop's work, one can see that he had a similar "global" vision. In fact, the three key men who have led Northrop since its founding in 1939 – Jack Northrop, Tom Jones, and Kent Kresa – have been leaders of the same essential vision framed to their respective times. As Jones fulfilled Northrop's vision of the Flying Wing, so Kresa is fulfilling Jones's vision of how to manage technology. With elegant closure, Kresa is also fulfilling Jack Northrop's concept of the team as key to sustained growth. In Kresa's vision the key to world growth is international teaming through technology, using technology both to manage such teaming and to produce new security systems. Jack Northrop would be pleased; it is through the team that the freedom and dignity of the individual is restored again.[131]

Finally the saga of the N-3PB comes to an end, though its mission goes on in different form. The heroic days when pilot and crew had to fly aircraft hands-on every minute and concurrently fight both the environment and the enemy were the days when success depended directly on the capability and courage of the aviator, with the airplane serving as the basic transport medium. It was the "Golden Age" when the individual made the difference. As this story has noted, the N-3PB was designed for a mission different from the one it was used in. But it succeeded, because of the individuals who built it, flew it and maintained it. The restoration of this airplane was more than that of an object for display in a museum. It was the restoration of the human team spirit that built and used the airplane that the restored airplane signifies; and that this story is about.

So the question posed in the beginning of the first chapter is now answered.

Still, one could ask, what does Icarus, the ancient Greek who donned wings of waxed feather, have to do with this story of restoration? The point is that Icarus crashed, Sevi Bulukin crashed, John Montgomery crashed, St. Exupery crashed, Jack Northrop's vision of the flying wing crashed, Tom Jones's vision of a commercialized defense market crashed: in effect, there are many forms of such falls to earth – the return to base, to reality, to the struggle for freedom from tyranny. Yet in none of these cases was there failure; what there was instead was restoration. Off the shore of Greece, there is today, the Icarian Sea, where Icarus fell from the sky in his eager ascent toward the sun; but was Icarus really headed for the sun? It's entirely possible he had another destination in mind, much further out in space and time. To make such voyages one must be prepared for restoration. Birds, between flights, restore themselves. Life is continual restoration: continual coming to earth and taking off again, until one is finally ready for the final ascent. That's the significance of Icarus in this story. Even the Federal Aviation Administration sees significance in the Myth of Icarus; at the FAA building in El Segundo, there is a large model of the Icarian Labyrinth in the lobby, unavoidable to the

---

[131] Kent Kresa succeeded Tom Jones as head of Northrop Corporation in 1990. Through his acquisition and merger strategy, the original "Northrop" is now Northrop Grumman Corporation and has grown from $3-billion in annual sales to $30 billion (including the July 1, 2002 acquisition of TRW). In aerospace, the company ranks second to first-ranked Boeing with Lockheed now third, the company having advanced from sixteenth since Kresa took over.

eye as one enters and has no choice but to walk by it. There is only one reason why it is there: to signify that in flight, man seeks and finds, if only symbolically, freedom from earthly bondage. To fly takes restoration. Figure 97 shows a few of the outstanding men who have proved this point.

Roy L. Wolford

Figure 97. At a Northrop Management Club meeting in 1985, the author (left) briefs (left to right) Jim Cassells, Northrop T-38 Aircraft Program Manager; Max Stanley, renowned test pilot of the Northrop XB-35 and subsequent flying wing bombers of the 1946-48 period; world-famous test pilot and USAF Brigadier General (rtd.) Charles Yeager, the first human to fly faster than the speed of sound. Roy L. Wolford, Northrop's noted aviation photographer checks the photo angle from Yeager's right.

Thus restoration, in its inescapable philosophical sense, has a mythical and even spiritual dimension beyond the physical that has been the principal focus of our story about the Northrop N-3PB airplane. This restoration, in all its dimensions, came to a fitting conclusion in 1995 when, at 1030 hours on July 19, a C-130H transport of the Royal Norwegian Air Force landed at Northrop Field in Hawthorne, California, with F-5A Freedom Fighter Serial No. 66-9207 onboard, being delivered by Major Erling

Markussen of the RNoAF[132]. This airplane, too, had been produced by Northrop, as the serial number indicates, in 1966, at the same facility as the N-3PB. It was one of an entire Fighter Wing of the F-5 aircraft series bought by Norway and one of 2,053 of the F-5 Freedom Fighter series operated in various allied countries around the world in 1995. It was being returned by the Norwegian government for permanent display by SCHAF at its Western Museum of Flight.

Valued at $2,793,693 for import purposes (as Norway's shipping document noted) this F-5 was being returned as fulfillment of an honorary debt Norway felt it owed Northrop and its volunteer team for having restored N-3PB SN320 for Norway's permanent historical exhibit. The F-5 tactical fighter, renowned for years as the "Freedom Fighter," represented Norway's return to secure nationhood following WWII. Its return, as an "honorary debt," memorialized the great team effort that had been put forth by the company and the Norwegians who fought during WWII to free their country from bondage to tyranny. Today, the two aircraft serve as a bond that integrates two great team efforts. Both the aircraft and the teams were truly freedom fighters.

But again, it is not the planes as objects but the act, that restores. With the arrival of Norway's F-5A, a cycle of restoration was completed; but with the end of one cycle a new one begins. It is an ascending cycle that has physical and spiritual meaning.

---

[132] Engineers Henrik Bjorna and Per Ingar Mortensen accompanied Major Markussen as F-5A transfer project assistants.

Appendices

APPENDED SUBJECT MATTER

APPENDIX A - KEY LIFE-CYCLE MILESTONES FOR EACH SQUADRON 330(N) N-3PB SEAPLANE

NORTHROP N-3PB

1.	2.	3.	4.	5.	6.	7.	8.
301	F. 1	27.03.41	19.05.41		GS-A (II)	25.04.42	FTR from ops. W of REYKJAVIK (Hvalfjord sweep
302	F. 2	05.02.41	.04.42	16.06.42	GS-N	17.09.42	Crashed at VATTARNES in fog. No survivors.
303	F. 3	10.02.41	-		-	21.02.41	Crashed off VANCOUVER, B.C. No survivors.
304	F. 4	15.02.41	.04.42	22.04.42	GS-V	24.11.42	Crashed on T/O from AKUREYRI. No. casualties.
305	F. 5	22.02.41	-	-	-	18.03.41	Crashed on T/O from VANCOUVER, B.C. One of th: survived with injuries.
306	F. 6	22.02.41	.04.42	.05.43	GS-K (II)	05.02.49	SOC SOLA, NORWAY. Sold for scrap.
307	F. 7	22.02.41	-	-	-	20.06.41	Crashed on T/O from TORONTO. No survivors.
308	F. 8	30.03.41	19.05.41	.06.41	GS-A (I)	.11.42	Withdrawn .02.42 and used for spares.
309	F. 9	25.03.41	19.05.41	.06.41	GS-K (I)	07.12.42	Scrapped.
310	F.10	18.03.41	19.05.41	.09.41	GS-B(II)	10.12.42	Scrapped.
311	F.11	25.03.41	19.05.41	.06.41	GS-B (I)	16.09.41	DBR at BUDAREYRI when D/C was dropped while l:
312	F.12	18.03.41	19.05.41	.06.41	GS-D	20.12.42	Scrapped.
313	F.13	18.03.41	19.05.41	.11.41	GS-L (II)	04.11.42	Crashed on ops. 12 mls. off SKAGATA. No survi: (ORB RAF STN REYKJAVIK mentiones this aircraf being S/330).
314	F.14	18.03.41	19.05.41	19.02.42	GS-E (II)	.03.43	Scrapped.
315	F.15	18.03.41	19.05.41	.06.41	GS-L (I)	22.10.41	Crashed on T/O from AKUREYRI. No casualties.
316	F.16	20.03.41	19.05.41	.06.41	GS-S	04.01.43	Scrapped.
317	F.17	20.03.41	19.05.41	.06.41	GS-M	22.10.42	Crashed on landing at FOSSVOGUR.. No casualti:
318	F.18	20.03.41	19.05.41	.06.41	GS-T	21.04.43	Crashed in river THJORSA. No casualties.
319	F.19	20.03.41	19.05.41	09.08.41	GS-G (II)	.02.43	Scrapped.
320	F.20	25.03.41	19.05.41	.06.41	GS-U	.04.43	Scrapped.
321	F.21	25.03.41	19.05.41	.06.41	GS-E (I)	04.02.42	Crashed on landing at BUDAREYRI. No casualtie:
322	F.22	27.03.41	19.05.41	31.07.41	GS-F	26.05.56	Scrapped at KJERVIK, NORWAY.
323	F.23	27.03.41	19.05.41	.06.41	-	24.07.41	Crashed on landing at FOSSVOGUR. No casualtie:
324	F.24	27.03.41	19.05.41	.06.41	GS-G (I)	30.07.41	FTR from ops. out of REYKJAVIK. No survivors.

Column 1.: Northrop c/n. Column 2.: Norwegian Naval Air Service Serial No. Column 3.: Acceptance date at Lake ELSINORE, CA. Column 4.: Date of arrival to ICELAND. Column 5.: Date of being taken on charge b: no. 330 (N) Squadron. Column 6.: Squadron Code (introduced end July, 1941). Column 7.: Date of crash or being SOC (Struck off charge). Column 8.: Remarks.

Abbrivations: FTR - Failed to return, T/O - Take-off, SOC - Struck off charge, DBR - Damaged beyond repa:

Six aircraft (c/n 302 - 307) were delivered to Canada for training purposes. Three of these (c/n 303,305 an: 307) crashed in Canada. The remaining three aircraft (c/n 302, 304 and 306) were shipped from TORONTO to ICELAND in March 1942, arriving in REYKJAVIK during April 1942.

Only two aircraft, c/n 306 and 322 (GS-K and GS-F) survived the operations in Iceland. These were flown fro: ICELAND to OBAN, SCOTLAND on June 12th. and 11th. resp.

Note: Shown above is a copy of the actual life-cycle record of 330(N) Squadron N-3PB aircraft from the date each was accepted by RNoAF Commander Kristien Ostby at Lake Elsinore, California, to the terminal date for each airplane's existence, as recorded for operations in Iceland and subsequent usage. Somehow Serial No. 318 was recorded as the plane that crashed-landed in the Thjorsa River, instead of Serial No. 320. For some years only the Thjorsa knew the truth. The clipped margins, left and right, are a result of the way the copy was originally reproduced. The flight log for N-3PB Serial No. 320 is shown in Appendix B. whiich follows.

APPENDIX B - SQUADRON 330(N) FLIGHT LOG OF NORTHROP N-3PB SEAPLANE SERIAL NO. 320 (GS-U)

THE LOG OF NORTHROP N3PB NO. 320 "GS-U"

The information listed below is an attempt to compile all available details of the N3PB No. 320.
The list is not complete but it will give a fair picture of the operational life of this aircraft.

DATE	STATION	TYPE OF MISSION	UP	DOWN	REMARKS
1940.03.12		The contract for delivery of 24 N3PB aircraft was signed. Price per plane was $ 61.899,- excluding engine.			
1941.04.25		No.330 (Norwegian) Squadron, R.A.F., was formed in Reykjavik, Iceland.			
1941.05.19		S.S. "fjordheim" arrived in Reykjavik with 18 N3PB's in crates.			
1941.06.02		The first aircraft was test-flown after assembly.			
1941.08.05	A-Flight	A/S-Sweep	11.10	17.00	First operational flight recorded for GS-U
1941.08.07	"	A/S-Sweep			
1941.08.10	"	Radiotest			
1941.08.10	"	Convoy-escort	08.36	11.40	
1941.08.12	"	A/S-Seep and escort	04.07	10.20	
1941.08.13	"	Speed-test			
1941.08.14	"	Transferred to service-section, Balbo			
1941.08.21	"	Returned to A-Flight from Balbo			
1941.08.21	"	Ambulance-flight to Budareyri/return			
1941.08.22	"	Testflight/nightflying			
1941.08.26	"	A/S-Sweep	17.20	23.00	
1941.08.27	"	A/S-Sweep	10.20	15.57	
1941.08.28	"	A/S-Sweep	05.15	17.35	Attack on german submarine
1941.08.28	"	Night flying			
1941.09.13	"	Convoy-escort	14.37	16.42	Attack on german submarine
1941.09.14	"	Convoy-escort	12.58	17.50	
1941.09.22	"	Anti-submarine bombing practice			

DATE	STATION	TYPE OF MISSION	UP	DOWN	REMARKS
1941.09.26	A-Flight	Ant-submarine bombing practice			
1941.09.28	"	Convoy-escort	06.46	11.33	
1941.09.30	"	Convoy-escort	06.45	11.50	
1941.10.02	"	Transferred to service-section, Balbo			
1941.10.07	"	Transferred from Balbo to A-Flight			
1941.10.10	"	Convoy-escort	15.47	19.55	
1941.10.11	"	Transferred from A-Flight to C-Flight as replacement for N3PB No.311 GS-B which was wrecked on september 16.			
1941.10.21	C-Flight	Proceeded from Budareyri to A-Flight			
1941.10.25	"	Proceeded from A-Flight to C-Flight			
1941.11.01	"	A/S-Sweep	11.31	17.04	
1941.11.04	"	Transport flight Budareyri-Reykjavik with an english officer.			
1941.11.05	A-Flight	Convoy-escort	09.27	14.08	
1941.11.06	"	Convoy-escort	07.30	12.40	
1941.11.06	"	Convoy-escort	13.55	17.30	
1941.11.07	"	Transferred from A-Flight to C-Flight			
1941.11.15	C-Flight	Assisted N3PB No.316, GS-S, which had made a forced landing in Hornafiord due to engine trouble.			
1941.12.11	"	Took off for B-Flight, Akureyri, but due to bad weather and icing, GS-U landed in Seydisfiord. Returned to C-Flight on December 14.			
1942.01.01	A-Flight	A/S-Sweep	14.50	16.55	
1942.01.02	"	Convoy-escort	10.40	13.00	
1942.01.09	"	Hvalfiord A/S-Sweep	16.09	17.30	
1942.01.18	"	Hvalfiord A/S-Sweep	07.35	13.08	
1942.01.21	C-Flight	Convoy-escort	09.50	10.25	
1942.01.23	"	Ambulance flight from Eskifjordur with sick icelandic woman. GS-U remained with A-Flight.			

(Continued next page.)

APPENDIX B (page 2 of 3)

Date	Flight	Operation		
1942.01.31	A-Flight	Test-flight		
1942.02.01	"	Hvalfiord A/S-Sweep		
1942.02.02	"	Convoy-escort		
1942.02.09	"	Hvalfiord A/S-Sweep		
1942.02.14	"	Test-flight		
1942.02.15	"	Test-flight		
1942.02.18	"	Hvalfiord A/S-Sweep		
1942.02.19	"	Proceeded to B-Flight, Akureyri		
1942.02.23	B-Flight	Proceeded to C-Flight, Budareyri		
1942.03.07	C-Flight	A/S-cross over patrol	12.50	18.15
1942.03.08	"	A/S-cross over patrol	10.30	16.35
1942.03.09	"	A/S-cross over patrol	13.40	16.35
1942.03.22	"	A/S-Sweep	05.55	12.40
1942.03.23	"	Convoy escort for naval unit	16.40	20.30
1942.04.09	"	A/S-Sweep	17.50	20.35
1942.04.10	"	A/S-Sweep	10.50	17.00
1942.04.17	"	A/S-Sweep	15.55	16.24
1942.04.18	"	A/S-Sweep. Returned to base due to unserviceable radio.	04.37	05.45
1942.04.18	"	A/S-Sweep	10.00	16.00
1942.04.19	"	A/S-Sweep	10.00 13.45	12.15 16.00
1942.04.22	"	Proceeded to A-Flight, Reykjavik		
1942.04.25	A-Flight	Short Hvalfiord A/S-Sweep	09.00	14.20
1942.05.13	"	Convoy-escort	06.35	12.05
1942.05.17	"	Convoy-escort	15.58	21.35
1942.05.21	"	Short Hvalfiord A/S-Sweep	08.02	13.30
1942.05.26	"	Convoy-escort	23.54	05.25
1942.05.27	"	Convoy-escort to SCL 84.	13.50	20.02
1942.05.31	"	Hvalfiord A/S-Sweep	22.56	04.33

Date	Flight	Operation			
1942.06.02	A-Flight	Hvalfiord A/S-Sweep	05.10	10.50	
1942.06.02	"	Transferred to service-section, Balbo			
1942.06.15	"	Transferred to A-Flight and tested			
1942.06.24	"	A/S-Sweep and escort	22.51	00.05	
1942.06.27	"	Proceeded to Budareyri for operations. Hit by anti-aircraft fire while flying over an american camp. GS-U force landed in Bløndous.			
1942.06.30	"	GS-U returned from Bløndous.			
1942.07.01	"	Transferred to service-section, Balbo			
1942.07.03	"	Returned from service-section			
1942.07.04	"	Transport flight to C-Flight,Budareyri			
1942.07.09	C-Flight	A/S-Escort	11.06	16.54	
1942.07.22	"	A/S-Cover for convoy	13.15	18.45	
1942.07.23	"	Proceeded to A-Flight, Reykjavik			
1942.07.24	"	Proceeded to C-Flight, Budareyri			
1942.07.25	"	Proceeded to A-Flight, Reykjavik			
1942.07.26	"	Proceeded to C-Flight, Budareyri			
1942.07.31	"	Anti Focke-Wulf patrol	10.20	14.55	
1942.08.12	"	Anti Focke-Wulf patrol	14.37	19.15	
1942.08.16	"	Anti Focke-Wulf patrol	16.00	20.30	
1942.08.17	"	Anti Focke-Wulf patrol	09.50	14.45	
1942.08.18	"	Anti Focke-Wulf patrol	13.00	18.05	
1942.08.22	"	A/S-Sweep Bud II	04.17	08.15	
1942.08.23	"	A/S-Sweep Bud II	07.57	09.50	
1942.08.24	"	Transport flight to Reykjavik/return			
1942.08.25	"	A/S-Sweep Bud I	04.14	09.05	Attack on german submarine.
1942.08.27	"	A/S-Sweep Bud I	04.10	09.25	
1942.09.05	"	Seydis cross-over patrol	16.40	20.00	
1942.09.06	"	Seydis cross-over patrol	05.10	09.18	Air combat with Focke-Wulf Fw.200 Condor.

(Continued next page.)

APPENDIX B (Page 3 Of 3)

1942.09.06	C-Flight	Seydis cross-over patrol	13.25	18.25
1942.09.07	"	Seydis cross-over patrol	05.19	07.40
1942.09.07	"	Convoy-escort	09.50	15.25
1942.09.07	"	Seydis cross-over patrol	15.20	20.15
1942.09.14	"	Convoy-escort	16.30	20.36
1942.09.17	"	A/S-Sweep Bud I. Assisted when GS-N crashed at Vattarnes peninsula.	05.40	09.20
1942.09.19	"	A/S-cover for convoy	10.00	15.52
1942.09.24	"	A/S-cover for convoy. Returned to base due to heavy snow storms and low temperature.	06.00	06.55
1942.09.26	"	GS-U transferred to A-Flight		
1942.09.	"	Returned to C-Flight		
1942.10.03	"	A/S-Sweep Bud I	06.17	11.30
1942.10.04	"	A/S-Cover to ship "Northern Sword"	06.15	12.28
1942.10.07	"	A/S-Cover for ship	13.30	16.25
1942.10.09	"	A/S-Cover for naval force	11.30	15.50
1942.10.11	"	A/S-Cover for naval force	09.13	14.50
1942.10.13	"	Transferred to A-Flight, Reykjavik		
1942.10.16	A-Flight	Training		
1942.10.17	"	Training		
1942.10.19	"	Bombing practice		
1942.10.20	"	Bombing and gunnery practice		
1942.10.22	"	Dive bombing practice		
1942.10.23	"	Proceeded to C-Flight, Budareyri		
1942.10.24	"	Arrived from Budareyri		
1942.10.28	"	Transferred to Service-section, Balbo		
1942.12.11	"	Testflight		
1942.12.17	"	Formation flying with GS-T		
1943.03.04	C-Flight.	A/S-Sweep	11.10	16.17
1943.03.11	"	Convoy escort	11.13	16.20

1943.03.12	C-Flight	Convoy-escort	06.50	10.15	
1943.03.13	"	A/S-Strike	17.00	20.30	Last recorded operatic flight of GS-U-
1943.04.21	"	GS-U crashed and sank during a forced landing on the river Thjorsa in Iceland. Pilot: W.W.Bulukin, Royal Norwegian Air Force.			

Note: The above flight log records mission objective and flight time for 131 sorties made by SN320 in Iceland from August 5, 1941 through April 21, 1943. These sorties represent 9.3 percent of the total flown by Squadron 330(N). Since this airplane represented 5 percent of the fleet, its sortie rate was almost double that of the average plane. This might be expected, since Lt. Sevi Bulukin flew it.

APPENDIX C - NORWAY'S WWII AIR FLEET

As a source of information on Norway's air force capabilities at the outset of WWII, the author had referred to an article titled "Norwegian Nemesis," by Robert McLarren, that was published in the April 1941 issue of *Model Airplane News*. This article was about the Douglas 8A-5 attack bomber that had been procured by Norway in a rush to upgrade its air force in the late-1930s, sensing the German threat. This "Douglas" airplane was a derivative of the Northrop N-2 designed by Jack Northrop while associated with Douglas Aircraft, 1932-37, and it was Douglas's decision to take over this design as a "Douglas" model for the international sales market (burgeoning due to the approaching war) that resulted in Jack Northrop selling his remaining shares in Northrop Aircraft Corporation to Douglas and starting his own company, Northrop Aircraft, Inc. McLarren's article assumed the airplanes bought by Norway had been delivered to England, where the royal family and provisional government were then located, Norway having been occupied by German forces one year earlier. As clarified by Cato Guhnfeldt, Norwegian journalist, author of a number of aviation history books, including one on Squadron 330(N), and president of the Norwegian Aviation Historical Society, the Douglas aircraft were actually delivered to Canada. Following is a listing of aircraft operated by Norway during the war, as provided by Cato Guhnfeldt by e-mail on February 4, 2002.

I'll now give you the complete list of where and when Norway operated aircraft during the war:

Canada 1941-45:
Fairchild Cornell, Douglas A-8, Northrop N-3PB (until 1942), Curtiss 75A-8 Hawk, Stinson Reliant (on both floats and wheels), Interstate Cadet, all used at Little Norway training camp in Toronto. When the basic training was moved to Muskoka in 1942, the Cornell followed, the advanced training remaining behind at Toronto).

Iceland 1941-43:
Northrop N-3PB and Consolidated Catalinas amphibiums (330 Squadron)

England 1941-44:
Hawker Hurricane (331 Squadron 1941), Supermarne Spitfire (331 Squadron, 332 Squadron from late 1941/early 1942. Both squadrons were stationed at RAF North Weald from May/June 1942). The two squadrons moved to France in August 1944, and later to bases in Belgium and Holland until April 1945.
North American Harvards (Little Norway training-camp at Winkleigh, Devon (March-November 1945)

Scottland 1942-45:
Consolidated Catalina flyingboats (333 Squadron A-Flight 1942-45),
DeHavilland Mosquito (333 Squadron B-flight, 1943-45)
Locheed Lodestars and C-47 Dakota (mostly Lodestars, flown by Norwegians within BOAC between Leuchars and Bromma, Sweeden 1942-45)

Shetland 1943-45:
Short Sunderland (330 Squadron).

That should more and less cover it.

Best regards

Cato Guhnfeldt
in Oslo

APPENDIX D - TEAM PERSONNEL AND SPONSORS WHO PARTICIPATED IN ICELAND DURING N-3PB RECOVERY PHASES ON THE THJORSA RIVER

1. NORTHROP RECOVERY PROJECT – PARTICIPANTS

(Sorted by country of origin then alphabetically by first names.)

A. From Iceland

Adalsteinn Adalsteinsson
Amundi Kristjansson
Arni Fridriksson
Baldur Sveinsson
Baldvin Thorsson
Bara Vestmann
Birgir Jonsson
Bjarni Magnusson
Eggert Jonsson
Einar Kristbjornsson
Einar L. Gunnarsson
Eirikur Einarsson
Eyjolfur Kr. Kolbeins
Gisli Sigurdsson
Gretar Felixson
Gudjon Jonatansson
Gudlaugur Leosson
Gudmundur Brynjolfsson
Gudmundur Hermanniusson
Gudmundur Jonsson
Gunnar Agustsson
Gunnar Gudmundsson
Gunnar P. Gunnarsson
Hallgrimur Marinosson
Hannes Thorsteinsson
Helgi Arason
Hermann Sigurdsson
Hildur Gudlaugsdottir
Hordur Eiriksson
Hreinn Sigurjonsson
Jon E. Bodvarsson
Jon Julirsson
Jon Karl Snorrason

APPENDIX D (Continued)

Junius Palsson
Leifur Benediktsson
Njordur Snaeholm
Olafur Gudmundsson
Olafur Palsson
Osk Solrun Kristinsdottir
Otto Vestmann Gudjonsson
Petur P. Johnson
Ragnar J. Ragnarsson
Sigurdur Ingvarsson
Sigurdur Pl Hardarson
Steingrimur Dagbjartsson
Thor Sigurdsson

B. From the U.S.A.

Sveinn Thordarson
Leo Gay

C. From Norway:

Cato Guhnfeldt
Dagfin Hansen
Georg Toftdahl
Jan Bulukin
Kjell Christiansen
Oluf Reed-Olsen
Richard Thomassen
Terje Persvand
Trygve Skaug
W. W. "Sevi" Bulukin

2. ICELANDIC SPONSORS WHO SUPPORTED THE RECOVERY

NAME	PLACE	DONATION
Alifuglabuid	Mosfellssveit	Foodstuff
Alifuglabuid Moar	Kjalarnes	Foodstuff
Arena Tours, Andres Petursson	Seltjarnarnes	Mobile Kitchen
Bandariski Flotinn (U.S.N.)	Keflavik Airport	E.O.D. group + misc. equip.
Bjorgunarsveitin "Albert" (Rescue team Albert)	Seltjarnarnes	Volvo Lapplander 4-wheel drive vehicle, first-aid tent and equipment, dingy, com. Equip. rescue equip.

(Continued next page.)

APPENDIX D (Continued)

Bogi Eggertsson	Vesturberg 4, Reykjavik	Transport/ pumice
Brandur Gislason	Reykjavik	Transport
Braud hf.	Reykjavik	Foodstuff
Burfell hf.	Reykjavik	Foodstuff
Brfellsstod (Buffell Hydro-Power Plant	Burfell	Mobile Air Compressor
Byggingavoruversl, Kopavogs	Kopavogur	Lumber
Fiskbudin Sarbjorg	Reykjavik	Foodstuff
Flugleidir hf. (Icelandair)	Reykjavik	Air Tickets
Flugmalastjorn (Directorate of Civil Aviation Admin.)	Reykjavik	Lifting Bags
Flygt Pumper A/S	Oslo	Pumps
Fotohusid	Reykjavik	Film
Fuglakynbotabuid Reykjum	Mosfellssveit	Foodstuff
Graenmetisverslun Landbunadarins	Reykjavik	Foodstuff
Gudnabakari	Selfoss	Foodstuff
Gudni Jonsson & Co.	Reykjavik	Gas Bottles, Gas
Gunnar Gudmundsson hf.	Reykjavik	Heavy Transport
Hagkaup	Reykjavik	Foodstuff
Hampidjan hf.	Reykjavik	Rope, etc.
Hamrakjor	Reykjavik	Foodstuff
Hans Petesen hf.	Reykjavik	Film
Haukar hf.	Reykjavik	Film
Hotel Esja	Reykjavik	Hotel Accomodation
Hotel Loftleidir	Reykjavik	Foodstuff
Hotel & Catering School of Iceland	Reykjavik	Catering Equipment
Husasmidjan hf.	Reykjavik	Lumber
I. Palmason hf.	Reykjavik	Fire Extinguishers
Innkaup hf.	Reykjavik	6" aluminum tube
Isbjorninn hf.	Reykjavik	Anchors
Jardraektarsamband Floa og Skeida	Selfoss	Caterpillar, Bulldozer
Kaupfelagid Hofn	Selfoss	Foodstuff
Kostakaup	Hafnarfjordur	Foodstuff
Kristofer Magnusson	Hraunbae 164, Reykjavik	Transport/Pumice
Kofunarstodin hf.	Gardabaer	Diving Equipment
Landhelgisgaeslan (Icelandic Coast Guard)	Reykjavik	High-press pump, and diving equipment
Landsvirkjun (Nat. Pwr. Co.)	Reykjavik	Mobile Crane

(Continued next page.)

X

APPENDIX D (Continued)

Lionsklubburinn "Freyr"	Reykjavik	Tent
Loftorka sf.	Reykjavik	Mobile Air Compressors
A/S Lowener, Mohn	Oslo	Diving Equipment
Mjolkurbu Floamanna	Selfoss	Foodstuff
Mjolkursamsalan	Reykjavik	Foodstuff
Norsk Sjofartsmuseum	Oslo	Diving Equipment
Norski Flugheinn (RnoAF)	Oslo	Tents, generator, etc.
Northrop Corp.	Hawthorne, CA	Misc. equipment
O. Johnson & Kaaber hf.	Reykjavik	Foodstuff
Oliufelagid hf. (Esso)	Reykjavik	Fuel oil, lubricants
Oliufelagid Skeljungur hf. (Shell)	Reykjavik	Fuel oil
Oliuverslun Islands hf. (B.P.)	Reykjavik	Fuel oil, gasoline
Orkustofnun (Nat. Energy Authority	Reykjavik	Misc. equipment
Osta- og smjorsalan	Reykjavik	Foodstuff
P. Arnason & Proppe sf.	Keflavik Airport	Transport
Polar hf.	Reykjavik	Batteries
Prentmyndastofan hf.	Reykjavik	Offset films
Rafmagnsveita Reykjavikur (Reykjavik Elec. Co.)	Reykjavik	Metal Detector
Reykjavikurborg, Ahaldahus (City of Reykjavik)	Reykjavik	Rope
Reykjavikurhofn (Port Authorities)	Reykjavik	Barge
Samband Isl. Samvinnufelaga (Union of Icelandic Coop.)	Reykjavik	Foodstuff
Saminnutryggingar	Reykjavik	Insurance
Sapugerdin Frigg	Gardabaer	Drums, containers
Sild og Fiskur	Reykjavik	Foodstuff
Silkiprent sf.	Reykjavik	Printing
Smjorliki hf.	Reykjavik	Foodstuff
Stalsmidjan hf.	Reykjavik	Air-lifter
Sefan Jonsson	Kotufelli 3, Reykjavik	Transport/pumice
Solufelag Gardyrkjumanna	Reykjavik	Foodstuff
Ulafar Jakobsen (Travel Agency)	Reykjavik	Sanitary Equipment
Vegagerd rikisins (State Roadbuilding Co.)	Reykjavik	Heaters, Lumber, etc.
Vita- og hafnarmalaskrifst. (Icelandic Lighthouse & Port Authorities)	Reykjavik	Anchors
Andres Arnason	Kopavogur	High Pressure hoses
Skograekt rikisins (Icelandic Forest Service)	Reykjavik	Access to land

APPENDIX E - COMMUNICATIONS EQUIPMENT SUPPLIED BY NORTHROP FOR RECOVERY OPERATIONS

Memorandum
Northrop Corporation

In reply refer to: 1001-1540

To: C. T. Page, Manager
Settlements & Property Management 9140/62

From: D. G. Page

Subject: RESALE OF USED EQUIPMENT FOR N-3PB PROJECT

Date: 18 June 1979

Copies:

Ref:

Attached is a list of equipment which has been purchased and forwarded to Iceland for the purpose of recovering the N-3PB from the River Thjorsa.

Per agreement, Sigurdur P. Hardarsson, Kanbsvegi 22, Reykjavik, Iceland, who is the Icelandic diver on the project, will purchase the first order of equipment following completion of the project at the rate of fifty cents on the dollar for a total of $364.40. He will purchase, at full price, the second order of $621.50 for a total of $985.90 for the lot.

Also attached is the Request for Disbursement and a copy of the invoice for the second order.

It is requested that the proper forms for effecting the resale, as outlined above, be accomplished utilizing the information submitted herewith.

Donald G. Page
Manager, Public Affairs
Administration

Att.

Note: The "Att." (Attachment) to this memo consists of the communications equipment list and pricing shown on the next page. At Northrop, the restoration of the Norwegian N-3PB seaplane was known as "Project Northrop." This name pertains to the restoration phase only. The author has chosen to downplay this particular terminology so as to emphasize and give principal credit to the international team by means of which the restoration was made possible and worth doing to return the airplane to Norway, where its genesis began. The provisioning of underwater communications equipment by Northrop shows the detailed level to which the recovery operation was planned and the care taken to cover every eventuality. In actual operations, however, the equipment was ineffective, because literally nothing could be seen by divers when submerged beneath the Thjorsa river's surface due to the lack of visibility in the silt-diffused water; and so with everything being done by feeling about to get a tactile sense of what was there and whether suctioning progress was being made, there was little or nothing to communicate in real-time voice contact back to the surface. After a few hours underwater, each diver developed a sense of orientation and tended to work their own areas of the plane and the riverbed. Furthermore, use of the equipment required a full water-free helmet or faceplate, of which only one was available. Nevertheless, the presence of the equipment gave a sense of backup and in the one instance where Gunnar Agustsson became trapped under the plane could have made the difference between life and death (cf., Chapter 9). Since this was special purpose equipment for underwater operations not usually engaged in by Northrop, it was acquired by Sigurdur P. Hardarsson after the recovery was completed.

NORTHROP

APPENDIX E (Continued)

PROJECT NORTHROP

1st ORDER

WPV-02	DIVER WET-PHONE	$ 236.50
WPS-02	SURFACE WET-PHONE	265.00
CWM-02	DIVER FULL FACE MASK	60.00
WBF-01	WET BEACON/WET FINDER SET	129.00
NB-01A	RECHARGEABLE BATTERIES	21.50
NB-06	CHARGER	16.80
	TOTAL	$ 728.80

NORTHROP CHECK $757.30, CREDIT ON 1st ORDER   28.50

2nd ORDER

WVA-02	WET-PHONE VOX (2 UNITS)	$ 530.00
CWM-02	DIVER FULL FACE MASK	120.00
	TOTAL	$ 650.00
	LESS CREDIT FROM 1st ORDER	28.50
		$ 621.50

NORTHROP CHECK $621.50.

PAYMENT DUE FROM SIGURDUR P. HARDARSSON,
    KANBSVEGH 22, REYKJAVIK, ICELAND

$$\frac{757.30}{2} + 621.50 = \$ 1000.15$$

APPENDIX F - NORTHROP SUPPLIERS/VENDORS WHO VOLUNTEERED PARTS AND DOCUMENTATION

Memorandum
Northrop Corporation

In reply refer to: 6150-80-081

To: D. McNeal

From: R. L. McAlpine

Subject: N3PB RESTORATION

Date: 20 November 1980

Copies: D. Bean
R. Cooper
J. Van Dorn

Ref: Memo 5003-80-292
dtd 18 Nov 1980

The undersigned became involved in the restoration program in May, 1980 when I received a request for some material to be donated to the N3PB. I personally contacted many of the Suppliers and told them of the history of the plane and the current project. As the needs increased, I involved many Buyers in the program.

The response from the Suppliers was overwhelming and without stint they proceeded to supply the necessary parts and materials. In several cases, such as Kai Kuhl, Inc., Kai went out and bought materials out of his own pocket to furnish to Northrop. Deft, Inc., Tony Desmond and Bud Levine, who furnished paint, also bought dope from a third party to give to the N3PB. Alcoa, Richard Mardock, arranged thru one of their distributors to give us some aluminum sheet. Pioneer, John Castle, President, had furnished much extrusion and aluminum sheet but near the end we needed extrusions he had in his Georgia warehouse which he had shipped in at his expense to support our schedule. In addition he bought extrusions from a competitor to give to us. Bendix Corporation furnished approximately $3,500.00 of walnut for the presentation plaques.

Rubbercraft, Stella Dancoes, Glen Werts and F. N. Merralls, set up and made a special run of rubber extrusions in one week to be used for the canopy seal. To do this, they overrode some priority production orders at no cost to Northrop. Liberty Engineering, Val Phiffer and Jeff Summers, worked on their own time to pull fasteners from stock to provide to us the next morning. Teledyne Linair, Bill Topliker and R. B. Entzminger, researched in their archives to identify a turnbuckle for the wing flaps. Tri Star, Inc., Gene Labelle, located in Fort Lauderdale, Florida air shipped some clamps. Aircraft Engine Maintenance Corporation, San Diego, Peter Pess, gave us the exhaust collector ring for the engine. Swedlow, Inc., Dave Swedlow and Irv Miller made the windshield glass twice because the lines provided them for the first one were wrong.

While all of the Suppliers performed admirably, the above incidents stand out. There may be other Supplier related stories which were not brought to my attention by other organizations. Some we have never done business with before.

In addition to the Supplier services, there were other human interest related activities provided by Procurement. When the call went out in July for more volunteers, I organized a group of Buyers and Managers who physically worked on the airplane. These people had never done this type of work before but cheerfully jumped in and learned how to rivet, form metal, and perform general work on the plane. All expressed pride and satisfaction for their participation. Attached is a roster of people who supported the project thru their buying efforts and those who physically worked on the plane.

As other stories come to light, I will pass them on to you. Good luck with the history.

R. L. McAlpine, Manager
Materials Procurement
Dept. 6150/32 Ext. 8352

APPENDIX F (Continued)

N3PB

LIST OF CONTRIBUTING SUPPLIERS

Adams Supply Company
Torrance, CA 90509

Aircraft Cylinder & Turbine
Sun Valley, CA 91040

Aircraft Engineering
Maintenance Corp.
San Diego, CA

Alpase, Inc
Downey, CA 90241

Aluminum Co. of America
Los Angeles, 90017

Aviation Warehouse
Hawthorne, CA 90250

Avlite Aviation
Van Nuys, CA

Bandy Hinge, Inc.
Burbank, CA 91504

Barco Aviation
Los Angeles, CA 90025

Bill & Chuck's Bonded
Locksmith
Gardena, CA 90249

W. W. Brownlow Company
Hawthorne, CA 90250

Burbank Aircraft Supply, Inc.
Sun Valley, CA 91352

Cableco Lifting Equipment
Los Angeles, CA 90058

Charles Aircraft
Torrance, CA 90505

China Lake Naval Weapon
Center
China Lake, CA

Clark Metals, Inc
Gardena, CA 90248

Copper & Brass Sales
Los Angeles, CA 90043

Davis-Monthan Air Force Base
Tucson, AZ

Deft, Inc
Irvine, CA 92714

Ducommun Metals & Supply Company
Los Angeles, CA 90054

EON Corporation
Los Angeles, CA 90065

G & H Air Parts
Santa Monica, CA 90404

Goodyear Aerospace Corporation
Los Angeles, CA 90022

Gudebrod, Inc
Glendale, CA 91201

Independent Lumber
Hawthorne, CA 90250

Insulation Supply Company
Torrance, CA 90501

J. D. Fields Lumber Company
Gardena, CA 90249

Kai R. Kuhl Company, Inc.
Los Angeles, CA

Liberty Engineering
Chatsworth, CA 91311

Lord Kinematics
Sherman Oaks, CA 91423

Moth Aircraft Company
Hawthorne, CA 90250

(Continued next page.)

APPENDIX F (Continued)

Motion Industries, Inc.
Gardena, CA 90248

Nagel Aircraft Sales, Inc
Torrance, CA 90505

Naval Weapons Support Center
Crane, IN.

Pacific Air Industries
Santa Monica, CA 90404

Pacific Missile Test Center
Point Magu, CA

Paul R. Briles, Inc.
P.B. Fasteners Division
Gardena, CA 90249

Pioneer Aluminun, Inc.
Los Angeles, CA 90023

Plastic Center Inc. of Los Angeles
Los Angeles, CA 90057

PR Fasteners, Inc.
Cerritos, CA 90701

Productool Inc.
Anaheim, CA 92801

Qualified Air Components
Santa Fe Springs, CA

Reliance Steel & Aluminum Company
Los Angeles, CA 90058

Rubbercraft Corporation of California
Torrance, CA 90507

Sky Controls, Inc.
Sun Valley, CA 91352

Southwest Plating
Los Angeles, CA 90044

Southwest Products Company
Monrovia, CA 91016

Sterling Lacquer Mfg. Company
St. Louis, MO 63139

Steward-Davis, Inc.
Long Beach, CA

Superior Thread Rolling Company
North Hollywood, CA 91605

Swedlow, Inc.
Garden Grove, CA

Task Research
Santa Paula, CA 93060

T. D. Materials, Inc.
Los Angeles, CA 90058

Teledyne Linair Engineering
Gardena, CA 90248

Textron, Inc.
Fafnir Bearing Co. Division
Carson, CA 90746

Tiernay Metals
Redondo Beach, CA 90271

Tri Process Company
Paramount, CA 90723

Tri-Star, Inc.
Fort Lauderdale, FL 33314

Tubesales
Los Angeles, CA 90040

U. S. Steal Corporation
U. S. Steel Supply
Vernon, CA 90058

VSI Corporation
Screwcorp Division
City of Industry, CA 91746

West Coast Instruments, Inc
Long Beach, CA 90808

West Coast Propeller Service
Burbank, CA

Air Industries Corporation
Garden Grove, CA 92641

Northrop University
Inglewood, CA

Barry Controls
Burbank, CA 91505

(Continued next page.)

APPENDIX F (Continued)

ADDITIONAL SUPPLIERS/VENDORS:

Aircraft Engine Maintenance Corporation
San Diego, CA 92073

Air Industries Corporation
Garden Grove, CA 92841

General Electric – Western District
Los Angeles, CA

Heady Aircraft
Long Beach, CA 90807

Northrop University
(Now Northrop Rice Aviation Institute of Technology)
Inglewood, CA 90301

P. B. Fasteners
Gardena, CA 90249

KEY U.S. DEPARTMENT OF DEFENSE PERSONNEL:

Captain W. B. Haff
Commander, China Lake Naval Weapon Center
China Lake, CA 93555

Colonel P. F. Dudley
Commander, Davis-Monthan Air Force Base
Tucson, AZ 85707

APPENDIX G - ROBERT G. GUNTER LETTER TO McNEAL SUMMARIZING HIS VOLUNTEER WORK ON THE RESTORATION OF THE N-3PB

At the completion of the restoration of the N-3PB, Darrell McNeal asked certain volunteers who had worked long hours diligently to write him a letter or memo summarizing their experiences on the project and what, in general they thought about it. Robert G. Gunter, a semi-retired engineer who had never worked at Northrop, read about the project in the newspaper and volunteered 142 hours of his time during the most crucial period when it was uncertain whether the rollout date would be met. His letter shows the drama of the project during that period and the fact that it was experienced, dedicated people like him who made it possible to meet the schedule. The letter is reproduced below in the same format as the original.

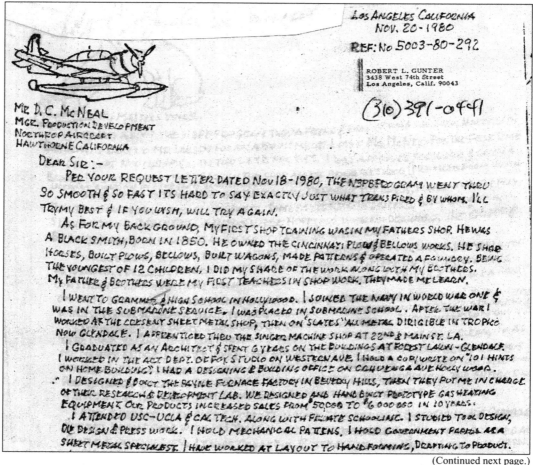

LOS ANGELES CALIFORNIA
NOV. 20-1980
REF: No 5003-80-292

ROBERT L. GUNTER
3438 West 74th Street
Los Angeles, Calif. 90043

(310) 391-0441

MR. D.C. McNEAL
MGR. PRODUCTION DEVELOPMENT
NORTHROP AIRCRAFT
HAWTHORNE CALIFORNIA

DEAR SIR:-

PER YOUR REQUEST LETTER DATED NOV 18-1980, THE N3PB PROGRAM WENT THRU SO SMOOTH & SO FAST ITS HARD TO SAY EXACTLY JUST WHAT TURNS PLACED & BY WHOM. I'LL TRY MY BEST & IF YOU WISH, WILL TRY AGAIN.

AS FOR MY BACKGROUND, MY FIRST SHOP TRAINING WAS IN MY FATHERS SHOP. HE WAS A BLACK SMITH, BORN IN 1850. HE OWNED THE CINCINNATI PLOW & BELLOWS WORKS. HE SHOD HORSES, BUILT PLOWS, BELLOWS, BUILT WAGONS, MADE PATTERNS & OPERATED A FOUNDRY. BEING THE YOUNGEST OF 12 CHILDREN, I DID MY SHARE OF THE WORK ALONG WITH MY BROTHERS. MY FATHER & BROTHERS WERE MY FIRST TEACHERS IN SHOP WORK. THEY MADE ME LEARN.

I WENT TO GRAMMER & HIGH SCHOOL IN HOLLYWOOD. I JOINED THE NAVY IN WORLD WAR ONE & WAS IN THE SUBMARINE SERVICE. I WAS PLACED IN SUBMARINE SCHOOL. AFTER THE WAR I WORKED AT THE CRESENT SHEET METAL SHOP, THEN ON "SLATES" ALL METAL DIRIGIBLE IN TROPICO NOW GLENDALE. I APPRENTICED THRU THE SINGER MACHINE SHOP AT 22ND & MAIN ST. LA.

I GRADUATED AS AN ARCHITECT & SPENT 6 YEARS ON THE BUILDINGS AT FOREST LAWN - GLENDALE. I WORKED IN THE ART DEPT. OF FOX STUDIO ON WESTERN AVE. I HOLD A COPYWRITE ON "101 HINTS ON HOME BUILDING" I HAD A DESIGNING & BUILDING OFFICE ON CAHUENGA AVE HOLLYWOOD.

I DESIGNED & BUILT THE PAYNE FURNACE FACTORY IN BEVERLY HILLS, THEN THEY PUT ME IN CHARGE OF THEIR RESEARCH & DEVELOPMENT LAB. WE DESIGNED AND HAND BUILT PROTOTYPE GAS HEATING EQUIPMENT OUR PRODUCTS INCREASED SALES FROM $50,000 TO $6,000,000 IN 10 YEARS.

I ATTENDED USC-UCLA & CAL TECH. ALONG WITH PRIVATE SCHOOLING. I STUDIED TOOL DESIGN, DIE DESIGN & PRESS WORK. I HOLD MECHANICAL PATTERNS, I HOLD GOVERNMENT PAPERS AS A SHEET METAL SPECIALEST. I HAVE WORKED AT LAYOUT TO HAND FORMING, DRAFTING TO PRODUCT.

(Continued next page.)

APPENDIX G (Continued)

I LEFT PAYNE & JOINED NORTHROP IN THE FORTIES & WAS PLACED IN TOOL PLANNING TO LEARN THE NORTHROP SYSTEM, THEN PLACED IN CHARGE OF DEVELOPMENT. THIS DEPT. CREATED WAYS & MEANS, TOOLS, EQUIPMENT & METHODS FOR FORMING & MAKING AIRCRAFT PARTS & EXPANDING THE USE OF NEW METALS AS REQUESTED BY MR NORTHROP. I WROTE A BOOK CALLED "NORTHROP MANUFACTURING METHODS." I ALSO TAUGHT IN THE NEW NORTHROP AERONOTICAL SCHOOL.

I WAS ON THE "METAL CONSERVATION COMMITTY" OF THE WAR PRODUCTION BOARD. CERTIFICATES OF MERIT, SIGNED BY MR. NORTHROP WERE AWARDED TO EMPLOYEES FOR SMALL IMPROVEMENTS - BUT A $25⁰⁰ BOND WAS GIVEN FOR OUTSTANDING SUGGESTIONS. MOST OF THE EMPLOYEES REQUESTED MR NORTHROP'S SIGNED CERTIFICATES IN LUE OF THE $25⁰⁰ BOND THE EMPLOYEES ALL LIKED JACK NORTHROP.

WHILE WORKING AT NORTHROP I ATTENDED A PRIVATE CLASS IN GEM CUTTING & JEWLERY MAKING. THERE I LEARNED TO WORK IN SILVER & GOLD, PATTERN MAKING & SAND CASTINGS. I MADE N3PB PINS & THE TACKS FOR MANY OF MY COWORKERS.

> Page 2 of letter continued from above.

HIS MASTERS VOICE.

I HEARD ABOUT THE N3PB PROGRAM THRU A FRIEND & THAT IT WAS FOR JACK NORTHROP'S BIRTHDAY. I CALLED MR LARSEN FOR AN APPOINTMENT. I MET MR McNEIL FOR THE FIRST TIME SINCE I LEFT NORTHROP CO. IN THE LATE FORTIES. I WAS APPROVED FOR WORK & GIVEN A BADGE. IT WAS SO NICE TO BE BACK IN THE SHOP AFTER BEING RETIRED. (I RETIRED FROM NORTH AMERICAN AVIATION IN 1968 THEN STARTED CONSULTING.)

I WORKED ON UNTANGELING THE BENT METAL, REMOVING THE RIVETS, FLATTENING THE PARTS FOR TEMPLATES THEN MAKING NEW PARTS. SOME PARTS REMOVED NEEDED ONLY CLEANING, STRAIGHTENING & PAINTING, OTHERS WERE HOPELESS. WITH NO DRAWINGS, THE "GUESS & BE DAMNED" METHOD WAS USED. IN MOST CASES WE WERE RIGHT.

I WORKED ALONE & ALSO HELPED OTHERS. I WORKED ON THE FUSELAGE ALINEMENT WITH ED WEAVER. I DRILLED & PLACED ANGLES ON THE FIREWALL. I HELPED ON THE INNER WING CONSTRUCTION & THE PONTOONS WITH MR LARSEN, AND WITH PAUL SPIKULA. I GAVE A HAND ON THE PEDESTALS. I MADE PARTS AS REQUIRED & HELPED MR STONE ON THE OUTER WINGS. I GAVE A HELPING HAND TO D. BROWNLOW IN FITTING THE COWLING & CLEANING ENGINE PARTS. I FURNISHED & INSTALLED TWO LIGHTS ON THE VERTICAL TAIL. THERE WERE SO MANY THINGS TO BE DONE, ERRANDS TO BE RUN FOR PARTS & TOOLS, SHOP TO BE KEPT WORKABLE CLEAN, SO AS MY MEMORY ASSURES ME - WE WERE KEPT BUSY AT ONE TASK OR ANOTHER. ALL THE FELLOWS WORKED AS IF IT WAS THEIR OWN SHIP - AND ENJOYED IT. THESE FINE CRAFTSMEN HAD THEIR OWN PRIVATE TOOLS & WERE WILLING TO SHARE THEM WITH THE OTHER WORKMEN. THE ENTIRE SHOP ATITUDE WAS THE FINEST THAT I HAVE EVER ENCOUNTERED ANYWHERE.

I MET & WORKED WITH CLEET ROBERTS, WHOSE FATHER WAS A BLACKSMITH & A CARRAGE BUILDER. HE WAS GOOD WITH HIS TOOLS. I MET OLD FRIENDS LIKE ROY WOLFORD & TALKED ABOUT PEOPLE & PAST HISTORY. IT WAS GREAT FUN & INTERESTING. ROY HAS MY LAPEL PIN. (N3PB)

ALL IN ALL, IT WAS A GREAT PLEASURE TO SEE A CORRODED PILE OF SCRAP METAL SLOWLY UNFURL & DEVELOP INTO A BEAUTIFUL "PROUD BIRD", LEAVE ITS NEST TO GREAT THE WORLD. IT'S THE MOST OUTSTANDING DEVELOPMENT OF THE YEAR: 1940 TO 1980.

IT WAS A THRILL & A WONDERFUL PROGRAM TO HONOR A GREAT MAN & THE WORLDS GREATEST AIRCRAFT CREATOR - MR JOHN (JACK) K. NORTHROP. HIS OTHER ACCOMPLISHMENTS IN OTHER FIELDS ARE NOT WELL KNOWN BUT THEY ARE NUMEROUS. HIS PROSTHESIS DEVELOPMENTS ARE OUTSTANDING. HE IS A MASTER IN HIS OWN RITE.

YOURS TRULY

Robert L. Gunter R.E.

APPENDIX H - KEY ICELANDIC AND NORWEGIAN REPRESENTATIVES AT THE NORTHROP ROLLOUT OF THE RESTORED N-3PB SEAPLANE

A complete list of the Icelandic and Norwegian dignitaries attending the Northrop rollout of the N-3PB seaplane was not available to the author, so the following list may be incomplete, as well as the names; however, the intent is to record that information which is available, with the objective of providing a starting point for some future historian, if one should be interested in the same subject. The names may not be spelled correctly in all cases, as the source of information was from a "Rollout Festivities Program" that the author had each of the key visitors sign; consequently, as might be expected, some deciphering of signatures was necessary.

FIRST NAME	LAST NAME	REPRESENTING
Alf	Steffen-Olsen	Norwegian Chief Navigation Officer
Baldur, Mr. & Mrs.	Sveinsson	President, Icelandic Aviation Historical Society
Birgir	Jonsson	Iceland Life Saving Association Rescue Team 'Albert'
Bredo	Thurman-Nielsen	Norwegian Pilot (most hours of any flying N-3PB)
Cato	Guhnfeldt	Norwegian Aviation Historical Society
Conrad	Skjoldhammer*	Norwegian Pilot (named Helgesen during WWII)
Einar L.	Gunnarsson	Icelandic Aviation Historical Society
Einar, Mr. & Mrs.	Kristbjornsson	Icelandic Divers Association
Gisli	Sigurdson	Icelandic Aviation Historical Society
Gudjon	Jonatansson	Iceland Life Saving Association Rescue Team 'Albert'
Gudmundur V., Mr. & Mrs.	Josefsson	Guests of Mr. & Mrs. Karl Eiriksson
Gunnar	Agustsson	Icelandic Divers Association
Jon Th.	Isaksson	Icelandic Aviation Historical Society
Jonatan	Gudjonsson	Iceland Life Saving Association Rescue Team 'Albert'
Kaare	Skabo	Norwegian Navigator
Karl, Mr. & Mrs.	Eiriksson	Icelandic Aviation Historical Society
Kjell	Christiansen	Norwegian Defense Museum
Luther	Tolimonsson	Iceland Guest
Nils M.	Joergensen	Norwegian Air Force
Olafur	Palsson	Icelandic Aviation Historical Society
Per Christian	Aas	Norwegian Pilot
Petur P.	Johnson	Icelandic Aviation Historical Society
Ragnar J.	Ragnarsson	IAHS N-3PB Recovery Project Manager
Sigurdur P.	Hardarson	Icelandic Aviation Historical Society
Sveinn & Wife Sigrid	Thordarson	Northrop Sr. Technical Specialist at Recovery Site
Sverre	Thuve	Einar Bakkevig Ocean Shipping Company
Wsewolod "Sevi"	Bulukin	Royal Norwegian Air Force Pilot of N-3PB SN 320

*Conrad Skjoldhammer flew the N-3PB and one of his mission exploits is described in Chapter 4, page 79. A person of similar Viking spirit to that of Oluf Reed-Olsen (cf., p. xviii), whose photos of mission operations are shown in Chapter 4 (see Figures 19 and 20 in particular), Skjoldhammer became a Norwegian airline pilot after the war, flying for Braathens South American & Far East Airlines. He retired at age 60 with 30,000 flying hours. He died December 20, 1998.

APPENDIX J - CATO GUHNFELDT "THANK YOU" LETTER FROM THE NORWEGIAN AVIATION HISTORICAL SOCIETY

NORSK FLYHISTORISK FORENING

Norwegian Aviation Historical Society Postadresse : Postboks 226- Sentrum, Oslo 1.

Mr. Darrell McNeal
Manager advanced production
NORTHROP CORPORATION - Aircraft Group
3901 West Broadway
Hawthorne,
California 90250
USA.

Oslo, December 1st 1980

Dear Darrell,

To find the appropriate words to open this letter was not easy, so I'll just say THANK YOU! For the wonderful way you and your men have restored the N-3PB, for the magnificent way you and your colleages looked after us all during our visit to Los Angeles. I think I can say on behalf of every Norwegian that was present: It was a dream come-through. It was something we'll never forget.

As Bulukin put it after the unvailing-ceremony: "She's never looked so pretty"! - You can all be proud of what you've done, for several reasons:
As far as "all we critical guys from the Aviation Society" could observe, the N-3PB looked just the way we all expected it to look, judging from all the war-time pictures we've collected. The Paint-scheme looked authentic, and as we all moved around it with our cameras, I think each one of us suddenly realized how much time and effort you've put into it. In a way, I whish you could keep it to stand by the gateway of the factory as a monument to Jack Northrop, and the early days.
But I remember your words during our dinner: "In Norway you can show it, saying, this is what we fought with during the war". I did not realize it at the time, but it so happens that the N-3PB will be the only aircraft (the original parts) that actually went into cambat during the war, that has been preserved. True, we have two Spitfires in Norway, the same type we flew during the war. But none of these aircraft fought, they were delivered to Norway after the war. The aircraft certaily will be a magnificent showpiece. And it will not only serve as a commemoration of the fighting during the war, but also of the remarkable will, dedication and effort of the people of Nothrop, that brought the N-3PB back to us. Big words, but they are true !

But there's another reason why you can be proud, and the fellows with you. It was not mentioned during the roll-out ceremony, but the fact is that 330 Squadron during the war not only was Norwegia but it was also very much forgotten. The personnel of the squadron fought on the outskirts of the war in Europe, accordingly their efforts were not given the appropriate attention by the heads of the government and military forces in London. There eyes were focused on 331 and 332 Squadron that almost daily flew their Spit-

(Continued next page.)

APPENDIX J (Continued)

fires across the English Channel, and 333 Squadron that flew Catalinas and Mosquitos over Norway, dropping parcels at Christmas,
sinking ships in the fjords.
"Sometimes London never quite knew what we were doing", Brigadier
Bredo Thurmann-Nielsen once told me (he spoke about the operations
after the unvailing-ceremony). "And we were the ones that sometimes
fought the toughest battles, not against Jerrys, but against nature
itself, repairing the aircraft outdoor, leaving the Icelandic coast
behind you, and not knowing if we would see it again. Thanks to the
Northrops, more of us survived than would have been expected".

330 Squadron was the forgotten squadron indeed, but thanks to your
people, Darrell, those that fought have been brought out into the
light of appreciation, and given the most fitting token of homage
that ever could be made, a real N-3PB. So you see, there was really
more to it than just the aircraft. You've lighted up a spark in many
a veteran, and for that we say THANK YOU!

I hope you can conway some of what I've told you here to the guys,
because their job have been more valuable than they might have
thought.

Finally, let me say it was a great honour and pleasure to meet you,
Darrell, and also please give my best regards to your lovely wife.
We had a long trip back to Norway onboard the Herkules, but every-
ting went fine. Right now we're planning a big meeting in January
for all the veterans of 330 Squadron here in Norway, to be held at
the Norwegian Defence Museum. We'll show slides, video-tape, models,
and large black and white photos put on exhibition. I can't wait to
see the faces of some of the old-timers.

As you've probably discovered, I'm sending you the first press
clippings that have come out here in Norway. I delayed my letter
to you, so they could be included. The smallest clipping is from
Norways principal newspaper, Aftenposten (Evening Post) in Oslo, and
the full page is from Bulukins home city Tønsberg, incidently the
oldest city of Norway, that traces its history back to 900. You and
the restoration-participants can keep these, as I have sent Donald
Page some copies as well. More clippings will come in January.

Then let me conclude by saying that now its your turn to come to
Norway. I'll be happy to show you around in Oslo, and with some
good timing, maybe you can be here when the N-3PB gets here next
summer. I know there's plans for a second roll-out, with all the
veterans present.

Well, thats all for now. Again thank you for all your help in getting
a favourite back to life.

All the best from

Cato Guhmfeldt

APPENDIX K - CAPILLARY ATTRACTION ANALYSIS

Phase V of the recovery effort, though exceedingly well planned in all the logistical details, overlooked one detail of nature that the Thjorsa River had as its plan for keeping the N-3PB airplane in its possession. The words of Farmer Bjorn Johannsson, "The Thjorsa never gives back anything it takes," kept recurring in everyone's mind throughout the recovery project, but everyone dismissed the saying as myth; pure balderdash, as the British might say. The focus, which became a mindset, was that "we know the plane is there and we're going to get it." The Thjorsa, however, had everything under control, because the commonsensical way of raising the plane wasn't the way the Thjorsa operated. Normally, in a body of water like a river, if you're going to raise something big and heavy from the bottom, common sense tells you to use the natural buoyancy properties of water and float the object to the surface using airbags. Air is a gas and so bubbles to the surface of water to join with atmosphere. Common sense says that if you put together a big enough air bubble, by pumping air into an airbag, the object will rise to the surface with the "big bubble" that is enclosed in the airbag. This approach is so obvious and so simple that it immediately becomes the way to proceed. The problem, however, is that it overlooks a fundamental physical parameter that affects objects sitting in water. This parameter is the attractive force of adhesion between water molecules and the material of the object sitting in the water. The figure below illustrates this attractive force. A glass plate G, put in contact with water, adheres to the water, because the adhesive force between glass and water molecules is greater than the cohesive force of the water molecules alone. This adhesive force, F, is measured by the weights in the left pan of the counterbalance and can be approximated by:

$$F = \pi r^2 T$$

where the area of the plate is multiplied by the surface tension of water, T = 5,285 dynes/cm^2. If the plate is assumed to be the N-3PB airplane, with an approximate radius of 20 feet, the area is 1,256 ft^2 or 97,239 cm^2 or approximately 514 million dynes, equating to about 37,000 pounds of force to break the plane free of the riverbed. Since this calculation assumes the plane to represent a circular plate, the actual force would have to

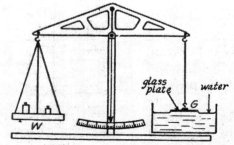

FIG. 26B—Experiment illustrating the forces of adhesion between glass and water.

From *Modern College Physics*, by Harvey E. White, published by Norstrand, New York, 1949.

be discounted. But even assuming a 50% discount, this force would still be about 18,000 pounds or 9 tons. A further factor is that "T" increases as water temperature decreases. The value noted above was measured at 20C, about 15C higher than the temperature of the Thjorsa during the N-3PB recovery operation. No wonder the airplane had to be yanked out of the Thjorsa's grasp with a heavy-duty crane.

APPENDIX L - ACRONYM GLOSSARY

ACRONYM	DEFINITION
AAHS	American Aviation Historical Society
Air Lifter	A suction device based on capillary action and pressure differential, with no moving parts.
CSCS	Cost Schedule Control System (C^2S^2)
DOD	U.S. Department of Defense
EAA	Experimental Aircraft Association
EOD GRP	Explosive Ordnance Disposal Group
EU	European Union
fps	feet per second
ft.	foot
IAHS	Icelandic Aviation Historical Society
IDF	Iceland Defense Force
in.	inch
km	kilometer
m	meter
MAF	Marine Amphibious Force
mph	miles per hour
N-	Northrop aircraft series designator.
NAHS	Norwegian Aviation Historical Society
NATO	North Atlantic Treaty Organization
NDM	Norwegian Defence Museum (Forsvarsmuseet)
PB	Patrol Bomber
RAF	Royal Air Force of Britain
RNoAF	Royal Norwegian Air Force
SCHAF	Southern California Historical Aviation Foundation
SDAM	San Diego Aerospace Museum
USAF	United States Air Force
USN	United States Navy
WBS	Work Breakdown Structure
WMF	Western Museum of Flight

APPENDIX M - METRIC AND ENGLISH MEASURING SYSTEM EQUIVALENTS

When you know:	Multiply by:	To find:
Length and distance		
inches (in)	2.54	centimeters[1]
feet (ft)	30.48	centimeters[1]
yards (yd)	0.9144	meters[1]
rods (rd)	5.029	meters
statute miles (mi)	1.609	kilometers
fathoms	1.829	meters
nautical miles	1.852	kilometers[1]
millimeters (mm)	0.03937	inches
centimeters (cm)	0.3937	inches
meters (m)	1.094	yards
kilometers (km)	0.6213	miles
Surface or area		
square inches (sq in)	6.452	square centimeters
square feet (sq ft)	929.0	square centimeters
square yards (sq yd)	0.8361	square meters
square miles (sq mi)	2.590	square kilometers
acres	0.4047	hectares
square centimeters (sq cm)	0.1550	square inches
square meters (sq m)	10.76	square feet
square kilometers (sq km)	0.3861	square miles
hectares (ha)	2.471	acres
Volume and capacity (liquid)		
fluid ounces	29.57	milliliters
cups, U.S.	0.2366	liters
pints, U.S.	0.4732	liters
quarts, U.S.	0.9464	liters
gallons, U.S.	3.785	liters
milliliters (ml)	0.03381	fluid ounces
liters (L)	4.227	cups, U.S.
liters (L)	2.113	pints, U.S.
liters (L)	1.057	quarts, U.S.
liters (L)	0.2642	gallons, U.S.
Weight and mass		
ounces (oz)	28.350	grams
pounds (lb)	0.4536	kilograms
tons	0.9072	metric tons
grams (g)	0.03527	ounces
kilograms (kg)	2.205	pounds
metric tons (t)	1.102	short tons
Temperature		
°Fahrenheit (°F)	5/9 (after subtracting 32)	°Celsius[1]
°Celsius (°C)	9/5 (then add 32)	°Fahrenheit[1]

[1] Answer is exact.

Note: When you know the metric unit, divide instead of multiplying to convert to the English unit.

APPENDIX N - PRINCIPAL INTERNATIONAL TEAM REPRESENTATIVES AT FINAL ROLLOUT IN NORWAY

Final and formal turnover of the N-3PB seaplane to Norway – where the plane had originally been intended for mission operations in coastal patrol – was on October 2, 1981. Thus 40 years after the plane was produced it arrived home, a restoration of earlier victory. Turnover took place at the Norwegian Air Defence Museum for historic aircraft at Gardermoen, Oslo, Norway. The schedule of events at the turnover program is shown below, followed by a listing of the key personnel from each of the international team members.

NORTHROP N-3PB.

OVERTAKELSESSEREMONI

GARDERMOEN FLYSTASJON
FREDAG 2 OKTOBER 1981

PROGRAM

1130 - 1200
Forsvarets stabsmusikk spiller.

1200 - 1245
Presentasjoner ved

- Sjefen for Gardermoen flystasjon,
- Representant for Northrop Corporation,
- Representant for 330 skvadrons veteraner,
- Generalinspektøren for Luftforsvaret.

Overrekkelse av erkjentligheter.

1245
Film fra bergings- og restaureringsarbeidet.

1300 - 1400
Visning av museumsflyene i Hangar E.

1400
Lunch i Befalsmessen for innbudte.
Fotoutstilling.

SPESIELLE OPPLYSNINGER:

Seremonien avholdes i Hangar E. Kjøreruten fra hovedporten til hangaren er spesielt merket.

Det er fotograferingsforbud på Gardermoen flystasjon. For denne anledningen er det imidlertid tillatt å fotografere i utstillingsområdene. Tillatelsen begrenser seg til museumsflyene og situasjoner fra seremonien.

Røyking er ikke tillatt i hangaren og området rundt den.

Gjestene og publikum bes vennligst følge anvisninger fra vaktene.

INTERNATIONAL TEAM REPRESENTATIVES AT FINAL ROLLOUT IN NORWAY		
NORWAY	ICELAND	NORTHROP CORPORATION
Bjorn Wallin	Baldur Sveinsson	Dr. Thomas O. Paine, COO
Capt. Conrad Skjoldhammer*	Einar Gunnarsson	Don Foulds
Col. Herud	Gudlaugur Gudjonsson	Leo Gay
Col. Nils M. Jorgensen	Gudmundur Gudmundsson	O. H. 'Bub' Larsen
Jene Nickelsen	Ragnar J. Ragnarsson	Les Epperly
Col. Wsevolod 'Sevi' Bulukin*	Sigurdur P. Hardarson	Dick MacKay
G. A. Sommerfelt		Ted Mothershead
Lt. Col. Odd Vollan		Bill Sheriffs
Lt. Col. S. Soelberg		

*N-3PB pilots with Squadron 330(N)

POSTSCRIPT

Historical Update: Discovery of Another Submerged Northrop N3-PB in Iceland

Ragnar J. Ragnarsson reported to the author on August 29, 2002 that a second crashed N-3PB had been discovered, this time submerged in the ocean. This discovery was made by the Icelandic Coast Guard. The serial number identity had not been determined as of this writing, but Lt. Adrian King of the ICG reported on September 14, 2002 that the plane was located off Reykjavik at Skerjafjodur in 12 meters (13.12 yards) of water. This would tend to narrow the candidates down to SN 301 and 324. SN 301 failed to return from its mission west of Reykjavik on April 25, 1942 and there were no survivors. SN 324 failed to return from a navigational training flight out of Reykjavik on July 30, 1941 and there were no survivors. Ironically, these were the first and last of the 24 airplanes produced.

An underwater 3-dimensional magnetic scan of the airplane, forwarded to the author by Ragnar J. Magnuson, is shown on the next page. The following is the detailed report provided by Lt. Adrian King:

The second wreck of a Northrop N-3PB aircraft to be found in Iceland since the end of WW II was discovered on August 28, 2002 by the Hydrographic Surveying Department of the Icelandic Coast Guard. The Surveying Department personnel on board the Hydrographic vessel "Baldur" were carrying out a routine measurement and examination operation in the area of Skerjafjörður, Reykjavík.

The aircraft was located by hull mounted multi-beam sonar, which was under test by the Hydrographic Department at the time. After the discovery the national Civil Aviation Authority was informed, as was the Coast Guard operations room. Considerable interest was immediately generated by the find, with the usual rash of experts coming forward to give their opinions and advice.

The large bay or fjörd known as Skerjafjörður is south of Reykjavík airport, which was an extremely busy airfield during WWII, being used by British, American and Canadian air forces. Several aircraft are known to have been lost in this area during WW II. The airport today serves mainly internal flight requirements with international flights now handled by the Leif Eriksson International Airport at Keflavík.

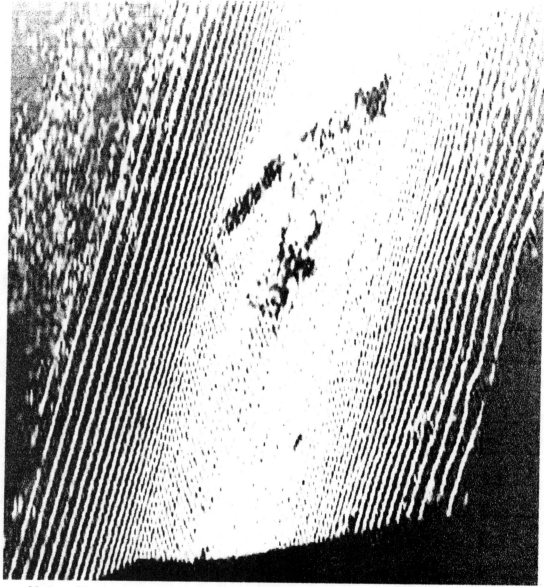

Note: Magnetic scan as transmitted by email on August 29, 2002, by Ragnar J. Ragnarsson. Airplane is lying inverted on seafloor.

At first, speculation by the many interested parties identified numerous possibilities as to the type of aircraft the find could be, although it was more random speculation, with some educated guesswork. In order to formally identify the wreck, the Coast Guard was asked to examine the wreck using divers and on 29 August the first of several dives was made. The objectives at this time were to: (a) identify the aircraft type; (b) search for human remains; and (c) identify any other hazards, especially if the aircraft was of military origin.

As a result of the first dive the aircraft was positively identified as a Northrop N-3PB, but the other objectives were not accomplishable at this time. Further dives were then made to sweep the area for possible unexploded ordnance and to establish whether human remains were present. These dives were only partially successful, although a good appreciation of the condition and geography of the wreck was gained. The aircraft being upturned and filled with sand coupled with poor visibility and a strong current made work difficult. The employment of pumping equipment in order to remove sand from the cockpit in an attempt to establish whether human remains were present was inconclusive and it is felt that this question will only be confirmed once and for all when/if the wreck is lifted.

During the operation various agencies and organisations were asked to assist in the identification of the aircraft and to provide technical information, including both the British and Norwegian embassies in Iceland, the RAF Historical and Casualty Branches, the NATO EOD Technical Information Centre, Northrop Grumman, and the Western Museum of Flight (in Hawthorne, California). A considerable historical record has now been established from the official documentation, and this information has enabled the Coast Guard to provisionally determine the aircraft serial number, subject of course to physical confirmation.

In the meantime the wreck is protected by a diving ban, but it is felt that due to the location of the site, this is only, in practice, a short-term measure, as the site is extremely vulnerable and easily accessible to interference. The Coast Guard has now suspended its operation on the aircraft as it was felt that due to the historical significance of the wreck, further work could only be justified if the aircraft was to be raised from the seabed.

Although considerable effort has been expended to try and positively identify the aircraft serial number through official records, a question mark still remains on this subject, which will only now be removed if a viable operation to remove the wreck by an interested party or organization is sanctioned by the Icelandic Government.[*]

---

[*]As reported by e-mail from Lt. King on September 30, 2002.

Other Ho Logos Press New, Great Themes!

Ho Logos Press publishes books, plays, and movies that provide new awareness and enlightened perspectives on the major social, political, and economic issues that confront us as we enter Millenium 2000. Go to the Ho Logos Press Bookstore on the internet at www.hlpress.com to see what's currently available; or call Ho Logos information at 1-877-407-7744.

David J. Bean not only knew Jack Northrop – the founder of present-day Northrop Grumman Corporation and one of the most memorably noted of aircraft designers and builders, who led the transition of manned flight to the aerospace age – he worked for him. Starting work at Northrop Aircraft, Inc., in 1946, after serving as an Air Force pilot during the Second World War, David J. Bean retired 38 years later, having been manager of new business proposals and Aircraft Group program manager for 22 years. The importance and presence of the Northrop N-3PB seaplane in his life occurred gradually, beginning in1977, when he was one of the key people called into a special meeting to evaluate a proposal from Ragnar J. Ragnarsson, co-founder of the Icelandic Aviation Historical Society. Ragnar had heard rumors from Icelandic farmers in the backcountry that a military seaplane had crashed in the great Thjorsa River during WWII and disappeared. For several years, Ragnar's waking hours and sleep were disturbed by the thought that he should find and recover this airplane for restoration, because he suspected that it was the Norwegian seaplane, from RAF Squadron 330(N), that had crash-landed in the river during a snowstorm in 1943. This airplane was historically important, because it signified the valiant effort by Norwegians to free their country from German occupation. Ragnar felt that the recovery of this airplane was a special mission ordained for his performance because, having been born in the U.S., he had a high regard for the determination of the Norwegians to fight for the freedom of their homeland. With the formation of the IAHS in 1972, recovery of this airplane became almost a full-time pursuit for Ragnar as it began to appear a "mission impossible" – the sort Icelanders find high adventure. The challenge intensified, because Norse legend says that once the Thjorsa takes something, it never gives it back.

Dave, with nephew Rod, at the end of WWII, headed for a career in aviation.

The meeting to evaluate this mission impossible restored memories the author had of the golden years of aviation and the beginning of Jack Northrop's company. The N-3PB had been important to Northrop, too, because it was the first airplane produced by the new company. Now, the company had the opportunity, if the airplane could be recovered, to restore it as a special tribute to Jack Northrop on his 85th birthday, 40 years after he had designed and built the plane under contract to Norway.

Two years of uncertainty followed, as first Ragnar tried to determine whether the airplane even existed. After two surveys of the last known position of the plane in the murky, frigid, swift flowing river, the plane was discovered, not just submerged, but buried in the lava silt, sand, and clay of the riverbed. The next question was whether the plane could be feasibly recovered: what was its condition, could it survive recovery, how could it be recovered, would it be restorable? The longer these questions persisted, the more the international team members doubted the plane should even be raised.

Finally it was necessary to bring in an international expert in marine archeology to survey the plane's situation and condition in a special diving session. Four months later it was recovered, after a tension-filled, life-threatening week in which the Thjorsa proved almost unbeatable in its means of retaining the object it had taken.

But recovery was just the beginning of this historical epic, for restoration was impacted by problems too. Had the restoration team, as one manufacturing executive predicted, "Bitten off more than it could chew, this time"? Would the plane be restored? And in time for Jack Northrop's 85th birthday?

The author tells an exciting, even philosophical story of how this mission impossible restored both the airplane and the "Golden Years" that Jack Northrop and all the restoration volunteers had experienced and evolved from professionally and personally. It was indeed a restoration of the spirit.